Pensions at a Glance 2021

OECD AND G20 INDICATORS

OECD
BETTER POLICIES FOR BETTER LIVES

Please cite this publication as:
OECD (2021), *Pensions at a Glance 2021: OECD and G20 Indicators*, OECD Publishing, Paris, *https://doi.org/10.1787/ca401ebd-en*.

ISBN 978-92-64-55744-4 (print)
ISBN 978-92-64-64133-4 (pdf)
ISBN 978-92-64-41177-7 (HTML)
ISBN 978-92-64-32518-0 (epub)

OECD Pensions at a Glance
ISSN 1995-4026 (print)
ISSN 1999-1363 (online)

Revised version, December 2021
Details of revisions available at: *https://www.oecd.org/about/publishing/Corrigendum_PAG2021.pdf*

Corrigenda to publications may be found on line at: *www.oecd.org/about/publishing/corrigenda.htm*.

Foreword

This ninth edition of *Pensions at a Glance* provides a range of indicators for comparing pension policies and their outcomes between OECD countries. The indicators are also, where possible, provided for the other major economies that are members of the G20. Two special chapters provide a review of the impact of COVID-19 on pensions and of recent pension reforms (Chapter 1) and an in-depth analysis of automatic adjustment in pension systems (Chapter 2).

This report is the joint work of staff in both the Pensions Team of the Social Policy Division of the OECD Directorate for Employment, Labour and Social Affairs and of the Insurance, Private Pensions and Financial Markets Division of the OECD Directorate for Financial and Enterprise Affairs. National officials – particularly delegates to the OECD Working Party on Social Policy and members of the OECD pension expert group – provided invaluable input to the report.

Chapter 1 on "Recent pension reforms" was written by Maciej Lis with contributions from Yuta Fujiki. Chapter 2 entitled "Automatic adjustment mechanisms in pension systems" was written by Wouter De Tavernier. Chapters 3 to 8 were written and the indicators therein computed by Andrew Reilly with contributions from Yuta Fujiki, while Chapter 9 was written by Romain Despalins with inputs from Pablo Antolin and Stéphanie Payet. Hervé Boulhol led the team and was responsible for revising and enhancing these chapters under the leadership of Stefano Scarpetta (Director of ELS), Mark Pearson (Deputy Director of ELS) and Monika Queisser (Senior Counsellor and Head of Social Policy). Maxime Ladaique provided extensive support for tables and figures. Liv Gudmundson prepared the manuscript for publication with inputs from Lucy Hulett. Alastair Wood prepared the work on infographics.

We are grateful to many national officials including ELSAC Delegates and to colleagues in the OECD Secretariat for their useful comments, notably Eliana Barrenho and Christian Geppert (ELS), Pablo Antolin, Romain Despalins, Elsa Favre-Baron, Diana Hourani, Jessica Mosher and Stéphanie Payet (DAF). The OECD gratefully acknowledges the financial support from the European Union, which co-financed this project with the OECD.

Table of contents

Follow OECD Publications on:

http://twitter.com/OECD_Pubs

http://www.facebook.com/OECDPublications

http://www.linkedin.com/groups/OECD-Publications-4645871

http://www.youtube.com/oecdilibrary

http://www.oecd.org/oecddirect/

This book has...

StatLinks

A service that delivers Excel® files from the printed page!

Look for the *StatLinks* at the bottom of the tables or graphs in this book. To download the matching Excel® spreadsheet, just type the link into your Internet browser, starting with the *http://dx.doi.org* prefix, or click on the link from the e-book edition.

Editorial - COVID 19 and ageing: Pension systems at a critical juncture

Almost two years into the pandemic, this new edition of *Pensions at a Glance* offers new insights on how pensioners and pension systems have fared during the crisis. In most OECD countries, retirees have not felt the economic impact of the crisis as pensions in payment were largely upheld. The same cannot be said for pension systems under pressure from lower contributions.

While pension benefits have been protected, retirement income systems had to deal with new financial pressures resulting from lower contributions due to crisis-related exemptions for companies and individuals, even though in many cases transfers from unemployment insurance and governments made up at least partially for the revenue losses. In addition, despite high mortality rates among older populations, savings on pension spending were overall small.

The impact of the crisis on pension systems, however, may be short-lived if the economic recovery observed in most countries over the past months is sustained. Many countries are now showing encouraging signs, and new hiring and a return to normal working hours will help replenish the coffers of public pension systems. If, however, public finance pressures intensify, for example with the increasing cost of debt, and sources of savings are sought, pension spending might also be affected. Currently, it is still early to assess the situation.

For future pensioners, by contrast, the crisis could cast a long shadow on retirement. Young people have been severely affected by the economic and social impacts of the crisis, and might see their future benefits lowered, especially if the pandemic results in longer-term scarring and difficulties in building their careers. Allowing early access to pension savings to compensate for economic hardship, as observed in some countries such as Chile, may also generate long-term problems: unless future higher savings offset these withdrawals, low retirement benefits will be the consequence.

All of these challenges pale in comparison to the long-standing effect of population ageing on pension systems. While it is natural that the COVID-19 pandemic has taken centre-stage in people's and policy makers' minds, the biggest long-term challenge for pensions continues to be providing financially and socially sustainable pensions in the future. As stressed regularly in previous editions of *Pensions at a Glance* and *Pensions Outlook*, putting pension systems on a solid footing for the future will require painful policy decisions: either asking to pay more in contributions, work longer, or receive less pensions. But these decisions will also be painful because pension reforms are among the most contentious, least popular, and potentially perilous reforms.

Long-term pension challenges have continued to be on countries' radar, even during the crisis. Over the past two years, Brazil and Sweden have tightened access to earnings-related pensions through higher pension ages. And a common feature of recent reforms in Chile, Germany, Latvia, Mexico, Slovenia and the Slovak Republic has been to pay particular attention to social sustainability by protecting benefits for low-income retirees. At the same time, political trade-offs can be seen in some of the recent reform packages. Higher pension ages were often accompanied by more lenient options for early retirement. Other countries backtracked, taking back more ambitious reforms and phasing change in more gradually.

According to European Commission projections, the average ratio of benefits to wages will decline by one-quarter by 2070, which would stabilise pension spending as a share of GDP in many countries despite ageing. But it remains to be seen whether these reductions will actually happen. Reviewing the situation over the past two decades, during which there was intense pension reform activity, the actual average ratio of benefits to wages in OECD countries remained broadly stable – implying that many trade-offs were made which partially unraveled the original reform packages.

Trying to avoid getting bogged down in long political debates every time changes to pension systems are made, many countries have introduced automatic adjustment mechanisms in their pension systems. Such mechanisms are a set of rules that automatically change pension system parameters, such as pension ages, benefits or contribution rates, when demographic, economic or financial indicators change.

About two-thirds of OECD countries use some form of automatic adjustment mechanism in their pension schemes. Six have notional defined contribution schemes, seven countries adjust qualifying conditions for retirement to life expectancy, and six adjust pension levels to changes in life expectancy, demographic ratios or the wage bill. Finally, seven countries have a financial balancing mechanism.

However, as this edition of *Pensions at a Glance* shows, these mechanisms can only address part of the challenges of pension systems facing population ageing. While they can reduce the need for governments to make ad hoc interventions and engage in lengthy negotiations of rules, they cannot isolate pension systems from political decision-making and certainly are not able to put pension systems on auto-pilot. In part, this is good news since governments must retain the flexibility to make changes in exceptional situations and adapt their pension policies to changes in labour market, health and social circumstances.

Automatic adjustment mechanisms have the advantage of defining the direction the systems should be heading for; deviating from that path will at least require explanations and discussions and make the trade-offs visible. The OECD analysis of countries' experiences shows that indeed, over the years, the automatic adjustment mechanisms were sometimes suspended or even eliminated in order to avoid pension benefit cuts and retirement-age increases, laid down in automatic adjustment mechanisms. While suspending automatic adjustments may be a necessary step to address concerns that such adjustments could generate harsh corrections at the lower end of the income distribution, governments should be sure to have a concrete alternative plan on how to finance pension expenditures in the longer term.

Overall, as countries gradually move away from COVID-19 crisis management response, governments should address the most pressing structural challenges to pension systems as part of their recovery plans. The use of automatic adjustment mechanism is an essential tool for sound pension systems. This edition of *Pensions at a Glance* sets out a number of principles on the design of automatic adjustment mechanisms to improve the financial and social sustainability of pension systems. It also provides countries with guidelines for their development and implementation.

Stefano Scarpeta
Director,
OECD Directorate for Employment,
Labour and Social Affairs

Mathilde Mesnard
Acting Director,
OECD Directorate for Financial, and Enterprise Affairs

Executive summary

This edition of *Pensions at a Glance* discusses the impact of COVID-19 on pensions and reviews the pension measures legislated in OECD countries between September 2019 and September 2021. As in past editions, a comprehensive selection of pension policy indicators is included for OECD and G20 countries. Moreover, this edition provides an in-depth analysis of automatic adjustment mechanisms in pension systems.

Limited impact of COVID-19 on pensions while ageing pressure might come back to the forefront

The past two years have been marked by the COVID-19 pandemic, which has taken a heavy toll especially among the older population. However, the income of current pensioners has been well protected. As exceptional policies supported incomes and cushioned the impact on labour markets, future pensions are not likely to be much affected in most OECD countries.

OECD countries have put concerns about public finance between parentheses, and shortfalls in pension contributions were largely covered by transfers from state budgets. But the long-term financial pressure from ageing persists. Although life expectancy gains in old age have slowed somewhat since 2010, the pace of ageing will be fast over the next two decades. The size of the working-age population is projected to fall by more than one-quarter by 2060 in most Southern, Central and Eastern European countries as well as in Japan and Korea.

Substantial measures, including strengthening first-tier pensions and extending early retirement

Many countries significantly reformed earnings-related pension benefits: Mexico substantially increased contributions, boosting future pensions; Estonia made contributions to private pensions voluntary and allowed to withdraw pension assets; and, Greece will replace pay-as-you-go auxiliary pensions with a funded defined contribution scheme. Measures boosting earnings-related pensions were also implemented in Hungary, Poland and Slovenia.

One clear recent trend has been to increase income protection for individuals who have recorded low earnings during their career, as in Chile, Germany, Latvia and Mexico.

Mandatory schemes provide an average future net replacement rate of 62% to full-career average-wage workers, ranging from less than 40% in Chile, Estonia, Ireland, Japan, Korea, Lithuania and Poland to 90% or more in Hungary, Portugal and Turkey. For workers earning half the average wage, net replacement rates are 12 percentage points higher on average.

Action on retirement ages was limited. Sweden increased the minimum retirement age for public earnings-related pensions, and plans a future link to life expectancy; the Netherlands postponed the planned increase while reducing the pace of the future link to life expectancy; and Ireland repealed the planned increase from 66 to 68 years. Denmark, Ireland, Italy and Lithuania have extended early retirement options. Among non-OECD G20 countries, Brazil has introduced minimum retirement ages and adjusted benefit calculation.

Based on legislated measures, the normal retirement age will increase by about two years in the OECD on average by the mid-2060s. The future normal retirement age is 69 years or more in Denmark, Estonia, Italy and the Netherlands, with links to life expectancy, while Colombia, Luxembourg and Slovenia will let men retire at 62. Women will maintain a lower normal retirement age than men in Colombia, Hungary, Israel, Poland and Switzerland.

Automatic adjustment mechanisms are crucial to help deal with the impact of ageing

Automatic adjustment mechanisms (AAMs) refer to predefined rules that automatically change pension parameters or benefits based on the evolution of a demographic, economic or financial indicator. AAMs protect pensions from uncertainties and are less erratic, more transparent and more equitable across generations than discretionary changes. Initially introduced to uphold pension adequacy through wage or price indexation, AAMs are increasingly used to maintain financial sustainability.

AAMs should be sustained politically over time, also when governments change, to achieve their medium- to long-term objectives. Wide political support for their introduction and a mechanism design that avoids harsh adjustments can contribute to that. As with discretionary changes, AAMs have distributional consequences: whether to make adjustments to pensions, contributions or retirement ages is fundamentally the subject of democratic debate. Even with AAMs, policy makers maintain full control over pensions and can intervene if they deem the triggered adjustments undesirable. At the same time, AAMs reduce the need for frequent pension reforms.

Some AAMs introduced at a time of crisis to restore financial sustainability might be questioned once the economy recovers. Hence, AAMs are not a substitute for bold discretionary measures in a financially unbalanced pension system: it is therefore important to distinguish changes that should take place in any case from those that are conditional to the evolution of circumstances.

Increases in life expectancy should at least partially be offset by increasing statutory retirement ages, as this protects both adequacy and financial sustainability. A supplementary correction is likely needed to adjust for changes in the size of the contributing population, as well as a balancing mechanism ensuring financial balance over time.

About two-thirds of OECD countries employ some form of AAM. Six have notional defined contribution schemes with built-in adjustments. Seven countries adjust pension qualifying conditions to life expectancy, and six adjust benefits to changes in life expectancy, demographic ratios or the wage bill. Finally, seven countries have a balancing mechanism. In funded defined contribution schemes, trends in life expectancy do not affect pension finances.

Sweden and Finland have the most far-reaching AAMs. Sweden combines the automatic adjustment of benefits to life expectancy with a balancing mechanism ensuring solvency. Finland adjust both benefits levels and retirement ages to life expectancy, supplemented by a balancing mechanism adjusting contribution rates if needed. Moreover, both Estonia and Italy account for changes in total contributions and GDP, respectively, while linking the statutory retirement age to life expectancy. The German balancing mechanism adjusts both pensions and contribution rates to demographics. Backstop mechanisms in the Canada Pension Plan ensure financial balance while explicitly prioritising a political solution in case of a deficit: the automatic balancing mechanism is triggered if there is no agreement on alternative interventions.

Overall, automatic adjustment mechanisms have the advantage of defining the direction pension systems should be heading for; deviating from that path will at least require explanations and make the trade-offs visible.

Infographic 1. **Key facts**

Pensions at a Glance 2021
OECD and G20 Indicators

Chapter 1

Recent pension reforms

This chapter looks into pension developments over the past two years, including both the effects of the COVID-19 crisis and pension reforms introduced in OECD and G20 countries between September 2019 and September 2021. In response to the COVID-19 crisis, measures were introduced to protect the income of workers and pensioners and to limit job losses, with limited impact on accruing pension entitlements. Moreover, recent pension reforms have focused on adjusting retirement ages, extending early retirement options, expanding first-tier pensions and adjusting benefits and contributions in earning-related schemes, including to encourage combining work and pensions. The chapter also summarises the extent to which ageing pressure affected pension spending since 2000 and assesses whether longevity gains had been slowing before the COVID-19 crisis.

Maciej Lis, Hervé Boulhol and Yuta Fujiki

Introduction

All over the world, the COVID-19 crisis has left its deep traces. Since the previous edition of *Pensions at a Glance* in 2019, the virus has taken a heavy toll, especially among the older population. OECD countries took unprecedented and swift measures to address health challenges, limit the impact on labour markets, support incomes and adjust macroeconomic policies.

The income of current pensioners is generally well protected during economic downturns, as already retired persons usually do not depend on the labour market and continue to receive their pensions, unless ad hoc cuts are made for fiscal reasons. This has been the case over the past two years, and in many countries older people even benefited from additional targeted support measures. Moreover, the expanded use of job retention schemes and the extension of unemployment protection significantly limited the impact of the COVID-19 crisis on future pensions. Entering the labour market, however, has become much harder during the crisis and career prospects of younger generations have worsened. The impact of the pandemic-related labour market turbulences on future pensions of the current youth is expected to be small but it will be visible in four decades when the current youth have retired. Policy changes too will have an impact. A few countries, Chile in particular, have for example allowed exceptional withdrawals of assets from individual funded pension accounts during the pandemic, which weakens future pension prospects.

In response to the pandemic, OECD countries have put concerns about public finance – and pension financial sustainability – between parentheses in their response to the crisis. While excess mortality due to COVID-19 has generated some small savings for pension providers in terms of fewer pension payments, the main impact for pension finances results from lost contributions, which, however, were mostly covered by transfers from state budgets. The medium-term impact on pension finances is generally expected to be relatively modest, even if in some countries the crisis may have exacerbated existing imbalances. Persistently low interest rates certainly ease short-term pressure on public finance, including pension finance. However, financial sustainability challenges will not disappear. They might come back to the forefront once macroeconomic policies normalise.

Population ageing has been accelerating over the last decade and the pace of ageing is projected to be fast over the next two decades, with significant differences in the shift of population structures among OECD countries. Pension systems in Greece, Japan, Latvia, Lithuania and Poland will face substantial challenges as the working-age population is projected to shrink by at least one-third by 2060. Estonia, Korea, Portugal, the Slovak Republic, Slovenia and Spain will also face acute demographic challenges affecting retirement income adequacy, financial sustainability or both.

Between 2000 and 2017, total (public and private) pension expenditure increased by 1.5% of GDP on average among OECD countries. Demographic changes alone are estimated to have contributed to raising pension expenditure by 2.5% of GDP; this increase was partly offset by strong labour market performance in many countries, especially among older workers; there were no common trends across countries on changes in pension benefit ratios (average pensions relative to average wages). Ageing is expected to further raise spending pressure in the OECD on average by an additional 3.5% of GDP by 2035. In the absence of new resources for pension financing, it is crucial to continue increasing employment prospects for older workers, including through the design of pension policies, in order to preserve the level of old-age benefits while limiting spending increases.

Beyond responding to COVID-19, many countries had already taken important pension measures over the past two years. Mexico implemented the most comprehensive reform among OECD countries, raising earnings-related contributions, as well as current and future first-tier benefits. The increases in first-tier benefits imply higher public spending and will significantly weaken the relation between benefits and contributions. Among non-OECD G20 countries, Brazil took big steps to improve pension finances, including by introducing minimum retirement ages. Estonia made funded pensions voluntary and allowed the withdrawal of accumulated assets, which is likely to negatively affect future pensions; one-quarter of pension assets were withdrawn so far. Greece created a new funded defined contribution (FDC) scheme to gradually replace the existing notional defined contribution (NDC) mandatory auxiliary pensions. Significant measures boosting earnings-related pension benefits also were implemented in Hungary and Slovenia as well as in Poland, which will further deteriorate future financial balances of the pension systems in the first two countries. Belgium has also boosted future pension entitlements among the self-employed without raising their contributions. The Netherlands is in the process of completing the transition of the quasi-mandatory occupational pensions from defined benefit into collective defined contribution schemes, which are FDC schemes in which individual choices are more limited in terms of both investment and asset withdrawals as the accumulated assets are only paid out as annuities.

One clear trend observed over the last two years has been to increase income protection for low or no pensions. Chile, Germany, Latvia and Mexico in particular, as well as the Slovak Republic and Slovenia raised the benefits of individuals who have recorded low earnings during their career.

Action on retirement ages, by contrast, was limited. Sweden started to raise retirement ages and plans to link them to life expectancy from 2026, while Ireland and the Netherlands postponed previously planned increases. In addition, the pace of the link between retirement age and life expectancy has been reduced in the Netherlands: from 2025, two-thirds of longevity gains will be passed into retirement-age increases; initially the plan had been to increase the pension age by all of the life expectancy increase. Early retirement options have been extended in Denmark, Ireland, Italy and Lithuania. Based on legislated measures, the normal retirement age will increase in the OECD on average by about two years in the next four decades during which life expectancy in old age is projected to increase by about four years. Colombia, Luxembourg, the Slovak Republic and Slovenia will be the only OECD countries with normal retirement ages of 64 years or less. Switzerland is making a new attempt to equalise retirement ages between men and women at age 65.

Different strategies are also being put in place to promote longer working lives. Canada, Greece, Japan and Slovenia have eased combining work and pensions. With the objective of making work at older ages more attractive, Hungary has exempted workers claiming old-age pension from paying pension contributions, while Spain considers the possibility to pay out the yearly bonus for deferring retirement as a lump-sum payment. In Sweden, a new "target retirement age" to be set at 67 in 2027, will be introduced to nudge retirement decisions in its flexible system, by providing a clear suggestion of what the adequate age to retire should be.

Key findings

Main findings related to how the COVID-19 crisis has affected pensions:

- For current pensioners, pension benefits have been safeguarded, and many countries introduced temporary and targeted income support measures.
- The impact of the crisis on future pensions has been limited thanks to the expanded use of job retention schemes – in which generally pension entitlements accrued -, subsidised pension contributions, the extension of unemployment protection, specific measures benefiting the self-employed and strong financial markets performance.

- Exceptional withdrawals of pension assets from individual funded pension accounts were allowed in a few countries to attenuate the impact of COVID-19; among them, Chile is the country where future pensions might be most affected.
- Pension finances deteriorated due to lost contributions, and shortfalls have been mainly covered by state budgets. In the aftermath of the COIVD-19 crisis, ageing pressure might come back to the forefront.
- Due to excess mortality, the number of people older than 65 has declined by about 0.8% in the OECD on average, which has slightly lowered pension spending.

Main recent pension policy measures in OECD and G20 countries:

- Mexico substantially increased mandatory contributions in their funded defined contribution (FDC) scheme, which will boost future pensions. Greece has created a new FDC scheme to replace mandatory NDC (notional defined contribution) auxiliary pensions over time. Estonia went the other way by making mandatory contributions to private pensions voluntary and allowing to withdraw pension assets.
- Brazil introduced minimum retirement ages, modified contribution rates and adjusted benefit calculation which should improve pension finances significantly.
- Hungary and Slovenia have increased earnings-related pensions, which will further deteriorate future pension financial balances; Poland also increased the benefits for current pensioners.
- Chile, Germany, Latvia, Mexico, Slovak Republic and Slovenia have significantly improved old-age safety nets or increased low pensions.
- Limited action took place on retirement ages: Sweden increased the minimum retirement age for public earnings-related pensions, and plans to link it to life expectancy from 2026 and to increase the eligibility age to the basic pension from 65 to 67 years; the Netherlands postponed the planned increase while loosening the future link to life expectancy; and Ireland repealed the planned increases from 66 to 68 years.
- Denmark, Ireland, Italy and Lithuania have extended early retirement options.
- Belgium substantially increased future pensions for the self-employed without adjusting their contributions while mandatory pension contributions of the self-employed in Greece has become flat-rate.
- Canada, Greece, Japan and Slovenia have eased combining work and pensions, and Hungary has exempted workers claiming old-age pension from paying pension contributions.

Current income of pensioners:

- On average in the OECD, people aged 65+ receive 88% of the income of the total population. Those aged over 65 currently receive about 70% or less of the economy-wide average disposable income in Estonia, Korea, Latvia and Lithuania, and about 100% or more in Costa Rica, France, Israel, Italy, Luxembourg and Portugal.

Retirement ages:

- For men retiring in 2020, the normal retirement age was the lowest at 52 years in Turkey and 62 years in Colombia, Costa Rica, Greece, Italy, Korea, Luxembourg and Slovenia, whereas it was 67 in Iceland and Norway, assuming labour market entry at age 22. In slightly less than half of OECD countries, the normal retirement age will not increase based on current legislation.
- The difference in the normal retirement age between men and women is being eliminated in Austria, Costa Rica, Lithuania and Turkey, but a gender gap will remain in the future for normal retirement ages in Colombia, Hungary, Israel, Poland and Switzerland.

- Based on current legislated measures, the normal retirement age will increase by about two years in the OECD on average, from 64.2 years in 2020 to 66.1 years in the mid-2060s for men. The future normal retirement age is 69 years or more in Denmark, Estonia, Italy and the Netherlands, which have all linked the retirement age to life expectancy, while it is 62 years in Colombia, Luxembourg and Slovenia.

Replacement rates:

- Future net replacement rates from mandatory schemes for full-career average-wage workers equal 62% in the OECD on average, ranging from less than 40% in Chile, Estonia, Ireland, Japan, Korea, Lithuania and Poland to 90% or more in Hungary, Portugal and Turkey at the normal retirement age.
- In countries with significant coverage of voluntary pensions – Belgium, Canada, Germany, Ireland, Japan, New Zealand and the United States – contributing to a voluntary pension boosts future net replacement rates by 24 percentage points on average for average earners contributing during their whole career and by about 11 percentage points when contributing from age 45 only, based on OECD modelling assumptions.
- Average-wage workers who experience a 5-year unemployment spell during their career face a pension reduction of 6.4% on average in the OECD compared to the full-career scenario. The loss exceeds 10% in Australia, Chile, Hungary, Iceland, Latvia, Korea, Mexico, Poland, the Slovak Republic and Turkey.
- For low-wage earners (at half the average wage), the net replacement rate from mandatory schemes is equal to 74% on average after a full career, hence 12 percentage points higher than for the average-wage worker, mainly due to redistributive mechanisms included in pension rules. The Czech Republic and Denmark record the largest difference in the replacement rates when comparing low-wage and average-wage workers.

Other findings:

- Between 2008 and 2018, the number of pensioners increased by 20% in the OECD on average, much less that the 27% increase in the number of people aged 65 or more, consistent with the increase in the effective age of claiming pensions.
- Between 2000 and 2017, total – public and private – pension expenditure increased by 1.5% of GDP on average among OECD countries. Population ageing alone would have triggered an increase in pension expenditure of 2.5% of GDP on average. This was offset by higher employment, which lowered pension expenditure by 1.1% of GDP on average.
- Even before COVID-19, old-age life expectancy has been growing less rapidly than between the mid-1990s and around 2010. There is strong evidence of a slowdown in old-age life expectancy in many countries from about 2010. For women, this slowdown brings the pace back to levels observed between 1970 and the mid-1990s, while for men the pace remains relatively fast.

This chapter is structured as follows. The next section discusses how the COVID-19 crisis affects pensions. The third section assesses changes in the pace of population ageing and the generated pension pressure. The last section focuses on the most recent pension reforms.

COVID-19 and pensions

Various policies greatly reduced the labour market impact of the COVID-19 crisis

The recession triggered by the COVID-19 outbreak was exceptionally large. Unusual macroeconomic policies succeeded in avoiding much sharper repercussions on individual incomes than feared. In particular, employment dropped much less than GDP, even though the labour market was severely affected in most countries.

The fall in employment was limited because a large share of the decrease in hours worked was absorbed by those who remained employed. The preservation of jobs combined with reduced hours was possible through job-retention schemes (JRS), which have been used at a much larger scale than in past downturns. Indeed, 19 of the 23 OECD countries that had such schemes before 2020 extended their coverage, simplified their access or increased their generosity. Moreover, 15 countries introduced new JRS in 2020 (OECD, 2021[1]).[1] Job-retention subsidies were claimed for more than one-fifth of dependent employees in many European countries, Australia and New Zealand. OECD (2021[1]) provides details about the unprecedented use of JRS among OECD countries during the COVID-19 crisis.

The exceptional labour-market policy response during the COVID-19 crisis has not been limited to JRS. Two-thirds of OECD countries eased or broadened the access to unemployment benefits. Sixteen countries reduced or entirely waived minimum contribution requirements to unemployment insurance, or granted unemployment insurance to new groups of workers (OECD, 2020[2]). In particular, the United States has expanded the coverage of unemployment benefits to the self-employed and Finland has broadened the coverage of the already existing scheme for the self-employed. Canada introduced a more generous (emergency response) benefit, which was not subject to social security contributions, for all who lost their income due to COVID-19 between March and September 2020. Chile permanently expanded the coverage of unemployment insurance to workers. New Zealand introduced a temporary benefit paid for up to three months to employees who lost their jobs and to the self-employed who stopped their activity. In addition, 12 countries extended the duration of unemployment benefits and ten raised benefit amounts.

Pension benefits were safeguarded and exceptional payments were made

Retirees generally suffer lower income losses during economic downturns than the working population. As a result of indexation rules, the exceptional measures discussed below and the income drop of the working-age population, the relative income situation of retirees is likely to have temporarily improved.[2]

When employment drops and wages are negatively affected, pensions in payment are usually more protected for two reasons. First, they are often linked only partially (or not at all) to wages. Second, floors to indexation may prevent reductions of benefits, which is the case for example in Australia (Age Pension), Austria, the Czech Republic, Germany, Latvia, Poland and the United States. The United Kingdom is an outlier in that respect as the currently used so-called triple lock guarantees that pensions increase with the highest of average wage growth, price growth and 2.5%. Thus, the benefits increased by 2.5% in April 2021 while average earnings decreased by more than 2%. As for 2022, the government announced that, upon parliamentary approval, the triple lock will be suspended and pensions will adjust to the higher of 2.5% and inflation to avoid that the catch-up in wages in 2021 causes an 8% hike in pension levels. In some countries, indexation also smooths abrupt changes by using averages over a longer period; e.g. Lithuania uses averages over the last three years, the current year and projections of the next three years.

Pensioners have also benefited from income support measures, population-wide in particular in the United States or towards low-income populations as in Spain. Additionally, some countries have targeted support for retirees or the older population: Australia, Belgium, Canada, Colombia, the Czech Republic, Denmark, Israel, Korea, Lithuania, Latvia, Hungary, New Zealand, Poland, Slovenia and Turkey.[3] In some specific circumstances, the cost of living of retirees might have increased due to limited opportunities for affordable shopping during the confinement. Some of them might have also lost earnings opportunities, for example when combining part-time or casual work with retirement.

However, those retiring during or shortly after a crisis might face a permanent benefit reduction. In earnings-related schemes, the calculation of the initial public pension is often linked to the labour market situation at the time of retirement through the valorisation of past wages, point values or notional accounts, depending on the scheme design. In particular, when average-wage growth is exceptionally weak, this affects the valorisation of all past wages, which reduces pension entitlements accrued in the past. When pension payments are indexed to wages, initially lower benefit levels would catch up during the economic recovery. However, a majority of OECD countries do not fully index pensions to wages (as discussed in greater detail in the next section), and short-term negative real-wage shocks can durably lower the benefits of those who are unlucky to retire in bad times. Symmetrically, short-term positive real-wage shocks can durably boost the pensions of those who are lucky to retire in good times. The magnitude of these effects is proportional to wage variations in the economic cycle, which have been exceptionally large in the COVID-19 crisis. Indeed, the real average-wage growth was negative at -0.1% in 2020 compared to 1.5% per year in the OECD on average over 2000-19. For example, it was almost -10% in Chile and -6% in Italy in 2020 and around -3% or less in Belgium, France, Iceland, Mexico and Spain.[4] Among those countries, Belgium, France, Italy and Spain include price indexation of pensions in payments.

Before the COVID-19 crisis, some schemes had included mechanisms to smooth the valorisation or prevent the reductions in entitlements. For example, after the global financial crisis, Latvia and Sweden provided an additional mechanism to their NDC schemes to cushion the fall in notional account values when labour and capital markets deteriorate abruptly. In Poland, the valorisation of notional accounts cannot be lower than inflation whereas in Austria, the Czech Republic, Italy, Latvia and Lithuania the uprating of past wages or the valorisation of notional accounts cannot be negative. Furthermore, Canada and Italy use a five-year average of the growth of the average wage and GDP, respectively, and Lithuania a seven-year average of the growth of the wage bill.

Impact of the COVID-19 crisis on future pensions

Job retention schemes and pensions

Workers enrolled in JRS accrue pension entitlements based on their subsidised wages depending on specific pension arrangements. In all minimum and contribution-based basic pension schemes in OECD countries, JRS accrued full pension rights by fully validating the corresponding periods. For example, periods of reduced hours accrued full eligibility to minimum pensions in Latvia and Poland.

In mandatory earnings-related pension schemes, pension rights generally continued to accrue on the subsidised part of wages. For example, in Chile, to qualify for JRS, the employers were required to pay pension contributions based on wages prior to the suspension of the employment contract. There have been, however, a few exceptions. In Korea and Turkey as well as in Japan, Latvia and Poland, wages paid in JRS have accrued no entitlements in mandatory earnings-related schemes but in the latter three countries the covered periods were fully validated as contribution periods fully counted towards eligibility conditions, e.g. for minimum pensions.[5] In Denmark, Iceland, the Netherlands, New Zealand and the United Kingdom, JRS covered at least some contributions to occupational schemes, which was not the case in Australia, Norway, Sweden and the United States.

In most countries, the state budget or other public funds subsidised mandatory pension contributions on subsidised wages. For example, Germany has reimbursed employers who have used JRS including for total social security contributions related to the lost worked hours, resulting in accruing full pension entitlements; during the global financial crisis, workers also accrued full pension rights but only half of contributions were subsidised. In Italy, the subsidised part, up to 80% of wages, has not been subject to pension contributions, but pension entitlements accrued on full wages. In France, after changes in the legislation in June 2020, contributions on subsidised wages have been paid by the newly created "solidarity fund", mostly financed by both the state budget and local governments, which is supposed to expire by end-2021.[6] Only in the United States were pension contributions not subsidised while being fully due.

Measures affecting pension contributions beyond job retention schemes

Beyond subsidising wages and pension entitlements through JRS, some countries reduced or subsidised pension contributions for hours worked. For example, France has subsidised employers' contributions in selected sectors without lowering individual accruals, and Greece has fully subsidised pension contributions for workers who stopped their activity due to the pandemic. Hungary has suspended pension contributions in sectors affected by the lockdown while entitlements kept accruing fully. Norway temporarily reduced social security contributions by 4 percentage points without affecting NDC entitlements. However, in Korea, all workers whose income was reduced due to the pandemic have been exempted from contributions on their remaining earnings; but there were no pension rights accruing for these workers. Finland lowered the mandatory pension contributions from May to December 2020 by 2.6 percentage points, without lowering future pension. The reduction will be covered by the buffer fund, which is supposed to be replenished by 2025 through higher contributions after 2021.

Many countries allowed for deferring pension contributions for a few months, and temporarily lowered or removed the penalties for delays in paying contributions, including Belgium, the Czech Republic, Estonia, Finland, France, Greece, Italy, Japan, Luxembourg, the Netherlands, Norway, Poland, Portugal, the Slovak Republic, Spain, Switzerland, Turkey and the United States. For example, in selected sectors, Italy allowed to defer pension contributions to the NDC scheme that were due between February and May 2020; the contributions are to be repaid by the end of 2022. The United States allowed to defer contributions between March and September 2020, to be repaid gradually by the end of 2022. Deferring contributions by a few months has no effect on entitlements in DB schemes and a very limited one in DC schemes, both funded and notional.

In Japan, individuals, such as some part-time workers, who are not covered by mandatory earnings-related pensions and have low household income can apply for a partial or full contribution exemption to the National Pension (contribution-based basic pension), which resulted in acquiring half of accruals on the non-paid contributions; however, it is possible for people to complement these retroactively by paying the missing contributions.

Unemployment benefits, late labour-market entry and pensions

The impact of career breaks on pension entitlements is cushioned by various mechanisms (Chapter 4). On average across OECD countries, those mechanisms offset about half of the impact of unemployment-related career breaks on pension (see last section of this chapter). The expansion of both labour income protection from JRS and unemployment benefits, as a response to the COVID-19 crisis, has provided significant additional pension protection against the labour market shocks in 2020 and 2021.

By contrast to dependent employees, non-standard workers have limited access to unemployment benefits when losing their job. Both the duration and the level of unemployment benefits often depend on tenure, thus providing better effective protection to older workers in stable jobs. Generally, many OECD countries eased the access to unemployment benefits, including for temporary employees, informal workers or the self-employed, increased their level and/or provided them for longer periods.

Youth employment has been severely hit (OECD, 2021[1]). Many young people work in the most affected sectors, such as accommodation and food services, and their employment opportunities were sharply reduced as the creation of new jobs dried up. Even in the fourth quarter of 2020 when total employment had largely recovered, the number of workers aged 15-24 was 10% lower than one year before. Due to short tenure and working in non-standard jobs, younger workers typically have a limited access to unemployment benefits.

Labour market difficulties during an economic crisis translate into delayed career starts and low earnings for young workers. Earnings losses related to graduating during a recession might be durable and visible even 10 years into the career (Oreopoulos, von Wachter and Heisz, 2012[3]). In addition to immediate effects, delayed career start and lower earnings will also have repercussion for future pensions. Compared with a full-career average-wage worker entering the labour market at age 22, individuals starting their career two years later at age 24 and earning successively 30%, 20%, and 10% less in the first three years of their career will receive 96% of pension benefits from mandatory schemes during the whole retirement period (Figure 1.1). That ratio is below 94% in Australia, Austria, Chile, Hungary, Latvia and Korea, while there is no pension impact in Colombia, Ireland, New Zealand and Spain. A lagged career start will result in retiring one year later in France and Portugal, and two years later in Luxembourg and Slovenia to avoid penalties. Hence, the impact of the COVID-19 crisis is strongly felt by many young workers who struggle to afford a decent living and the effect – albeit small in proportion – will be felt also several decades later when they retire.

Figure 1.1. **Difficulties in entering the labour market will lower future pensions**

Pensions from mandatory schemes of people facing difficulties in entering labour markets compared to full-career average earners

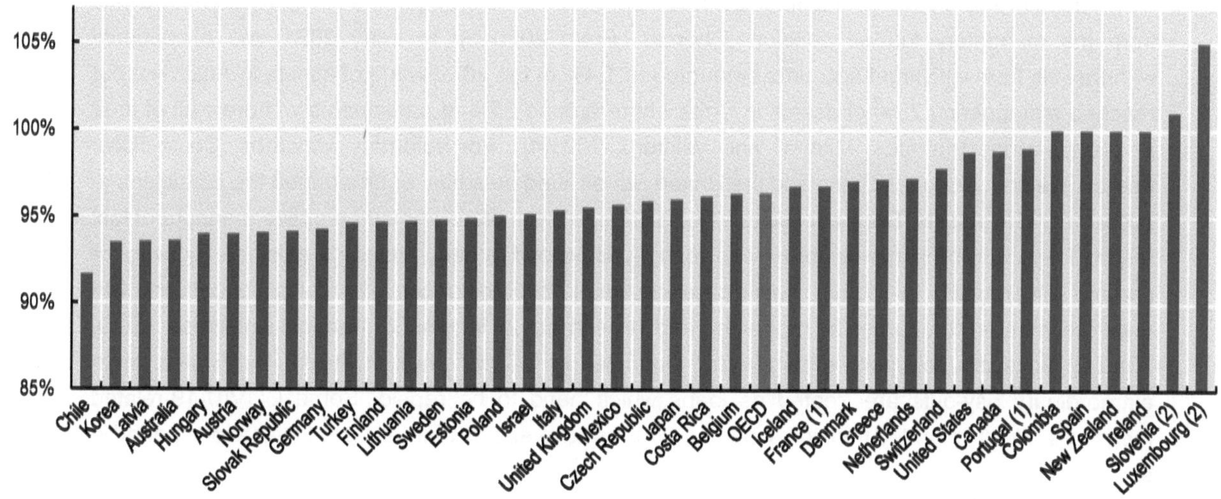

Note: People facing difficulties in entering labour market are assumed to start career at age 24 (in 2022) instead of 22 (in 2020) and earn 30%, 20%, and 10% less than the average earnings in the first three years of their career. Numbers in brackets indicate increases of normal retirement age (in years) due to delayed entering labour market, where relevant.

StatLink https://stat.link/nulh26

Pension entitlements of the self-employed

In normal times already, the self-employed tend to be less protected against old-age risks and pay fewer pension contributions than employees. After a full career, self-employed workers can expect pensions from mandatory schemes to be about one-fifth lower than those of employees with similar earnings, on average across the OECD (Chapter 5).[7]

The COVID-19 crisis hit especially strongly sectors such as culture, event management, personal services and tourism, where many workers are self-employed. Some countries have provided temporary and targeted cash transfers to the self-employed.[8] Pension entitlements accrued on income support measures for the self-employed in Canada, Estonia, Finland, Ireland, Lithuania, New Zealand, Norway and Spain. Moreover, in Belgium, pension entitlements accrued on some special benefits for the self-employed whose activity was interrupted between March 2020 and September 2021 (bridging benefits), similar to regular unemployment benefits. Ireland introduced a special unemployment benefit giving rights to public pension entitlements in March 2020, which also covered the self-employed.

Some countries deferred, subsidised or suspended social security contributions for the self-employed while pension entitlements kept accruing. This was important because mandatory pension contributions for the self-employed are set based on their income in the previous year (e.g. Austria, Slovenia, the United States) or at the minimum required amount (e.g. Poland, Spain). In addition, Estonia, France, Hungary, Italy, Poland, the Slovak Republic, Slovenia and Spain granted subsidised social security contributions and thereby pension entitlements to the self-employed whereas Portugal reduced pension contributions of the self-employed without harming their entitlements.[9]

Other countries provided temporary relief from pension contributions to the self-employed without subsidising their entitlements. For example, Austria allowed the self-employed to reduce their contributions to the required minimum, similarly reducing pension entitlements. Belgium, the Czech Republic, Finland, Greece and Switzerland allowed the self-employed to defer pension contributions which, however, are required to accrue entitlements.

Extraordinary measures in funded schemes

Australia and Chile provided financial relief to workers by allowing some exceptional withdrawals from the mandatory funded pension schemes. From 2020 up to early 2021, the exceptional withdrawals from individual accounts amounted to 1.4% of the 2019 value of assets in Australia, but reached a staggering 25% of assets in Chile where around 35% of participants withdrew all of their pension savings (Fuentes, Mitchell and Villatoro, 2021[4]). For voluntary schemes, Costa Rica, France, Iceland, Portugal, Spain and the United States lifted penalties or broadened the conditions to access pension assets. Early access to savings in retirement plans should be only a measure of last resort. There can be some flexibility, and many jurisdictions already include provisions allowing for partial withdrawals in some specific exceptional circumstances: hardship situations like unemployment accompanied by protracted and large losses of income, or terminal illnesses (OECD, 2020[5]). In some voluntary schemes, for examples in DC schemes in the United States, such extraordinary pay-outs are treated as loans which need to be repaid. Some COVID-19-related measures affecting funded pension schemes will thus have effects that will be felt over a long period in some countries.

Australia, Canada and the Netherlands also took measures in funded occupational schemes to cushion the impact of the crisis on pensioners. To prevent cashing in losses in the funded schemes, Australia and Canada relaxed the minimum withdrawal requirements for pensioners. In the Netherlands, to avoid benefit cuts, the required value of assets compared to pension liabilities in defined benefit pension funds, i.e. the funding ratio, was temporarily, before the crisis in 2019 and 2020, lowered from 104.2% to 90%. During the COVID-19 crisis, the reduction of the required funding ratio was prolonged until 2027 (Chapter 2).

In Estonia, a legislative process to make the mandatory funded DC scheme voluntary started before the outbreak of the COVID-19 pandemic and was finalised in 2020 (see the last section of the chapter). During this process, temporary COVID-19-related measures were introduced. The mandatory employer's contributions of 4% financing the private funded DC scheme were temporarily retained in the public scheme from July 2020 to August 2021 and the employees were given the option to suspend their DC contributions of 2% for the same period. The value of missing contributions, uprated by the average return of all DC funds between 1 July 2020 and 31 December 2022, will be transferred to the DC individual accounts in 2023-24 except for employees who use the newly introduced possibility to opt out of the DC scheme or suspended their DC contributions in 2020.

COVID-19 and demographics

Excess mortality

The pandemic has been causing enormous human suffering and the number of COVID-19 deaths exceeded 2.5 million in OECD countries by mid-2021 (OECD, 2021[6]). As older populations have been particularly affected, this unexpected crisis also implies that, on average, fewer pensions will be paid, temporarily lowering annual pension spending and generating savings for pension providers. The ultimate impact on the number of deaths and on shortening the longevity of the different cohorts still remains subject to a large uncertainty.

Although governments have tracked the number of deaths due to COVID-19, the reporting of deaths differed across countries depending on whether deaths took place in hospitals, whether the presence of the virus was confirmed by a medical test and whether the COVID-19 was acknowledged as the main cause of death. Additionally, this measure does not account for the deaths indirectly caused by the virus though e.g. less resources serving other diseases. Excess mortality – the actual number of deaths divided by the expected number of deaths based on data from previous years minus one – allows to better measure the total impact of the virus on the number of deaths across countries (Morgan et al., 2020[7]).[10]

Excess mortality totalled 12% on average among OECD countries between January 2020 and August 2021, which means that 12% more people died in this period than would have been expected based on data from previous years (Figure 1.2). In Australia, Denmark, Iceland, Ireland, New Zealand and Norway excess deaths did not exceed 3% while they reached 15% or more in Chile, Colombia, the Czech Republic, Mexico, Poland, the Slovak Republic and the United States. As a result of excess mortality, life expectancy (at birth) declined in 24 out of 30 OECD countries in 2020, and by one year or more in Belgium, Italy, Lithuania, Poland, Slovenia, Spain, the United Kingdom and the United States (OECD, 2021[6]).

Figure 1.2. **Excess mortality between January 2020 and August 2021**

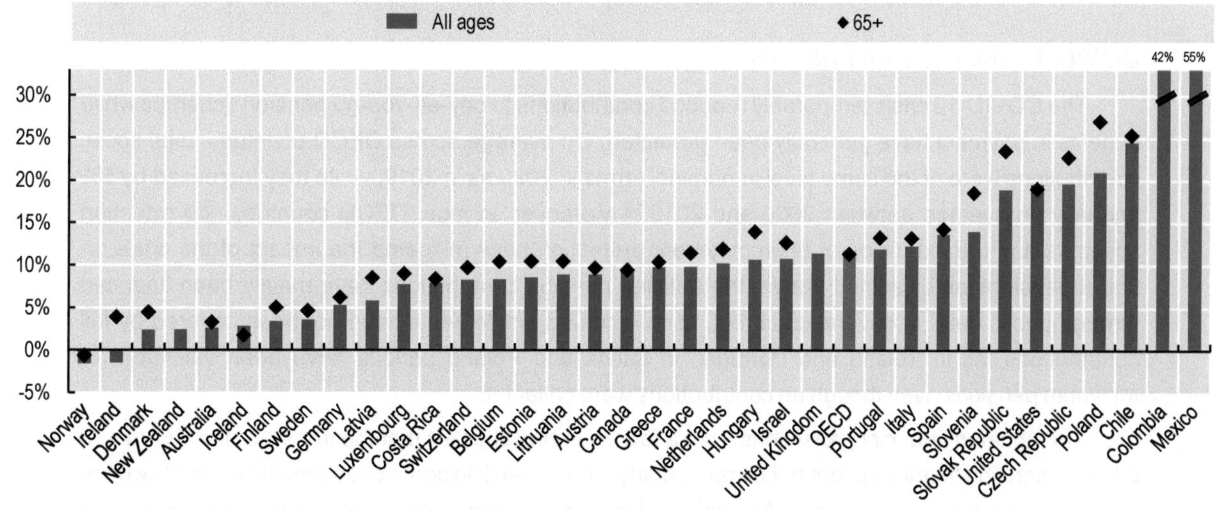

Note: Excess mortality is calculated for most countries through dividing actual number of deaths by the average number of deaths over 2015-19 for most countries, and by 2019 number of deaths due to data availability for Costa Rica for all ages, and for Costa Rica and Ireland for the 65+ age group, based on data provided by these countries. For most countries data include deaths recorded until week 36 of 2021, except for: Australia (week 25), Canada (26), Colombia (23), the Czech Republic (34), Greece (35), Iceland (32), Italy (30), Luxembourg (35), Mexico (35), the Netherlands (35) and the Slovak Republic (34). For Costa Rica and for people aged 65 or more in Ireland, data cover only 2020.

Source: OECD Excess Deaths database (*https://stats.oecd.org/index.aspx?queryid=104676#*) and data provided by countries.

StatLink *https://stat.link/rdnehm*

Due to excess mortality, the number of people over 65 declined by 0.8% on average in OECD countries between January 2020 and August 2021.[11] Pension spending is expected to fall temporarily in similar proportions. The higher mortality is having a direct impact on pensions in schemes that link retirement ages or benefits to life expectancy. For example, in the Polish NDC scheme, lower period life expectancy observed in 2020 has raised the value of newly granted pensions by 6%,[12] while the Swedish Pension Agency expects a much smaller immediate impact, because, for pension calculations, mortality data are averaged over the five previous years, which smooths the impact of the abrupt mortality increase. In private DC schemes, higher mortality improves the finances of annuity providers given that this excess mortality was not expected in the mortality tables used to compute annuities. The impact of COVID-19 on future mortality is highly uncertain as those who died tended to have had other health risks before the COVID-19 (Pifarré i Arolas et al., 2021[8]; Cairns et al., 2020[9]), while, on the other hand, there might be negative longer term effects on the health of the surviving population (Lopez-Leon et al., 2021[10]). The Belgian Federal Planning Bureau estimates that after a short disruption mortality rates will be back to the long-term trend from 2022 (Duyck, Paul and Vandresse, 2020[11]).

Fertility

The COVID-19 crisis might have affected fertility due to higher economic and health uncertainty. Aassve et al. (2021[12]) compare the observed birth rates from November 2020 through February 2021 against past trends in 22 countries and found a statistically significant declines in Austria, Belgium, Hungary,[13] Italy, Portugal, and Spain and no significant changes in other countries. Similarly, in the United States the actual number of births declined by 6% in November and 8% in December 2020, compared to the same months in 2019.[14] Other countries also reported a substantial decline in births in December 2020 or January 2021 (depending on data availability): Poland by 25%, Estonia, France, Latvia and Lithuania by more than 10%, England and Wales, and Israel by around 10%.[15] McDonald (2020[13]) estimates for Australia that a large part of the decline in the fertility rate will likely be offset by higher fertility over the next decade. It is too early to assess whether the current crisis could have a substantial impact on total fertility that would affect the pace of population ageing.

COVID-19 and pension finances

The COVID-19 crisis temporarily reduced contributions to pay-as-you-go pension schemes while benefits in payment have generally been protected. On average across OECD countries, total social contributions were at the same level in nominal terms in 2020 as in 2019, while they increased by 5% annually on average between 2000 and 2019.[16] Moreover, in most OECD countries, job retention schemes and the extension of unemployment protection have mitigated the impact of the crisis on future pensions as explained above; the missing pension contributions have mainly been financed through public debt. In several countries, some accrued entitlements have not been covered by full contributions, as in Ireland and Portugal; in Latvia and Poland periods have been validated for minimum pensions even though no contributions were collected.

The updated financial projections from a few countries suggest that the impact of the COVID-19 crisis on pension finances might not be particularly large, even if in some countries the crisis may have exacerbated existing imbalances. As explained above, a reasonable order of magnitude is that the COVID-19-related excess mortality would slightly limit pension expenditure, by about 0.8% in the OECD in 2021, but less so in the following years. An estimate by the Pensions Advisory Agency (COR) for France implies a similar decrease in pension spending due to increased mortality.

However, given that GDP fell with the economic slump, pension spending as a share of GDP increased in most countries. This temporarily weakens pension finances even though subsidies have helped contributions fall less or increase more than GDP, transferring some of the costs to state budgets. Overall, as this effect might be offset in the recovery phase, the total medium-term impact on pension finances would be modest, although some cost might still be covered by public finances in some countries. In Finland, ETK (2021[14]) estimated in March 2021 that lower pension contributions will be offset by the increase in contribution rates in 2022-25 and by around 2027 the ratio of pension liabilities to pension assets (the so-called solvency ratio) would be back to the pre-crisis trajectory. In France, due to the economic contraction (i.e. denominator effect) pension expenditure increased from 13.7% to 14.7% of GDP between 2019 and 2020. With the projected economic recovery, pension spending as a percentage of GDP is supposed to come back close to its pre-crisis level in 2022 (COR, 2021[15]). In the United States, there will be some impact in the medium term: based on the estimates of the Social Security and Medicare Boards of Trustees, the reserve pension fund (Trust Fund) is now expected to be depleted is 2033 instead of 2034 before the COVID-19 crisis (SSA, 2021[16]).

Pension finances have also been affected through the impact of COVID-19 on financial markets, and therefore on assets held in public reserve funds and funded DB schemes. However, those effects were temporary given that financial markets bounced backed strongly after the crash in the first half of 2020, in part thanks to new policies implemented by central banks. For example, rates of return of pension schemes in 2020 exceeded 10% in the Netherlands and Sweden (OECD, 2021[17]).[17] Likewise, within funded DC plans, pension assets have benefited from exceptionally high returns from mid-2020, also in relation to central banks' measures.

Ageing pressure and pensions – where do we stand?

Population ageing has been accelerating although paces vary strongly across countries

Populations have been ageing in all OECD countries. On average across OECD countries, the median age was 41 years in 2020, eight years higher than in 1990 and is expected to further increase by six years by 2050 (Figure 1.3) – meaning that half of the population will be younger than 47 and half older. This rapid rise results from people living longer on average and having fewer babies. The median age is expected to increase by more than 10 years in Chile, Colombia, Korea, Mexico and Turkey and by less than three years in Denmark and Sweden, where relatively high birth rates will increase the size of younger age groups, and in Latvia, where high past emigration would limit the growth in the number of older people. Populations started to age at a fast pace in the 1980s, but that pace is expected to slow down from the late-2030s (Figure 1.4). The fall in fertility rates has a direct impact on the median age but takes one generation to affect the demographic ratio that is more relevant for pensions, i.e. the old-age to working-age ratio – the number of people older than 65 years per 100 people of working age (20 to 64 years).

Population ageing has been accelerating in recent years based on this ratio. Over the last 30 years, the number of people older than 65 years per 100 people of working age (20 to 64 years) increased from 21 in 1990 to 31 in 2020 in the OECD on average (Figure 1.4). Over the next 30 years, it is expected to reach 53. Although ageing trends are largely common across countries, one striking feature of the below chart is the growing dispersion of projected old-age to working-age ratios among OECD countries during the first half of the 21st century.

The pace of ageing is projected to be fast until about 2060 on average, from when it would slow down substantially, but uncertainty is large when projecting so far in the future. However, that pace is already largely determined for the next 30 years. While in the baseline the old-age to working-age ratio is projected to increase by 23 points on average between 2020 and 2050 (from 30 to 53), a low-fertility scenario assuming that fertility ratios are 0.5 lower from 2020, which would be a big difference, would imply an increase of 24 points instead. If one assumes that there were no future mortality improvements, the increase in the average demographic ratio would be of 16 points.

Figure 1.3. **Median age is increasing fast**

OECD countries, in 1990, 2020, and 2050

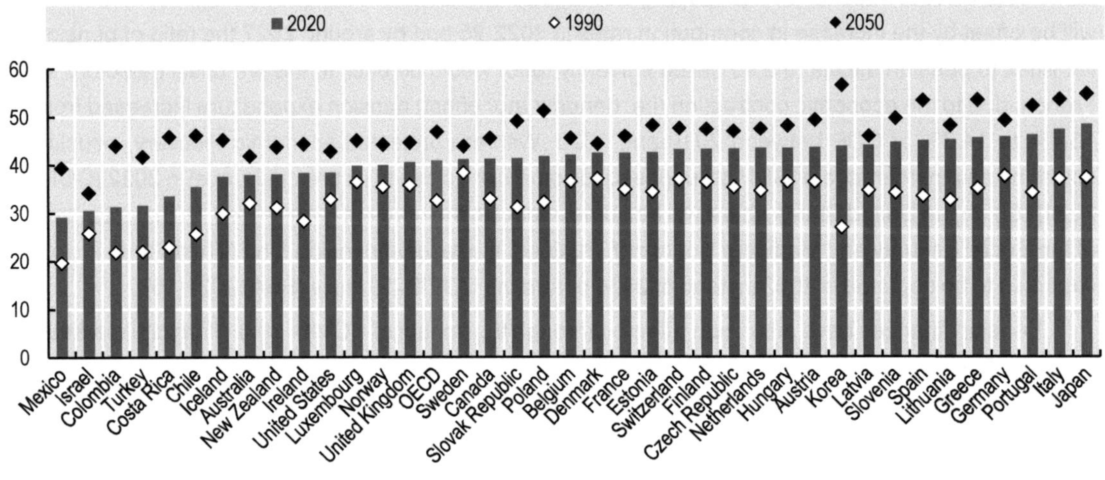

Source: United Nations World Population Prospects: The 2019 Revision.

StatLink https://stat.link/p0j2t3

Over the decade preceding the COVID-19 crisis, improvements in longevity have slowed in many countries (Box 1.1). For women, this slowdown brings the pace back to levels similar to those that prevailed between 1970 and the mid-1990s, while for men the pace remains relatively fast. This means that the acceleration of old-age life expectancy between the mid-1990s and around 2010 seems to have ended.

Figure 1.4. **The old-age to working-age ratio is accelerating**

Number of people older than 65 years per 100 people of working age (20-64), 1950-2100

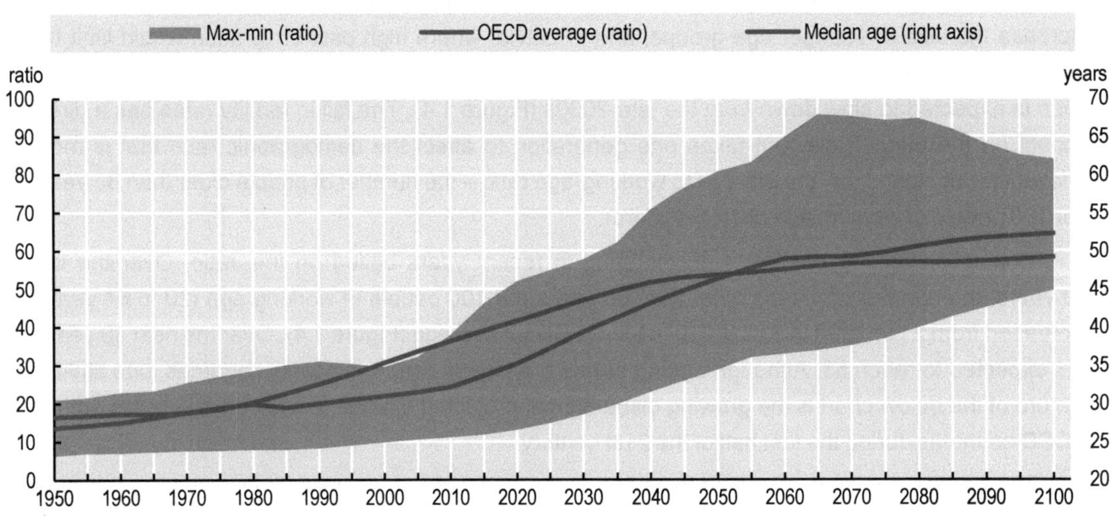

Note: The centre line is the OECD average old-age to working-age ratio. The shaded area indicates the range between the country with the lowest old-age to working-age ratio and the country with the highest old-age to working-age ratio.

Source: United Nations World Population Prospects: The 2019 Revision.

StatLink https://stat.link/gcinw5

Box 1.1. **Has there been a slowdown in pre-COVID-19 old-age life expectancy?**

Recent OECD work has provided some evidence that there have been recent changes in the pace of life expectancy improvements (Raleigh, 2019[18]). This analysis aims to go one-step further and systematically test whether significant structural breaks in life-expectancy gains can be identified. This assessment is done based on the Bai-Perron test, which has been used in previous OECD work to identify structural breaks in labour productivity trends (Boulhol and Turner, 2011[19]). The focus is on remaining life expectancy at age 65 among women and among men by country until 2019, which is the last available data point, hence not accounting for the COVID-19 crisis.

For the OECD on average, the method identifies a significant structural break after 2010 for women, with the annual change being equal to 0.11 years on average (1.1-year gain per decade) compared with 0.14 years between 1996 and 2010 (1.4-year gain per decade) (Figure 1.5, Panel A). The slowdown brings the pace of life-expectancy improvements roughly back to where it was between the early 1970s and the mid-1990s. That is, long-term trends suggest that there has been a slowdown from a period of acceleration of longevity between the mid-1990s and around 2010. There are some exceptions within countries: no recent slowdown is found in the Baltic countries, the Czech Republic, Denmark, Iceland, New Zealand, Portugal, the Slovak Republic and the United States. The estimated reduction in the pace of improvements has been particularly strong, of more than 0.7 years per decade, in Australia, Finland, Ireland (from a high level), Italy, Japan, the Netherlands and the United Kingdom. Details by country are provided in Figure 1.5.

Figure 1.5. **Structural breaks in life-expectancy gains in the OECD on average**

Yearly change in life expectancy at age 65, in years, OECD average

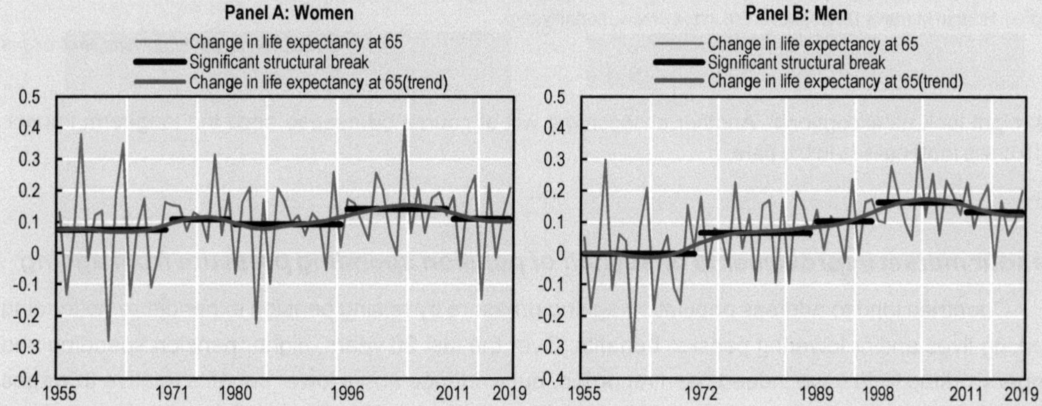

Note: The breaks are significant at the 99% confidence level. To limit interferences from short-term fluctuations in change in period life expectancy, the breaks are estimated on the Hodrick-Prescott filtered trend series (lambda=100). The OECD average does not include Colombia, Costa Rica, Mexico and Turkey due to data missing in the in the Human Mortality Database (2020).
Source: Human Mortality Database (2020), https://www.mortality.org/.

StatLink https://stat.link/jw6o1e

For men, there is a similar pattern on average, from a gain of 1.6 years per decade to 1.3 years (Figure 1.5, Panel B), which implies that the current pace remains faster that what prevailed until the mid-1990s. However, this masks a stronger heterogeneity across countries than among women. In more than one-third of countries – Belgium, the Czech Republic, Denmark, Hungary, Iceland, Italy, Korea, Latvia, Lithuania, the Netherlands, Norway, Poland, the Slovak Republic and Sweden – there is no recent slowdown. The case of the Czech Republic is illustrated in Figure 1.6, Panel A. Chile and France are the only two OECD countries in which there has been no structural break for males even since 1980.[1] For the remaining countries, there has been a recent slowdown around 2010 among males. The slowdown is between 2009 and 2013 in all of these countries except in Japan where it was in 1986. Panel B illustrates the case of Australia (see Annex 1.B for more details).

Overall, there is strong evidence that many countries have experienced a slowdown in old-age life expectancy improvements from about 2010. For women, this slowdown brings the pace back to similar levels as those that prevailed between 1970 and the mid-1990s, while for men the pace remains relatively fast. This means that the acceleration of old-age life expectancy between the mid-1990s and around 2010 seems to have ended. In the future, this period of about

Box 1.1. **Has there been a slowdown in pre-COVID-19 old-age life expectancy?** *(cont.)*

Figure 1.6. **Structural breaks in life-expectancy gains in the Czech Republic and Australia**

Yearly change in remaining life expectancy at age 65, in years, men, the Czech Republic and Australia

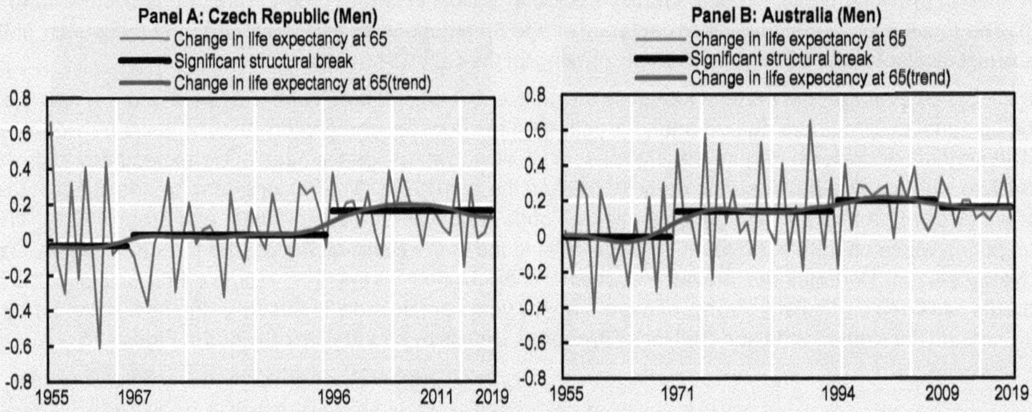

Note: The breaks are significant at the 99% confidence level. To limit interferences from short-term fluctuations in change in life expectancy, the breaks are estimated on the Hodrick-Prescott filtered trend series (lambda=100).
Source: Human Mortality Database (2020), https://www.mortality.org/.

StatLink https://stat.link/40d3n6

15 years might look as exceptional. Another assessment will of course be needed once the long-term impact of the COVID-19 crisis materialises in the data.

Labour market improvements offset half of pension spending pressure from ageing

Countries tend to address population ageing pressure by raising pension expenditure, extending working lives and/or lowering pension benefits. Over the last 20 years, higher pension spending and longer working lives have indeed been recorded, but evidence about lower benefits relative to wages is mixed.

Pre-COVID-19 employment increased among older workers and people worked longer

Since 2000, employment rates of older individuals have increased substantially. This is a major achievement. Among individuals aged between 55 to 64 years, the employment rate grew from 44% in 2000 to 62% in 2020 in the OECD on average (Figure 1.7); the increase was also large in the Russian Federation, but not in other non-OECD G20 countries. The increase exceeded 30 percentage points in the Czech Republic, Estonia, Germany, Hungary, Latvia, the Netherlands and the Slovak Republic. During the same period, the employment rate among people aged between 25 and 54 years increased much less – from 76.5% to 79.5% on average. Improvements in employment have benefited the 55-59 and 60-64 age groups in similar proportions. But, employment still falls abruptly in most countries after around age 60, with average employment rates being equal to 72% among the 55-59 in 2020 and 51% among the 60-64 (Chapter 5).

Higher employment rates at older ages have been driving up the average age when people leave the labour market which increased by 2.2 and 2.8 years between 2000 and 2020 for men and women, respectively, on average across OECD countries (Chapter 6). Over the past decade, ages of labour market exit on average increased faster than life expectancy in EU countries (EC, 2021[20]). On top of the increasing female employment and the effects of higher levels of education (Geppert et al.,

Figure 1.7. **Employment rates of older workers have grown strongly**

Change in employment rates, 2000-20, percentage points

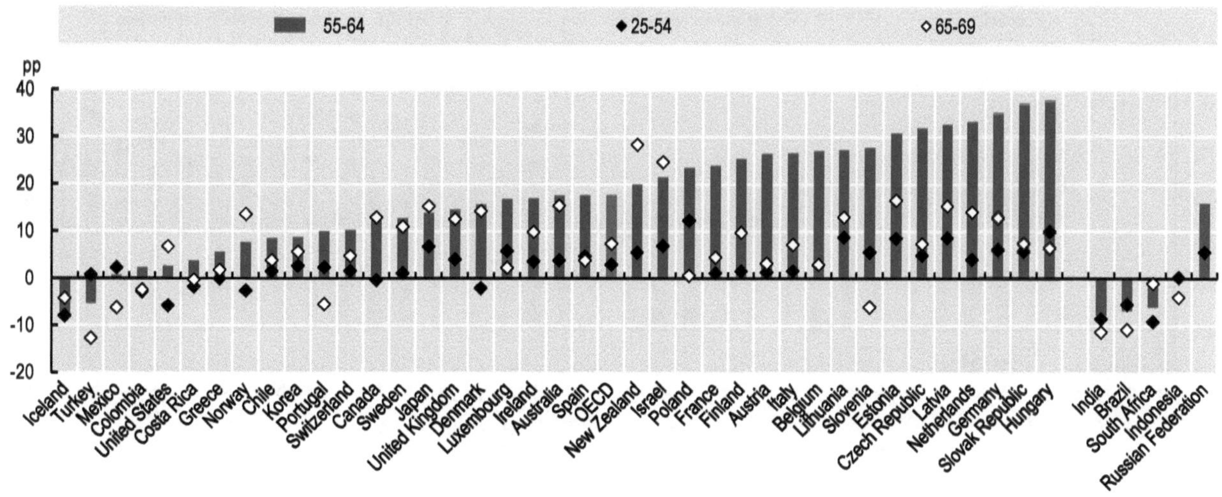

Source: OECD Labour Force Statistics (*https://stats.oecd.org/Index.aspx?DataSetCode=LFS_SEXAGE_I_R*).

StatLink *https://stat.link/nkom8e*

2019[21]), pension policies have played a crucial role, for example through the tightening of early retirement options and the increase in statutory retirement ages.

Pension rules changed for cohorts born in 1940 and 1956, retiring around 2005 and 2020, respectively, depending on countries. On average across OECD countries, men born in 1940 or 1956 with an uninterrupted career from age 20 could have retired without penalty at ages 62.9 or 64.2 years, respectively, hence an average increase of 1.3 years (OECD, 2019[22]). Italy and Japan had the largest increase, while the normal retirement age did not change in slightly more than half of OECD countries for these cohorts. The average increase in the normal retirement age thus represents about half of the average increase in the labour market exit age.

The increase in retirement ages has helped limit the impact of population ageing on pension systems. Between 2008 and 2018, the number of pensioners increased by 20% – whether or not disability pensioners are accounted for -, much less than the 27% increase in the number of people aged 65 or more on average in the OECD (Figure 1.8). The tightening of pension eligibility conditions contributed to the slower increase in the number of pensioners, particularly in the Czech Republic, Denmark, France, Greece, Hungary, Italy, the Netherlands, Poland, Portugal, the Slovak Republic and the United Kingdom. In Finland and Sweden, there was a sharp decrease in the number of disability pensioners; by contrast, in Belgium, Estonia and Hungary, the increase in the number of disability pensions had a big impact on the change in the total number of pensioners. Mexico is an outlier with the introduction of a nationwide non-contributory scheme (*Pensión para Adultos Mayores*) for people aged 70 or more in 2007 while the contributory funded scheme is still maturing.[18]

Figure 1.8. **The number of pensioners increased less than the number of older people**

Change in the number of pensioners and the number of people aged 65 or older, 2008-18

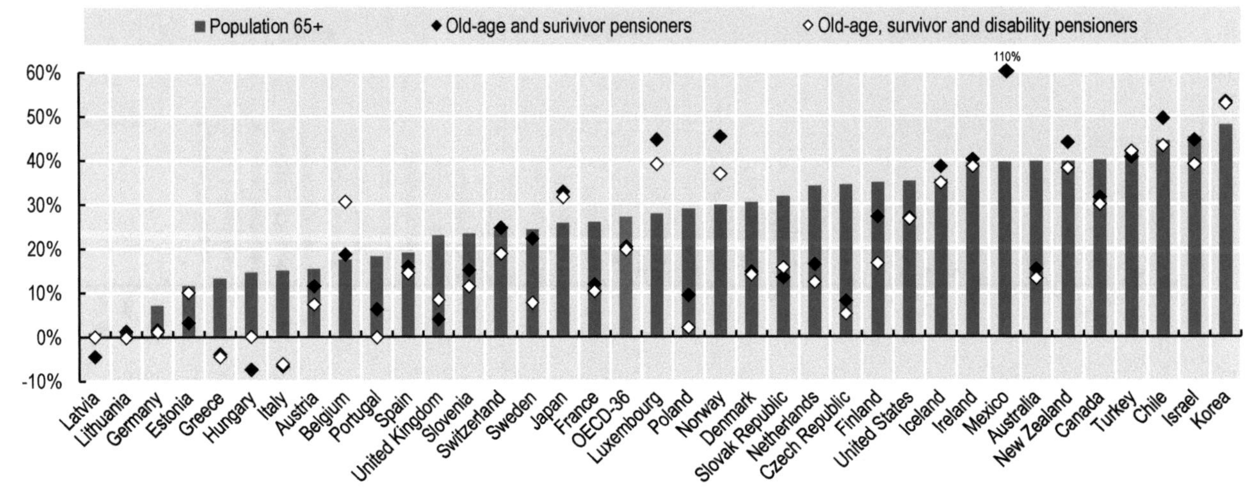

Source: OECD Social Benefit Recipients (SOCR) Database (https://www.oecd.org/social/social-benefit-recipients-database.htm) and ESSPROS (https://ec.europa.eu/eurostat/web/social-protection).

StatLink https://stat.link/gvu5mx

Pension expenditure

Total (private and public) pension expenditure increased by 1.5% of GDP between 2000 and 2017, from 7.9% to 9.4%, on average in the OECD. The increase was larger than 4% of GDP in Finland, Greece and Portugal, while Chile, Germany, Ireland, Latvia and Lithuania recorded a decrease in the spending ratio (Table 1.1).

The increase in pension expenditure as a share of GDP can be decomposed into changes in four contributing factors: the demographic structure; employment; the average benefit ratio; and, the labour share in GDP (Box 1.2). It is estimated that population ageing captured by the shift in demographic structures alone would have triggered an increase in pension expenditure of 2.5% of GDP on average, which is 1.0% of GDP more than the actual increase. Germany, Italy, Japan, the Netherlands and Slovenia faced the largest ageing pressure on spending over this period, of more than 4% of GDP.

Higher employment lowered total pension expenditure by 1.1% of GDP on average, absorbing about 40% of the demographic pressure. Higher employment reduces the pension spending ratio through two channels: through stronger productive capacity (denominator or GDP effect) and more specifically at older ages as it implies fewer pension beneficiaries. Improved labour market outcomes have substantially limited the growth of pension expenditure as a share of GDP in Estonia, Germany, Hungary and Latvia. By contrast, lower employment rates generated additional pension spending pressure in several countries, including Greece, Portugal and Turkey. Given available data, changes in the average benefit ratio, i.e. the average pension divided by the average wage, cannot be distinguished from changes in the pension coverage, e.g. through expanding pensions to previously uncovered population or higher prevalence of combining work and pensions. Based on the best proxy, the average benefit ratio increased over the period, leading to higher pension spending of 0.4% of GDP on average in the OECD between 2000 and 2017. This is consistent with the fact that economic replacement rates – defined as pension spending per old-age population over GDP per working-age population – in European countries have been higher than before the Global Financial Crisis (Fouejieu et al., 2021[23]).

Given demographic projections, the increase in the old-age to working-age ratio is estimated to generate an additional pressure on pension spending, by around 3.5% of GDP between 2017 and 2035. In the absence of new resources that would be available to finance pensions, continuing to raise employment prospects, including through pension policies, is therefore crucial to preserve the level of old-age benefits while limiting the increase in pension expenditure.

Table 1.1. **Higher employment offset almost half of the demographic pressure on pension expenditure over 2000-17**

Change in pension expenditure in GDP between 2000 and 2017 and contribution from different factors, in percentage points

Country	Pension exp./GDP	Contribution from				Residual
		Demography	Labour market	Benefit ratio	Labour share	
Latvia	**-1.9**	2.9	-2.8	-2.2	1.4	-1.2
Chile	**-1.7**	2.2	-1.3	-1.6	-0.5	-0.5
Ireland	**-1.0**	1.7	-0.5	-0.3	-1.5	-0.4
Lithuania	**-0.9**	2.6	-1.9	-0.8	-0.1	-0.7
Germany	**-0.6**	4.1	-3.7	-0.1	0.5	-1.4
New Zealand	**0.0**	1.6	-1.5	0.7	-0.2	-0.5
Slovenia	**0.1**	4.3	-1.1	-2.1	-0.1	-1.0
Poland	**0.1**	3.8	-1.7	-1.0	-0.2	-0.8
United Kingdom	**0.3**	1.7	-1.2	0.3	-0.3	-0.2
Estonia	**0.5**	1.9	-2.6	1.8	0.6	-1.3
Israel	**0.7**	1.0	-1.3	1.3	0.1	-0.4
Czech Republic	**1.0**	3.0	-1.7	-0.6	1.1	-0.8
Hungary	**1.1**	1.8	-2.6	0.5	2.4	-1.1
Slovak Republic	**1.2**	1.9	-1.4	1.0	0.0	-0.4
Austria	**1.2**	3.0	-1.8	0.2	0.3	-0.4
Luxembourg	**1.4**	-0.2	-0.1	1.8	0.0	-0.1
Australia	**1.5**	2.1	-1.2	0.4	0.4	-0.2
Belgium	**1.5**	1.3	-0.9	1.3	-0.1	-0.1
Netherlands	**1.6**	4.3	-2.1	-0.4	0.6	-1.0
Denmark	**1.6**	3.5	-1.1	0.7	-0.9	-0.6
Korea	**1.6**	1.7	-0.2	0.4	-0.1	-0.1
Japan	**1.7**	8.2	-2.4	-1.7	0.2	-2.5
Sweden	**1.8**	1.5	-1.4	1.9	0.1	-0.3
Switzerland	**1.9**	2.2	-0.5	0.1	0.1	-0.1
Mexico	**1.9**	0.2	0.1	1.0	0.0	0.5
France	**2.2**	3.3	-1.1	0.0	0.2	-0.3
Italy	**2.2**	4.3	-2.5	-0.6	1.8	-0.7
Canada	**2.2**	2.9	-0.9	1.0	-0.5	-0.3
Iceland	**2.3**	1.0	0.7	0.4	0.0	0.3
Norway	**2.6**	0.5	1.1	0.4	0.2	0.3
Spain	**2.9**	1.5	-0.7	1.9	0.2	0.1
United States	**3.1**	2.5	0.3	0.7	-0.4	0.1
Turkey	**3.5**	1.0	0.6	4.7	-1.6	-1.3
Finland	**4.4**	3.9	-1.8	2.2	0.5	-0.4
Portugal	**5.4**	3.0	0.5	1.1	0.1	0.7
Greece	**5.4**	3.7	0.9	1.4	-1.0	0.3
OECD	***1.5***	***2.5***	***-1.1***	***0.4***	***0.1***	***-0.5***

Note: Details are described in Box 1.2.

Box 1.2. Decomposition of the change in pension expenditure as a share in GDP

Pension spending in GDP evolves in response to changes in the demographic structure, changes in employment – which also affect the number of retirees -, changes in the average wage and pension, coverage of pensions and the labour share:

$$\frac{Pension\ spend.}{GDP} = \frac{\frac{Pension\ spend.}{Pensioners}}{\frac{Wage\ bill}{Employment}} \frac{Pensioners}{Retirees} \frac{Retirees}{Pop65} \frac{1}{\frac{Employment}{Pop2064}} \frac{Pop65}{Pop2064} \frac{Wage\ bill}{GDP}$$

The equation could be equivalently written as:

$$\underbrace{\frac{Pension\ spend.}{GDP}}_{e} = \underbrace{\underbrace{\left(\frac{AvP}{AvW}\right)}_{b-benefit\ ratio} \underbrace{\left(\frac{Pensioners}{Retirees}\right)}_{c-coverage\ ratio}}_{ab-approximated\ benefit\ ratio} \left(\underbrace{\frac{Retirees}{Pop65}\frac{1}{ER}}_{l-labour\ market}\right) \underbrace{\left(\frac{Pop65}{Pop2064}\right)}_{d-demographics} \underbrace{(LS)}_{ls-labour\ share}$$

Where: *AvP* – average pension spending per retiree; *AvW* – average wage; *ER* – employment rate (total employment / population aged 20-64); *P65* – number of people 65 or older, *P20-64* – number of people aged 20-64, *LS* – labour income share (wage bill / GDP).

Private and public expenditure on old-age and survivor pensions is described in Chapter 7. Demographic pressure is measured by the size of the population 65 or older divided by the population aged 20-64, called the "old-age to working-age demographic ratio". The labour market affects the share of pension expenditure in GDP through the total employment rate and the number of retirees divided by the number of people 65 or older. The number of retirees is proxied as the number of people at 55 or older being economically inactive. While the average pension and the coverage ratio cannot be calculated separately because data about the number of pensioners are not available in cross-country comparison, the approximated benefit ratio combines both and is simply equal to the ratio of pension spending per retiree divided by the average wage.

Relative old-age income

The increase in the old-age relative income over the last two decades is consistent with the estimation that ageing pressures have not yet affected benefit ratios. On average among OECD countries, people older than 65 had an average disposable income equal to 88% of the total population in 2018. It was about 70% or less in Estonia, Korea, Latvia and Lithuania, but about 100% or more in Costa Rica, France, Italy, Israel, Luxembourg and Portugal (Figure 1.9). Since around 2000 the average relative old-age income increased by 6 percentage points in the OECD across the 32 countries for which data are available. It increased by more than 10 points in Denmark, Hungary, Greece, Iceland, Ireland, Israel, Italy, Norway, Portugal, and Spain and the United States, while it decreased by 10 points in Poland, 8 points in Chile, and by about 3-5 points in the Czech Republic, Japan, Latvia and Lithuania.

Pension indexation

One way to contain rising spending while preserving pension replacement rates at retirement is to reduce pension indexation. Many countries have already reduced indexation. In 17 OECD countries, the rules for pension indexation were the same in 2020 as in 2000 and, among them, 11 countries indexed benefits to prices throughout the whole period (Table 1.2). In some countries the shift from wage to price indexation took place earlier, e.g. in Italy in 1992. Over the last 20 years, 11 countries made pension indexation less favourable through linking it only to prices, or through increasing the weight of prices in the total indices, or as in the case of Germany, Japan and Sweden through introducing automatic adjustment mechanisms (Chapter 2). In the Netherlands, earnings-related occupational pensions are indexed fully to prices only if the value of asset compared to liabilities (the so-called funding ratio) is high enough (Chapter 2). After the global financial crisis the average funding ratio of Dutch pension funds declined and stabilised at a low level, leading to benefit

Figure 1.9. **Relative income of older population increased**

The average disposable income of people aged over 65, percentage of average disposable income of total population

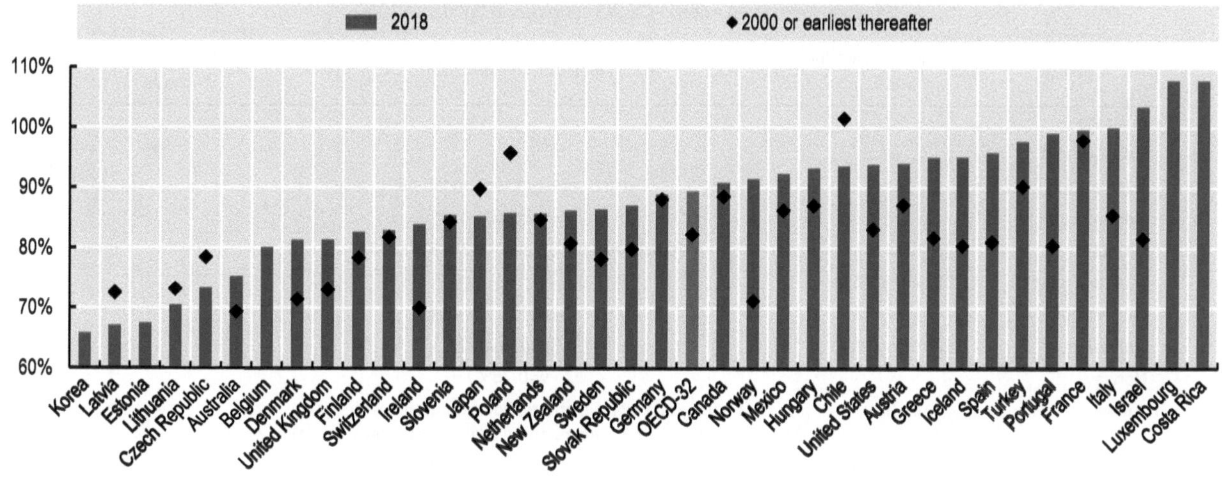

Note: 2018 or latest available year. All income from employment, self-employment, capital and public transfers are included. Incomes are measured on a household basis and equivalised with the square root equivalence scale to adjust for differences in household size.
Source: Chapter 7.

StatLink https://stat.link/1vms8c

indexation below prices, even though some supervisory rules were relaxed (Gerard, 2019[24]) By contrast, five countries made pension indexation more generous. Among them, the United Kingdom is an outlier with the triple-lock rule. In Austria, Latvia, Italy and Portugal higher indexation has applied to low pensions.

Actual indexation sometimes deviates from what the rules imply. Upward discretionary adjustments have been frequent for example in Mexico and Turkey, whereas some countries have applied a lower pension indexation than implied by the rule during and after the global financial crisis to reduce fiscal pressure.

Table 1.2. **Pension indexation rules have remained stable in most OECD countries since 2000**

Pension indexation rules in OECD countries in 2000 and 2020

Country	Indexation rule around 2000	Indexation rule in 2020	Change in the rule
Belgium	p	p	0
Canada	p	p	0
Chile	p	p	0
Costa Rica	p	p	0
France	p	p	0
Korea	p	p	0
Mexico	p	p	0
Spain	p	p	0
Turkey	p	p	0
United States	p	p	0
Italy	p (less for higher pensions)	p (less for higher pensions)	0
Finland	80%p + 20%w	80%p + 20%w	0
Ireland	w, d	w, d	0
Poland	80%p + 20%w	80%p + 20%w	0
Switzerland	50%p + 50% w	50%p + 50%w	0

Table 1.2. **Pension indexation rules have remained stable in most OECD countries since 2000** *(cont.)*

Pension indexation rules in OECD countries in 2000 and 2020

Country	Indexation rule around 2000	Indexation rule in 2020	Change in the rule
Australia	w	w	0
New Zealand	w	w	0
Austria	w	d: p (more for lower pensions)	-
Germany	w	w – sustainability factor	-
Greece	p	p or lower, but 0 between 2009 and 2022	-
Hungary	30%p + 70% w	p	-
Luxembourg	w	w, subject to fiscal space	-
Netherlands	p (funding ratio)	p (funding ratio)	-
Norway	w	w-0.75%	-
Japan	p+ d: w	p from age 68 (and automatic adjustment mechanism) w until age 68 (and automatic adjustment mechanism)	-
Slovak Republic	50%p + 50%w	p (with a minimum fixed amount adjustment guaranteed)	-
Slovenia	w	40%p+60%w	-
Sweden	p	w-1.6%, (and automatic adjustment mechanism)	-
Czech Republic	67%p+33%w	50%p+50%w	+
Denmark	w with constraints	w	+
Estonia	50%p + 50% wb	20% p + 80% wb	+
Latvia	p	70%wb (less for higher pensions)	+
United Kingdom	p	triple lock: max(p, w, 2.5%)	+
Lithuania	d	wb	x
Portugal	d: p, GDP	Between p-0.75 percentage points. and 120%*GDP growth, depending on the GDP growth and individual pension amount	x

Note: p – prices, w – wages, wb – wage bill, d – discretionary, "-" – indexation became less favourable, "+" –indexation became more favourable, "x" – the impact of reforms is not obvious. For Australia (Age pension), Denmark, New Zealand and the United Kingdom, the rules concern basic pensions while for other countries earnings-related schemes. Exceptional measures stopped any pension indexation in Greece between 2009 and 2022. Hungary indexed pension to wages up to 1998, when it was reduced to 50% of the real wage growth, and since 2012, pensions have been indexed only to prices. The Norwegian Parliament is likely to approve the shift of the indexation rule from the wage growth minus 0.75 point to the average of the price and wage growth by the end of 2021. In Sweden, a discount factor of 1.6% increases initial pension amounts, which is offset by indexation of pensions in payment being lowered by 1.6 points, resulting in that pensions in payment were indexed effectively to inflation over the last 20 years. Additionally, an automatic adjustment mechanism.

Over 2000-20, the real annual indexation of pensions is equal to 0.8% on average among OECD countries, half of the average real wage growth of 1.6% (Figure 1.10). In 15 countries indexation did not differ significantly from inflation, whereas in 12 countries pensions in payment increased by at least 1 percentage point faster than prices. Countries with the strongest real wage growth, Estonia, Hungary, Latvia and Lithuania, indexed pensions in payment by more than 2 points on top of prices. Indexation was larger than the average wage growth in the United Kingdom through the effect of the triple lock.[19] The Netherlands is the only country where the indexation of contributory occupational pensions was substantially less than price inflation: -1.1% in real terms per year on average because the solvency rule links indexation to funding ratios (Chapter 2). The funding ratio reflects what part of pension liabilities are backed by assets.[20]

Figure 1.10. Pension indexation was above inflation in most OECD countries

Average annual real indexation of pensions in payments and real-wage growth, 2000-20

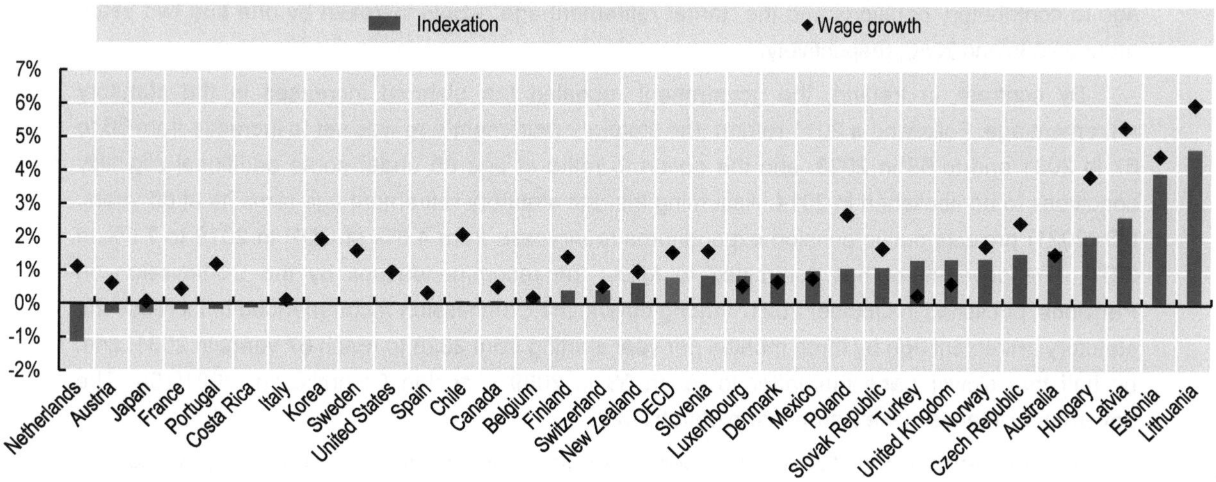

Note: The growth of the gross average wage in Lithuania was inflated by lowering employer's social contributions by 28.9 points in 2019.
Source: OECD Taxing Wages (*https://stats.oecd.org/Index.aspx?DataSetCode=AWCOMP*) and information provided by countries.

StatLink *https://stat.link/akptzn*

Recent pension reforms

This section summarises pension reforms introduced in OECD and G20 countries between September 2019 and September 2021. Several countries implemented substantial pension reforms. Overall, there was limited action on retirement ages while several countries extended early retirement options. Pension benefits in earning-related schemes have been increased in a few countries and there has been a trend towards expanding old-age safety nets or to increase low pensions.

Mixed changes in retirement ages over the last two years

Recent retirement age measures

Over the past two years, limited policy action took place to directly change retirement ages; exceptions are the increase in Sweden, cancellation in Ireland and postponement in the Netherlands. Other retirement-age measures were taken in the Slovak Republic and Slovenia, and among non-OECD G20 countries Brazil introduced minimum retirement ages.

In 2020, Sweden increased the earliest age to draw public contributory pensions from 61 to 62 years.[21] There is an official plan to increase it further to 63 years in 2023 and 64 in 2026. In parallel, the eligibility age for the residency-based basic pension (so-called guarantee pension)[22] is planned to be raised from 65 years today to 66 in 2024 and 67 years in 2027.[23] In 2021, the "target retirement age", introduced in 2019, was set at 67, to be effective from 2027. The "target retirement age" aims to nudge retirement decisions, by providing a clear suggestion of what the adequate age to retire should be.[24] Finland first introduced a "target retirement age" in 2017 to indicate the age until which consecutive cohorts need to work to offset the impact of the life expectancy coefficient on replacement rates.

Provided that these plans, which are based on a 2019 agreement of most political parties present in the Swedish Parliament, are implemented, the earliest age to draw public contributory pensions and the "target retirement age" would be indexed to life expectancy at 65 years, transmitting two-thirds of changes in life expectancy into retirement ages, from 2026 onwards upon governmental approvals. However, it has not yet been decided whether the link will apply also to the eligibility age to access the basic pension and to the mandatory retirement age, at 68 currently and 69 from 2024. As these likely changes in future retirement ages have not yet been legislated, *Pensions at a Glance* indicators do not take them into account. Based on national Swedish demographic projections, the minimum eligibility age to contributory pensions and the "target retirement age" would increase by one and two years around 2035 and 2050, respectively.

By contrast, in Ireland, the government repealed the planned increases in the statutory retirement age. Following a 2011 reform, the statutory retirement age was set to increase from 66 to 67 in 2021 and to 68 in 2028, and the option to retire at age 65 under some additional eligibility conditions to be abolished in 2014. Assuming that the statutory retirement age remains at 66 years, EC (2021) projects public pension expenditures to increase from 4.6% of GDP in 2019 to 7.6% in 2070. The government has committed to follow the recommendations by the Commission on Pensions, published in October 2021. Among others, the Commission recommended to increase the statutory retirement age by three months per year starting from 2028 to reach 67 years in 2031, and, by half that slower pace thereafter to reach 68 in 2039 (Pension Commission, 2021[25]). The government intends make a proposal in March 2022.

The Netherlands modified the link between retirement age and life expectancy (Chapter 2 provides details about automatic adjustment mechanisms). For each year of life expectancy gains at age 65, the pace of the increase in the retirement age applying to the basic pension will be eight months in 2025 rather than the initially foreseen one year increase. The one-to-one link was fast, implying that all longevity improvements were passed into the retirement age, hence steadily reducing the share of adult life spent in retirement. At the same time, the increase of the retirement age from 66 and 4 months to 67 was postponed from 2021 to 2024. As a result, based on current life-expectancy projections, the retirement age for someone entering the labour market at age 22 now will reach 69 against 71 years in the previous edition of *Pensions at a Glance*.[25]

In the Slovak Republic, while the retirement age is increasing by two months per year to reach 64 years in 2030, the retirement-age cap of 64 years – introduced in 2019 along with the cancellation of the link between the retirement age and life expectancy – was abolished from the Constitution in 2020. In 2021, the government prepared a proposal to re-establish a link between the retirement age and life expectancy. Additionally, the retirement age of mothers was lowered by six months for each child up to three children. This right is, under certain conditions, transferable to fathers. Apart from the Slovak Republic, only the Czech Republic, Italy and Slovenia in the OECD allow mothers to retire earlier without penalties than single women.

Against the general trend among OECD countries, Slovenia introduced in December 2020 a mandatory retirement age – i.e. an option for employers to terminate the employment contract above a certain age. The reform removed the requirement to provide a justified reason when dismissing an employee who has met eligibility conditions to the old-age pension (OECD, 2022[26]). Thus, the mandatory retirement age would apply in Slovenia as early as age 60 for people who worked for at least 40 years. Only in Japan and Korea does the mandatory retirement age apply to private-sector workers from age 60, while in nine other countries it applies only from age 65 or higher (OECD, 2022[26]).[26] However, the implementation of this amendment is uncertain as it has been appealed in the Constitutional Court on the ground of discrimination.[27]

Among G20 countries, Brazil took significant steps to improve pension finances in 2019, which required amending the constitution and included introducing minimum retirement ages. The option to retire after a career of 35 and 30 years for men and women, respectively, without any age restriction, was eliminated. These loose conditions had led to the average effective age of labour market exit of 56 years for men and 53 years for women. From 2020, men and women can retire when older than 65 and 60 (being gradually increased to 62 by 2024), respectively, after a 15-year long career, which will increase to 20 years for men who will start to contribute after the reform. Some exceptions were made for rural workers and those working in arduous occupations. Those who had qualified for pensions before the legislation are not affected, with a transition for those who are close to retirement. Other measures affecting the pension replacement rate are discussed in the corresponding section below.

Implications for normal retirement ages

Normal retirement ages – the age at which individuals are eligible for retirement benefits from all pension components without penalties, assuming a full career from age 22 – differ significantly among OECD countries. For men retiring in 2020, the normal retirement age was the lowest at 62 years (except for Turkey) in Colombia, Costa Rica, Greece, Italy, Korea, Luxembourg and Slovenia, whereas it was 67 in Iceland and Norway. Turkey is currently an outlier at 52 years. Given current legislation, the future normal retirement age – i.e. after having entered the labour market in 2020 and therefore retiring after 2060 – will range from 62 years in Colombia, Luxembourg and Slovenia and 64 years in the Slovak Republic to 74 years in Denmark. On average across OECD countries, it will increase by about two years, from 64.2 in 2020 to 66.1 in the future. Over the same period, life expectancy at age 65 is expected to grow by 4.1 years on average. The current normal retirement age is lower for women than for men in Austria, Colombia, Costa Rica, Hungary, Israel, Lithuania, Poland, Switzerland, and Turkey, on average by 2.8 years in these countries (Chapter 3). Austria, Costa Rica, Lithuania and Turkey will eliminate the gender gap in normal retirement ages.

Over this period, the normal retirement age is set to increase by more than five years in Denmark, Estonia and Italy through links with life expectancy, which are discussed in detail in Chapter 2, as well as in Turkey but there from a low level (Figure 1.11). Meanwhile, 17 OECD countries have not passed any legislation that will increase the normal retirement age. In Luxembourg, the Slovak Republic and Slovenia where future retirement ages are comparatively low, pension spending is projected to increase by more than 5% of GDP between 2019 and 2070, the highest increases in the European Union (EC, 2021). Moreover, all non-OECD G20 countries will have retirement ages of 65 years or below, and even lower than 60 years in India and Saudi Arabia.

Figure 1.11. **The normal retirement age is rising in many OECD countries**

Normal retirement age for men entering the labour market at age 22 with a full career

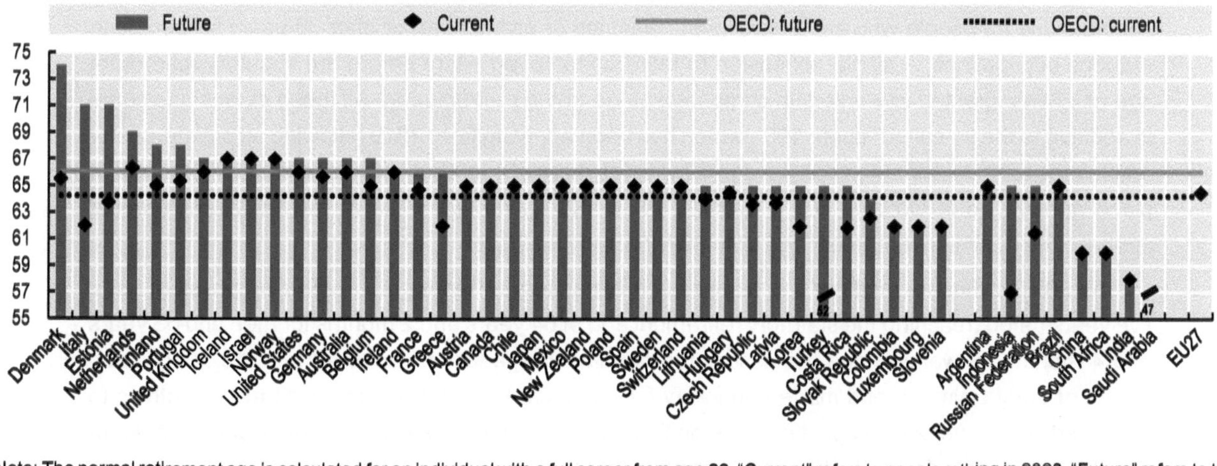

Note: The normal retirement age is calculated for an individual with a full career from age 22. "Current" refers to people retiring in 2020. "Future" refers to the age from which someone is eligible to full retirement benefits from all mandatory components (without any reduction), assuming a full career from age 22 in 2020. Educational credits are not included. The current normal retirement age for Italy is based on a temporary measure "quota 100" which was introduced for 2019-21 and allows to retire below the statutory retirement age.
Source: Chapter 3.

StatLink https://stat.link/fprg42

Expanding early retirement

Early retirement options have been expanded in Denmark, Ireland, Italy and Lithuania. In Denmark, from January 2022, those who have been insured for at least 42 years before the age of 61 will be able to receive a benefit equal to the basic pension amount up to three years before the normal retirement age of 67.[28] Other countries allow early retirement without penalty for individuals with a long career from an early start, including Austria, France, Germany, Greece, Luxembourg, Portugal, Slovenia and Spain. In Denmark, another new option to retire early was introduced: it allows individuals who have at least 20 to 25 years (depending on occupations) of full-time employment and are unable to work more than 15 hours a week (18 hours from 2024) in their most recent jobs to receive a pension up to six years before the normal retirement age. These new early retirement options were introduced within the context of Denmark's previously legislated increase of the retirement age from 65 to 67 years between 2019 and 2022, and to 68 in 2030. Related to early retirement for long careers, Austria legislated a new pension top-up (*Early Starter Bonus*) in 2020, which will come into force for people retiring from 2022.[29] People who have worked for at least 25 years in total will receive a monthly top-up of EUR 12 for each year of work between ages 15 to 20.

Ireland introduced a benefit for those who: are at least 65, which is one year before the statutory retirement age; have ceased either regular employment or self-employment; and, meet the eligibility conditions to unemployment benefits.[30] The benefit replaces, at the same amount of EUR 203 per week, the unemployment benefits for those older than 65, but it does not require any job-search effort, hence potentially generating disincentives to work longer.

Italy extended some early retirement options which were supposed to be temporary and to expire in 2020. The so-called women's option, initially introduced for a year in 2017, was extended again by one year, until the end of 2021. This option allows women to retire at age 58 (or 59 if self-employed) after a 35-year career, but it requires that pensions are fully calculated based on the notional defined contributions (NDC) rules while pensions from defined benefit (DB) and NDC schemes are prorated when retiring at the statutory retirement age. In Italy, NDC rules generally result in benefits being lower than those based on the DB scheme, due to the automatic actuarial adjustments in NDC and low penalties in DB. Additionally, the government prolonged the options to retire at age 63 with 30 years of contributions for people who are unemployed, disabled or giving care, or after 36 years for people in arduous occupations. A similar extension to retire up to seven years before the statutory retirement age of 67 was granted to workers in companies undergoing restructuring. All these extensions come in addition to the so-called "quota 100", which has been applying from 2019, allowing all private-sector employees to retire without penalty at age 62 with 38 years of contributions. According to government plans announced in October 2021, "quota 100" would be replaced by "quota 102", which would increase the minimum retirement age from 62 to 64, only for 2022.

In 2021, Lithuania modified the early-retirement scheme. Retiring early remains possible up to five years before reaching the statutory retirement age of 64 years and 2 months for men and 63 years and 4 months for women, and the associated penalty was reduced from 0.40% to 0.32% for each month of early claiming, and made temporary for some workers.[31] This increases the incentives to retire early with a negative impact on pension finances and pension levels. For public pensions, apart from Lithuania, only Korea, Turkey and Colombia (for women) allow early retirement for private-sector workers before the age of 60.

Expanding first-tier pensions

Over the past two years, several countries made substantial efforts to improve the minimum standards of living of retirees. Social protection at the lower end of the old-age income distribution was substantially improved in Chile, Latvia, Mexico and the Slovak Republic. Moreover, the minimum pension was raised in Slovenia and Germany introduced an individual supplementary benefit to contributory pensions.[32] Australia, Canada, Norway and Sweden also took some measures to improve old-age safety nets.

Chile legislated a large increase in the levels of both the basic (solidarity) pension (*Pensión Básica Solidaria – PBS*) and the publicly financed pension supplement (*El Aporte Previsional Solidario – APS*) in 2019, by 50% each by 2022. The basic pension is granted to individuals not receiving any pension from the earnings-related DC scheme and the supplement tops up the individual DC pension, with a 67% withdrawal rate. As a result, based on OECD modelling assumptions, the future pension of full-career low-wage earners will be increased by one-third. Additionally, the government expanded the pension supplement by subsidising programmed withdrawals at very old ages to those with low pensions.[33] This is meant to avoid that those opting for programmed withdrawals face drops in payments at older ages.

Both Latvia and Mexico substantially increased the old-age safety-net benefit and reformed their minimum (contributory) pensions. In Latvia, both the minimum pension and the non-contributory old-age benefits were increased by 25% in 2020, from a low level. In 2021, the non-contributory old-age benefit was set at 25% of the median disposable income, which meant an additional increase by 70% of both benefits as the minimum pension that is accessible after 15 years of contributions is set at 110% of the non-contributory old-age benefit. The level of these benefits had been frozen in nominal terms for 13 years, so linking them to the median disposable income is an important innovation. Additionally, the design of the minimum pension changed and the benefit levels now increase by 2% for every year of contribution beyond 15 years while before the benefit increased only stepwise at 20, 30 and 40 years of contributions. This reform is fully consistent with recommendations made in the *OECD Pension System Review of Latvia* to address the high level of old-age poverty.

In Mexico, the non-contributory residency-based basic pension (*Programa Pensión para el Bienestar de las Personas Adultas Mayores*), introduced in 2019, is paid to all eligible citizens from age 65 since July 2021, against 68 before. On top of the nominal increase of 120% documented in the previous edition of *Pensions at a Glance*, the amount of this benefit will increase gradually by 75% in real terms by 2024. After these increases, the basic pension will be around 25% of the gross average wage. Moreover, in December 2020, the government increased substantially the amount of the minimum pension (*Pensión Mínima Garantizada*) and changed it from a flat-rate benefit to a benefit, the level of which increases with career length up to 24 years, with the individuals' average wage and with the effective retirement age. Penalties of around 1.3% for each year of claiming the minimum pension before the statutory retirement age are far from actuarial neutrality; they may encourage early labour market exit and create a net cost for public finances. The minimum pension reform will be gradually implemented between 2023 and 2030. Accessing the minimum pension before the statutory retirement age with no or limited penalty is unusual among OECD countries.

Concretely, for a person aged 65 who earned the average wage and contributed for at least 24 years, the Mexican minimum pension amount has doubled from 30% to 63% of the gross average wage while the minimum pension does not exceed 40% of the average wage in any other OECD country. As the benefits are to be indexed to prices, the minimum pension is projected to fall back to about 37% of the average wage for those who will retire in the 2060s.This compares to future theoretical replacement rates from the DC scheme – i.e. without including a top-up from the minimum pension – at age 65 of an average-wage earner of 28% after 24 of contributions and 46% after 43 years, based on OECD modelling assumptions. Such a high level of the minimum pension has two main implications. First, it implies that for many pensioners the pension level will no longer depend on accumulated assets financed by past contributions, and that the state budget will provide a supplement. The lower the future financial returns, the larger the fiscal cost, which will be visible only over time because the state subsidies finance minimum pensions once DC assets are depleted. Second, as the minimum pension is likely to play a much larger role, future pensions will depend less on past earnings and differences in pension benefits across individuals will be lower. Overall, this reform has a systemic component: it increases future pension levels and tends to make the funded DC scheme at least in part more like a DB scheme partly funded by contribution assets and partly funded by the state budget.

In 2020, the Slovak Republic shifted the calculation of the minimum pension accessible after 30 years of contributions from 136% of the minimum subsistence level to 33% of the gross average wage, implying an immediate increase of 17% and steadily more as the average wage tends to grow faster than the minimum subsistence level. However, just one year later and effective from January 2021, the minimum pension was permanently delinked from the average wage.[34] In 2019, as part of the reform to the contributory pension (see below), Slovenia gradually increased the minimum pension, available after 15 years of contributions, by 11% for men such as to equalise benefit levels between men and women by 2025; in 2021 the measure was moved forward and became effective in May 2021.

In 2021, Germany introduced an individual pension supplementary benefit (*Grundrente*) to those who contributed for at least 33 years on the basis of low income. Both the eligibility conditions and the benefit calculation are complex (Börsch-Supan et al., 2021[27]). The full amount of the supplement is paid to pensioners with monthly income[35] of up to EUR 1 250 (29% of the gross average wage) for a single person or EUR 1950 for a couple. For higher income, up to EUR 1 600 and EUR 2 300, respectively, the supplementary benefit is withdrawn at a 60% rate, and at a 100% rate for income above these thresholds. Overall, the supplement may raise contributory pensions by as much as around 90% for retirees who worked for at least 35 years at low wages. However, the impact of the supplement on total individual income is expected to be much lower given that it reduces the amount of safety-net benefits.[36] The German Pension Insurance Agency (*Deutsche Rentenversicherung*) estimated that 1.3 million pensioners (7% of population aged 65 or more) would receive the new supplement, at EUR 75 per month on average (about 4% of median disposable income of population aged 65 or older).[37] The new benefit is financed from the state budget and is estimated by the Federal Ministry of Labour and Social Affairs to generate an additional cost of around 0.04% of GDP per year.in 2021-25., which suggests it will have a small impact.

Australia eased the asset condition used in the income test when calculating the old-age safety-net benefit (Age Pension) in 2020 to reflect the potential impact of low interest rates on the future income from accumulated assets. Part of Australia's age pension income test assumes that individual financial assets will generate a fixed rate of return, regardless of actual returns. The assumed rates of return are called the deeming rates. In 2020, the deeming rates were substantially reduced from 1% to 0.25% for yearly income below AUD 53 600 for singles (89 000 for couples) and from 3% to 2.25% above that threshold. The reduction was implemented to reflect the low interest rate environment leading to lower income earned on savings. These changes reduce income support recipients' deemed income, resulting in higher Age Pension payments for many recipients.

In 2021, Canada passed a legislation to increase the basic pension (Old Age Security) for seniors aged 75 and over by 10% from July 2022. In 2021, Sweden introduced a new pension supplement to increase monthly pensions between SEK 9 000 and SEK 17 000 (between 23% and 44% of gross average wage, respectively) by up to 6.7%. This benefit will be paid to people who receive none or a small amount of the basic pension, which is fully withdrawn when monthly earnings-related pension exceeds SEK 12 529 (in 2020). The supplement is financed by the central government budget and is estimated to cost 0.1% of GDP annually. Norway discretionarily increased the minimum pension benefit for single pensioners in the old DB scheme by 6.5% on top of regular indexation over 2019-21.

Adjusting benefits and contributions in earning-related pensions

Changes in pay-as-you-go pensions

Several countries decided to increase earnings-related pensions over these last two years. Hungary and Slovenia took the measures with the biggest impact, which will affect future pension financial balances in these two countries. Greece, Poland and the Slovak Republic also took action in this area, and Japan broadened the pension coverage of part-time workers. Among non-OECD G20 countries, the 2019 pension reform in Brazil will affect future benefits substantially.

In Hungary, an additional pension benefit, the so-called 13th-month pension, was introduced in January 2021, at the amount of 25% of the monthly pension and gradually increasing to 100% in 2024, hence representing eventually an increase of 8.5% in pensions.[38] The employer's social contribution rate, which finances both pensions and health care, was reduced from 17.5% to 15.5%, following previous reductions from 27% in 2016. The immediate impact of the lower contribution rate on the pension balance has been partly offset by a strong labour market performance in recent years. However, the current financing gap is likely to widen in the future given population ageing; EC (2021) projects that pension expenditure will increase from 8.3% to 11.2% of GDP between 2019 to in 2050.

In December 2019, Slovenia cancelled the planned decrease of accrual rates for women and instead gradually increased those for men so that men's net replacement rates after 40 years at the average-wage level will be converging from 57.25% in 2019 to women's levels of 63.50% in 2025. The 2021 reform accelerated this transition which will be fully effective in 2023.

In 2020, Poland turned the thirteenth month pension payment, initially introduced as a one-off benefit in 2019, into a permanent annual benefit, paid to all pensioners at the level of the minimum pension, which is equal to 24% of the monthly average wage. Additionally in 2021, a one-off benefit called fourteenth month pension was paid to pensioners with low pensions. These new tax-financed benefits are expected to increase old-age pension spending by 9.5% in 2021.[39] The new measures will help address the challenge of very low future replacement rates to a small extent (see further in this section) while both the average relative income of older people and relative old-age income poverty rates are around the OECD averages (Chapter 6).

In 2020, following a ruling of the Supreme Court, the Greek Government cancelled the recalculation of pensions (both accruing and being paid) introduced in 2016, that had led to benefit cuts. In 2016, all auxiliary pension entitlements – mandatory PAYG occupational pensions which are part of public pensions on top of the general DB scheme – that accrued before 2014 had been fully recalculated based on NDC rules for pensioners whose total pension was higher than EUR 1 300. This generally meant benefit cuts of up to 40% for the auxiliary component for 200 000 pensioners (OECD, 2017[28]).[40] The reversal of previous benefit cuts is expected to increase pension expenditure by around 1% of GDP (Fouejieu et al., 2021[23]). Additionally, a 13th pension payment, introduced in 2019 was abolished after only one payment was made in May 2019. Moreover, Greece changed the annual accrual rates in the public DB scheme, which have increased by 0.5-0.9 points between 30 and 39 years of contributions and decreased by 1.5 points for more than 40years.

In the Slovak Republic, the Christmas bonus – a targeted pension payment equal to EUR 200 and decreasing to zero for pensions higher than EUR 658.50 – was replaced in April 2020 by a more generous 13th monthly pension payment at a flat-rate amount equal to the average monthly pension of EUR 460.40 (in 2020), paid to all pensioners. Yet, in November, the level of the new benefit was cut substantially, especially for high pensions: at EUR 300 only for those with pension below EUR 214.83 and decreasing to EUR 50 for pensions higher than EUR 909.30.

In May 2020, Japan expanded the mandatory coverage of earnings-related pensions to more part-time workers, who represented 26% of total employment in 2020 compared to 20% in 2010. In Japan, all individuals working at least 30 hours a week are mandatorily covered by earnings-related pensions while those working less than 20 hours or earning less than JPY 88 000 (20% of the monthly average wage) are not covered by the earnings-related scheme. So far, those working between 20 and 30 hours and earning more than JPY 88 000 have been covered only if working in companies employing more than 500 full-time employees. The new law will expand this obligation to companies employing more than 100 and 50 full-time employees by 2022 and 2024, respectively. Furthermore, the mandatory coverage will be expanded to workers in unincorporated firms which provide professional attorney and advisory services.[41]

In January 2021, Italy reduced pension contributions for some groups, in order to lower labour costs and boost employment, which will not affect future pensions as the missing contributions will be covered by the central government budget. For example, for newly employed people who are younger than 35 and for unemployed women, pension contributions will be reduced by up to EUR 6 000 per year (20% of the gross annual average wage) in 2021 and 2022. Moreover, in seven economically depressed regions of Southern Italy (Abruzzo, Basilicata, Calabria, Campania, Molise, Puglia, Sardinia, and Sicily), the government reduced pension contributions by 30% between 2021 and 2025, by 20% in 2026 and 2027 and by 10% in 2028 and 2029.

Among G20 countries, beyond changing eligibility conditions to pensions, discussed above, Brazil modified employees' contribution rates from 8%-11% to 7.5%-14%, depending on income, and modified benefit calculation in the following way. The reference wage will be based on lifetime earnings uprated with prices while before one-fifth of the periods with the lowest earnings were excluded. Accrual rates are set at 60% for the first 20 years for men and 15 years for women. As a result, for men entering the labour market at age 22 in 2020 and working without any breaks at the average wage, the gross replacement rate is projected to be 88% at age 65 compared to 59% at age 57 before. Replacement rates for women will be 5 points higher and they will be able to retire three years earlier than men; before the reform the replacement rate was 13 points lower with retirement five years earlier. Additionally, survivor benefits were lowered to 50% of the deceased's benefit plus 10% for each additional dependant (up to 100%).

Changes in funded defined contribution schemes

Mexico substantially increased mandatory contribution rates in their funded DC (FDC) schemes, thus sharply increasing future replacement rates (Figure 1.12). Greece has created a new DC scheme to replace over time the existing NDC scheme for mandatory auxiliary pensions. Estonia went in the other direction.

As a result of the 2021 pension reform in Mexico, the employer's contribution rate in the mandatory FDC scheme will start to increase in 2023 from 5.15% to reach 13.875% in 2030, at the average-wage level, leading to an increase of the total contribution rate from 6.5% to 15%. Such an increase is consistent with recommendations in the 2016 *OECD Pension Review of Mexico* (OECD, 2016[29]). At the same time the contribution subsidies from the government (*social quota*) will be more targeted at low income workers.[42] In addition, the minimum contribution period required to qualify for an old-age pension was reduced from 1 250 weeks (around 24 years) to 750 weeks (around 15 years), but is set to reverse course and increase by 25 weeks per year to reach 1 000 weeks (around 20 years) in 2031.

In Estonia, the FDC scheme, which used to be mandatory for people born from 1982, has become voluntary since January 2021. Opting out requires taking action while remaining is the default. Re-joining is possible 10 years after having opted out. Before the reform, FDC complemented the basic pension and the mandatory PAYG points system, with a contribution rate of 6% on top of 16% for public pensions, so 22% in total. For individuals opting out from FDC, accumulated assets can be withdrawn. As of mid-2021, about one-fifth of members opted out and withdrew their money (representing 25% of total assets).[43] Moreover, when opting out the contribution rate to the PAYGO scheme is raised to 20% – hence a lower total contribution rate of 2 points in total – which leads to 25% more points being granted while the basic pension level has not changed.

Estonia has followed Hungary, Poland and the Slovak Republic in abolishing the obligation to participate in the funded schemes introduced in the early 2000s, which is expected to have a substantial impact on future benefits. Based on the assumptions in the OECD pension model, this will lead to much lower replacement rates for those opting out due to the unchanged basic pension amount, lower total contribution rates and low returns in the Estonian points scheme (see Figure 1.11). Lower replacement rates from the public pension scheme are due to the strong future decline in the working-age population (Chapter 5), which will severely weigh on the indexation of the points value, while financial returns in DC schemes remain constant in the OECD pension model despite ageing pressure.[44] Hence, this reform carries significant risks for the future pension adequacy of those opting out. At the same time, net wages might be slightly higher and the extra contributions financing the PAYG system generate additional revenues. The popularity of the opting out strategy might be surprising in this context and may have several explanations: a strong appetite for the cash being withdrawn; mistakes in the choice made by individuals; and/or low confidence in the future of FDC in Estonia, either due to very low expected returns or to the perception of high future political risks for FDC.

A new fund for auxiliary pensions, the "Hellenic Auxiliary Pensions Defined Contributions Fund", was established in Greece in September 2021 and will be effective in January 2022. Auxiliary pensions, which used to be fragmented mandatory defined benefit schemes, differing by sector, have been largely unified over the last decade and transformed into an NDC scheme for entitlements accrued after 2014. With the creation of the new fund, auxiliary pensions will be gradually transformed from NDC to FDC. The new FDC scheme will cover new entrants to the labour market while workers younger than 35 would be able to join voluntarily. Other workers and pensioners will not be affected as the decrease in NDC contribution revenues will be covered by the state budget. The contribution rate will remain unchanged at 6.5% until mid-2022, and then be lowered to 6% for employees (equally divided between employees and employers) or a fixed amount for the self-employed.

Future replacement rates

Future theoretical replacement rates are computed by the OECD in order to distinguish some key characteristics of pension systems that allow the comparison across countries. One main indicator is the net replacement rate for the best-case scenario, which assumes a full career in the private sector starting at age 22 in 2020 until reaching the country-specific normal retirement age. This theoretical replacement rate is equal in that case to the pension benefit at retirement as a percentage of the last earnings. The projections take into account all legislative measures adopted until September 2021.

Future pension replacement rates display a large dispersion across countries. Figure 1.12 shows theoretical net pension replacement rates across OECD and G20 countries for a full-career average-wage worker. Net replacement rates from mandatory schemes are equal to 62% on average in the OECD, ranging from less than 40% in Chile, Estonia, Ireland, Japan, Korea, Lithuania and Poland to 90% or more in Hungary, Portugal and Turkey at the normal retirement age. The measures taken over the past two years, which are described in this section, have the largest impact on this indicator in Brazil (G20), Hungary, Mexico and Slovenia (increase), and Estonia (decrease). Auto-enrolment in the United Kingdom has succeeded in generating broad coverage over recent years (Box 1.3), such that voluntary pensions are now classified in the indicators of *Pensions at a Glance* as quasi-mandatory as in Denmark, the Netherlands, Norway and Sweden, and therefore included in the "mandatory" series in Figure 1.12.

Among countries with significant coverage from voluntary private pensions – Belgium, Canada, Estonia, Germany, Ireland, Japan, Lithuania, New Zealand and the United States – contributing to a voluntary pension for the whole career would boost future replacement rates for average earners by 24% points on average in these countries based on the modelling assumptions used in the OECD projections (see Chapter 4 for more detail). The coverage of voluntary pensions is much lower for people at early stages of their careers and voluntarily contributing only from the age of 45 would raise future replacement rates by 11 points on average in the nine above listed countries compared to mandatory pensions.

Figure 1.12. **Future net replacement rates for full-career average-wage workers**

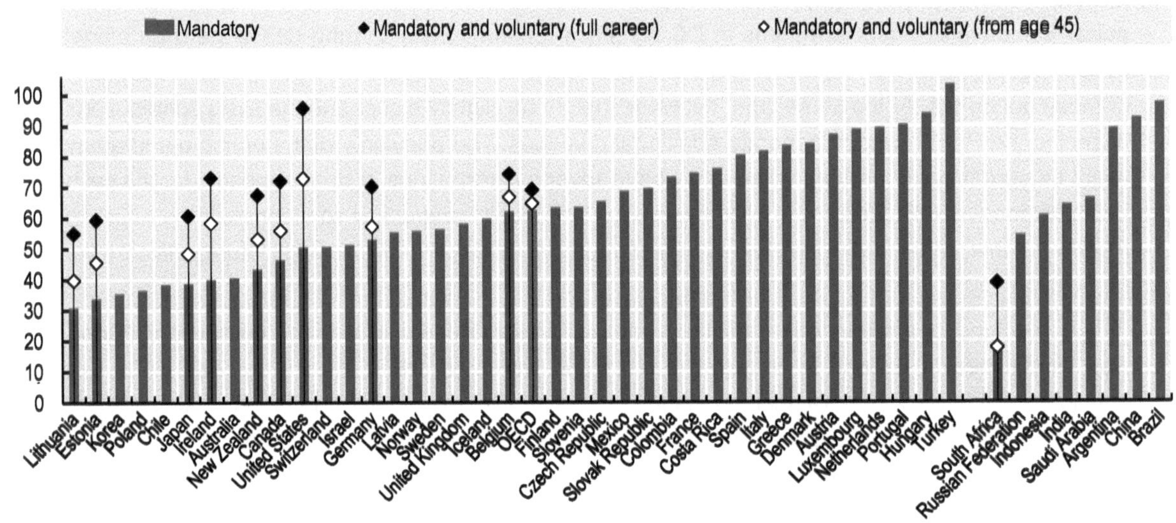

Note: OECD calculations based on the pension model. Pension entitlements are based on current legislation in OECD countries. The values of all pension system parameters reflect the situation in 2020 onwards. The calculations show the pension benefits of a worker who enters the system that year at age 22 and retires after a full career. The baseline results are shown for single individuals. See Chapter 4 for details.

Source: Chapter 4.

StatLink https://stat.link/05a4fe

Chapter 4 also includes replacement rates for a large range of career scenarios. For example, for low-wage earners (at 50% of the average wage), the net replacement rate from mandatory schemes is equal to 74% on average after a full career, hence 12 percentage points higher than for the average-wage worker mainly due to the impact of redistributive mechanisms included in pension rules. The Czech Republic and Denmark record the largest difference in replacement rates when comparing low-wage and average-wage workers. Measures taken over the past two years have the largest impact for the replacement rate of full-career low-wage workers in Chile, Germany, Mexico and Slovenia (increase in all countries) and Estonia (decrease).

Interrupted careers typically lead to lower pensions, but entitlements are not equally sensitive to career breaks across the OECD. Average-wage workers who experience a 5-year unemployment spell in the middle of the career face a pension reduction of 6.3% in mandatory schemes compared to the full-career scenario on average in the OECD (Figure 1.13). A one-to-one relation between earnings and entitlements would imply the impact to be around 13% (Chapter 4). This means that instruments such as pension credits for periods of unemployment cushion about half of the impact of the employment shock on pension benefits on average.

The loss exceeds 10% in Australia, Chile, Hungary, Iceland, Latvia, Korea, Mexico, Poland, the Slovak Republic and Turkey. Conversely, in Ireland and New Zealand there is no impact of such career breaks on pensions from mandatory schemes, which only include a basic pension. In Spain and the United States, a 5-year career break does not influence pension benefits either, as full

Box 1.3. **Auto-enrolment in occupational pensions in the United Kingdom**

In the United Kingdom, the coverage of private-sector employees by occupational pensions increased gradually from about 40% in 2012 to 88% in 2019 (DWP, 2020[30]), following the implementation of the auto-enrolment, with the government established NEST scheme being the largest provider. In the public sector, the coverage by occupational pensions is even higher at 94%. However, the coverage among the self-employed decreased from 20% in 2012 to 16% in 2020. Thus, as the coverage exceeds the 85% threshold used by the OECD to qualify for quasi-mandatory (Chapter 3), the occupational pension scheme is now considered quasi-mandatory for future retirees in the United Kingdom as in Denmark, the Netherlands, Norway, and Sweden.

Minimum contribution rates have also increased. They started from 3% in 2012 and gradually increased to 8% in 2019, of which employers pay a 3% rate. Occupational schemes for new entrants are defined contribution, and the 8% contribution rate will add 27.4 points to the replacement rate of 21.6% from the basic pension for a person with a full career from age 22 in 2020 until the future normal retirement age of 67, earning the average wage and contributing throughout career. Hence, future pension adequacy will substantially improve.

benefits in the earnings-related scheme are reached after 38.5 and 35 years of contributions, respectively. In Colombia, a five-year career break has no impact on public pensions because the reference wage is based on earnings from the last 10 years of the career, the maximum accrual of 80% is reached after 35.5 years and unemployment benefits cover pension contribution for half a year.[45] To avoid penalties, workers experiencing such a break have to retire one year later than full-career workers in France, Greece and Portugal and three years later in Luxembourg and Slovenia.

Figure 1.13. **Career breaks significantly lower pension entitlements in most countries**

Gross pension entitlements from mandatory pensions of an average earner with 5-year unemployment break relative to a full-career worker, percentage

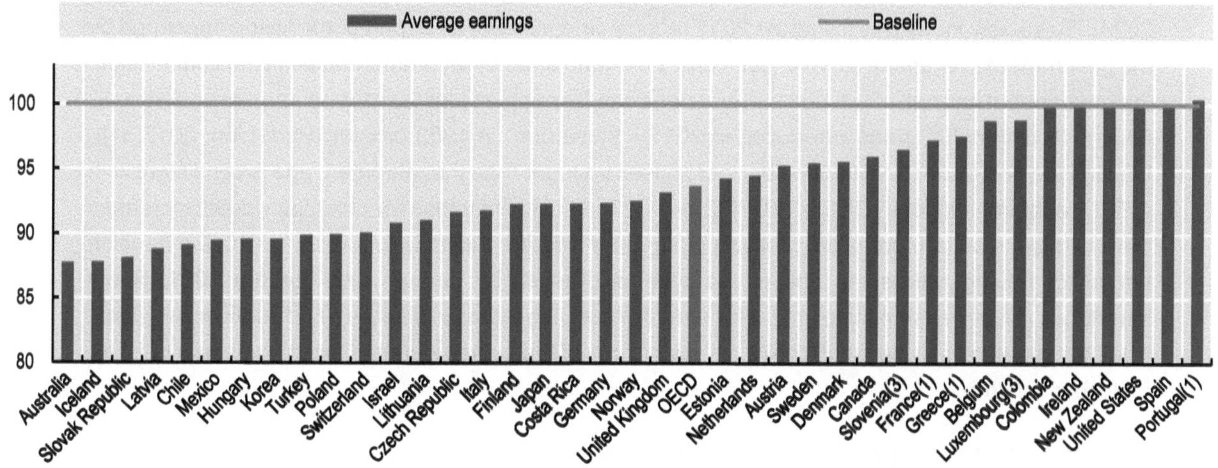

Note: Figure in brackets refers to increase in retirement age to get a full pension given the career break. See Chapter 4 for details.
Source: Chapter 4.

StatLink https://stat.link/n24vj1

Pensions of self-employed workers

Belgium and Greece took measures that will affect the future pensions of the self-employed. Belgium substantially increased their future pension levels without adjusting their contributions. So far, pension entitlements of the self-employed were set at 69% of those of dependent employees to reflect their lower contribution rate of 13.07%, compared to 20.5% for employees. For careers starting from 2022, the 69% coefficient will be removed, increasing new entitlements of the self-employed by

45% while keeping the contribution rate constant. While pension expenditure was already projected to increase by 3% of GDP between 2019 and 2070, the third highest increase in the EU (EC, 2021), this will create additional financing pressure and might unduly discourage dependent employment.

Greece also reformed the pension scheme for the self-employed. From 2021, the self-employed will be required to pay only flat-rate pension contributions while they can voluntarily contribute more. Previously, contributions were based on profits from the self-employed activity. Auxiliary pensions remain voluntary for the self-employed while they are mandatory for employees. Mandating only flat-rate contributions makes them independent from actual taxable earnings and thereby immune from any tax-evasion practices, but it implies that a self-employed worker having the same taxable earnings as an average-wage employee and not contributing more than what is mandatory can expect to receive a pension equal to less than half of the employee's pension (Chapter 4) compared to 12% lower before the change.

Family-related pension benefits

Lithuania, Norway, Slovenia and Spain took some measures affecting family-related pension benefits. From July 2021, Lithuania is gradually introducing a benefit for single pensioners not receiving survivor pensions, at a low flat rate of around 2% of the gross average wage, equal to the survivor pension. This benefit means to initially cover the poorest pensioners while in the future all single pensioners will receive the benefit.[46] Providing higher pensions to single pensioners aims at compensating them for not benefiting from economies of scale compared to couples for the consumption of basic goods such as accommodation. In Norway, from 2024, survivor pensions for spouses younger than the retirement age of 67 years will be granted for only up to three years whereas currently the benefit is paid until the spouse has reached the retirement age, and the benefit will no longer be based on the deceased's pensions but paid at a fixed rate. Additionally, survivor pensions in payment for people older than the retirement age will be frozen in nominal terms from 2024. These new measures follow the 2017 recommendations of an expert commission appointed by the government to examine survivor pensions. Following another recommendation of the commission, the government has not introduced survivor pensions for people older than the retirement age who will fully retire under NDC rules introduced in 2011 – those born in 1963 or later (Pedersen, 2017[31]). Limiting the access to survivor pensions of spouses younger than the retirement age is consistent with OECD recommendations (OECD, 2018[32]), while their full elimination for older individuals increases the risk of substantial income drop following a partner's death. Slovenia introduced in 2019 a pension bonus for having children to one of the parents (women by default). In February 2021, Spain introduced a new pension supplement for parents receiving old-age, disability and survivor pensions. The new supplement is set at EUR 378 per year (1.5% of the average annual gross wage) per child for up to four children.

Measures facilitating the combination of work and pensions

Canada, Greece, Japan and Slovenia have eased combining work and pensions, and Hungary has exempted workers claiming an old-age pension from paying pension contributions. Creating obstacles to retirees working while receiving their earned pension entitlements, such as earnings tests for benefits, effectively increases taxation of labour income. OECD (2017[28]) recommended removing such obstacles to make combining work and pensions more attractive. More generally, in order to efficiently promote more gradual forms of retirement, conditions to withdraw partial pensions should not depend on the amount of work or on labour income after the normal retirement age.

In July 2020, for both employees and the self-employed, Canada eased the earnings test that applies to the old-age targeted income supplement (GIS). The threshold to avoid the GIS benefit being reduced was raised from an annual earning of CAD 3 500 to CAD 5 000 (from 6 to 9% of the gross average wage) and an exemption of 50% on the next CAD 10 000 was introduced. Greece increased the part of pension that can be received while working from 40% to 70%.

Japan introduced a more beneficial recalculation of benefits for working pensioners. From April 2022, pension amounts will be recalculated once a year even when a beneficiary is still working. Before the amendment, if a beneficiary continued to work after the retirement age, the old-age pension amount was recalculated only at the time of termination of employment or on reaching the age of 70. Also the threshold of income (including both salaries and pensions) beyond which earnings-related pensions are reduced for people aged 60 to 64 will increase from JPY 280 000 to JPY 470 000, i.e. from 65% to 109% of the gross average wage.

Slovenia eased the restrictions on combining work and pensions (OECD, 2022[26]): when working full time after having met the eligibility conditions to pensions, 40% of the pension can be claimed for the first three years and 20% thereafter. Before, only 20% of pensions could be claimed.[47] Combining work with full time work was first allowed in 2012 and in 2019 almost 20% of new pensioners combined claiming pension with full-time work. Finally, in 2020, Hungary exempted those combining work with pensions from both employers' and employees' pension contributions, lowering labour costs and increasing their take-home pay, thereby potentially providing strong incentives to work longer for people who highly value current income.

Pension reforms in progress

The Netherlands is in the process of making a systemic reform to the quasi-mandatory occupational pension schemes by shifting members from defined benefit to defined contribution schemes in which individual choices are limited in terms of both investment and asset withdrawals, with the accumulated assets being only paid out as annuities. The latter are generally classified as collective defined contribution (CDC) schemes. Canada and the United Kingdom have also enacted a legal framework for occupational CDC schemes. Switzerland is finalising the law to increase women's retirement age and improve financial sustainability of the pension system. The comprehensive reform to introduce a universal points system in France was suspended, while Spain has not yet decided on measures to improve financial sustainability and Ireland postponed the introduction of auto-enrolment. Turkey is planning to introduce a mandatory FDC pension scheme.[48]

In July 2020, the Dutch Government reached an agreement on several major occupational pension reforms, which include transferring members of existing defined benefit (DB) plans to CDC plans, and eliminating age-based contribution rates. The main trigger for this reform moving away from DB plans is the persistent solvency issues encountered by funded DB pensions in the Netherlands, as in many countries, as well as the related opposition to the needed adjustments of DB benefits and pension promises to deal with ageing trends and pressures arising from persistently low interest rates. In CDC schemes, changes in the financial returns and in projected longevity directly affect newly granted benefits. The government aims to introduce the legislation by 2023, while the funds will be required to be transformed into CDC by 2027, after having reached a funding ratio of at least 95% (Chapter 2).[49]

In December 2020, to limit the shift from DB to pure DC schemes, the Quebec Government in Canada has approved legislation to introduce the Target Benefit Pension Plan (TBPP) within mandatory occupational schemes. The governing regulations have to be finalised, and employers and their employees must agree to form a TBPP and negotiate its core terms. The calculation of individual benefits in a TBPP plan will follow DC rules or DB rules based on career-long earnings but with possible adjustments to both entitlements and benefits in payment so that all the risks are borne collectively by employees while the contribution rate evolves over time – e.g. adjusting to changes in expected rates of return and longevity – to meet the initially set target replacement rate. A legal framework to create CDC pension schemes was enacted in the United Kingdom in 2021 and Royal

Mail is planning to be the first company to launch such a scheme in the United Kingdom in 2022.[50] In CDC schemes in the United Kingdom, benefits could be calculated with a DC formula or a DB formula but with potential collective adjustments to both entitlements and benefits, depending on funds' returns and longevity developments.

Switzerland is in the process of increasing the retirement age of women from 64 to 65, by three months a year from 2023 at the earliest, to equalise the retirement age between men and women around 2027. As an offsetting measure, women aged 58 or older when the law becomes effective would receive pension supplements when retiring at the new retirement age; the amounts and coverage of the compensation package are under debate and considered to be crucial to gather a broad support for the reform. If the change is implemented, the future normal retirement age will differ between men and women in only Hungary, Israel and Poland in the OECD. Final parliamentary approval is expected by the end of 2021, but this law is likely to be brought into a referendum; a similar reform was rejected by referendum in 2017. As a complementary measure, an increase of VAT to finance pensions is discussed, which would require an amendment of the constitution and therefore a referendum. A commission of the lower chamber of Swiss Parliament is also preparing a new proposal to address the impact of higher longevity on the finances of occupational pensions; the so-called conversion rate – used to convert pension assets into annual pensions – would be reduced from 6.8% to 6.0% which would lower future benefits by 12% all other things equal. To cushion the impact of the reform, a targeted benefit would be introduced for 15 years. Additionally, mandatory pension coverage would be expanded for low earners and young people. Indeed, the minimum earnings threshold to be mandatorily covered by occupational pensions would almost be halved, to around 12% of the average wage, and the obligation to contribute would start at age 20 against 25 now.[51]

France attempted to unify its pension system by adopting a universal points system covering private- and public-sector employees as well as the self-employed. The core of the proposal was to merge the 42 mandatory pension schemes, often based on very different rules. In January 2020, the pension reform bill was voted by parliament in the first phase of the legal process, but in March the process was suspended with the outbreak of the COVID-19 pandemic.

In Spain, the government and social partners reached a preliminary agreement in 2021 and the government presented a reform proposal in August as requested by the European Commission as part of the Resilience and Recovery plan. The proposal is expected to be implemented by the end of 2023. The proposal includes a change in the future penalties for early retirement from 6-8% to 4.75%-15.5% per year, depending on the contribution period and period missing to the statutory retirement age, which would generally lead to lower penalties but for the case of retiring 23 or 24 months before the statutory retirement age.[52] Moreover, incentives to defer pensions would be raised as benefits would be increased by 4% per year of deferral compared to 1.5%-4% today depending on the career length. Alternatively, it would be possible to pay out the yearly bonus for deferring retirement as a lump-sum payment ranging from around 30% to 50% of yearly benefits for those with high pensions and short careers, and low pensions and long careers, respectively.[53] To provide adequate incentives to work longer, those payments should be calibrated close to actuarial neutrality. However, the agreement does not include concrete measures to address the issue of financial sustainability. It includes the indexation of pensions fully to prices, and thereby the final elimination of the indexation adjustment (IRP), which resulted in the fall of pensions in real terms in 2017 and 2018. Additionally the suspended (and never applied) sustainability factor, which was supposed to lower initial pension amounts proportionally to improvements in life expectancy, would be fully removed. Instead, a new mechanism, called Intergenerational Equity Factor, is expected to improve the financial sustainability and become effective from 2027; so far this mechanism is still vague and no agreement has been made on its design. The agreement does acknowledge that tackling imbalances in pension finances will require additional financing from the state budget. State subsidies to the pension schemes increased in 2020 and 2021.

In Ireland, the introduction of auto-enrolment, announced by the government in 2019 and initially planned for 2022, is postponed to at least 2023. It is assumed that the minimum contribution rate would gradually reach 12%, equally shared between employers and employees. If this succeeds in generating a broad coverage, as in the United Kingdom (see above), future pensions will substantially increase. Currently, the contribution-based basic pension is the only widespread pension scheme in Ireland, providing a benefit equal to 28% of the gross average wage in 2020.

Turkey is planning to introduce a new private pension plans to be mandatory for those entering the labour market from 2022, while for the others it will remain optional. The scheme is to be FDC with contribution rates of 3% for employers and between 0.5% and 3% for employees; additional 5.33% contribution rate would finance an associated severance pay scheme. This reform follows the introduction of a subsidised auto-enrolment scheme (OKS) in 2017, which has had a disappointing coverage. Introducing an additional scheme and raising total pension contributions is useful to help Turkey prepare for an acceleration of population ageing from still an early phase. The current public DB pension is generous leading to a future net replacement rates of 101% at age 65.

Notes

1. Two crucial aspects of all job retention schemes are that employees keep their contracts with the employer even if their work is fully suspended and the labour costs are partially of fully subsidised by the government (OECD, 2021[1]). Most new JRS that were introduced in response to the crisis take the form of furlough schemes that only subsidise jobs whose hours are temporarily reduced to zero (e.g. Denmark, Slovenia, and the United Kingdom).
2. For example, in France, the relative income of retirees compared to that of the general population would have increased from 105% to 110% in 2020 (COR, 2020).
3. Australia provided up to four additional payments to eligible beneficiaries of the means-tested Age Pension: AUD 750 for the first two and AUD 250 for the other two, which in total amounts to around 5% of the maximal annual Age Pension benefit. Belgium temporarily (for 2020 and 2021) increased the minimum amount of the safety-net benefit by 6% (EUR 50 per month (as a reference, the safety-net benefit for someone living alone was EUR 1 131.78 in January 2020). Canada granted a one-off allowance of CAD 300 to pensioners receiving the basic pension (Old Age Security) and an additional CAD 200 to those with the lowest income who therefore receive the Guaranteed Income Supplement; the total allowance of CAD 500 is about 1% of the average annual disposable income among the 65+. Canada granted a further one-time payment of CAD 500 in 2021 to all Old Age Security pensioners age 75 and over, regardless of whether they received the Guaranteed Income Supplement. In Colombia, the old-age safety net benefit (so called Colombia Mayor), was increased by 87% as a response to the COVID-19 in 2020 and the increase is expected to remain permanent. In Denmark, all recipients of public benefits – including pensioners – received a lump-sum payment of DKK 1 000 (0.5% of the average annual disposable income among the 65+, free of income taxation) in the summer 2020. Israel granted up to NIS 4 000 for those aged 67+ who lost their job due to COVID-19, on top of their state pension. New Zealand doubled the Winter Energy Payment benefit paid to all pensioners between May and October 2020 at NZD 20.45 per week, representing 4% of the basic pension. Slovenia introduced a so-called solidarity bonus to temporarily increase the lowest pensions.
4. OECD Labour Market Statics: *https://stats.oecd.org/Index.aspx?DataSetCode=AV_AN_WAGE*.
5. In France, the criteria to validate one-quarter in the main DB scheme (*régime general*) combine both number of hours worked and earnings. Initially the quarters for those working very few hours were not fully validated, but legislation adopted at the end of 2020 retroactively granted full pension entitlements for these periods.
6. Under short-time work (STW) schemes, the subsidised income is largely exempt from social contributions in France and, before June 2020, workers did not accrue pension entitlements in the main public scheme for the part of wages that was subsidised. However, the impact on pension entitlements for those covered by STW schemes is probably small as the non-subsidised part (corresponding to the time spent working) is often enough to validate quarters of contributions while the reference wage for pension purposes is based on the best 25 years in the private sector. According to the June 2020 COVID-19 related law, the subsidised part of wages paid between March and December 2020 will also be accounted for to validate quarters for the computation of future pensions and the contributions are financed by the "solidarity fund".

7. The self-employed are required to contribute to mandatory earnings-related pensions in a similar way as employees in only 9 OECD countries. In another 14 countries, self-employed workers are mandatorily covered by earnings-related schemes, but they are allowed to contribute less than employees through reduced contribution rates or discretion in setting their income base, or when they have low income. In Greece, Poland, Latvia and Turkey, only flat-rate contributions are require while contributions and entitlements are proportional to earnings for employees. In Australia, Denmark, Germany, Ireland, Japan, Mexico, the Netherlands and the United Kingdom the self-employed are not mandatorily covered by earnings-related scheme.
8. These transfers often depend on previous earnings or income losses during the crisis, as for example in Australia, Austria, Chile, Denmark, Ireland, Iceland, Latvia, Norway, Portugal, the Slovak Republic, Switzerland and the United Kingdom. In Chile for example, the self-employed have received income benefits amounting up to 70% of the drop in their monthly income for up to 3 months. In Denmark, self-employed workers experiencing an income loss of more than 30% have received a cash support amounting to 75% of the loss for up to 3 months. Iceland introduced a subsidy of 80% of average earnings benefiting the self-employed for 3 months. In Portugal, the self-employed who suspended their business activity or experienced an income loss of more than 40% have received a subsidy compensating their income loss. In the Slovak Republic, the allowance depended on the income loss and ranged from EUR 330 and 879 a month. Belgium, Canada, Colombia, the Czech Republic, France, Greece, Italy, Israel, Korea, Lithuania, the Netherlands, Slovenia and Spain and introduced flat-rate payments or lump-sum transfers. For example, Italy provided compensation of EUR 600 in March and April, and of EUR 1 000 in May to the self-employed while the self-employed who earned less than EUR 50 000 in 2019 and who experienced at least a 33% decrease in income in 2020 compared to 2019 will be exempted from payment of their 2021 contributions. Lithuania has subsidised the self-employed through an allowance of EUR 257 a month. In Spain, half of the self-employed have been granted a new benefit at EUR 660 or more.
9. Greece, Hungary, Slovenia and Spain provided full exemptions from contributions for some of the self-employed. Greece has fully subsidised the pension contributions of the self-employed (as for employees) who stopped their activity due to the pandemic, while for others 25% of the contributions from February through May have been reduced by 25% without affecting pension entitlements provided they are paid by April 2021. In Hungary, employers, private entrepreneurs and business partnerships pursuing some activities were not be liable for paying pension contributions for the months of March, April, May and June 2020. In the Slovak Republic, the self-employed persons could request a deferral of the social insurance contributions in March, May-July and December 2020 and from January to May 2021; and a remission for April 2020. In Slovenia, the self-employed who have been affected by the crisis have been exempted from paying contributions while continuing to accrue pension entitlements. Spain exempted the self-employed whose revenues dropped by at least 75% from pension contributions, without harming their entitlements. France and Lithuania have subsidised pension contributions of the self-employed. In France, self-employed workers and non-salaried agricultural workers, who met certain conditions, received a bonus of EUR 600 per month in reduced social security, including pension, contributions. In Lithuania, a flat-rate benefit for the self-employed was included in their taxable income and thereby it raised pension entitlements and contributions. Portugal allowed the deferral of two-thirds of pension contributions due in April through June 2020 for up to six months without harming pension entitlements.
10. Morgan et al. (2020[7]) approximate the expected mortality by the average mortality rates from the previous five years and they show that adjusting the numbers for long-term trends in mortality have a minor effect on the final numbers.
11. Due to excess mortality, in Chile, Colombia, the Czech Republic, Hungary, Mexico, Poland, the Slovak Republic, Slovenia and the United States the number of people over 65 decreased by more than 1% between January 2020 and August 2021. The decline of population due to excess mortality is calculated by dividing the number of excess deaths by the population size.
12. *https://www.bankier.pl/wiadomosc/Prezes-ZUS-Wzrost-smiertelnosci-w-czasie-epidemii-wplynal-na-wysokosc-emerytur-8083969.html.*
13. The raw monthly numbers of birth rates until August 2021 in Hungary show that there were year-to-year declines in birth rates by 7.4% and 9.4% in December 2020 and January 2021, while no clear trend has been noted beyond these two months.
14. *https://www.cdc.gov/nchs/data/vsrr/vsrr014-508.pdf.*
15. Yet, in the Czech Republic, Germany and the Netherlands the birth rates dropped by less than 2%. Based on UN data: *https://unstats.un.org/unsd/mbs/app/DataSearchSeries.aspx.*
16. *https://stats.oecd.org/Index.aspx?DataSetCode=QNA.*
17. *https://www.ipe.com/news/dutch-pension-funds-return-an-average-102-for-2020/10051732.article* https://www.pionline.com/pension-funds/2-swedish-ap-funds-record-almost-10-returns-2020.

18. When ignoring Mexico, the number of pensioners increased by 18% on average (instead of 20% when including Mexico).

19. In Turkey data on the average wage might be underestimated as the real GDP per capita grew by 3.2% on average between 2000 and 2020 compared to the reported average annual wage growth of 0.3%.

20. Additionally, public basic pension in the Netherlands increased by 0.3% in real terms on average annually, which was not enough to offset the negative indexation of occupational pensions which are expected to deliver 58% of pension income for an average earner (Chapter 5).

21. This measure had been included in the reform proposals by the Parliamentary Pension Group in 2017.

22. This eligibility age applies also to Housing Benefit for Pensioners and the Pension Supplement. The age thresholds to which the sickness and unemployment insurance apply are expected to be adjusted accordingly.

23. At the guarantee pension age, it is also possible to receive the housing benefit for the elderly while other working age benefits (sick insurance, disability insurance, unemployment insurance etc.) cease.

24. The target retirement age will be set six years before it will actually be applied, i.e. 67 was set on 1 July 2021 and will be applicable from 2027. Any further increase will need to be approved by the parliament.

25. In Greece, the one-to-one link of retirement age to life expectancy, which was legislated in 2010, has become effective in 2021. Partly thanks to this link (EC, 2021[37]) projects public pension expenditure to decrease by 2% of GDP between 2019 and 2070, from the highest level among EU countries at 15.7% of GDP in 2019.

26. Mandatory retirement regulations could allow employers to change employment conditions unilaterally upon reaching the mandatory retirement age. This is for instance the case in the wage peak system in Korea allowing older workers to continue employment at a lower wage level, or the requirement in Japan to offer a new, typically less generous, employment contract to workers whose employment contracts are automatically terminated when they turn 60.

27. The Constitutional Court suspended the implementation of these statutory provisions until its final decision. Moreover, the Norwegian Parliament is debating on abolishing the mandatory retirement age for public-sector workers, which takes a strict form as civil servants are obliged to resign from their position when reaching 70 – it is lower for some arduous occupations (e.g. policemen, firemen). In addition, in 2020, Japan increased the maximum age until pensions could be deferred, both for the basic and earnings-related pension, from 70 to 75 years, effective from April 2022. Australia increased from 65 to 67 the age until which it is possible to make voluntary contributions to occupational pensions (Superannuation) without working.

28. More precisely, retiring one, two or three years earlier will be allowed after 42, 43 or 44 years of work between ages 16 and 61, respectively. The benefit is equal to the amount of the full basic pension received at the normal retirement age and is subject to means-, earnings- and asset-testing.

29. In 2019, Austria removed penalties for early retirement for those who have contributed for at least 45 years, being effective from January 2020. In 2020 the penalties were restored (to be effective from 2022).

30. Two or three years of contributions for employees or the self-employed, respectively.

31. The penalty applies also for pensions received after the retirement age only if the early pension had been claimed for more than three years and the insurance record is shorter than 40 years, which is set to increase by 3 months every year until having reached 42 years and six months in 2031.

32. The new individual pension supplement (*Grundrente*) is classified as neither a basic pension nor a minimum pension because its amount increases with the amount of individual lifetime earnings. According to OECD definitions (Chapter 3), the level of a basic pension is independent of the earnings' level during the career. Minimum pensions either define a minimum for total contributory lifetime entitlements, which may increase in level once the length of the contribution period exceeds certain thresholds, or are based on minimum pension credits that calculate year-by-year entitlements of low earners based on a higher earnings level.

33. In Chile, older individuals who receive DC pension payments from programmed withdrawals faced, before this new measure, sharp drops in their benefits as they aged. From now on, the supplement, in the case of beneficiaries of the solidarity pillar, will offset drops of payments in programmed withdrawal plans as beneficiaries age, operating as a subsidised annuity.

34. Additionally, in 2021, the eligibility requirements to the minimum pension were tightened: validating one year of contribution requires reporting earnings of at least 24.1% of the average wage while before there was no earnings-related condition.

35. The relevant income refers to the taxable income and tax-free pension components as well as certain investment income not included in taxable income.

36. Without the new supplement, a single person who earned 40% of the average wage throughout a 35-year career, would receive an earnings-related pension of EUR 479 and a safety-net benefit of EUR 359 in 2020.

The new supplement would be EUR 419 and, thus, the total benefit would exceed the maximum income, of EUR 838, to qualify for the safety-net benefit. Hence, in this case, the supplement would increase the earnings-related pension by 88% and the total benefit amount by 7%. In a similar case, but with average earnings equal to 70% of the average wage, the earnings-related pension is EUR 838 and the new supplement at EUR 105 would increase the total pension amount by 13%.

37. https://www.deutsche-rentenversicherung.de/SharedDocs/Downloads/DE/Broschueren/national/grundrente_zuschlag_zur_rente.pdf?__blob=publicationFile&v=20

38. Moreover, from July 2020, pension, health and unemployment contributions for employees were merged into a single contribution at the unchanged rate of 18.5%. This change will not affect pension finances in the short term, as 54% of the new contributions will flow into pensions, which is equal to the previous 10% pension contribution rate.

39. *https://dziennikustaw.gov.pl/D2021000019001.pdf.*

40. Understanding this changes requires coming back to pension reforms introduced during the global financial crisis. In 2011, some fragmented state-backed occupational (auxiliary) pension schemes were unified and transformed from defined-benefit (DB) into notional defined contribution (NDC) while others remained pure private pensions without any guarantees form the states. In 2016, this unification process covered almost all auxiliary schemes. Yet, until 2016, the NDC rules applied only to entitlements accrued after 2014 which made the transition to NDC very slow.

41. Additionally, in September 2020, the ceiling to pensionable earnings was discretionarily raised by 4.8%.

42. As for 2020, the government pension subsidies are twofold: a universal contribution top up of 0.225% to everyone and a redistributive one (*social quota*) that is paid to those earning less than 3.6 times the average wage. The 2021 law assumes that the universal top up to contributions will disappear in 2023, while the redistributive part will apply only to earnings up to 170% of the average wage in 2023 and up to the average wage from 2024. Employees' contribution rate will remain unchanged at 1.125%, which means that the total contribution rate will increase from 6.5% to 15%.

43. *https://news.err.ee/1608327707/pensionikeskus-has-transferred-99-percent-of-second-pillar-funds.*

44. A person entering the labour market today at age 22 and with a full career at the average wage and at half the average wage is projected to have a gross replacement rate of 52% and 71%, respectively, if remaining in the funded scheme against 28% and 48% when opting out. When assuming a real rate of return of 1% per year – which is the actual number for Estonia on average in 2015-19 – instead of 3% in the OECD baseline assumption, the gross replacement rate for people remaining in the FDC would be 41% for average earners and 59% for low earners.

45. The result would be different for a person covered by a DC scheme instead of a DB scheme, which is possible in Colombia within mandatory earning-related pensions.

46. The decision on the indexation mechanism of the benefit would be taken in autumn of 2021.

47. The accrual rate for working the 41st, 42nd and 43rd years was decreased from 4% to 3% compared to the regular accrual rate of 1.36% for 15th through 40th years. The combination of higher accrual rates and mandatory deferral of 60% of benefits is close to actuarially neutrality.

48. After this chapter was sent to publication, in Spain a draft law has been presented to the Parliament according to which pensions in payment will be indexed to price inflation. The proposal includes a so-called Intergenerational Equity Mechanism based on an increase in the contribution rate of 0.6 p.p. (0.5 p.p. for employers and 0.1 p.p. for employees) up to 2032. The additional contributions will be accumulated in the public pension reserve fund, which will help mitigate the financial impact of the retired baby-boom generations.

49. The required funding ratio is dependent on the decisions social partners make on how they transition to a new contract. The 95% is a temporary (minimum) benchmark for as long as these decisions are not made.

50. *https://www.ipe.com/news/royal-mail-could-launch-first-uk-cdc-scheme-in-2022/10055078.article.*

51. *https://www.ipe.com/news/swiss-parliamentary-committee-shifts-to-alternative-reform-proposal/10054585.article?utm_campaign=468714_23.8.21%20ipe%20daily%20news&utm_medium=email&utm_source=IPE&dm_i=5KVE,A1NU,C5BZU,17DW3,1.*

52. *https://www.elcorreo.com/economia/tu-economia/nuevas-penalizaciones-jubilacion-anticipada-cantidades-aprobadas-gobierno-20210825195306-nt.html?ref=https%3A%2F%2Fwww.elcorreo.com%2Feconomia%2Ftu-economia%2Fbanco-espana-pensiones-clave-20210912135841-nt.html.*

53. *https://cincodias.elpais.com/cincodias/2021/08/24/economia/1629801448_838275.html.*

References

[12] Aassve, A. et al. (2021), "Early assessment of the relationship between the COVID-19 pandemic and births in high-income countries", *Proceedings of the National Academy of Sciences*, Vol. 118/36, p. e2105709118, http://dx.doi.org/*10.1073/pnas.2105709118.*

[36] Aburto, J. et al. (2021), *Quantifying impacts of the COVID-19 pandemic through life expectancy losses: a population-level study of 29 countries*, Cold Spring Harbor Laboratory, http://dx.doi.org/*10.1101/2021.03.02.21252772.*

[27] Börsch-Supan, A. et al. (2021), "Targets missed: three case studies exploiting the linked SHARE-RV data", *Journal of Pension Economics and Finance*, pp. 1-21, http://dx.doi.org/*10.1017/s1474747220000359.*

[19] Boulhol, H. and A. Turner (2011), *Recent trends and structural breaks in the US and EU15 labour productivity growth*, Applied Economics, No. 43 (628).

[9] Cairns, A. et al. (2020), "The Impact of COVID-19 on Future Higher-Age Mortality", *SSRN Electronic Journal*, http://dx.doi.org/*10.2139/ssrn.3606988.*

[15] COR (2021), *Évolutions et perspectives des retraites en France. Rapport annuel du COR – Juin 2021, https://www.cor-retraites.fr/node/562.*

[11] Duyck, J., J. Paul and M. Vandresse (2020), *Perspectives démographiques 2019-2070*, Bureau fédéral du Plan, *https://www.plan.be/uploaded/documents/202006020558410.REP_POP1970Covid19_12154_F.pdf.*

[30] DWP (2020), *Workplace Pension Participation and Savings Trends of Eligible Employees Official Statistics: 2009 to 2019, https://assets.publishing.service.gov.uk/government/uploads/system/uploads/attachment_data/file/892841/workplace-pension-participation-and-saving-trends-2009-2019.pdf.*

[37] EC (2021), *The 2021 Ageing Report. Economic and Budgetary Projections for the EU Member States (2019-2070)*, European Commission, http://dx.doi.org/*10.2765/84455.*

[20] EC (2021), *The 2021 Pension Adequacy Report: current and future income adequacy in old age in the EU, Volume 1*, European Commission, http://dx.doi.org/10.2767/013455 K.

[14] ETK (2021), *TyEL-eläkkeiden rahoitus koronavuoden 2020 jälkeen.*

[23] Fouejieu, A. et al. (2021), "Pension Reforms in Europe. How Far Have We Come and Gone?", *IMF Departmental Paper, https://www.imf.org/en/Publications/Departmental-Papers-Policy-Papers/Issues/2021/09/10/Pension-Reforms-in-Europe-464651.*

[4] Fuentes, O., O. Mitchell and F. Villatoro (2021), *Chile's Experience with COVID-19 Early Pension System Withdrawals, https://cepar.edu.au/sites/default/files/07-Fuentes.pdf.*

[21] Geppert, C. et al. (2019), "Labour supply of older people in advanced economies: the impact of changes to statutory retirement ages", *OECD Economics Department Working Papers*, No. 1554, OECD Publishing, Paris, *https://dx.doi.org/10.1787/b9f8d292-en.*

[24] Gerard, M. (2019), "Reform Options for Mature Defined Benefit Pension Plans: The Case of the Netherlands", *IMF Working Papers, https://www.imf.org/en/Publications/WP/Issues/2019/01/25/Reform-Options-for-Mature-Defined-Benefit-Pension-Plans-The-Case-of-the-Netherlands-46542.*

[10] Lopez-Leon, S. et al. (2021), "More than 50 long-term effects of COVID-19: a systematic review and meta-analysis", *Scientific Reports*, Vol. 11/1, http://dx.doi.org/*10.1038/s41598-021-95565-8.*

[13] McDonald, P. (2020), *A Projection of Australia's Future Fertility Rates*, The Australian Government, Canberra., *https://population.gov.au/docs/2020_mcdonald_fertility_projections.pdf.*

[33] Minister of Labour, Social Affairs and Family of the Slovak Republic (2021), *Návrh ústavného zákona o primeranom hmotnom zabezpečení v starobe [Draft Constitutional Law on Adequate Material Security in Old Age], https://hsr.rokovania.sk/291792020-m_opva/.*

[7] Morgan, D. et al. (2020), "Excess mortality: Measuring the direct and indirect impact of COVID-19", *OECD Health Working Papers*, No. 122, OECD Publishing, Paris, *https://dx.doi.org/10.1787/c5dc0c50-en.*

[26] OECD (2022), *OECD Reviews of Pension Systems: Slovenia*, OECD Reviews of Pension Systems, forthcoming, OECD Publishing, Paris.

[6] OECD (2021), *Health at a Glance 2021: OECD Indicators*, OECD Publishing, Paris, *https://dx.doi.org/10.1787/ae3016b9-en.*

[35] OECD (2021), *OECD Economic Outlook, Interim Report September 2021: Keeping the Recovery on Track*, OECD Publishing, Paris, *https://dx.doi.org/10.1787/490d4832-en.*

[39] OECD (2021), *OECD Economic Outlook, Volume 2021 Issue 1*, OECD Publishing, Paris, *https://dx.doi.org/10.1787/edfbca02-en*.

[1] OECD (2021), *OECD Employment Outlook 2021: Navigating the COVID-19 Crisis and Recovery*, OECD Publishing, Paris, *https://dx.doi.org/10.1787/5a700c4b-en*.

[17] OECD (2021), *Pension Markets in Focus*, OECD Publishing, Paris, *https://www.oecd.org/pensions/private-pensions/pensionmarketsinfocus.htm*.

[2] OECD (2020), *OECD Employment Outlook 2020: Worker Security and the COVID-19 Crisis*, OECD Publishing, Paris, *https://dx.doi.org/10.1787/1686c758-en*.

[5] OECD (2020), *OECD Pensions Outlook 2020*, OECD, http://dx.doi.org/*10.1787/67ede41b-en*.

[34] OECD (2019), *Pensions at a Glance 2019: OECD and G20 Indicators*, OECD Publishing, Paris, *https://dx.doi.org/10.1787/b6d3dcfc-en*.

[22] OECD (2019), *Will future pensioners work for longer and retire on less?*, *https://www.oecd.org/pensions/public-pensions/OECD-Policy-Brief-Future-Pensioners-2019.pdf*.

[32] OECD (2018), *OECD Pensions Outlook 2018*, OECD Publishing, Paris, *https://dx.doi.org/10.1787/pens_outlook-2018-en*.

[28] OECD (2017), *Pensions at a Glance 2017: OECD and G20 Indicators*, OECD Publishing, Paris, *https://dx.doi.org/10.1787/pension_glance-2017-en*.

[29] OECD (2016), *OECD Reviews of Pension Systems: Mexico*, OECD Reviews of Pension Systems, OECD Publishing, Paris, *https://dx.doi.org/10.1787/9789264245938-en*.

[3] Oreopoulos, P., T. von Wachter and A. Heisz (2012), "The Short- and Long-Term Career Effects of Graduating in a Recession", *American Economic Journal: Applied Economics*, Vol. 4/1, pp. 1-29, http://dx.doi.org/*10.1257/app.4.1.1*.

[31] Pedersen, A. (2017), "Towards a fully individualised pension system in Norway", *ESPN Flash Report*, *https://ec.europa.eu/social/BlobServlet?docId=17189&langId=en*.

[25] Pension Commission (2021), *Report of the Commission on Pensions*, *https://www.gov.ie/en/publication/6cb6d-report-of-the-commission-on-pensions/*.

[8] Pifarré i Arolas, H. et al. (2021), "Years of life lost to COVID-19 in 81 countries", *Scientific Reports*, Vol. 11/1, http://dx.doi.org/*10.1038/s41598-021-83040-3*.

[18] Raleigh, V. (2019), *Trends in life expectancy in EU and other OECD countries: Why are improvements slowing?*, OECD Health Working Papers, No. 108.

[16] SSA (2021), *The 2021 Annual Report of the Board of Trustees of the Federal Old-Age and Survivors Insurance and Federal Disability Insurance Trust Funds*, *https://www.ssa.gov/oact/TR/2021/index.html*.

[38] University of California, Berkeley and Max Planck Institute for Demographic Research (2020), *The Human Mortality Database*, *https://www.mortality.org/*.

ANNEX 1.A

Recent pension reform overview

Annex Table 1.A.1. Pension reform decided between September 2019 and September 2021

	Retirement age	Coverage	Pension benefits	Contributions	Minimum and basic pensions, income and means testing	Taxes and fees	Other
Australia				July 2020, People aged 65 and 66 are no longer required to meet the 'work test' in order to make voluntary concessional (before tax) and non-concessional (after tax) contributions to their superannuation. To satisfy the work test, an individual must work at least 40 hours during a consecutive 30 day period in the financial year they make or receive the contributions. It continues to apply for individuals aged 67 to 74 years. May 2021 Accounts from Eligible Rollover Funds to be transferred to the ATO for consolidation with members' active accounts starting 30 June 2021 and finishing 31 January 2022.	May 2020 The asset condition used in the income test when calculating the old-age safety-net benefit (Age Pension) was reduced. Australia's deeming rules assume that a person will generate a fixed return from their financial assets, regardless of actual returns. This process forms part of Australia's income test, which is used to determine the rate of social security payments paid to recipients, including the Age Pension. The lower deeming rate was reduced from 1.0% to 0.25%, and the upper deeming rate was reduced from 3.0%to 2.25%. In 2021, the lower deeming rate applies to amounts up to AUD USD 53 600 for singles, and USD 89 000 for couples combined. The upper deeming rate applies to amounts above the aforementioned thresholds. These changes reduced income support recipients' deemed income, resulting in higher income support payments for many recipients.		2020 Pension Loans Scheme (PLS, similar to a reverse mortgage scheme).On 1 January 2020, the compound interest rate was reduced from 5.25% to 4.50% per annum. The reduced interest rate eases borrowing costs which are realised when the balance of the loan is repaid. 2021 In the 2021-22 Budget, the Australian Government announced changes to the PLS which will increase the flexibility of the scheme for recipients. From 1 July 2022, pending passage of legislation, the government will introduce a No Negative Equity Guarantee to the PLS, which means recipients will never have to repay more than the equity in the property used to secure the PLS loan. PLS recipients will also be able to access a portion of their annual PLS payment as an advance, capped at 50%of the annual maximum rate of Age Pension. The government will also raise awareness of the PLS to inform older Australians of how accessing the equity in their home can improve their living standards in retirement.

Annex Table 1.A.1. **Pension reform decided between September 2019 and September 2021**

	Retirement age	Coverage	Pension benefits	Contributions	Minimum and basic pensions, income and means testing	Taxes and fees	Other
Austria	2020 As of January 2020, people with at least 45 years of (employment) contributions face no penalty when claiming a pension (early old age or invalidity pension) before the statutory retirement age. This possibility will end with the beginning of 2022 as this law was revoked one year later in November 2020, the penalties of 4.2% were reintroduced along with introducing the Early Starter Bonus, to be effective from 1 January 2022. The Early Starter Bonus grands a bonus to the pension for those who have at least 25 years (300 months) of active contribution due to employment to the pension system, who have worked between the age of 15 and 20 and have earned at least 12 months of active contribution due to employment in that stage of life. The benefit for the individual pension equals EUR 1 per month for every month worked before age 20 and will be at least EUR 12 for the minimum of one year and a maximum of EUR 60 for the maximum of 5 years. The Early Starter Bonus will be paid out monthly (14/year) with the pension benefit.		January 2021 Pension indexation in 2021 deviated from the rule (price indexation) for low and high pensions (CPI would be 1.5%): - Up to EUR 1 000: 3.5% EUR 1 000-1 400: linear decline from 3.5% to 1.5% EUR 1 400-2 333: 1.5% Above EUR 2 333: fixed increase of EUR 35				

Annex Table 1.A.1. **Pension reform decided between September 2019 and September 2021**

	Retirement age	Coverage	Pension benefits	Contributions	Minimum and basic pensions, income and means testing	Taxes and fees	Other
Belgium			2021 Pension entitlements of the self-employed were increased without adjusting their contributions. So far, the pensions of the self-employed were set at 69% of those of employees to reflect the lower contribution rate paid by the self-employed compared employees. For periods of work starting from 2022 the 69% coefficient will be removed. The wage ceiling for the calculation of pensions of employees is increased by 2.38% as of the career year 2021.		2021 The minimum pension after a full career (45 years worked or credited) is gradually increased to EUR 1 500 net per month between 2021 and 2024. In 2021, social assistance benefits for older people were also increased by 2.58%.		
Canada			December 2020 The Quebec Government has approved legislation to introduce the Target Benefit Pension Plan (TBPP), an occupational pension plan that combines the specific features of an existing Defined Contribution (DC) and Defined Benefit (DB) plan. Employers and their employees must agree to form a TBPP and negotiate its core terms (Multi-employer TBPP is also available). As part of the negotiation, employers and employees must set target benefit levels for the plan.		July 2020 The government enhanced the GIS earnings exemption so that low-income seniors who work are able to keep more of what they earn. The enhanced exemption applies to both employment and self-employment income, and provides a full exemption on up to USD 5 000 of annual earnings, as well as a 50% exemption on the next USD 10 000 of earnings. 2021 The government introduced an increase to the regular Old Age Security (OAS) pension for seniors age 75 and older. This measure will be implemented in two steps: a one-time payment of USD 500 in 2021 and a permanent increase to the OAS pension for seniors 75 and over		

Annex Table 1.A.1. **Pension reform decided between September 2019 and September 2021**

	Retirement age	Coverage	Pension benefits	Contributions	Minimum and basic pensions, income and means testing	Taxes and fees	Other
					by 10%, beginning in July 2022.		
Chile					Solidarity Pillar law was approved in December 2019: Starting in January 2020, new recipients of solidarity pension benefits under programmed withdrawals have full longevity risk coverage, so their total pension will not decrease over time. The formula that applied before only to pensioners with self-financed pension below the basic pension now applies to all new recipients. In these cases, the total pension amount is financed initially through the pensioners' remaining balance and later through public spending, when the retirement capital is exhausted. Additionally, the law established a 50% increase in the parameters PBS (basic solidarity pension) and PMAS (maximum pension with solidarity complement), over the following years, starting in December 2019. This increase will benefit both old and new PBS and APS (solidarity pillar top-up benefit) recipients. After the 50% increase, the PBS will be near the poverty line.		
Colombia	2020 The old-age safety net benefit (so called Colombia Mayor), was increased by 87% as a response to the COVID-19 and the increase is expected to remain permanent.						

Annex Table 1.A.1. **Pension reform decided between September 2019 and September 2021**

	Retirement age	Coverage	Pension benefits	Contributions	Minimum and basic pensions, income and means testing	Taxes and fees	Other
Costa Rica			October 2020 Lump sum pay-outs of pensions are forbidden in the mandatory DC scheme (called ROP, Law 9 906)				October 2020 1.5% of contribution for mandatory DC scheme (ROP) are transferred directly to pension provider (OPC). Before this contributions transfer was deferred for up to 1 year (Law 9 906).
Czech Republic							
Denmark	December 2020 The parliament approved legislation for the introduction of a new early pension (tidlig pension) starting in 2022. From January 2022, those who have been employed for at least 42 years before the age of 61 will be able to receive a pension starting three years before the normal retirement age of 67. Early retirement is allowed up to one year after 42 years of service between the ages of 16 and 61, two years after 43 years of service, and three years after 44 years of service, with a benefit reduction of 4.2% per year. January 2020 An early retirement pension, known as the Senior Pension, was introduced for individuals who have lost the ability to work after a long career. The senior pension allows individuals who have at least 20 to 25 years of full-time employment (depending on						

Annex Table 1.A.1. **Pension reform decided between September 2019 and September 2021**

	Retirement age	Coverage	Pension benefits	Contributions	Minimum and basic pensions, income and means testing	Taxes and fees	Other
	the occupations worked) and are unable to work more than 15 hours a week in their most recent jobs to receive a pension up to 6 years before the normal retirement age (currently age 65 and 6 months and gradually rising to age 67 by 2022 and to age 68 by 2030).						
Estonia				January 2020 (approved by the Constitutional Court in October 2020, coming into force in January 2021). The membership in the funded defined-contribution scheme (FDC), which used to be mandatory for people born in 1982 or later, became voluntary. Opting-out means that 4% out of 6% contribution rate to FDC remains in the public PAYGO scheme while the remaining 2% lowers the total mandatory pension contribution rate from 22% to 20%. Option-out allows withdrawing all assets from the scheme. Rejoing is possible 10 year after having opted out.			October 2020 (effective from September 2021) The participants of the second pillar will be able to manage their own investments. Currently, the second pillar of individual account savings are exclusively held in pension funds managed by professional fund managers.
Finland		2020 The right to pension assistance for the long-term	2020 Full national pensions are increased by EUR 34 and the guarantee pension by EUR 50				The act with the goal to promote the return to work of employees on disability pension, initially introduced

Annex Table 1.A.1. **Pension reform decided between September 2019 and September 2021**

	Retirement age	Coverage	Pension benefits	Contributions	Minimum and basic pensions, income and means testing	Taxes and fees	Other
		unemployed is expanded on 1 October 2019 to persons born before 1 September 1958. Pension assistance is aimed at providing income security for elderly long-term unemployed persons living in Finland who have been unemployed for five years with no or few interruptions. The amount of the assistance is the same as guarantee pension.	per month as of the beginning of 2020.				in 2010 and extended a few times afterwards, was extended until the end of 2022. It is likely to be extended again until new rules are implemented in 2024.
France			October 2021 Social partners agreed to uprate the point value in the supplementary pensions AGIRC and ARRCO by 1% in November 2021, which is 0.5 percentage point below what the regular rule would imply.				
Germany			January 2021 Germany introduced an income-related pension supplement (Grundrente) as part of the first-tier old-age pension to those who have made compulsory contributions to the statutory pension insurance for at least 33 years on the basis of relatively low earnings throughout the whole working life. The number of points earned are doubled, but only to a maximum of 0.8 per year (corresponding to 80% of				

Annex Table 1.A.1. **Pension reform decided between September 2019 and September 2021**

	Retirement age	Coverage	Pension benefits	Contributions	Minimum and basic pensions, income and means testing	Taxes and fees	Other
			the average income) for a maximum of 35 years. Only contribution periods with average earnings points of at least 0.025 per month (corresponding to 30% of the average income) are eligible. The specific provisions are complex. The full amount of the supplement is paid to pensioners with monthly relevant income (including salary, pensions, rental income, etc.) of up to EUR 1 250 for a single person or EUR 1 950 for a couple. With monthly relevant income above these amounts but not exceeding EUR 1 600 for a single person or EUR 2 300 for a couple, the supplement is reduced by 60% of monthly income above EUR 1 250 or EUR 1 950, respectively. No supplement is paid with monthly income greater than EUR 1 600 for a single person or EUR 2 300 for a couple.				
Greece		September 2021 A new fund for auxiliary pensions was established in Greece (Law 4826/2021). This new fund, called "Hellenic Auxiliary Pensions Defined Contributions Fund" will be effective on 1 January 2022 and will start replacing the existing mandatory NDC	2020 Law 4670/2020 modified annual accrual rates, being effective from 1.10.2019 onwards, as follows: from 30 to 32 years: 1.98% from 33 to 35 years: 2.50% from 36 to 39 years: 2.55% 40 onwards and every year: 0.50% Readjustment of auxiliary pensions introduced in May 2016 was abandoned and pension amounts were restored	January 2020, A new regime for the social security contributions is introduced for self–employed persons and farmers. Self–employed pay per month for the main insurance the fixed amount of the insurance category which choose, with minimum the amount of the 1st insurance category. Six insurance categories			March 2020 The Unified Agency for Auxiliary Social Insurance and Lump-sum Benefits (ETEAEP) were integrated as an Auxiliary insurance branch into the Unified Agency for Social Insurance (EFKA). The latter is renamed "digital National Agency for Social Insurance" (e-EFKA). All services provided by the e-EFKA are to be digitalised (L.4670/2020).

Annex Table 1.A.1. **Pension reform decided between September 2019 and September 2021**

Retirement age	Coverage	Pension benefits	Contributions	Minimum and basic pensions, income and means testing	Taxes and fees	Other
	scheme for auxiliary pensions. The new DC scheme will cover new entrants *to the labour market* while workers younger than 35 would be able to join voluntarily. Other workers and pensioners will not be affected as the decrease of contribution amounts paid to the NDC scheme will be covered by the state budget.	according to the 2014 rules (*L.4670/2020 art.44*). 2021 An advance payment of old-age *pensions and temporary* pensions were introduced for persons who applied for a pension: with 15 years and 67 years old, EUR 384; with 15 years and between 62 to 67 years old, EUR 360; with 20 years and age between 62 to 67, EUR 384; under 62 years old and with special pension requirements, EUR 360; Advanced payment for survivors and disability pensions is EUR 384. Survivors pensions for orphans changed: if a child has lost both parents the amount received is doubled (from 25% to 50%) and cannot fall short of the statutory minimum amount applied for survivors pension (EUR 345-384).	are available, and a special for new self–employed for the first 5 years of insurance. *Farmers:* pay per month for the main insurance the fixed amount of the insurance category which choose, with minimum the amount of the 1st insurance category. Six insurance categories are available. From 1 January 2020 the self–employed, free lancers, salaried engineers and the employed lawyers insured in the Unified Supplementary Insurance and Lump Sum Fund – ETEAEP (Auxiliary insurance branch of e-EFKA from 1-3-2020,-Law 4670/2020), pay per month for the supplementary insurance the fixed amount of the insurance category they choose, with minimum, the amount of the 1st insurance category. The employers of salaried engineers and employed lawyers, cover 50% of the monthly contribution (L. 4670/2020, art.45, L.4756/2020 art.35).			

Annex Table 1.A.1. **Pension reform decided between September 2019 and September 2021**

	Retirement age	Coverage	Pension benefits	Contributions	Minimum and basic pensions, income and means testing	Taxes and fees	Other
Hungary			January 2021 The 13th month pension has gradually been introduced. Those persons are entitled who has been receiving for at least one day in the preceding year before the introduction (thus in 2020) and is receiving a pension benefits for January 2021. The amount of the extra one month pension equals to the amount of the benefit due for the month of January of the current year, paid at least for one day of the preceding year. The amount of the 13th month pension is gradually introduced, therefore in 2021 25% of the monthly amount, in 2022 50%, in 2023 75% and from 2024 onwards a full month extra pension is paid. The 13th month pension is paid to the entitled persons in February 2021 On the basis of the government decree No. 257/2021. (V. 19.) the minimum monthly amount of the orphan's allowance will be HUF 50 000 from 1 Jan 2022.	2020 The new Act CXXII of 2019 on Entitlements to Social Security Benefits and on funding these Services stipulates only one individual social security contribution (employees' contribution), aggregating the former individual contributions. The rate of the new, aggregated social security contribution is 18.5%. There are certain groups of people who pay 10% pension insurance contribution. Of the social security contribution received, the state tax authority shall allocate 54% (equals to the former rate cca. 10% out of 18.5%) to the Pension Insurance Fund as pension contributions, 37.9% to the Health Insurance Fund as health insurance contributions (equals to the former rate cca. 7% out of 18.5%), and 8.1% to the National Employment Fund as labour market contributions (equals to the former rate cca. 1.5%) on a daily basis. From 1st of July 2020 the social contribution tax (employers			

Annex Table 1.A.1. **Pension reform decided between September 2019 and September 2021**

	Retirement age	Coverage	Pension benefits	Contributions	Minimum and basic pensions, income and means testing	Taxes and fees	Other
				contribution) was reduced from 17.5% to 15.5%. Due to the change in the legal background from 1 July 2020 all pensioners receiving a benefit on their own right and pursuing any kind of gainful activity are exempt from contribution payment obligation (and employers are exempt from the payment of social contribution tax as well), however they are still eligible for in-kind health care services.			
Iceland							
Ireland	December 2020 The Irish Government has suspended the planned increase in the State Pension Age (currently 66, scheduled to rise to 67 in 2021 and 68 in 2028), pending a report from the Commission on Pensions (published in October 2021) and consequent Government consideration.		February 2021 The government introduced a benefit payment for people aged 65 who have ceased regular employment or self-employment and satisfied the (PRSI) contribution conditions. The benefit stops when the State Pension Age (currently 66) is reached. The rate of payment is EUR 203 per week (same rate as Jobseeker's Benefit) with an increase for dependants.				A Commission on Pensions has been set up to examine sustainability and eligibility issues in respect of the State Pension and the Social Insurance Fund. The Pensions Commission's Report was published on 7 October 2021. The report has been referred to a Cabinet Committee, a Joint Oireachtas Committee and the Commission for Taxation and Welfare for consideration over the following six months. This is with a view to bringing a recommended response and implementation plan

Annex Table 1.A.1. **Pension reform decided between September 2019 and September 2021**

	Retirement age	Coverage	Pension benefits	Contributions	Minimum and basic pensions, income and means testing	Taxes and fees	Other
							to Government by the end of March 2022.
Israel							2020 In January 2020, elderly disabled people received an additional NIS 190 to their monthly pension. As of January 2021, this amount was updated to NIS 379.
Italy	January 2021 The government extended an early retirement option for women: women who are 58 years of age or older by the end of 2020 (59 years or older if they are self-employed) and have at least 35 years of contributions may choose an early retirement option in 2021. The government extended the Early Retirement Allowance programme. Unemployed, disabled, a care-giver or a hardship worker who have contributed for more than 30 years (a hardship worker in 36 years) will receive an old-age pension from the age of 63. (until 2021) Extended an early retirement option for restructuring. Employees of overstaffed firms can retire up to 7 years before the normal retirement age if the firms have negotiated special agreements with their unions and the government to restructure (until 2023).			January 2021 The government waived employer contributions for certain younger hires, and certain women hires. Employers are exempt from paying a maximum annual contribution of EUR 6 000 per person if they hire a person under the age of 35 under an open-end employment contract in 2021 or 2022. Employers who hire unemployed women in 2021 and 2022 will be exempt from paying up to EUR 6 000 per person per year in contributions. The government temporarily reduced employer contributions in economically depressed regions.			

Annex Table 1.A.1. **Pension reform decided between September 2019 and September 2021**

	Retirement age	Coverage	Pension benefits	Contributions	Minimum and basic pensions, income and means testing	Taxes and fees	Other
Japan	May 2020. From April 2022, it will be possible to defer the claim until 75 years old under the National Pension System, the Employees' Pension System (EPS) and defined contribution pension schemes. Before the amendment, receiving old-age pension benefits can be deferred until being 70 years old.	May 2020. From October 2022, the coverage of the Employees' Pension System (EPS) will be expanded to workers employed by unincorporated firms which provide professional attorney and advisory services such as legal or accounting firms. The coverage of Employees' Pension System (EPS) for part-time employees will be expanded to companies with more than 100 full-time employees in October 2022 and more than 50 full-time employees in October 2024. Before the amendment, part-time workers who meet the requirements such as working hours of 20 hours or more per week and earnings of JPY 88 000 or more per month are covered by the only employed by companies with more than 500 full-time employees. From May 2022, the age requirement for	May 2020. From April 2022, with regard to the employees' old-age pension paid to people aged 60 to 64, the threshold for the total amount of wages and monthly pension, over which the pension is reduced as income increases, will be raised from JPY 280 000 to JPY 470 000. From April 2022, the old-age employees' pension amount will be recalculated once a year, even while the beneficiary is still working. Before amendment, if a beneficiary continues to work after retirement age, the old-age employees' pension amount is recalculated only at the time of termination of employment or on reaching the age of 70, taking account of the insured period after the normal retirement age\	May 2020 From September 2020, the ceiling of wage on which the Employees' pension contributions are levied has been raised from JPY 620 000 to JPY 650 000 per month.			

Annex Table 1.A.1. **Pension reform decided between September 2019 and September 2021**

	Retirement age	Coverage	Pension benefits	Contributions	Minimum and basic pensions, income and means testing	Taxes and fees	Other
		joining defined contribution pension plans will be extended as follows: corporate defined contribution: from under 65 to under 70; individual defined contribution: from under 60 to under 65.					
Korea				November 2020 The maximum number of years that could be contributed at a later date when paying contributions to the National Pension Plan was set at 10 years. Previously, there was no limit.			
Latvia					2020 The minimum old age pension calculating base was set at EUR 80 (for persons with disabilities since childhood – EUR 122.69). Previously minimum base was equal to state social security benefit (EUR 64.03, for persons with disability since childhood – EUR 106.72). The amount of the state social security benefit is used to calculate the minimum disability pension by applying a coefficient – 1.6 for persons with I disability group and 1.4 for persons with II disability group. From 2021, the minimum base for calculating old-age	Non-taxable minimum for pensioners is gradually increasing: from EUR 270 in 2019, to EUR 300 in 2020, and to EUR 330 in 2021. There is also an additional tax relief for persons with disability (EUR 154 for persons with I, II disability groups, EUR 120 for persons with III disability group), politically repressed persons (EUR 154) and for a dependent (EUR 230	

Annex Table 1.A.1. **Pension reform decided between September 2019 and September 2021**

	Retirement age	Coverage	Pension benefits	Contributions	Minimum and basic pensions, income and means testing	Taxes and fees	Other
					pensions is set at EUR 136 (25% of median income), for persons with disabilities since childhood EUR 163 (30% of median income). The amount of the minimum old-age pension has changed: it is equal to 1.1 times the base for the first 15 years plus 2% of the base for each subsequent year. Therefore, the minimum monthly amounts vary from EUR 149.60 in case of 15 years of insurance to EUR 247.52 in case of 51 years of insurance. For those with disabilities since childhood, the minimum monthly amounts vary from EUR 179.30 in case of 15 years of insurance to EUR 296.66 in case of 51 years of insurance.	in 2019, EUR 250 in 2020/2021).	
Lithuania			January 2021 Pensions are subject to a reduction by 0.32% for each full month remaining until the date when the person reaches the old-age pension age. The amount of the old-age pension is not reduced if the person has received the early old-age pension for no more than 3 years and the record of pension insurance is at least 40 years when person applies for the early old-age pension (from 2022 the requirement of the record of pension insurance annually is increased by 3 months until it will reach 42 years 6 months in 2031). Since July 2021, a new benefit for single pensioners (old age and disabled) not receiving		January 2020 The social assistance pension base is calculated as 56% of minimum consumption needs in the previous year (EUR 140 in 2020 and EUR 143 in 2021). The minimum social assistance pension is set to 100% of social assistance pension base. This tying of the social assistance pension base with the amount of minimum consumption needs entails indexation to prices in the future. Recipients of statutory old-age pensions whose pensions are less than 100% of the amount of the minimum consumption needs (EUR 260 per month for 2021) are eligible to receive a pension supplement from the state budget. Supplements for		

Annex Table 1.A.1. **Pension reform decided between September 2019 and September 2021**

	Retirement age	Coverage	Pension benefits	Contributions	Minimum and basic pensions, income and means testing	Taxes and fees	Other
			survivor pensions is gradually introduced. In 2021, the new benefit is covering only poorest pensioners: the receivers of social assistance pensions or pension supplements. Since 2022 the benefits will cover all lonely pensioners (old age and disabled). The system will function in parallel with the widows/ers pensions providing the same amount for both – widows/ers and lonely pensioners. The amount in 2021 will be EUR 28.63 and in 2022 – EUR 32. The decision on the indexation mechanism of the benefit will be taken in autumn of 2021.		small social insurance pensions – top up to the ceiling (100% of minimum consumption needs) depends on service years (full amount with obligatory service years requirement; minimum amount with 15 years minimum requirement).		
Luxembourg							
Mexico			January 2021 The minimum work period in regular employment to access pension was reduced from 1 250 to 750 weeks. However, 25 weeks will be added per year, and from 2031 the minimum work period will be 1 000 weeks.	January 2021 The employer contribution rate for contributions to individual pension investment accounts will be based on salary level, and will increase from the current level of 5.15% to 13.875% between 2023 and 2030. The workers' contribution will remain unchanged at 1.125%. The government contribution rate previous, and until year 2023 is 0.225% of the salary, plus the "social quota" which is a fixed amount depending on the salary level up to 15	December 2020 The guaranteed (minimum) fixed-rate pension was redefined to depend on past earnings, the number of weeks paying contributions, and the age upon retirement. There is a non-contributory and non-means testing pension paid for all Mexican people above 68 years old, and from 65 years old to the indigenous and African-Mexican people. The President announced in March of 2021 that since July 2021, the benefit will be paid to all Mexican people above 65 years old, and will have increase gradually by 75% in real terms by 2024, to be approved by the parliament.	December 2020 Fees of pension funds managers (AFORE) which used to be defined in terms of the market's conditions was changed. The new rule states the fees cannot be higher than the average of the fees from the 3 countries: United States, Colombia, and Chile.	

Annex Table 1.A.1. Pension reform decided between September 2019 and September 2021

	Retirement age	Coverage	Pension benefits	Contributions	Minimum and basic pensions, income and means testing	Taxes and fees	Other
				UMA. The government's fixed rate will disappear in year 2023 and the "social quota" will be paid on salaries below 7.09 UMA, also a fixed amount depending on the salary level, and from year 2024 the "social quota" will be only for salaries below 4 UMA, also a fixed amount depending on the salary level. The fixed amounts are increased in March, June, September and December of each year, according to the quarterly inflation rate.			
Netherlands	December 2020 The retirement age was scheduled to increase from 66 to 67 in 2021, but the Dutch Parliament postponed this change to 2024. As of 2025, the retirement age will increase by 2/3rds of the increase in life expectancy instead of 1-to-1.						
New Zealand					November 2020 Qualified superannuitants no longer have the option to include their partner (who does not qualify) in their rate of New Zealand Superannuation or Veteran's Pension. People already including their non-qualified partner can continue to do so. A superannuitant's New Zealand Superannuation or Veteran's Pension is no		

Annex Table 1.A.1. Pension reform decided between September 2019 and September 2021

	Retirement age	Coverage	Pension benefits	Contributions	Minimum and basic pensions, income and means testing	Taxes and fees	Other
					longer reduced because their partner has an overseas pension that exceeds that partner's entitlement to a New Zealand benefit or pension. A single superannuitant who lives alone in a self-contained mobile home is now entitled to receive the single living alone rate. These changes were originally scheduled for July 2020, but delayed due to COVID-19.		
Norway			2021 Reform of the survivors' benefits in the National Insurance Scheme has been approved by the Storting and will be implemented in 2023 or 2024. Main changes include: - The current permanent survivor's pension for persons under the age of 67 will be replaced by a time-limited adjustment benefit. The benefit will no longer be calculated as a pension on the basis of the deceased's earnings, but determined at a fixed level approximately corresponding to the current minimum level. The new benefit will be taxed as salary and reduced to the survivor's earned income. An activity requirement will be introduced. - Children's pension is significantly improved. - Current supplements to survivors' old-age pension or disability benefit will be phased out over time.		September 2019 The minimum pension level (special rate for single pensioners) was raised by NOK 4 000. December 2020 A decision was made to further increase the minimum pension by NOK 4 000 as a lump sum. February 2021 It was decided that the amount of NOK 4 000, adopted in December 2020, should be sustained as a permanent increase in the minimum pension level for single persons from January 2021, in addition to the regular indexation for 2021, and that the minimum pension level (special rate for single pensioners) should be raised again by NOK 5 000 from July 2021.		January 2021 Rules on "individual pension accounts" in private defined contribution schemes were set into force. The rules facilitate collection of pension accrual from various DC schemes on a single account and introduces increased freedom of choice in the management of pension capital.

Annex Table 1.A.1. **Pension reform decided between September 2019 and September 2021**

	Retirement age	Coverage	Pension benefits	Contributions	Minimum and basic pensions, income and means testing	Taxes and fees	Other
			In 2021, pensions in payment were indexed to the average wage growth while the indexation rule indicated an indexation to the average wage growth minus 0.75 percentage points.				
Poland			January 2020 The government introduced an additional annual cash benefit for all pensioners (the so-called 13th pension) equal to the minimum old-age pension on 1 March. In 2020, the minimum pension was PLN 1 200 gross. In 2021 amount 13th pension will be PLN 1250.88 gross. March 2021 A one-off benefit, the so-called 14th pension in the amount of the lowest old-age pension, was introduced. In November 2021, benefits of PLN 1, 250, 88 gross were paid to pensioners whose pensions did not exceed PLN 2 900. People whose pensions were higher than PLN 2 900 received reduced amounts. 2020, at 100% withdrawal rate. September 2021 Calculation of pensions granted in June was adjusted to make sure that they are not lower compared to those granted in May. In previous years, the quarterly indexation of notional accounts did not apply to those retiring in June; the yearly indexation applied instead but people retiring in June could have received lower pensions	February 2020 The government reduced the social security contributions for self-employed workers (the so-called "Little ZUS plus") whose annual income was lower than PLN 120 000. Their contributions are based on 50% of income (before deducting any costs) as opposed to 100% of profits.		October 2019 The income tax rate in the first income bracket (which covers most pensioners) was reduced from 18% to 17%.	October 2019 Persons incapable of independent existence, including retirees and pensioners, receive a supplementary benefit of maximum PLN 500 per month. The supplementary benefit and the old-age / disability pension may not exceed the amount of PLN 1, 772, 08 gross per month in 2021 (PLN 1 700 in 2020, PLN 1 600 in 2019). The supplementary benefit is intended to provide additional financial support to people with disabilities due to increased costs related to nursing, rehabilitation and medical care.

Annex Table 1.A.1. **Pension reform decided between September 2019 and September 2021**

	Retirement age	Coverage	Pension benefits	Contributions	Minimum and basic pensions, income and means testing	Taxes and fees	Other
			than those retiring in other months.				
Portugal			May 2020 Extraordinary pension indexation. Pensions indexed between 2011 and 2015 were increased by EUR 6.00; pensions not updated between 2011 and 2015 increased by EUR 10. In 2021, pensions were not indexed according to legal framework; pensions up to 1.5 x IAS (EUR 658, 20) increased by EUR 10.				
Slovak Republic	December 2020. The Slovak Government removed the cap on the retirement-age increases at 64. The future pathway for retirement age is to be enacted the by parliament in the next 2 years. Currently, the retirement age is increased by 2 months a year until the retirement age reaches 64 years. Increasing the retirement age by two months mirrors the trend in the change of the life expectancy in the Slovak Republic. The retirement age for mothers was lowered by at least 6 months for each child, up to three children.		April 2020 The government introduced an additional pension payment (13th pension), equal to the average pension, at EUR 460 in 2020, to replace the so-called Christmas bonus. The new 13th pension amount has been set at the average pension amount for each type of pensions (e.g. old-age pensions, disability pensions). If one receives more than one pension benefit (for example old-age and survivor pension), he or she is entitled only to the higher of the two 13th pensions. All pensioners will receive the new benefits while, before, only pensioners with their benefits lower than 65% of the average wage were eligible. November 2020 The new 13th pension was reduced especially for high pensions: at EUR 300 only for those with pension below EUR 214.83 and decreasing to		2020 The minimum pension for individuals with 30 years of contributions was set at 33% of the average wage two years before. For each extra year of contributions, the minimum pension increases by 2% of the subsistence level threshold up to 39 years of career and by 3% thereafter. October 2020 Effective from January 2021, the mechanism determining the minimum pension is dropped, and their amounts are frozen at the level of 2020. Additionally, from 2021, only those years with contributions from a contributory base above 24.1% of the average wage are taken into account to determine the minimum pension amount.		

Annex Table 1.A.1. **Pension reform decided between September 2019 and September 2021**

	Retirement age	Coverage	Pension benefits	Contributions	Minimum and basic pensions, income and means testing	Taxes and fees	Other
			EUR 50 for pensions higher than EUR 909.30.				
Slovenia			December 2019 A reform increased men's total accruals from 57.25% to 58.50% in 2020, to 59.50% in 2021 and then gradually to the women's level of 63.50% by 2025. A pension bonus for having children, at 1.36% accrual per child up to three children, was introduced. The restrictions on combining work and pensions were eased: when working full time after having met the eligibility conditions to pensions, 40% pension can be claimed for the first 3 years and 20% thereafter. Before, only 20% of pensions could have been claimed. The additional accrual for working 41st, 42nd and 43rd years was decreased from 4% to 3% compared to the regular accrual rate of 1.36% for 15th through 40th years. May 2021 The Act Amending The Pension and Disability Insurance Act has shortened the transitional period for the gradual equalisation of the assessment scale by gender from 2025 to 2023. That increased men's total accruals to 61.50% in 2022 and 63.50% in 2023.		December 2019 The minimum pension is set at 29.5% of the minimum pension base and from 1 May 2021 amounts to EUR 279.56, and will continue to be adjusted in the same way as pensions. The guaranteed pension for beneficiaries of an old-age or disability pension with at least 40 years of completed pension period from 1 May 2021 onwards amounts to EUR 620.00. Furthermore, the guaranteed pension will be co-ordinated in the same way as pensions. From 1 May 2021 onwards, the lowest disability pension is set at 41% of the minimum pension base, amounting to EUR 388.54. This pension will continue to be adjusted in the same way as pensions.		December 2020 A requirement to provide a justified reason when dismissing an employee who has met eligibility conditions to the old-age pension was removed. However, the implementation of this amendment, which effectively introduces the mandatory retirement age, is uncertain as it has been appealed in the Constitutional Court on the ground of discrimination. The Constitutional Court suspended the implementation of these statutory provisions until its final decision.
Spain			February 2021 The government introduced a new pension supplement for parents receiving old-age, disability, and survivor pensions.		June 2020 The Social Security implemented the Minimum Vital Income. The Minimum Vital Income is a benefit aimed at preventing the risk of poverty		

Annex Table 1.A.1. **Pension reform decided between September 2019 and September 2021**

	Retirement age	Coverage	Pension benefits	Contributions	Minimum and basic pensions, income and means testing	Taxes and fees	Other
			The new supplement starts from a fixed amount of EUR 378/year, per child, up to a maximum of 4 children.		and social exclusion of people who live alone or are integrated in a cohabitation unit and lack basic economic resources to cover their basic needs. In general, the guaranteed income was set at EUR 469.93 per month for an adult person living alone. In the case of a cohabitation unit, this amount is increased by EUR 140.98 per month for each additional person, adult or minor, up to a maximum of EUR 1 033.85 per month. In addition, for single-parent families, a supplement of EUR 103.39 is added.		
Sweden	January 2020 The government increased the earliest age to draw public contributory pensions from 61 to 62 years and the mandatory retirement age was increased from 67 to 68 in 2020 and to 69 in 2023. The planned further reforms require enacting amendments to the law: - increasing minimum retirement age to 63 in 2023 and to 64 in 2026; - increasing the minimum age to access the basic pension from 65 to 67 by 2026; - introducing a "target retirement age"; the target retirement age will undergo annual review, but any increase would take effect 2026 later and remain				2021 The government introduced a new pension supplement to increase monthly pensions between SEK 9 000 and SEK 17 000 (between 23% and 44% of gross average wage, respectively) by up to 6.7%. This benefit will be paid to people who receive none or a small amount of the basic pension, which is fully withdrawn when monthly earnings-related pension exceeds SEK 12 529 (in 2020).		

Annex Table 1.A.1. **Pension reform decided between September 2019 and September 2021**

	Retirement age	Coverage	Pension benefits	Contributions	Minimum and basic pensions, income and means testing	Taxes and fees	Other
	unchanged for at least three years; - linking all retirement ages to changes in life expectancy.						
Switzerland							
Turkey			April 2021 A holiday bonus amount was increased to TRL 1 100 for each holiday to total of TRL 2200.				
United Kingdom							February 2021 A legal framework to establish and operate occupational CDC schemes was enacted. Government tightened abuse rules for pension schemes by the Pensions Regulator's powers. Government strengthened the Pensions Regulator's ability to take stronger, more effective, action to protect members' pensions of Defined Benefit Pension Schemes.
United States							

ANNEX 1.B

Results of the Bai – Perron test

Annex Table 1.B.1. **Yearly change in life expectancy at age 65, in years**

The reported measure indicates the average change for each sub-period during which no break is identified

Country	Women					Men					
		Break1	Break2	Break3	Break4		Break1	Break2	Break3	Break4	Break5
Australia	1955-72	1973-82	1983-2008	2009-19		1955-70	1971-93	1994-2008	2009-19		
	0.06	0.12	0.16	0.08		0.00	0.14	0.20	0.16		
Austria	1955-70	1971-80	1981-2019			1955-71	1972-81	1982-96	1997-2008	2009-19	
	0.06	0.17	0.13			-0.01	0.10	0.15	0.19	0.10	
Belgium	1955-72	1973-93	1994-2019			1955-73	1974-84	1985-2019			
	0.06	0.16	0.11			-0.02	0.10	0.15			
Canada	1955-63	1964-82	1983-99	2000-10	2011-19	1955-66	1967-75	1976-97	1998-2010	2011-19	
	0.09	0.13	0.07	0.13	0.09	0.01	0.05	0.10	0.19	0.13	
Chile	1993-2003	2004-19				1993-2019					
	0.15	0.09				0.12					
Czech Republic	1955-63	1964-86	1987-2019			1955-66	1967-95	1996-2019			
	0.10	0.02	0.15			-0.03	0.03	0.17			
Denmark	1955-63	1964-78	1979-98	1999-2019		1960-95	1996-2006	2007-19			
	0.07	0.14	0.03	0.15		0.00	0.11	0.19			
Estonia	1960-94	1995-2019				1955-63	1964-72	1973-86	1987-95	1996-2009	2010-19
	0.03	0.19				0.00	-0.05	0.02	0.13	0.17	0.12
Finland	1955-67	1968-81	1982-93	1994-2008	2009-19	1955-69	1970-93	1994-2008	2009-19		
	0.05	0.20	0.11	0.18	0.09	0.01	0.11	0.19	0.13		
France	1955-72	1973-82	1983-91	1992-2010	2011-19	1955-74	1975-2019				
	0.11	0.15	0.18	0.14	0.08	0.05	0.14				
Germany	1991-2002	2003-07	2008-11	2012-19		1991-2010	2011-19				
	0.17	0.13	0.10	0.06		0.17	0.09				
Greece	1982-87	1988-99	2000-11	2012-19		1982-88	1989-97	1998-2002	2003-11	2012-19	
	0.08	0.11	0.15	0.09		0.05	0.08	0.11	0.14	0.10	
Hungary	1955-64	1965-85	1986-96	1997-2010	2011-19	1955-63	1964-82	1983-94	1995-2019		
	0.10	0.03	0.10	0.13	0.07	0.01	-0.04	0.04	0.10		
Iceland	1955-68	1969-78	1979-94	1995-2019		1955-69	1970-78	1979-91	1992-2019		
	0.03	0.18	0.05	0.08		0.00	0.09	0.04	0.13		
Ireland	1955-76	1977-98	1999-2009	2010-19		1955-79	1980-96	1997-2010	2011-19		
	0.06	0.11	0.22	0.14		0.00	0.08	0.25	0.18		
Israel	1984-90	1991-98	1999-2009	2010-19		1984-98	1999-2010	2011-19			
	0.18	0.15	0.17	0.14		0.11	0.17	0.12			
Italy	1955-76	1977-2007	2008-19			1955-70	1971-80	1981-2019			
	0.10	0.16	0.08			0.00	0.05	0.15			
Japan	1955-63	1964-73	1974-2003	2004-19		1955-64	1965-73	1974-85	1986-2019		
	0.08	0.17	0.22	0.11		0.05	0.15	0.19	0.12		
Korea	2004-10	2011-19				2004-12	2013-19				
	0.31	0.24				0.26	0.25				

Annex Table 1.B.1. **Yearly change in life expectancy at age 65, in years** *(cont.)*

The reported measure indicates the average change for each sub-period during which no break is identified

Country	Women					Men					
		Break1	Break2	Break3	Break4		Break1	Break2	Break3	Break4	Break5
Latvia	1960-94	1995-2004	2005-19			1960-77	1978-95	1996-2005	2006-19		
	0.01	0.10	0.15			-0.05	-0.03	0.07	0.12		
Lithuania	1960-68	1969–1994	1995-2019			1960-68	1969-94	1995-2008	2009-19		
	0.08	0.01	0.11			0.01	-0.04	0.04	0.09		
Luxembourg	1961-74	1975-2011	2012-19			1961-74	1975-97	1998-2011	2012-19		
	0.07	0.16	0.11			-0.02	0.13	0.20	0.14		
Netherlands	1955-71	1972-83	1984-2000	2001-10	2011-19	1955-74	1975-97	1998-2019			
	0.10	0.15	0.04	0.13	0.06	-0.02	0.06	0.18			
New Zealand	1955-64	1965-2019				1955-69	1970-80	1981-89	1990-2010	2011-19	
	0.02	0.10				-0.03	0.06	0.12	0.20	0.16	
Norway	1955-69	1970-87	1988-99	2000-19		1955-69	1970-90	1991-99	2000-19		
	0.04	0.10	0.15	0.13		-0.06	0.04	0.13	0.18		
Poland	1959-76	1977-93	1994-2010	2011-19		1959-93	1994-2019				
	0.07	0.03	0.17	0.10		0.01	0.13				
Portugal	1955-72	1973-2019				1955-73	1974-99	2000-10	2011-19		
	0.04	0.15				0.02	0.11	0.18	0.12		
Slovak Republic	1955-63	1964-89	1990-2000	2001-09	2010-19	1955-63	1964-72	1973-86	1987-95	1996-2004	2005-19
	0.11	0.04	0.09	0.13	0.16	0.02	-0.06	-0.01	0.03	0.09	0.15
Slovenia	1984-2011	2012-19				1984-2000	2001-12	2013-19			
	0.18	0.12				0.12	0.22	0.15			
Spain	1955-73	1974-84	1985-2010	2011-19		1955-73	1974-84	1985-2000	2001-10	2011-19	
	0.10	0.18	0.15	0.12		0.05	0.13	0.10	0.16	0.13	
Sweden	1955-63	1964-75	1976-84	1985-95	1996-2019	1955-71	1972-80	1981-90	1991-2019		
	0.10	0.13	0.12	0.10	0.09	0.01	0.04	0.10	0.14		
Switzerland	1955-68	1969-80	1981-89	1990-2009	2010-19	1955-68	1969-93	1994-2009	2010-19		
	0.11	0.18	0.15	0.12	0.08	0.04	0.11	0.17	0.14		
United Kingdom	1955-76	1977-98	1999-2010	2011-19		1955-70	1971-79	1980-95	1996-2010	2011-19	
	0.07	0.10	0.16	0.08		0.02	0.06	0.12	0.21	0.11	
United States	1955-2019					1955-68	1969-98	1999-2010	2011-19		
	0.08					-0.01	0.10	0.16	0.09		
OECD	**1955-70**	**1971-79**	**1980-95**	**1996-2010**	**2011-19**	**1955-71**	**1972-88**	**1989-97**	**1998-2010**	**2011-19**	
	0.07	**0.11**	**0.09**	**0.14**	**0.11**	**0.00**	**0.07**	**0.10**	**0.16**	**0.13**	

Note: The breaks are significant at the 99% confidence level. To limit interferences from short-term fluctuations in change in life expectancy, the breaks are estimated on the Hodrick-Prescott filtered trend series (lambda=100).

Source: Human Mortality Database (2020), *https://www.mortality.org*.

Pensions at a Glance 2021
OECD and G20 Indicators

Chapter 2

Automatic adjustment mechanisms in pension systems

The chapter describes automatic adjustment mechanisms in mandatory pension schemes in OECD countries. About two-thirds of OECD countries employ such mechanisms, including notional defined contribution (NDC) schemes, links of the statutory retirement age to life expectancy, benefit adjustments to changes in life expectancy, demographic ratios or the wage bill, and balancing mechanisms. The chapter discusses what automatic adjustment mechanisms can and cannot do, as well as possible alternative policies. AAMs can be useful tools to prevent pension schemes from becoming increasingly unsustainable as populations age. Finally, it proposes some guidelines for designing and implementing automatic adjustment mechanisms based on OECD countries' experiences with revising or overturning such mechanisms. This includes the need for wide political agreement on their introduction and avoiding mechanisms that reduce pension benefits in payment in nominal or real terms.

Wouter De Tavernier and Hervé Boulhol

Introduction

Pension systems are a crucial element of social protection for older people. They are designed to provide individuals with an income in the (distant) future, which makes them susceptible to uncertainties surrounding demographic and economic developments. How can pension adequacy be upheld if the evolution of wages and prices over the next decades is unknown? And how can financial sustainability of pension systems be ensured in the long term in light of population ageing with an increasing ratio of pensioners to contributors?

In the face of demographic, economic or financial trends, policy makers can choose not to act and accept the negative consequences these trends might have for financial sustainability or for the adequacy of the pension system. Alternatively, they can adjust pension parameters. These adjustments can be discretionary, by undertaking regular legislative action as circumstances change. Or, changes can occur automatically by setting rules about how pension parameters should be adjusted. Even though automatic rules cannot eliminate all the uncertainty, this last option can be attractive to policy makers as, while for example the precise extent of future ageing trends is unknown, the broad impact of how a given demographic evolution affects the pension system is typically well understood. Moreover, automatic rules are one way to better include future generations who have neither a vote nor a voice today.

Automatic adjustment mechanisms (AAMs) refer to predefined rules that automatically change pension parameters or pension benefits based on the evolution of a demographic, economic or financial indicator. They can protect pensions from uncertainties: pension indexation can protect pension adequacy against current and future inflation trends, and, more generally, automatic adjustments to benefits, contribution rates and retirement ages can serve various objectives. This chapter provides an overview of why AAMs came into being and what they look like, as well as of what they can and cannot achieve.

About two-thirds of OECD countries employ some form of AAM in mandatory or quasi-mandatory pension schemes. Six have notional defined contribution (NDC) schemes. Seven countries adjust qualifying conditions for retirement to life expectancy, and six adjust benefits to changes in life expectancy, demographic ratios or the wage bill. Finally, seven countries have a balancing mechanism.

As population ageing is the result of several demographic trends, several AAMs may be required to reach financial sustainability in the pension system, with each AAM linked to one specific demographic evolution. Increases in life expectancy should at least partially be offset by increasing the statutory retirement age, as this protects both adequacy and financial sustainability of the pension system. A supplementary correction is also likely to be needed to adjust for changes in the size of the population contributing to the pension system, thus determining its revenues. Moreover, those adjustments might not be sufficient to reach or maintain financial balance over time, and hence a balancing mechanism may be needed.

Whether to make adjustments to pensions, contributions or retirement ages depends on a wide array of factors, and is fundamentally the subject of democratic debate for both discretionary changes and automatic adjustments. When putting an AAM in place, choices for which pension parameters to adjust depend among others on their initial level and people's preferences. However, some AAMs introduced at a time of crisis to restore financial sustainability – meaning that measures are needed irrespective of how some indicators will develop – might be questioned once the economy recovers. Hence, AAMs are not a substitute for bold discretionary measures in a financially unbalanced pension scheme. It is therefore important to distinguish changes that should take place in any case from those that are conditional to the evolution of circumstances in order to fulfil agreed objectives.

The **main findings** of this chapter are the following:

- Automatic adjustment mechanisms (AAMs) protect pension systems from demographic, economic and financial uncertainties affecting pension adequacy and/or financial sustainability.
- While AAMs emerged as a tool to uphold pension adequacy through wage or price indexation, there has been a shift in focus over the last decades towards maintaining financial sustainability.
- As AAMs are conditional on a changing indicator, they reduce the risk of under- or over-shooting the mark compared to discretionary adjustments aiming to reach the same target. Uncertainty can further be reduced through procedures smoothing the adjustments over several years.
- Compared to the alternative of discretionary changes, AAMs can be designed to generate changes that are less erratic, more transparent and more equitable across generations.
- AAMs reduce the political cost of maintaining or improving financial sustainability of a pension system as well as the need for frequent pension reforms.
- Since AAMs are meant to operate in the medium or long term, it is critical that they remain politically sustainable. This can be reached through wide political support for their introduction and by designing mechanisms that avoid harsh adjustments.
- As for discretionary changes, AAMs have distributional consequences and their design should be subject to democratic debate. Once AAMs are in place, policy makers maintain full control over the development of pensions and can intervene if they deem the triggered adjustments undesirable.
- AAMs are meant to adjust for future trends and are not a substitute for bold discretionary measures in a financially unbalanced pension scheme. Countries in that situation should ideally have a wider reform plan consisting of discretionary steps that restore financial balance and of a set of AAMs that can in particular deal with ageing trends. If measures have not been taken to ensure a sound pension system, the AAMs used to restore financial balance are likely to be overturned if they lead to nominal or real losses in retirement income or too rapid increases in the retirement age.
- Automatic adjustments of pension parameters are unlikely to be sufficient to meet the main objectives of the pension system. In particular, they need to be complemented by an automatic balancing mechanism which aims at ensuring a balanced budget of the pension scheme.
- About two-thirds of OECD countries have at least one AAM in place. Mechanisms include those embodied in notional DC (NDC) schemes (6 countries), links of the statutory retirement age to life expectancy (7 countries), benefit adjustments to changes in life expectancy, demographic ratios or the wage bill (6 countries), and balancing mechanisms (7 countries). In funded DC (FDC), trends in life expectancy do not affect pension finances by design, but retirement-income adequacy may be weakened.
- Countries with no AAM are: Austria, Belgium, the Czech Republic, France, Hungary, Ireland, Israel, Korea, New Zealand, the Slovak Republic, Slovenia, Spain, Switzerland and Turkey. However, some of these countries have some medium-term plans to change pension parameters based on a set timetable, i.e. adjustments are not conditional on change in an indicator even though they were planned based on ageing projections. The Czech Republic and the Slovak Republic will continue to raise the retirement age until 2030 while France will extend the contribution period required for a full pension until about 2035.
- Sweden and Finland have the most effective AAMs. Sweden combines NDC pensions and a balancing mechanism to ensure solvency, and plans to introduce a link between retirement age

and life expectancy. Finland adjusts to changes in life expectancy in a DB scheme, by changing future retirement ages by two-thirds of changes in life expectancy and by adjusting new pensions. Finland supplements these with a balancing mechanism adjusting contribution rates if needed.

- Both Estonia and Italy account for changes in the size of the working population through adjusting benefits to changes in total contributions and GDP, respectively, while the statutory retirement age is linked to life expectancy. However, Italy has developed a temporary workaround for retirement age increases by facilitating early retirement without actuarial adjustments (Chapter 1). The German balancing mechanism adjusts to the ratio of pensioners to contributors through adjustments of both pensions and contribution rates.
- Backstop mechanisms in the Canada Pension Plan ensure a financially balanced pension system while explicitly prioritising a political solution in case of a deficit: the automatic balancing mechanism is only triggered if policy makers cannot agree on an alternative set of interventions.

This chapter is structured as follows. The next section briefly presents what AAMs are, which purposes they serve and how they came about. Some common criticisms of AAMs are dealt with in this section as well. The subsequent section delves into different types of AAMs in OECD countries and provides an in-depth overview of the mechanisms in place and their main characteristics. The fourth section discusses the limitations of AAMs in terms of their design and the politics surrounding them, as well as possible alternatives. The final section highlights the advantages of AAMs, and sets out some guidelines for their design and introduction to improve their chances of succeeding.

Automatic adjustment mechanisms: objectives and common criticisms

Automatic adjustment mechanisms (AAMs) in pension systems refer to predefined rules that automatically change pension parameters or pension benefits linked to the evolution of a selected indicator. Hence, rules regularly changing pension parameters without adjustment to an indicator, such as a one-month increase in the retirement age every year, are not considered as AAMs in this chapter. The indicators used in these AAMs can be demographic (e.g. life expectancy at a given age), economic (e.g. wage or wage-bill growth) or financial in nature (e.g. funding balance), or a combination of those. The mechanism can affect benefit levels, contribution rates and/or the statutory retirement age. 'Automatic' means that the parameters or the benefits are adjusted in accordance with a predefined rule when the indicator changes or crosses a critical threshold without the need for discretionary decisions or political interventions. While fully automatic mechanisms require no legislative intervention, some others can be classified as 'semi-automatic' or 'soft' mechanisms (Vidal-Meliá, Boado-Penas and Settergren, 2009[1]): in that case, the changes they trigger require parliamentary confirmation. Finally, others function as a backstop triggering a predefined set of adjustments in case no political agreement can be reached on an alternative way to improve pension finances – such backstops are needed as a disciplining device to help take difficult decisions –, which could be classified as automatic backstop mechanisms (the next section provides more details).

Objectives of automatic adjustment mechanisms

AAMs help insulate pension systems from the impact of a changing and uncertain environment, and protect pension benefit levels or pension finances from changing demographic and economic circumstances. While AAMs come in different forms and with different goals, one common purpose is to reduce the impact of uncertainties affecting pension systems, including the future development of inflation, life expectancy and financial returns. In pay-as-you-go (PAYG) systems financial uncertainties also arise from trends in the ratio of the number of contributors per retiree, which in turn depend on changes in longevity, fertility rates, employment and migration. AAMs avoid that pension adequacy or the financial sustainability of the pension scheme is undermined as a result of these uncertainties by adjusting pension parameters.

AAMs cover a wide range of pension policy areas. Indexing pensions in payment and rules to uprate past wages when calculating pension benefits reduce uncertainty surrounding the purchasing power of pensioners. Other AAMs, such as automatic balancing mechanisms, aim to ensure solvency or improve financial sustainability, reducing uncertainty surrounding the pension system's capacity to fulfil its future commitments. Links between the statutory retirement age and life expectancy can serve a wider set of goals, including financial sustainability, pension adequacy, intergenerational equity and higher labour supply.

AAMs can reduce the political cost of improving financial sustainability. By providing a default scenario that adjusts some pension parameters, they increase the required political efforts of those who want to deviate and potentially undermine sustainability (Bosworth and Weaver, 2011[2]): as AAMs reveal the trade-off between short-term interests, such as contribution and benefit levels, and long-term financial sustainability, the long-term consequences of pension policy interventions become much clearer if AAMs have to be overturned. Instead of pleading for interventions improving financial sustainability, AAMs result in policy makers having to legitimise interventions negatively impacting sustainability – not only towards their electorate, but for example also towards the capital markets that might respond adversely to abandoning commitments to financial sustainability. Hence, AAMs reduce the asymmetry in ease with which policy makers spend surpluses compared to the difficulty they face to reduce deficits in the pension system (Diamond, 2004[3]). By reducing the frequency of the need for interventions and by making decisions that deviate from the mechanism – whether interventions negatively affecting financial sustainability or, though less likely, harsher reductions in pension adequacy than needed to maintain financial sustainability – more politically costly, AAMs reduce uncertainty surrounding future changes in the pension legislation. Moreover, if AAMs are consistently applied, they can also contribute to maintaining or restoring trust in the pension system by providing long-term financial sustainability and/or upholding pension adequacy.

Development of automatic adjustment mechanisms

AAMs in pension systems have existed since the 1930s, initially as pension indexation, i.e. increasing pensions automatically in line with price or wage increases in order to sustain pension adequacy. Pensions were introduced from the late 19th century, and when, decades later, concerns rose about the long-term purchasing power of pensions, pension indexation emerged (Fernández, 2012[4]). Initially benefit increases were discretionary, meaning that the value of a pension depended on economic and political cycles. In order to reduce uncertainty and improve social sustainability, Denmark introduced the indexation of pensions in payment to prices in 1933, followed by France after the Second World War and most other OECD countries in the following decades. Indexation of pensions to average wages was first introduced in the Netherlands in 1956, followed by Germany the year after. Periods of high inflation encouraged countries to introduce indexation mechanisms, in particular the high inflation rates following the oil crisis in the 1970s (Hohnerlein, 2019[5]). Moreover, pension indexation was supposed to reduce class conflict by avoiding recurring political discussions on revaluing pensions (Fernández, 2012[4]). By accounting for inflation and removing the need for political agreement to maintain the purchasing power of pensioners, indexation provided certainty through offering older people a predictable real income stream.

With population ageing resulting in increasing concern about the financial sustainability of pension systems, several countries adjusted their pension indexation rules to generate savings. Some countries that were previously at least partially indexing pensions to wages moved towards price indexation; others made indexation of pension benefits conditional on economic metrics other than consumer prices or average wages, such as the growth in the total wage bill or GDP. In this way, indexation took into account changes in the size of the working population. Germany, for example, adjusted pensions to the ratio of pensioners to contributors and Sweden introduced an adjustment to financial balance of the system, defined as the ratio of future pension expenditures to future revenues. Several countries are linking benefit levels or statutory retirement ages to changes in life expectancy. Finally, some countries completely changed the structure of their pension systems and moved away from defined benefit pension schemes to defined contribution schemes, both funded and notional, which include some forms of automatic adjustments (see below).

Common criticisms of automatic adjustment mechanisms

AAMs have been presented as 'depoliticising' pension policy (Fernández, 2012[4]; Vidal-Meliá, Boado-Penas and Settergren, 2009[1]) as political interventions in pension management would be less necessary. However, implementing an AAM is a highly political process balancing interests of different stakeholders and allocating risks, which in turn have implications on who bears which risks. Both setting objectives for AAMs and deciding which parameters to adjust require open political debate as they have important distributional implications. Policy makers, of course, maintain the power to change the AAM if they no longer deem its outcomes desirable, confirmed by the frequent changes observed in pension indexation rules over time (Chapter 1). Several countries introduced AAMs more recently and then suspended their implementation or even removed the mechanisms altogether, which shows that it is not always politically easy to keep AAMs in operation once they have been introduced.

AAMs, such as those linking benefit levels at the moment of retirement to life expectancy in old age, are sometimes criticised because with rising life expectancy they automatically reduce replacement rates at a fixed age, and thus could be seen as improving financial sustainability at the expense of retirement income security. While that argument might be true, it misses the fact that if no additional financial resources can be allocated to pensions, upholding the replacement rate will require increasing the pension age or the contribution levels in order to keep the system financially sustainable. This might generate more insecurity, especially if these changes are discretionary, with potentially some erratic timing and magnitude of adjustments. Thus, AAMs should not be criticised against the scenario of no policy change, which is not credible, but should rather be assessed against a sustainable policy alternative. That is, the challenges driven by increasing longevity need to be addressed in any case through a parametric change, whether automatic or discretionary.

The no-policy-change scenario, maintaining the same promises at the same retirement age while keeping the same contribution rate, is likely to result in financial imbalances that will ultimately entail uncertainty about pension adequacy: governments cannot guarantee that pension levels will be sustained in a financially unsustainable system. At some point, as happened in fact to various countries facing intense financial pressure, adjustments need to take place, and they may then be made hastily, be more erratic, abrupt and potentially inequitable across various groups than what carefully designed AAMs, decided after a broad consultation, could deliver.

It should, however, be noted that while AAMs can improve pension finances, they might not, depending on their design, be sufficient to provide financial sustainability in the long term, and some might even be difficult to sustain politically over time. For instance, by fixing the amount of years cohorts can expect to live in retirement, as is the case in Denmark, the share of adult life spent in retirement will fall as life expectancy increases, which raises questions of intergenerational justice. On the other hand, AAMs can also result in a better relative income position of older people over time. The UK's triple-lock indexation, adjusting pensions to whichever is the highest of three options – inflation, wage growth or 2.5% –, might improve the situation of pensioners relative to workers while increasing pension expenditure.[1] These measures change the status quo, with some distributive implications.

One criticism of AAMs refers to the unequal impact they may have within generations on different social groups as they are linked to average and aggregate indicators. This is particularly a concern regarding links between the retirement age and life expectancy and is discussed in greater detail below (in the section on Adjustment of the retirement age to life expectancy). This potential criticism actually extends beyond AAMs to pension policy more generally, as even fixed pension parameters such as a common retirement age for everyone may produce unequal outcomes.

Types of automatic adjustment mechanisms

Automatic adjustment mechanisms (AAMs) come in a variety of forms. Table 2.1 provides a summary of AAMs in place in OECD countries, with details provided throughout the section. As this chapter hones in on AAMs related to mitigating the impact of demographic changes, 'pure' wage or price indexation or a combination of both is not included here, but is discussed in Chapters 1 and 3.

About two-thirds of OECD countries employ at least one type of automatic adjustment for at least one of the (quasi-)mandatory components of their pension systems. The countries without any AAM are Austria, Belgium, the Czech Republic, France, Hungary, Ireland, Israel, Korea, New Zealand, the Slovak Republic, Slovenia, Spain, Switzerland and Turkey. None of the non-OECD G20 countries currently has an AAM.

Defined contribution (DC) schemes adjust pension benefits to demographic and economic changes in several ways (see below). Twelve OECD countries have mandatory or quasi-mandatory funded DC (FDC) schemes and six operate notional or non-financial DC (NDC) schemes. In addition, seven countries adjust qualifying conditions for retirement to life expectancy, and six adjust benefits to changes in life expectancy, demographic ratios or the wage bill. Finally, seven countries have a balancing mechanism.

Most of these mechanisms are fully automatic, while some are semi-automatic as each adjustment requires political approval in order to be activated. One scheme (Canada) could be described as an automatic backstop mechanism: when the contributory public pension plan is estimated to be financially unsustainable, this triggers a political process and the back-up adjustment is only automatically applied in the absence of a political agreement on an alternative solution. This section presents these different adjustment mechanisms and discusses similarities and differences in how countries have been operationalising the mechanisms.

Funded defined contribution schemes

In an FDC scheme, retiring individuals can draw the money accumulated in their account. This can take various forms, from lump sums to annuities; the latter are priced taking into account expected mortality rates: the longer the life expectancy, the lower the value of the pension annuity, thus automatically including an adjustment of pension levels to life expectancy. Retirees choosing a lump sum will have to manage their pension assets throughout their remaining life themselves. Hence, FDC schemes with lump sum withdrawals by definition allocate the risk of increasing life expectancy to pensioners as accumulated pension assets have to cover longer average retirement periods at a given retirement age, and pensioners have to account for this when withdrawing their pension assets. Moreover, the individual retiree and not the pension provider is exposed to longevity risks, i.e. to the risk of living longer than projected on average and of consuming all the assets.[2] Programmed withdrawals fall in between these two polar cases, mixing lump sums and annuities.

An FDC pension system is thus financially sustainable in the face of economic fluctuations and demographic trends as no pension promise is made until a person starts drawing an annuity upon retirement. Economic and financial shocks as well as demographic changes affect FDC pensions through the realised return on investment of the pension fund. While financial sustainability is ensured in FDC schemes – unless pensions are paid out as annuities and mortality rates are consistently overestimated, resulting in the annuities being mispriced –, pension adequacy might be at risk without further automatic adjustments as increases in longevity then translate into lower retirement income. The pension replacement rate is likely to fall gradually if the minimum age to draw the FDC pension

Table 2.1. **Automatic adjustment mechanisms in mandatory pension schemes**

AAMs mitigating the impact of demographic changes in mandatory pension schemes in OECD countries

	Funded defined contribution (FDC)	Notional defined contribution (NDC)	Retirement age linked to life expectancy	Benefits linked to life expectancy, demographic ratios, wage bill or GDP (incl. sustainability factors)	Balancing mechanism
Australia	A				
Austria					
Belgium					
Canada					B
Chile	A				
Colombia	A				
Costa Rica	A				
Czech Republic					
Denmark	A		S		
Estonia	A		A	A	
Finland			A	A	A
France					
Germany					A
Greece		A[a]	A	A	
Hungary					
Iceland	A				
Ireland					
Israel					
Italy		A	A		
Japan				A	
Korea					
Latvia	A	A			
Lithuania				A	
Luxembourg					S
Mexico	A				
Netherlands [b]			A		A
New Zealand					
Norway	A	A			
Poland		A			
Portugal			A	A	
Slovak Republic					
Slovenia					
Spain					
Sweden	A	A			A
Switzerland					
Turkey					
United Kingdom	A				
United States					A

Note: A = fully automatic adjustment; S = semi-automatic adjustment (adjustment requires political approval each time in order to be activated); B = automatic backstop mechanism (a political process is triggered and the back-up adjustment is only automatically applied in the absence of a political agreement on an alternative solution). [a] The NDC scheme in Greece applies to auxiliary pensions, which account for 12% of total public pension expenditure. As of 2022, the auxiliary pension for new entrants in the labour market will build up as FDC instead of NDC; workers younger than 35 will be able to join the FDC scheme voluntarily. [b] The Dutch Pension Agreement foresees a transition from DB to DC occupational pensions by 2027, but this has not been legislated yet.
Source: OECD based on information provided by the countries.

and/or the contribution rate are not increased as life expectancy increases. Without an automatic link between life expectancy and retirement age, workers would have to decide themselves to postpone retirement in order to uphold pension adequacy. As many people tend to retire as early as possible or fail to correctly estimate their future financial needs (Davidoff, Brown and Diamond, 2005[6]; O'Dea and Sturrock, 2018[7]), counting on individuals' own decisions to delay retirement may not work for many. Hence, even in FDC schemes, either the minimum retirement age or pension contributions should be linked to life expectancy to help achieve adequate pensions over time.

Notional defined contribution schemes

NDC schemes are modelled after FDC schemes and hence share many of their characteristics, but are financed on a pay-as-you-go (PAYG) basis. Pension accounts accumulate as individuals pay contributions at a set contribution rate and interest is credited to the account with a notional rate of return. At retirement the account value is transferred into an annuity, based on a conversion formula that takes into account life expectancy at retirement (or more generally mortality rates in old age) in a very similar way to that of FDC schemes. However, unlike in an FDC scheme these accounts are notional: the contributions of active workers are used to pay the pensions of current retirees instead of being saved in individual accounts.

NDC schemes are meant to automatically adjust pension benefits to changes in life expectancy through both the conversion formula (directly) and the notional interest rate (indirectly), and the financial balance of NDC pensions is in principle immune to longevity trends. In its ideal-typical, generic form, an NDC scheme ensures financial sustainability over time by adjusting to the effects of demographic changes beyond the sole effects coming from changes in longevity. As for all PAYG pensions, the internal rate of return – i.e. the highest rate of return that can apply to paid contributions in a financially sustainable way – of NDC pensions is equal to the growth rate of the contribution base (total amount of contributions paid) which is well proxied by the growth rate of the wage bill under a constant contribution rate. Generic NDC schemes are thus based on a notional interest rate equal to the growth rate of the contribution base, while pensions in payment are indexed at the same rate and the pension at retirement is equal to the value of the accumulated notional account divided by the projected remaining life expectancy. In short, longevity trends are accounted for in the conversion of the notional account value into pension benefits, and changes in the working age population driven in part by demographics are reflected in the notional interest rate. Changes in the wage bill affect pensions through both the notional interest rate and the indexation during retirement.[3]

None of OECD countries with an NDC scheme, however, has introduced the generic NDC model, and these countries deviated in the way they calculate the pension at retirement. Italy, Latvia, Norway, Poland and Sweden have an NDC scheme with varying rules (Table 2.1, column 2). Deviations from generic NDC may pertain to: the notional interest rate, the measure of life expectancy and the formula calculating the initial pensions based on the chosen indexation.[4] Greece has applied NDC to its auxiliary pension scheme for contributions paid as of 2015, but has very recently decided to transform the auxiliary pension scheme from NDC to FDC for new labour market entrants as of 2022 (Chapter 1).[5]

Table 2.2 summarises the NDC parameters in these six countries. In contrast to the generic NDC, no country applies the same rate for compounding notional assets (notional rate of return), for indexing pensions in payment and for discounting pension flows to convert the accumulated NDC assets into pension benefits. Moreover, countries differ widely in their notional rates of return. For example, both Latvia and Poland use the growth rate of the total wage bill and Italy uses GDP growth which equals wage-bill growth if the labour share is constant, while Norway and Sweden use the average wage. In these two latter countries, the notional rate of return, therefore, does not account for the evolutions in the size of the working age population. Greece uses the growth rate of total contributions as the notional interest rate in calculating new pensions and the lowest of either total contribution growth or CPI inflation to index pensions in payment.

Table 2.2. **NDC schemes in OECD countries**

Basic characteristics and risks covered by different NDC schemes

	Notional interest rate applied to the contribution assets *(growth rate of)*	Indexation of pensions in payment	Automatic balancing mechanism	Risks covered for pension finances	
				Changes in labour force size	Changes in life expectancy*
Italy	GDP	CPI		•[a]	•
Latvia	Wage bill	CPI + 75% of real wage bill growth		•	•
Norway	Average wage	Average wage – 0.75%[d]			•
Poland	Wage bill (but no less than price inflation)[b]	CPI + 20% average wage		•[c]	•
Sweden	Average wage	Average wage – 1.6%[d]	•		•
Greece[e] (being phased out)	Total contributions	lowest of total contributions and CPI		•	•

Note: [a] Italy's NDC scheme only partially covers risks posed by a declining labour force and declining productivity. The annuity conversion factor assumes growth of the covered wage bill by 1.5% in real terms, but indexation of pensions in payment is not adjusted to deviations from this 1.5% assumption. Hence, the scheme would be in deficit if growth of the covered wage bill is below 1.5% in real terms. [b] For the funds that were transferred from FDC schemes to the NDC scheme in 2011, the notional rate equals GDP growth, not growth of the wage bill. [c] As the applied rate cannot be below inflation, changes in the size of the labour force are only accounted for to the extent that the growth rate of the wage bill does not fall below inflation. [d] In Norway and Sweden, the subtraction of 0.75% and 1.6% from wage growth, respectively, is actuarially offset by using a discount rate of 0.75% and 1.6%, respectively, applied to *mortality rates* when computing the conversion factor (instead of full indexation and 0% in the generic NDC). [e] Entitlements to Greek auxiliary pensions are built up in the NDC scheme as of 2015 (2014 for new entrants in the labour market), but for new labour market entrants as of 2022 auxiliary pensions will be built up as FDC. Workers younger than 35 will be able to join the FDC scheme voluntarily (Chapter 1). Currently, auxiliary pensions cover 12% of public pension expenditure. * These NDC schemes account for remaining period life expectancy at the time of retirement, not for projected life expectancy, and therefore likely underestimate a retiring cohort's average longevity.
Source: OECD based on information provided by the countries.

All NDC schemes base their annuity conversion on *period* life expectancy, calculated from observed mortality rates, whereas the generic NDC design is based on *cohort* life expectancy, which accounts for expected gains in longevity. As period life expectancy likely entails an underestimation of a retiring cohort's average longevity, annuity conversion factors based on period life expectancy are likely to set benefits at a higher level than what actuarial calculation would warrant.[6] This might generate financial imbalances, which need to be subsequently offset. On the other hand, as period life expectancy is observed, not projected, the adjustment procedure is more transparent and less dependent on assumptions. The choice of assumptions is a potential source of relatively invisible political intervention in the functioning of the AAM.

Yet, even if the generic NDC principles were followed, economic shocks can still result in imbalances in the short term while unanticipated changes in life expectancy might generate structural issues (Valdes-Prieto, 2000[8]). Hence, solvency is not ensured over time and corrective measures are needed. A supplementary automatic balancing mechanism is thus required to ensure long-term financial sustainability of the pension system. Sweden is the only NDC country with such a mechanism (see the section on Balancing mechanisms).

Adjustment of the retirement age to life expectancy

By automatically linking the statutory retirement age to life expectancy, countries can prevent increasing life expectancy from negatively affecting the financial sustainability of DB pensions or the retirement income adequacy of FDC and NDC pensions. Several OECD countries have introduced such a link so that cohorts that can expect to live longer also have to work longer: Denmark, Estonia,

Finland, Greece, Italy, the Netherlands and Portugal (Table 2.1, column 3). Such a link has also been in effect in the Slovak Republic from 2017, but it was abolished from 2020.

Countries differ in the exact way they link their statutory retirement age to life expectancy (Table 2.3). The link is fully automatic in all countries except Denmark, where parliamentary approval is required to change the statutory retirement age when applying the link.[7] Denmark, Estonia, Greece and Italy link their statutory retirement age one-to-one to life expectancy, meaning that a one-year increase in life expectancy at 65 (60 for Denmark) leads to a one-year increase in the statutory retirement age. This basically implies that all additional expected life years are supposed to be spent working, while the average length of the retirement period will be constant: this thus leads to a steady decline in the length of the retirement period relative to the period spent working. In Denmark, the link is made by fixing the period people can expect to live in retirement at 14.5 years.

Table 2.3. **The retirement age is linked to life expectancy in seven OECD countries**

Basic characteristics of the link

	Increase in retirement age as proportion of increase in life expectancy	Need for parliamentary approval of retirement-age increase	Link based on life expectancy at age	Years between retirement age revisions	Period between setting new retirement age and it taking effect	Minimum increase per retirement age revision	Maximum increase per retirement age revision	Retirement age goes down with decreasing life expectancy
Denmark	1	•	60	5	15 years	6 months	1 year	
Estonia	1		65	1	2 years	1 month	3 months	•
Finland	2/3		65	1	3 years	1 month	2 months	•
Greece	1		65	3	Max 1 year	No	No	•
Italy	1		65	2	2 years	1 month	3 months	
Netherlands	2/3		65	1	5 years	3 months	3 months	
Portugal	2/3 *		65	1	2 years	1 month	No	•

Note: * For someone with more than 40 years of contributions, the normal retirement age increases by only half of life-expectancy gains.

Source: OECD based on information provided by the countries.

In Finland, the Netherlands and Portugal, the statutory retirement age is increased by two-thirds of the increase in life expectancy at 65, and average retired life is extended by one-third. In addition, in Portugal, someone with more than 40 years of contributions can retire without penalty four months earlier for each year over 40 years of contributions. This implies that in fact only half of life-expectancy gains are reflected in the normal retirement age applying to full-career workers. While the Netherlands had legislated a one-to-one link from 2025, in the 2019 Pension Agreement social partners and the government agreed to instead apply a two-thirds adjustment (see the section on Design problems in automatic adjustment mechanisms). Also Sweden is in the process of legislating a two-thirds link between the retirement age and life expectancy (Chapter 1). Among countries with a one-to-one link, taking into account additional increases before the link applies, the normal retirement age – that is, the age at which someone who entered the labour market at 22 can retire after a full career without any reduction to the pension – is expected to rise by 4.5 years in Denmark and Estonia between 2021 and 2050, and by 2.8 and 2.5 years in Greece and Italy, respectively (Figure 2.1).[8] In Finland, the Netherlands and Portugal, where the statutory retirement age increases with two-thirds of the increase in life expectancy, it is expected to increase by around two years.

A two-thirds link roughly keeps the share of adult life that people can expect to spend in retirement constant across cohorts. Indeed, retirement periods are approximately half as long as career lengths. Such a link is equitable as it keeps this ratio between time spent working and in retirement roughly constant across cohorts. If the starting point is a financially balanced pension system – with pension revenues covering pension expenditure – and if fertility rates are close to the population replacement rate of about 2.1, a two-thirds link in a PAYG system basically ensures a stable pension replacement rate across generations financed by a stable contribution rate in a sustainable way. In this case, if the retirement age increases by less than implied by a two-thirds link, then either the contribution rate must rise or pensions must fall in order to maintain the long-term financial balance.

Increasing the statutory retirement age often is politically unpopular and the need for the increase when life expectancy improves must be made clear to the wider population. Unlike discretionary increases in the statutory retirement age, a link to life expectancy makes clear why changes in the statutory retirement age are needed and provides a transparent mechanism to determine the size of the adjustment. Public support for a link may increase if it can widely be perceived as fair, as for example with a link that keeps the share of adult life in retirement constant.

Figure 2.1. **Evolution of normal retirement ages for those retiring between 2005 and 2050 in countries now linking the statutory retirement age to life expectancy**

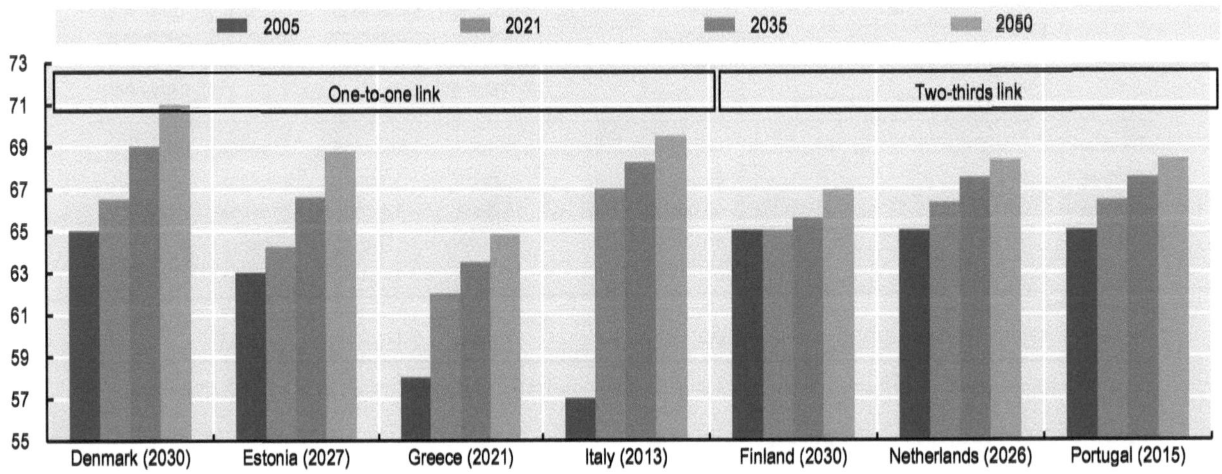

Note: The normal retirement age is defined as the age at which someone who entered the labour market at 22 can retire after a full career without any reduction to the pension. The year in parentheses is the year from which the link started or will start to apply. The numbers shown also include discretionary increases before the link kicks in. For Denmark, the statutory retirement age projected for 2050 is slightly lower than in the most recent projections from Statistics Denmark, according to which it would be 71.5 years. The data for Estonia in 2005 show the normal retirement age for men; the statutory retirement age for women was at 59 years during the first half of 2005 and at 59 years and 6 months in the second half of that year. The data for Finland show the age from which a person has access both to the earnings-related and the targeted pension scheme. In the earnings-related scheme, the normal retirement age was 63 years in 2005 and is 63 years and 9 months in 2021.

StatLink https://stat.link/wpvui3

While linking the statutory retirement age makes the pension system more robust in the face of increasing life expectancy, a two-thirds link does not protect it against other factors, such as low fertility rates. If the initial situation is financially unbalanced or if sub-replacement fertility is expected, a faster link is needed to ensure financial sustainability in case the retirement age is the only policy lever that is used. Furthermore, an increase in the statutory retirement age, while in general succeeding to prolong working lives, does not necessarily result in the same increase in the labour market exit age, at least in the short-to-medium term (Geppert et al., 2019[9]; Mastrobuoni, 2009[10]).

When the objective is to avoid financial imbalances while maintaining the same replacement rates, the retirement-age link should be combined with a mechanism that proportionally reduces accrual. Otherwise, increasing the retirement age results in additional build-up of pension entitlements leading to higher pension replacement rates at retirement age in PAYG pensions, thereby limiting net savings. Hence, increases in the statutory retirement age might not be sufficient to ensure the financial sustainability of standard DB pension systems based on constant accrual rates. This can be established through a sustainability factor such as the Finnish life expectancy coefficient.

In Estonia, Finland, Greece and Portugal, the link is symmetrical so that the retirement age is supposed to adjust both when life expectancy increases and decreases, whereas in Denmark, Italy and the Netherlands, the link is not activated when life expectancy decreases. These three latter countries have a mechanism that ensures that, after a decline in life expectancy, the statutory retirement age does not increase until life expectancy reached the same level as it was before declining.[9] Although declining life expectancy was often seen as a theoretical scenario before the COVID-19 pandemic, the effect of COVID-related excess mortality through the application of the link will become visible in 2022 only. However, the responsiveness of a link to short-term changes in life expectancy is an issue going well beyond the life expectancy shock due to COVID-19. As mortality rates fluctuate from year to year due to environmental factors even in normal times such as weather conditions and contagious diseases like the flue, changes in life expectancy are not a stable indicator. By linking the statutory retirement age to the moving average of life expectancy over multiple years, changes in the statutory retirement age are more stable and predictable.

Most countries with an automatic link between the statutory retirement age and life expectancy proceed with incremental changes. Estonia, Finland and Portugal assess the link on a yearly basis, Italy every second year. If the mechanism prescribes a change in the statutory retirement age, it takes effect two or three years after. The statutory retirement age changes with one or two months per revision in Finland, and with one to three months in Estonia and Italy. If the increase in life expectancy would result in an increase in statutory retirement age exceeding this maximum, the excess increase in the statutory retirement age is implemented with the next revision. The mechanism in the Netherlands is somewhat different in that the statutory retirement age increases in increments of three months, with the increase taking effect five years after it was triggered. Denmark's link deviates from all others in a number of ways. In Denmark, revisions only take place every five years, with the increase in the statutory retirement age only taking effect 15 years later. As a result of the longer periods between revisions, the Danish statutory retirement age does not follow the same incremental path as that in other countries, and instead increases in leaps of either half a year or a full year, potentially generating larger differences for close cohorts.[10]

How socio-economic differences in longevity interfere with the link between retirement age and life expectancy deserves some specific attention (Boulhol, Lis and Queisser, 2022[11]). There is substantial inequality in life expectancy between socio-economic groups in all countries (OECD, 2017[12]). Income redistribution from those dying early to those dying late is the core insurance function of pension systems. As low earners have a shorter life expectancy and thus receive benefits over a shorter period, this reduces the progressivity of pension systems. Therefore, even schemes that appear to be distribution-neutral, such as those delivering annuities from pure DC pensions, are in fact regressive as annuities are typically computed from common mortality tables.[11]

Addressing longevity inequality is a challenge for pension policies. Policy makers should take this inequality into account when determining benefit levels for low-income workers as large longevity gaps can justify increasing redistribution in pension systems (Diamond and Orszag, 2004[13]).[12] Bommier et al. (2005[14]) estimated that differential mortality offsets about one-third of the income redistribution built into the French PAYG pension system, while Sánchez-Romero, Lee and Fürnkranz-Prskawetz (2019[15]) suggest it offsets redistribution fully in the United States. OECD (2017[12]) estimates that the average 3-year gap in remaining life expectancy at retirement reduces total pensions received by low earners by 13% relative to those of high earners, on average across countries, on top of the effects from lower earnings.

However, the issue of accounting for life-expectancy inequality in a pension benefit formula is sometimes mixed up with the question of how retirement ages should respond to changes in life expectancy. Raising the retirement age with average mortality tables means that the increase will shorten low earners' average retirement period more due to their lower life expectancy and thus be regressive, although this effect is quantitatively very small (OECD, 2017[12]).[13] This does not mean that applying an automatic link that raises retirement ages in line with increasing life expectancy is regressive. The reason is the following: if nothing is done and pension ages are kept at the same level despite longevity gains, those gains will, based on the same argument, benefit relatively more those with shorter expected lives, when longevity gains are broadly shared across socio-economic groups. Therefore, implementing such a link to accompany health improvements will be neutral in terms of redistribution, i.e. neither progressive nor regressive. However, if life expectancy gaps between socio-economic groups widen, linking the retirement age to life expectancy does raise equity concerns.

The evidence on changes in socio-economic inequality in longevity is mixed, varying across countries and measures, such as those based on education, income or location. Banks et al. (2021[16]) highlight that assessing these changes raises serious methodological issues. Using a wide range of analyses,[14] over the last decades, inequality in longevity is found to have: increased in Finland,[15] Lithuania, Norway and the United States; decreased in Estonia, Greece, Hungary, Italy, Poland and Spain; and been stable in France and Korea. In the Czech Republic, Canada, Denmark, Japan, Portugal, the Slovak Republic, Slovenia, Sweden, Switzerland, Turkey and the United Kingdom the picture is unclear.

Benefits linked to demographics, wage bill or GDP

A wider group of measures automatically corrects benefit levels in order to reduce the impact of demographic changes on pension expenditures. This includes linking benefits to life expectancy, the size of the working population, GDP or the wage bill.

Linking benefits to life expectancy

A sustainability factor adjusting pensions to changes in life expectancy across cohorts improves financial sustainability and may contribute to intergenerational equity by accounting for differences in the length of benefit receipts.[16] As discussed above, such a mechanism applies by design in DC schemes. Moreover, in principle, it provides an incentive for people to postpone the exit from the labour market without increasing the statutory retirement age, as this is the way for them to achieve the same pension level they would have in the absence of the AAM. However, as many people do not delay retirement in response to changing incentives, sustainability factors may still need to be combined with an increase in the statutory retirement age in order to uphold pension adequacy.

The Finnish life expectancy coefficient adjusts new pensions in a similar way as the annuity conversion factor in NDC schemes. It is calculated based on mortality rates as of age 62 (Box 2.1) to account for changes in the present value of the total pension benefits due to changes in longevity. As such, the mechanism ensures that pension wealth, i.e. the total amount of pension benefits received during the retirement period, does not increase as a result of increases in life expectancy. The life expectancy coefficient decreased from 1 in 2009 (the reference year) applying to the 1947 birth cohort to 0.957 in 2021 for the 1957 birth cohort, implying a 4.3% reduction of new pensions through this effect (Table 2.4). In addition, as of 2030, the statutory retirement age will be linked to life expectancy. From that moment onward, the calculation of the coefficient will be based on life expectancy the year before the earliest eligibility age for an old-age pension (for example life expectancy at age 65 years and one month in 2040 based on current projections). The coefficient is projected to be 0.869 in 2066, meaning that the pension of a person entering the labour market at age 22 in 2020 will be reduced by

13.1% through this effect. The Portuguese sustainability factor was introduced in 2007 and subsequently reformed with the introduction of the automatic link between the statutory retirement age and life expectancy in 2013. Its calculation has the big advantage of simplicity: the sustainability factor is equal to the ratio of life expectancy at 65 in 2000 over life expectancy at 65 in the year before the old-age pension becomes accessible, similar to what is used for the NDC schemes in Latvia and Poland. However, both the purpose and the calculation are very different from Finland's life expectancy coefficient and from annuity conversion factors in NDC schemes. The Portuguese sustainability factor now only applies to early pensions taken up before the normal retirement age for people with a contribution record of less than 40 years at age 60. The factor generates substantial pension reductions for early retirement on top of penalties of 0.5% per month of early retirement – the factor alone reduces further pension benefits in case of early retirement by 16.7% in 2021, and the reduction would rise to 30.3% in 2066. Hence, the factor is not designed to adjust pension systems to life expectancy consistent with actuarial principles.

Table 2.4. **Life expectancy coefficients in OECD countries**

Basic characteristics of sustainability factors correcting for life expectancy

	Life expectancy at age	Sustainability factor based on…	Sustainability factor projected value			Mortality period assessed	Corrects also when life expectancy decreases	Frequency of calculation
			Reference year	2021	2066			
Finland	62	Survival rates	2009	0.957	0.869	Last 5 years available	•	Yearly
Portugal *	65	Period life expectancy	2000	0.833	0.697	Last year	•	Yearly

Note: The sustainability factor for 2066 is the factor that applies to the cohort entering the labour market at age 22 in 2020. * The Portuguese sustainability factor only applies in case of early retirement.
Source: OECD pension model; OECD based on information provided by the countries.

Portugal thus stands out among other OECD countries in terms of penalties for early retirement: as the sustainability factor does not currently apply to retirement at the normal retirement age, early retirement triggers sweeping benefit reductions. OECD (2019[17]) highlights that the policy objective pursued by penalising early retirees so strongly is unclear. Retiring early does not seem rational in most cases given these very strong penalties. This suggests that people who retire early despite these rules either do not understand the drastic consequences of their decision or have no other choice, for example due to bad health conditions. Hence, the big difference with Latvia and Poland is that in these two NDC countries the adjustment applies actuarially to all the pensions of a given cohort.

Finland and Portugal also differ in terms of smoothing the adjustments made by the life expectancy coefficient. In Finland, mortality is assessed over a five-year period, compared to a one-year period in Portugal. As a result, the Finnish mechanism provides a smoother correction over cohorts and ensures that cohort differences in pension benefit levels reflect longer life expectancy trends rather than yearly fluctuations in mortality rates (see the section on Adjustment of the retirement age to life expectancy). In theory, both the Finnish and the Portuguese calculation methods also make upward pension adjustments in case of decreases in life expectancy, although this has never happened until 2020.

When benefits are adjusted to remaining life expectancy, either through an annuity conversion factor or a sustainability factor, an additional link between the retirement age and life expectancy can help improve pension adequacy. If the statutory retirement age remains unchanged, sustainability factors and annuity conversion factors will result in an erosion of replacement rates over time with population ageing, unless individuals decide by themselves to claim their pensions at older ages. This is supposed to provide financial incentives to delay retirement. However, beyond the rational choice made by some individuals, many people tend to retire as early as possible even with low pensions as a result of cognitive limitations, underestimation of longevity and low levels of financial literacy (O'Dea and Sturrock, 2018[7]). Through linking the statutory retirement age to life expectancy, this erosion of pension levels at a given age is counteracted by keeping people in the labour market longer. Finland linked the statutory retirement age to life expectancy seven years after it introduced the life expectancy coefficient and Sweden is likely to follow suit with the introduction of a two-thirds link to delay retirement, reducing the erosion of new pensions due to the annuity conversion factor.

Box 2.1. Finland's life expectancy coefficient

The life expectancy coefficient is calculated for each cohort at the age of 62. In year *y*, the life expectancy coefficient (LEC) of the cohort born in year *y – 62* equals the longevity indicator (LI) of the year 2009 over the longevity indicator in year *y*:

$$LEC_{y-62} = \frac{LI_{2009}}{LI_y}$$

Hence, the life expectancy coefficient decreases as the longevity indicator increases, which is used to correct new pensions calculated from the DB formula. The longevity indicator in year *y* is calculated as follows (Merilä, 2019[18]):

$$LI_y = \sum_{x=62}^{100} 1.02^{-(x+0.5-62)} \cdot \frac{L_{x,y}}{l_{62,y}}$$

in which x is age, ranging from 62 to 100. $L_{x,y}$ equals the average of the number of persons alive at age *x* ($l_{x,y}$) and at age *x+1* ($l_{x+1,y}$) in year *y*. These numbers are based on mortality rates over a 5-year period in order to provide smoothing: it is established by multiplying $l_{x,y}$ with the mortality rate at age *x* over the 5-year period. The calculation assumes an annual mortality rate at age 100 of 1, and a 2% discount rate.

The longevity indicator is thus related to mortality rates in old age (remaining life expectancy). It is similar to the conversion factor in an NDC scheme where 2% would be equal to the notional interest rate minus the indexation rate of pensions in payment: in NDC schemes, the pension benefit in year *y* for an individual retiring at age *x* is computed by dividing the accumulated notional account by the conversion factor, $A_{y,x}$, which is:

$$A_{y,x} \equiv \sum_{l=x}^{\infty} \frac{s_{y,l}(1+z_l)^{l-x}}{(1+r_l)^{l-x}} \approx \sum_{l=x}^{\infty} \frac{s_{y,l}}{(1+r_l-z_l)^{l-x}}$$

where *s* denotes survival rates, *z* the pension indexation rates and *r* the nominal discount rates. In a generic NDC scheme, *r* is the notional interest rate, itself equal to the growth rate of the contribution base (close to the wage bill). When *z* and *r* are equal, the conversion factor simplifies into remaining life expectancy at age *x* in year *y*. The Latvian and Polish NDC schemes indeed use remaining (period) life expectancy as the conversion factor even though the indexation of pensions in payment is equal to price inflation plus 50% of the real growth rate of the wage bill in Latvia and to price inflation plus at least 20% real average-earnings growth in Poland. In Finland, pensions in payment are indexed to 80% prices and 20% wages, implying that the wage bill growth ("notional interest rate") is equal to 2% plus this indexation rate only if one assumes that 2% is equal to 80% of annual real-wage growth rate plus the annual employment growth rate.

Linking benefits to the size of the working population, GDP or the wage bill

Several countries link the benefit levels to the size of the working population in a variety of ways. These mechanisms affect pensions in payment, and in some countries also new pensions (Table 2.5). Indexation of pensions, even partially, to the real growth of GDP or the total wage bill implicitly adjusts for trends in the size of the working population: pensions are not only adjusted to the average wage, but also to the number of contributors – indexation based on GDP growth is similar to indexation to wage bill growth when assuming a constant labour share in GDP. This thus accounts for the impact of demographic changes affecting the size of the workforce. Perhaps more importantly, indexing to a proxy for the contribution base (wage bill or GDP) in a PAYG system makes good economic sense as it closely relates to the internal rate of return of what the scheme can ensure on paid contributions (see above). All these measures have in common that they seek to improve financial balance in the pension scheme. Estonia, Greece, Japan and Lithuania have such a mechanism in place. Germany also accounts for shifts in the population structure; its mechanism functions as a balancing mechanism and is thus described in greater detail in the corresponding section below.

The Estonian pension system includes an adjustment of pensions to the evolution of the wage bill (more precisely, the contribution base) through the value of the pension point within their points system. This mechanism affects both new pensions and pensions in payment as both the base amount of the pension and the value of the point (called "year of pensionable service") are indexed for 20% to the CPI and for 80% to total contributions in the last year over total contributions the year before.

Similarly, in Lithuania, both the value of the pension point and of the basic pension are linked to changes in the wage bill, albeit over a seven-year period: for a given year, the average wage bill growth comprises the average for the last three years as well as projections of wage bill growth in the current and next three years. Lithuania also ensures a certain level of pension adequacy by not adjusting pension benefits and entitlements if the wage bill falls in nominal terms. While the long reference period provides smoothing, it also creates a need for supplementary corrections in case the seven-year moving average deviates too much from economic conditions in the current year. This need is addressed through a reserve fund mitigating the impact of short-term economic shocks (see the section on Are there alternatives to automatic adjustment mechanisms?) and by applying the indexation only if total pension expenditures are projected to fall short of total contributions during both the current and the next year; and if total contributions exceed expenditures in the current year, a maximum of 75% of the surplus can be used for indexation. The seven-year smoothing procedure does not contain a mechanism to correct indexation if the projections on which indexation was based in previous years turn out to be incorrect. The lack of such a correction mechanism makes the AAM vulnerable to manipulation by changing projection methods or assumptions.

Japan's system of 'macroeconomic indexation' applies a correction both to price indexation of pensions in payment and, for new pensions, to the uprating of past wages based on the average wage. Both are adjusted by changes in the number of contributors to public pensions. The change in the total number of active participants is calculated as an average over the three-year period between four and two years prior. Macroeconomic indexation also adjusts in principle for the rate of growth of life expectancy at 65, although this factor is fixed at 0.3% since its introduction in 2004 based on long-term projections to avoid short-term fluctuations (Sakamoto, 2005[19]). If the sum of the growth rate of the number of active participants and -0.3% is negative, it is added both to the growth of average wages in the uprating of past wages to calculate pension entitlements and to CPI growth in the indexation of pensions in payment. However, by fixing the factor at 0.3%, it no longer accounts for uncertainties in the development of life expectancy, placing the measure in the realm of long-term planning (see below) rather than AAMs. Indeed, the fixed factor was significantly lower than increases in life expectancy between 2004 and 2019 especially for males.[17]

Adjustments in both Estonia and Japan contain little smoothing as both countries assess change over a period of one year and three years, respectively. Yet, the pension systems in both countries include a mechanism to limit the size of the adjustment. In Estonia, as in Lithuania, negative indexation is not possible. Japanese pensions are indexed to inflation with no additional correction at times of negative inflation (and partial correction in case of small positive inflation) as the adjustment itself cannot result in a nominal decrease in pensions. The same applies to uprating in case of negative wage growth. Indexation has been negative in several years since 2004, particularly in 2013 and 2014, when pensions were reduced to account for previous periods of negative inflation. Due to a

Table 2.5. **Adjustment of pension benefits to size of the working population, GDP or the wage bill in OECD countries**

Basic characteristics of adjustments to evolutions in size of the working population, GDP or the wage bill

	Affects new pensions	Affects pensions in payment	Based on change in...	Extent of indexation	Period assessed	Mechanism to protect adequacy
Estonia	•	•	Total contributions	80% (+ 20% CPI)	1 year	No negative indexation
Greece		•	GDP (nominal)	50% [a] (+50% CPI)	1 year	
Japan [b]	•	•	Total number of active participants across schemes [c]	added to both wage growth (uprating of past wages) and CPI growth (indexation of pensions in payment)	3 years	Replacement rate for standard pension not below 50%
Lithuania	•	•	Total wage bill	100%	7 years	No negative indexation
Portugal		•	Real GDP	Ranging between CPI – 0.75% and CPI + up to 20% real-GDP growth [c]	2 years	

Note: [a] Pensions are indexed to the lowest of two options: either full CPI or 50% CPI and 50% GDP. Hence, partial indexation by GDP only applies if real GDP falls. [b] Increases in life expectancy are also accounted for in indexation of new pensions and pensions in payment in Japan, but it is proxied by a fixed rate based on long-term projections in life expectancy. Japan opted for this fixed rate to avoid fluctuations in pensions due to circumstances such as pandemics. [c] If the sum of the change in the number of active participants and -0.3% is negative, it is added both to the growth of average wages in the uprating of past wages to calculate pension entitlements in build-up and to CPI growth in the indexation of pensions in payment. [c] In Portugal, indexation varies depending on the level of the pension itself and growth in real GDP.

Source: OECD based on information provided by the countries.

combination of factors, the correction mechanism from "macroeconomic indexation" was applied for the first time in 2015. In 2018, a catch-up system was introduced, which carries over downward benefit revisions in years of negative inflation to later years. The Japanese AAM also contains a safeguard limiting its application that should prevent that pensions become inadequate due to the adjustment to the size of the contributing population: if the actuarial review conducted every five years projects that the replacement rate of a "standard pension"[18] will fall below 50% before the next review, adjustments can be suspended.

Replacement rates from the points scheme in Estonia and Lithuania will likely be eroded significantly over the next decades due to the impact of demographic changes on the indexation of the point value. Indeed, the size of the working-age population is projected to fall sharply by about 30% in Estonia and 40% in Lithuania by 2060 (Chapter 5). This means that in both countries the value of total contributions or the wage bill will grow significantly less than wages, lowering replacement rates.

Greece adjusts pensions in payment by 50% of CPI and 50% of nominal GDP growth. Indexation cannot exceed CPI growth, hence, partial indexation to GDP growth only applies if real GDP falls.[19] In Portugal, indexation of pensions in payment depends on average growth in real GDP over the last two years and the pension level itself, with more favourable indexation of the lowest pensions. The lowest indexation applies to the highest pensions when real-GDP growth is below 2%, in which case pensions in payment are indexed to CPI inflation minus 0.75%; the most favourable indexation applies to the lowest pensions when real-GDP growth exceeds 3%, in which case pensions in payment are indexed to CPI plus 20% of real-GDP growth.

Balancing mechanisms

AAMs are designed to adjust pensions to demographic or economic changes, in particular to improve financial sustainability. Automatic balancing mechanisms (ABMs) are AAMs with a specific objective: they are designed not just to improve financial sustainability, but to ensure a balanced budget of the pension scheme (Gannon, Legros and Touzé, 2015[20]). ABMs can be designed to ensure long-term financial equilibrium or to avoid short-to-medium term imbalances. They can contain a variety of adjustments to both pension benefits and contributions triggered by current or projected imbalances in the pension system. Table 2.6 summarises the main characteristics of the ABMs which exist in seven OECD countries: Canada, Finland, Germany, the Netherlands, Sweden and the United States as well as Luxembourg to some extent.

The ABM for the main component (base) of the Canada Pension Plan (CPP) is an automatic backstop mechanism in the sense that the mechanism is automatically activated in the absence of a political agreement. Every three years, the Chief Actuary calculates the minimum contribution rate required to finance pensions over the following 75 years.[20] If the calculated minimum contribution rate exceeds the legislated contribution rate and the finance ministers of the federal and provincial levels cannot agree on how to restore long-term financial sustainability, then a safety mechanism (known as the insufficient rates provisions or the self-sustaining default provisions) is activated. In that case, indexation of pensions in payment is frozen and contribution rates are increased by 50% of the difference between the legislated and the calculated minimum contribution rate for a three-year period, until the next report of the Chief Actuary. Hence, in case of a forecasted deficit in the pension scheme the procedure first induces a political debate, and it only triggers the adjustment mechanism if policy makers fail to converge on a solution. The mechanism thus acts as a safety valve avoiding that financial pressure on the pension system increases over time when policy makers cannot agree on a course of action. The recently introduced CPP enhancement, which unlike the base CPP is meant to be fully funded, also has a distinct but similar backstop mechanism.

Finland has a balancing mechanism adjusting only contribution rates. Reserve funds for private sector employees should at least equal 20% of expected PAYG pension expenditure in the coming year. If the reserve fund size is projected to fall below this standard, then the contribution rate is automatically increased to the level required to meet the 20% threshold. However, as reserve funds currently hold 65% of annual PAYG expenditure, more than three times the minimum required amount of assets, it is unlikely that the mechanism will be triggered in the foreseeable future.

Germany's pension system contains a sustainability factor adjusting the pension point value on the one hand and an adjustment of the contribution rate on the other hand that, together, function as a balancing mechanism. Unlike in the Canadian and Swedish mechanisms, future revenues and expenditures are not taken into account. However, it balances current revenues and expenditures, and by doing that successively every year, long-term solvency would be achieved by default.

Since 2005, the German pension point value is adjusted to three components accounting for the change in average earnings, the change in the contribution rate, and a sustainability factor (Box 2.2). The sustainability factor links pensions to the demographic ratio of contributors over pensioners, which is critical for PAYG pensions: in a pure PAYG pension (i.e. fully financed by current contributions), this ratio multiplied by the contribution rate is mathematically equal to the average replacement ratio, defined as the average pension divided by the average wage. By adjusting the pension point value, both pensions in payment and accruing pension entitlements are adjusted.

Through the so-called alpha coefficient, the costs of balancing are divided between contributors and pensioners: with the alpha-level currently at 0.25, the sustainability factor actually adjusts the pension point value to 25% of the change in the ratio of pensioners to contributors between last year and the year before.[21] Were the alpha level set at 1, then the balancing would happen entirely through adjusting pensions and the contribution rate would be kept constant.

A nominal decline in the pension point value is not possible. Until 2019, non-implemented negative indexation has been compensated by the 'catch-up factor' that reduces subsequent positive

Box 2.2. The mechanics of the German points system

For every year of work, a person earns points based on her individual gross annual earnings. One point is granted to an individual whose earnings equal the average earnings in Germany in the same year. Higher individual earnings up to a ceiling generate proportionally more points, based on the principle of equivalence between contributions and benefits (*Äquivalenzprinzip*).

The pension point value (PPV) is set every year on 1 July following the below formula. Demographic and economic changes are accounted for through three parts: growth in gross average earnings, growth in the contribution rate, and a sustainability factor, where PCR is the pensioners-to-contributors ratio (see below).

$$PPV_t = PPV_{t-1} \cdot \frac{average\ earnings_{t-1}}{average\ earnings_{t-2}} \cdot \frac{100 - contribution\ rate_{t-1}}{100 - contribution\ rate_{t-2}} \cdot \overbrace{\left(1 - 0.25 \cdot \frac{PCR_{t-1} - PCR_{t-2}}{PCR_{t-2}}\right)}^{Sustainability\ factor}$$

In addition, an increase (decline) in the contribution rate has to be legislated once the account balance managed by the public pension authority drops below (exceeds) a certain level. The contribution-rate component of the formula implies that the benefit level declines when the contribution rate increases and vice versa. This makes current contributors and pensioners suffer or benefit jointly from current financial developments, for example driven by a deteriorating or an improving labour market. Since the introduction of tax subsidies for voluntary private pensions (Riester pensions) in 2001, the contribution-rate factor includes the maximum voluntary contribution rate that is subsidised, which is currently equal to 4%.

The last factor was introduced in 2004 to help deal with financial sustainability. It is determined by changes in the ratio of pensioners to contributors. An increase in the pensioners-to-contributors ratio means that the point value is not fully indexed to earnings growth. An increase of 1% in the relative number of pensioners decreases the adjustment of the point value by 0.25%. The 0.25 factor was determined to fulfil the objective of ensuring that the contribution rate remains below 22% by 2030 and that the replacement rate for an average-wage worker with a 45-year career remains above 43%. Overall, the sustainability factor is meant to capture the demographic and labour market developments that affect the financial sustainability of the system.

A law passed at the end of 2018 introduces a floor in the pension point value such that the net replacement rate of an average-wage worker with a 45-year career is at least 48% until 2025. That law also imposes a ceiling of 20% on the contribution rate until 2025 (*Doppelte Haltelinie*). From 2026, when population ageing is expected to have its largest impact as the demographic old-age to working-age ratio is projected to increase sharply between around 2025 and 2035, the pension adjustment formula will be in force again if no renewal of the replacement rate floor and contribution rate ceiling is legislated.

A decline in the real value of the pension point is allowed and also intended if, for example, demographic change deteriorates the ratio of contributors to pensioners. Nominal declines of the pension point value are ruled out by a restrictive clause. That clause was activated in 2005, 2006 and 2010, when the adjustment was calculated to be lower than one. Non-implemented negative indexation had to be offset in following years by a lower indexation than implied by the formula, which happened until 2013. However, this 'catch-up factor' was suspended in 2019 until 2025 to ensure the 48% replacement rate throughout the period (*Haltelinie*).

Source: Updated based on Boulhol, 2019 ([28]).

indexation. In 2018, the catch-up factor was suspended until 2025, leading to an asymmetric indexation mechanism.[22] The asymmetry can result in a higher level of the pension point value, and thus total spending, if the average wage falls and subsequently increases to the previous level (Börsch-Supan and Rausch, 2020[21]).

The second part of the balancing mechanism entails adjusting the contribution rate, which does not affect the number of points being acquired in contrast to the main occupational scheme in France (Agirc-Arrco). The contribution rate must be increased in Germany if the pension account balance deteriorates beyond a certain threshold, which in turn automatically lowers the point value (Box 2.2), thereby sharing the burden of the adjustment between current workers and current pensioners. If at the start of the year, the contribution rate is projected to result in the public pension reserves (totalling about 1% of GDP) falling below 0.2 times or growing above 1.5 times average monthly pension expenditure by the end of the year, the contribution rate has to be adjusted in such a way that the reserve fund is forecasted to remain within these limits (see the section on Are there alternatives to automatic adjustment mechanisms?). However, this adjustment of the contribution rate can be circumvented by directly financing the pension system from the State budget through legislative action. At the same time, the contribution rate component in the formula reduces the pension point value if the contribution rate is increased.

To avoid that the balancing mechanism creates too high a burden on the contributing population while ensuring a certain level of pension adequacy in the short term, there is a ceiling for the contribution rate and a floor for the pension point value until 2025 (Box 2.2). There currently are no limits to the impact the balancing mechanism can have on pension levels or contribution rates after 2025, although in 2020 the commission tasked with developing a proposal on what should happen after 2025 proposed to maintain both a ceiling to the contribution rate and a floor to the pension point value.[23]

In the Netherlands, an ABM currently is in place for funded DB schemes. The uprating of pension entitlements and indexation of pensions in payment are directly linked to funding ratios, that is, the ratio of the funds' current value over its future estimated liabilities. In case of persistent underfunding, indexation can be suspended or pension benefit levels reduced. A pension fund can index pension benefits and uprate pension entitlements by the full growth of CPI only if it has a funding ratio above a certain threshold that varies across pension funds, and it can uprate and index to less than CPI growth if the ratio is above 110%. Funding ratios below 110% lead to a freeze in pension benefits and pension entitlements. Funding ratios below 104.2% for more than five years lead to cuts in entitlements and benefits. The funding ratio in that case should be brought back to 104.2%, with associated cuts being spread over up to 10 years. The mechanism triggered cuts in entitlements and benefits in several pension funds in the wake of the 2008 financial crisis as funding ratios needed to be increased while interest rates remained low and life expectancy increased. The resulting public dissatisfaction with the system led to a decision to partially suspend the ABM and to a more structural reform (Chapter 1 and the section Design problems in automatic adjustment mechanisms).

Sweden supplements its NDC scheme with an ABM, in particular as its NDC scheme does not adjust for the size of the working population; indeed, the notional interest rate is only set to equal the average-wage growth by default. The Swedish Pensions Agency calculates a balance ratio dividing the sum of estimated contribution assets and the market value of the reserve fund by pension liabilities (accrued notional pension entitlements and pensions in payment). If a deficit is identified a brake is activated, reducing the notional interest rate below the wage growth rate in order to help restore solvency by both limiting accumulation in notional accounts and reducing indexation of pensions in payment. In the aftermath of the 2008 financial crisis, the mechanism resulted in a decline in the value of pensions both in nominal and in real terms, mainly as a result of the fall in the value of financial assets in the reserve fund (Sundén, 2009[22]). Following this experience, smoothing was introduced in the ABM. Since 2017, the potential reduction of the notional interest rate and the pension indexation rate triggered by the balancing mechanism is spread over a three-year period. For instance, if wages grow by 2% per year and the balancing mechanism requires a downward correction of 1%, then the interest rate on pension accounts and indexation of pensions in payment will equal 1.66% for three consecutive years. This smoothing offers more income stability to pensioners (del Carmen Boado-Penas, Naka and Settergren, 2020[23]; Bosworth and Weaver, 2011[2]). Once rebalancing is achieved, any surplus can be used to boost the interest and indexation rates during a catch-up phase to the level they would have been if no negative correction had occurred. The mechanism provides a catch-up but does not distribute surpluses in the financial balance (Barr and Diamond, 2011[24]).

The United States has a 'fiscal cliff' balancing mechanism (Gannon, Legros and Touzé, 2020[25]). As the Social Security pension scheme is not allowed to borrow, it is obliged to cut benefits when its reserve fund is fully depleted so that total benefits can be covered by total contributions.[24]

This is currently estimated to happen in 2033, the date after which pension benefits are expected to make a sudden drop of 24% (Board of Trustees, 2021[26]). The ABM used in the US Social Security is not unlike Canada's automatic backstop mechanism as it is meant to act as a disciplining device to trigger policy action to prevent its activation. However, the Canadian system makes the conditionality on political disagreement explicit, which is not the case in the United States where in addition the impact of a non-agreement is much more abrupt.

Table 2.6. **Automatic balancing mechanisms in OECD countries**

Basic characteristics of automatic balancing mechanisms

	Affects new pensions	Affects pensions in payment	Affects contributions	Based on change in...	Period assessed	Mechanism to protect adequacy	Fully automatic
Canada		•	•	Estimated minimum contribution rate	75 years	No negative indexation	Backstop
Finland			•	Ratio of reserve fund size to expected pension expenditure	1 year	No	•
Germany	•	•	•	Equivalised pensioners to contributors ratio	1 year	No negative indexation	•
Netherlands	•	•		Funding ratio (fund value over liabilities)	1 year	No	•
Sweden	•	•		Balance ratio of notional assets over liabilities	Long term	No	•
United States	•	•		Ratio of total assets plus income over scheduled benefits	1 year	No	•
Luxembourg	•	•	•	Ratio of reserve fund size to expected pension expenditure	10 years	No	Semi-automatic

Source: OECD based on information provided by the countries.

Luxembourg has a semi-automatic balancing mechanism, forcing the government to take action. The total pension contribution rate for old-age, disability and survivors' benefits is fixed in the law for a 10-year period based on projections by the General Inspectorate of Social Security (IGSS). It is fixed in such a way that the public pension reserve fund is projected to be at least 1.5 times annual pension expenditure at all times over the 10-year period. The IGSS also performs a mid-term evaluation to see if the contribution rate needs to be adjusted.[25] Hence, the semi-automatic balancing mechanism primarily adjusts contribution rates, although indexation of benefits in payment is also adjusted in case contributions fall short of covering expenditures nonetheless. As long as contributions cover expenditures, CPI indexation is supplemented by the growth of real average wages. However, once current contributions no longer suffice to cover expenditures, the law determines that the government must make a proposal to parliament to reduce indexation (i.e. move from full wage indexation to indexation between prices and prices plus 50% of real wage growth). The semi-automatic adjustment of the contribution rate has not been brought to the test yet, as the first revision of the contribution rate under the current mechanism is due in 2022; pension expenditures are expected to exceed total contributions in 2027 if the contribution rate is not changed (Inspection générale de la sécurité sociale, 2021[27]). As pension expenditures are projected to almost double from 9.2% of GDP in 2019 to 18.0% of GDP in 2070 (Chapter 7), the pension contribution rate would almost have to double if the semi-automatic adjustment mechanism was to be applied. Given the current contribution rate of 24%, the semi-automatic link will thus not ensure the financial balance over the long term.

Limitations of automatic adjustment mechanisms

AAMs should be designed to meet clear objectives given the specific context of each country. Whether to adjust contributions, benefits or retirement ages depends on their initial levels, demographic evolutions and people's preferences, and is therefore ideally subject to democratic debate. AAMs are likely to be reformed, replaced or removed if they do not fit well with the context they are implemented in.

This section presents instances where AAMs were changed or cancelled, and discusses whether there are alternatives to deal with the challenges faced by pension systems as populations age. The first part discusses political pitfalls in the implementation of AAMs and the second part presents problems in the design of AAMs that led to their reversal. While political and design elements are often intertwined and both at play to some extent in reversals, as the case of Spain illustrates, some appear to be more politically motivated than others. The final part presents other policy tools to make pension systems more sustainable and argues why they are not full alternatives to AAMs. The section shows that for AAMs to succeed in pursuing financial or social sustainability and providing trust in the pension system, both a careful AAM design and an inclusive political process to implement it are essential.

Political pitfalls of implementation

Populations may differ in their preference for certain policies, as well as how they value time and income (Börsch-Supan, 2007[29]). Depending on the initial pension parameter levels, the same AAM may not be as acceptable to people in different countries. In some cases, for example if pension benefit levels are relatively high or contribution rates relatively low, adjusting pension benefits or, at least temporarily, contribution rates to life expectancy may be preferable to adjusting the retirement age. Even if countries face the same challenges, the political feasibility of specific AAMs to overcome these challenges may differ and opposition against their introduction may be fiercer in some countries than in others. Therefore, it is necessary for policy makers to convince the wider population of the need for AAMs by highlighting the cost and consequences of inaction, and to argue how the proposed AAMs solve this problem while accounting for people's preferences.

AAMs require a continuous application to reach their objectives of financial or social sustainability and trust in the pension system, and are hence best introduced through wide political support. AAMs that are decided by simple majority may not be upheld when coalitions change. For example, even with standard pension indexation, discretionary changes or repeated deviations from the indexation rule – which might be needed in the absence of a well-designed balancing mechanism – highlight time inconsistency in policy decisions, which in the end hurts transparency, equity and confidence in the pension system.

Germany's demographic factor, legislated in 1997, which adjusted benefits to half of the growth in life expectancy at age 60, was withdrawn when a new government came to power a year later. In 2004, the sustainability factor was introduced, linking pensions to the ratio of pension recipients to contributors. In order to ensure sufficient trade union and political support, the application of the mechanism is subject to some constraints such as a minimum net replacement rate (Bosworth and Weaver, 2011[2]). In contrast, Sweden's NDC scheme with the ABM discussed in the preceding section was developed through political collaboration beyond the governing coalition. While the 2008 global financial crisis provided a stress test for the ABM, the broad principles of the ABM have remained largely unchallenged even though this experience shows that in periods of large volatility interventions by politicians are still needed (Weaver and Willén, 2014[30]). The Swedish ABM is thus more likely to succeed in fulfilling its long-term objectives due to its design and political sustainability, strengthened by the extensive process of consensus-building among all political parties prior to the pension reform.

The short-lived link between the retirement age and life expectancy in the Slovak Republic is also the consequence of a lack of wide political agreement, although the experience is somewhat different. Here, the main party in the government, which had approved the introduction of the one-to-one link between statutory retirement age and life expectancy in 2012, subsequently decided under political pressure to cap the increase in 2019 at the age of 64 (to be reached in 2030) and to abolish the link.[26] The link was only in effect for three years between 2017 and 2020. The cap on the retirement age was removed again in December 2020, and the Ministry of Labour, Social Affairs and Family prepared a proposal to re-establish a link between the retirement age and life expectancy.

On top of changing the AAM itself, policy makers may seek to intervene in the calculation of the indicator the AAM is based on to modify the outcomes of the adjustment mechanism. Particularly projection-based indicators may be prone to such interventions, as they are based on a series of assumptions. Policy makers can then affect the indicator through challenging or changing the assumptions the indicator is based on. For instance, the activation of the Canadian balancing mechanism is rather sensitive to the assumptions made by the Chief Actuary (Baldwin, 2020[31]), and there is some controversy surrounding the dismissal of the Chief Actuary in 1998 in this regard. According to Bosworth and Weaver (2011[2]), the dismissed Chief Actuary would have claimed to have been pressured into adjusting assumptions when initial calculations showed that the contribution rate at the time fell just short of being financially sustainable. This case illustrates not only the importance of political independence of the body that calculates the indicators for AAMs, but also the need for transparency in how the indicator is calculated. By clearly stating the methodology used in the calculations, transparency and trust in the pension system are improved as changes in the methodology would require clear explanations.

Design problems in automatic adjustment mechanisms

Some might be tempted to consider that because an AAM is in place all pension problems are solved and the system can run on auto-pilot. However, not all AAMs are well designed, and badly designed AAMs may generate opposition resulting in their cancellation or reform. Moreover, not all AAMs are equally suitable to tackle the specific challenges a country faces, and supplementary reforms might be required in order for the mechanism to fulfil its objectives.

The capacity of AAMs to account for demographic and/or economic changes largely depends on the indicator used. The accuracy of the indicator determines the extent to which the mechanism will correctly adjust to changes. For instance, an annuity conversion factor, a life expectancy coefficient or a link with the statutory retirement age only really adjust to changes in ex post longevity if the ex post observed longevity corresponds to the (ex ante) life expectancy estimate (at retirement). Even projection-based automatic balancing mechanisms cannot avoid imbalances if the projections of changes in life expectancy differ from ex post longevity changes. However, unless the projections prove to be totally wrong, the AAM is likely to substantially reduce the size of the imbalances compared to a scenario without any AAM.

AAMs designed to mask cuts in pension benefits in real terms are more likely to fail as they may result in increasing pressure on policy makers to soften the impact of the AAM or even abandon it altogether. Spain introduced the Revalorisation Pension Index (IRP) without wide political consensus in 2013, a mechanism indexing all pensions to account for the difference between the growth rate of total contributions and that of total expenditures, albeit with a minimum nominal indexation of 0.25% per year. Every year between 2014 and 2017, pensions were indexed at the floor of 0.25%, and, based on projections, the floor was likely to be persistently applied in the future given expected difficulties in financing public pensions in Spain. After protests of pensioners against this index resulting in a loss of purchasing power in 2017 and 2018 and as a new government came into power that same year (Montserrat Codorniu and Rodríguez Cabrero, 2018[32]), the parliament deviated from this mechanism and instead indexed pensions to the CPI, resulting in significantly higher indexation rates. In 2019, the IRP was suspended. This example illustrates not only the need for political consensus, but also that the introduction of an AAM leading to a steady decline in pensions in real terms during retirement is questionable as retirees have little possibility to adjust their income, for example by working more. This also implies that corrective measures – through AAM or more generally – need to be implemented soon enough, as modifying pension calculations for current retirees is very difficult. Otherwise, when pension promises that were made are not financially sustainable, the burden of adjustment is unlikely to be well shared across generations or, even worse, macroeconomic stability may ultimately be threatened.

The protests against the Spanish IRP and its subsequent suspension ultimately spilled over to the sustainability factor that was legislated in 2013 to adjust new pension benefits at retirement to increases in life expectancy. The sustainability factor was supposed to take effect as of 2019, but its implementation was suspended until 2023. As of yet, the design of a mechanism that is supposed to replace both the IRP and the sustainability factor is unclear (Chapter 1).

When AAMs trigger a decline of real pension benefit levels, policy makers may also seek to counteract this negative indexation. In Sweden, the 2008 global financial crisis provided a stress test for the ABM, as the rule would have generated a decline in the value of pensions (see the section on Balancing mechanisms). The rule was therefore altered through a small smoothing adjustment. In addition, the government attempted to counteract the impact of negative indexation by reducing taxation of pension incomes. In doing so, a deficit in the pension system was avoided by transferring the cost to the general budget, which is what NDC schemes aim to avoid.[27]

Large adjustments triggered by AAMs may generate political pressure not to apply them. Initially, Italy's conversion factor adjusting NDC benefits to life expectancy was updated every 10 years and the adjustment required political approval. However, given the size of the adjustment to be applied when the coefficient was to be updated for the first time in 2005, the government backtracked and suspended the adjustment until 2010 (Turner, 2009[33]; Guardiancich et al., 2019[34]). More frequent adjustments diminish the need for substantial corrections, and therefore generate less pressure to intervene in the mechanism's working.

The Netherlands provides another example where substantial and sustained reductions in indexation have led to public dissatisfaction with the AAM. The balancing mechanism forced several pension funds to make nominal reductions in pensions in the aftermath of the 2008 financial crisis and pension providers felt resentment over the last decade when the mechanism did not allow them to share high investment returns with pensioners through increased indexation, instead having to use the money to build up reserves to increase their funding ratio. This led to the 2019 Pension Agreement between the Dutch Government, trade unions and employers' organisations prescribing that funded DB occupational pension schemes will be replaced by FDC pension schemes. The transition is yet to be legislated, but it is expected that funds can transition to FDC as of 2023 and that all funds will have to have transitioned before 2027 (Chapter 1).

The Dutch balancing mechanism will be partially suspended until funds make the transition from funded DB to FDC: pension funds will not be forced to reduce pensions if their funding ratio is above 90%, instead of the legislated 104.2%. The social partners have to determine the minimum funding ratio required for a pension fund to transition to FDC, but it cannot be below 90%. Until the social partners reach an agreement, pension funds have to employ a funding ratio target of at least 95%. If the mechanism had not been suspended, many pension funds would have had to reduce pensions in nominal terms.[28]

Not only AAMs reducing pension benefits in real terms are vulnerable to being reformed, also one-to-one links of the statutory retirement age to life expectancy may not be politically sustainable. They might be used in the medium term in countries that need to restore financial sustainability, but over the long term the steady reduction they imply in the share of life spent in retirement relative to the length of the working period is difficult to justify. The Slovak Republic withdrew its one-to-one link, although new attempts are being made to re-establish a link as described in the previous section. The Netherlands replaced its one-to-one link with a two-thirds link as part of the implementation of the Pension Agreement. Denmark has no concrete plans to deviate from its current one-to-one link, but a committee has been set up to look into the effects of easing the link after 2040. The committee will present its recommendations in early 2022.

Finally, the design of an AAM should take into account the administrative capacity of the country: sufficient administrative capacity is needed for a successful implementation of AAMs as it may require specific knowledge and expertise as well as data collection (Guardiancich et al., 2019[34]). The required capacity varies according to the chosen measure, with some AAMs such as adjustments of the statutory retirement age to observed changes in period life expectancy being relatively easy to implement whereas measures based on forward-looking indicators require some forecasting capacity.

Are there alternatives to automatic adjustment mechanisms?

AAMs are not the only measures available to tackle the challenges population ageing poses to pension systems, as this can also be done through discretionary adjustments. However, to reach long-term financial sustainability through discretionary measures while maintaining citizens' trust in the pension system requires forward-looking policy makers and a stable political environment. Beyond AAMs, two policy tools are of particular importance to assist policy makers in making pension systems more robust in the face of a changing demographic environment: long-term planning and reserve funds. In this section, both policy tools are presented and their main advantages and drawbacks discussed.

Long-term planning entails legislating a schedule of adjustments in pension system parameters over a relatively long period, usually based on long-term projections. Hence, changes in parameters can be legislated to take effect only decades later. In contrast to AAMs that link pension parameters to a specific indicator, under long-term planning the parameter path is fixed. It essentially is a form of extreme smoothing. Both the Czech Republic and the Slovak Republic, for instance, are increasing their statutory retirement ages until 2030 according to a fixed timetable that is set based on assumptions about the evolution of life expectancy. However, the pre-determined changes in parameters are also the Achilles' heel of long-term planning, as the projections they are based on have to be correct: political intervention remains required at the end of the planning period or when economic and demographic changes deviate from the forecasted evolution, hence to a much larger extent than with AAMs.

One of the advantages of long-term planning is that it can give people sufficient time to adjust their lives accordingly (Goss, 2010[35]). However, fixing parameters in the long term may give people a false sense of security, as there is no guarantee that circumstances evolve as predicted and, therefore, that the scheduled change in parameters is respected. Hence, to present long-term planning as generating certainty for people regarding retirement benefits is misguided: the sense of certainty it may project comes from its lack of adjustment to changing circumstances, which actually might become a source of financial unsustainability.

While long-term planning could offer an alternative to AAMs in theory, the lack of flexibility to adjust to changing circumstances entails a strong reliance on policy makers in the future to make changes in pension parameters, especially if previous estimations have turned out to be too optimistic.

The example of the United States makes this abundantly clear, as the fiscal cliff moved forward from 2057 at the time when the long-term plan was developed to 2033 in the most recent estimate (Board of Trustees, 2021[26]). The Canadian procedure in case of a forecasted deficit combining long-term planning with an automatic backstop mechanism, in case policy makers cannot find an alternative way to restore long-term financial sustainability, can be a way to overcome this issue. Moreover, by starting the procedure at the time the deficit is projected rather than when it materialises is likely to result in much less harsh corrections which, as discussed above, is important to uphold the mechanism.

Long-term planning, like AAMs, is vulnerable to reversal. In 2011, the Czech Republic decided that, once the statutory retirement age reached 65 in 2030, it would increase by two months per year indefinitely. The policy entailed a faster future increase in the retirement age than the expected increase in any country where the retirement age is linked to life expectancy. In 2016, merely five years after its introduction and before the policy would take effect, the increase in the retirement age was capped at 65 (OECD, 2020[36]).

Public pension reserve funds can also contribute to making pension systems more robust, and are often an important component of long-term planning efforts. These funds hold reserves established by governments or social security institutions to support public pension systems. The United States was the first country to create a reserve fund, with the Old-Age and Survivor Insurance Trust Fund having been established in 1937. Reserve funds were particularly established in the 1990s and early 2000s, as concerns rose over the financial sustainability of pension systems in the face of population ageing, particularly in relation to the forthcoming retirement of the baby-boom generation. The size of these funds varies between countries, with funds exceeding one-quarter of annual GDP in Canada, Finland, Japan, Korea, Luxembourg and Sweden (Chapter 9).

Reserve funds serve three main purposes. First, they can be used as a buffer to smooth the impact of short-term economic or demographic fluctuations on pension finances. Second, they can partially prefund pensions to account for demographic changes, either through a generation-specific reserve fund that is fully depleted after retirement of the larger generation or through a system of permanent prefunding. Reserve funds created to cushion the temporary, medium-term financial impact of a large generation such as the baby-boom generation reaching retirement are built up while these large cohorts are of active age and then depleted when they are in retirement. In a PAYG scheme, they can prevent that larger retiring generations result in either an increased burden on subsequent generations through higher contributions (or additional financing from the state budget) or in reduced pensions (OECD, 2012[37]). In a system of permanent prefunding, on the other hand, each generation partially funds its own retirement. This is the case in Canada and Finland, where the size of the buffer fund is taken into account in their respective ABMs. Third, reserve funds can provide a permanent diversification of pension financing through financial returns on investment, which is otherwise financed on a PAYG basis. Beyond these, reserve funds can be an important component of the balancing mechanism, as in Sweden for example.

Only the second objective clearly, but partly, connects to those pursued by AAMs, and might then be seen as operating for a couple of decades as an alternative to AAMs on the condition that pension assets have been accumulated over a sufficiently long phase while the baby-boom generation was in the labour market. Even in that case, reserve funds created for that purpose are supposed to be depleted in the long term, making them useful to partially prefund the retirement of the baby-boom generations, but unsuited to manage long-term ageing trends unlike AAMs. Moreover, the success of reserve funds in prefunding the retirement costs of numerous generations depends on the accuracy of long-term demographic projections and consistency in the regulatory framework over time, much like in the case of long-term planning. As with long-term planning, reserve funds are vulnerable to reversals, with several funds being depleted earlier than initially intended or used for other purposes when the government faces an urgent funding need. For example, when the 2008 financial crisis hit,

Ireland first used its reserve fund to support its banking sector and subsequently for strategic investment in the domestic economy (Casey, 2014[38]). In 2014, the reserve fund was abolished and its remaining assets transferred to the newly established Ireland Strategic Investment Fund, as economic growth and employment were considered a greater priority at the time than long-term sustainability of public pension provision.

Automatic adjustment mechanisms: Where to go and how to get there

Pension expenditures have been increasing and the level of pension benefits might be under pressure in many OECD countries due to demographic changes driven by improvements in longevity, the retirement of the baby-boom generation and low fertility rates. Given the high cost of inaction, policy makers thus have the choice to take measures mitigating the effects of population ageing on pension parameters or increasing pension system revenues in an automatic or a discretionary way. This section first argues why automatic adjustments are the best way to tackle these challenges, at least when pension systems are initially on a solid footing, and sets out a number of principles on the design of automatic adjustment mechanisms (AAMs) to improve financial and social sustainability of pension systems. Subsequently, some guidelines regarding the process for the development and implementation of AAMs are presented to improve their political sustainability.

Why automatic adjustment mechanisms are needed

Automatic adjustment mechanisms are often claimed to be the most important innovation of pension policy over the last decades. Indeed, they reduce uncertainty surrounding future changes in the pension system in response to demographic and economic developments. While there is no doubt that population ageing is happening, the exact extent of future demographic shifts remains subject to large uncertainty. Yet, even though it is difficult to forecast precisely the development of mortality, fertility and employment, the consequences of changes in these indicators for pensions are easier to predict. This predictability makes it possible to design and implement AAMs that can substantially reduce the impact of demographic changes on financial sustainability.

Political choices are essential in implementing AAMs, as there unavoidably is a trade-off between financial sustainability and pension adequacy, although some mechanisms, such as adjustments of contribution rates or statutory retirement ages can limit this trade-off. Well-defined AAMs thus raise the credibility of the pension system and the promises it makes, and of public finance management more broadly (OECD, 2012[37]), which can ultimately also increase trust in the pension system. In theory, these outcomes could also be reached through a combination of close monitoring of the pension system, long-term planning and recurrent discretionary reforms. Pensions can for instance be balanced without an automatic balancing mechanism through reserve funds or transfers from the state budget. However, the political reality of pension reforms, with many stakeholders and high political costs, makes relying on such continuous efforts of both current and future governments a risky strategy. Hence, discretionary reforms may provide solutions in the short to medium term, but are unreliable to provide long-term financial sustainability. AAMs, on the other hand, can reverse the political process: rather than having to argue for measures improving financial sustainability, policy makers instead would have to legitimise any decisions reducing sustainability.

It is crucial to distinguish AAMs that accompany long-term trends from those that are used to correct imbalances due to entitlements that already accrued. AAMs should ideally be used to prevent the deterioration of financial sustainability, as mechanisms implemented or activated only when the pension system faces financial problems are likely to result in harsh adjustments in benefit levels. Hence, mechanisms preventing insolvency are preferable to those that are triggered in case of insolvency. Preventive AAMs provide frequent small adjustments depending on demographic or economic evolutions, smoothing corrections over time. To that end, AAMs should be introduced and activated well before sharp corrections are required, and the period in between assessments should be limited to avoid the need for sharp corrections.

However, AAMs have also been used to restore financial sustainability. AAMs triggered only in the face of insolvency are likely to be painful and therefore to generate political pressure to circumvent their impacts. This is the case with the suspension of the AAMs in Spain (Chapter 1). If the pension system is not financially sustainable given already accrued entitlements, necessary changes are immediate and not conditional on the developments of some future indicators. In that case, measures should be taken in any case, and the long-term planning of predetermined measures is probably better suited than AAMs. For example, if pension promises are made in such a way that less than price indexation is needed to help improve financial sustainability – something that must be avoided in the first place – then it is probably too late to introduce an AAM. In short, AAMs are meant to adjust for future trends and are not a substitute for bold discretionary measures in a financially unbalanced pension scheme. Countries in that situation should ideally have a wider reform plan consisting of discretionary steps that restore financial balance – there is little reason to condition those steps to some indicators – and of a set of AAMs that can in particular deal with ageing trends.

What should automatic adjustment mechanisms look like

For AAMs to be successful over the longer term, they should fulfil some basic characteristics. One such characteristic is that every AAM should be designed to pursue one specific objective. Different instruments are needed to deal with different sources of imbalance, and a combination of AAMs is necessary to protect pension schemes against the various challenges posed by population ageing. To fulfil different objectives, various pension parameters can be adjusted. It is important to strike the right balance between adjustments to the three main parameters – retirement age, contribution rate and pension level – depending on their initial levels and on social preferences. The choice of pension system parameters to adjust through AAMs as well as through discretionary measures has distributional consequences. Even financial sustainability alone requires that different AAMs are in place. First, an adjustment to longevity trends is needed. However, as adjusting retirement ages or benefit levels to life expectancy might not be sufficient to deal with the overall shifts in the population structure, accounting for changes in the size of the contribution base through another AAM is also needed. For instance, the recent review of the Finnish pension system indicates that, although this is not an urgent problem, the current adjustments to life expectancy are insufficient to ensure long-term financial sustainability, among others due to a sustained low fertility rate (Andersen, 2021[39]). In addition, even if they are well designed, these AAMs cannot guarantee financial solvency, and a balancing mechanism ensuring that total contributions equal total benefits over time should complement them.

One serious difficulty comes from the possible inconsistency of different goals given ageing prospects. For example, in a PAYG pension scheme, financial balance is ensured when total contributions finance total pensions, either every year or on average over time. This means that the contribution rate should be equal to the average benefit ratio (i.e. the average pension divided by the average wage) multiplied by the pensioners-to-contributors ratio. If one goal is to stabilise pension benefit ratios without changing the contribution rates, then the AAM should adjust the retirement age to stabilise the pensioners-to-contributors ratio. If another goal is to ensure that the length of retirement remains at roughly half the working period, which is generally considered to be fair across generations, then the retirement age should be linked to about two-thirds of longevity gains. However, increasing the retirement age will not suffice to prevent the decline in the relative size of the labour force in many countries (Boulhol and Geppert, 2018[40]). This difficulty exists whether pension parameters are adjusted automatically or discretionarily.

Given distributional implications and the need to find a compromise between different goals, the choice of which parameters to adjust should be the topic of political debate. If the choice were made to act on the contribution rate of a PAYG pension scheme to stabilise replacement rates or the average benefit ratio, then the contribution rate would have to be linked one-to-one to the pensioners-to-contributors ratio. The problem is that the demographic old-age to working-age ratio is projected to double by around 2060 on average in the OECD (Chapter 5). This implies that the contribution rate would have to double if the total employment rate does not change, which is not realistic. Thus, while contribution rates may be adjusted to help deal with ageing, this would only be one (small) part of the equation: to preserve pension levels, the adjustment must involve limiting the increase in the pensioners-to-contributors ratio, by raising employment, in particular at older ages and especially by raising the retirement age to accompany improvements in life expectancy. Only four OECD countries have automatic adjustments of contribution rates, and in three of them there is a political option to avoid or limit the automatic adjustment of contribution rates: the backstop mechanism in Canada, the semi-automatic balancing mechanism in Luxembourg and the adjustment of the contribution rate in Germany that is limited by transfers from the State budget to the pension system. In the fourth country, Finland, the automatic balancing mechanism is not expected to be triggered in the foreseeable future (see above).

Linking the statutory retirement age to life expectancy is a good way to improve financial sustainability without reducing pension adequacy. It is therefore a key policy if the objective is to maintain replacement rates. In generic DB schemes, replacement rates are equal to the number of years spent working multiplied by the accrual rates. However, a retirement age link without adjustment of accrual rates also results in higher pension entitlements when life expectancy increases as career length is increased. If there is no fiscal space to raise pension spending, accrual rates should be negatively linked to the retirement age and therefore to life expectancy, hence stabilising replacement rates. This is similar to what Finland does by linking the retirement age to life expectancy improvements and through the life expectancy coefficient. Also in France, although there is no link, the gradual increase in the contribution period to get a full pension in its core DB scheme (*régime général*), decided to cope with increasing longevity, is being implemented without modifying the replacement rate.

The pace of the link could vary depending on people's preferences and the initial retirement age, pension contribution rates and benefit levels. One alternative implemented in Denmark, Estonia, Greece and Italy is a one-to-one link between statutory retirement age and life expectancy. While such a fast link may be beneficial from a perspective of financial sustainability, the political sustainability of such a link might be weak over the long term, as suggested by policy reversals in the Slovak Republic and the Netherlands. When introducing life expectancy links, it is also important to monitor changes in social inequalities in life expectancy. While there currently is no clear pattern in the development of inequalities in life expectancy across countries, a link would disproportionately affect low-income groups if these inequalities were to continuously grow over time, as has been the case in some countries.

An automatic increase in the statutory retirement age when life expectancy increases, does not necessarily translate one-to-one into increases in effective retirement ages in the medium term (Geppert et al., 2019[9]). To strengthen the effectiveness of retirement age links to boost employment in old age, these links should ideally be accompanied by labour market policies that facilitate older people to remain in the labour market longer. While these policies are beyond the scope of *Pensions at a Glance*, the OECD publication *Working Better with Age* provides a synthesis of the main challenges and policy recommendations together with a set of international best practices to foster employability, labour demand and incentives to work at an older age (OECD, 2019[41]).

Automatically adjusting benefit levels of new pensions or pensions in payment might still be needed. Adjustment of new pensions is particularly suitable to account for changes in remaining life expectancy at retirement, as these changes are specific to the cohort retiring. This is in line with adjustments made by annuity conversion factors in NDC schemes and in Finland through the life expectancy coefficient in its DB scheme. Over time, however, adjustments to new pensions may become socially unsustainable if people do not work longer. Therefore they might be best combined with an automatic adjustment of the retirement age. Introducing an adjustment affecting new pensioners does have distributional consequences as it does not affect already retired generations.

Estonia, Japan and Lithuania adjust both new pensions and pensions in payment to changes in total contributions or a proxy thereof. These mechanisms will significantly erode pension replacement rates over time given the large projected decline in the size of the working population in these countries, although in Japan the adjustment mechanism can be suspended to protect a certain level of pension adequacy.[29] Most balancing mechanisms in place in OECD countries adjust both new pensions and pensions in payment as well, which is an effective way to restore financial balance in a short time. However, making demographic changes part of pension indexation has its limits, especially in countries that have already opted for price indexation as they have basically no room to further reduce indexation in order to generate savings: sharp or sustained decreases of pensions in payment in real terms will likely lead to strong discontent against the AAM and increase pressure on policy makers to adjust, suspend or remove it, defeating the main *raison d'être* of AAMs.

Even if different AAMs adjust to changes in life expectancy and in the wage bill, financial sustainability is substantially strengthened when including a well-designed automatic balancing mechanism (ABM). ABMs specifically aim at ensuring a balanced budget over time and therefore are the final cornerstone of any sustainable pension scheme. By adjusting both new pensions and pensions in payment, balancing mechanisms distribute the burden of restoring balance across generations. While ABMs can ensure a balanced budget in absence of other AAMs such as a link between retirement age and life expectancy, as a standalone policy they might trigger sharp or sustained corrections in benefit levels that could undermine public and political support for the mechanism. This means that an ABM should rather complement some main AAMs, as in Sweden for example. Although the balancing mechanism in Canada does not complement other AAMs, it provides another good example of this principle of reliance on ABMs as a last resort. Here, priority is given to political solutions, but the backstop mechanism automatically restores financial balance if policy makers cannot agree on a set of adjustments sufficient to restore it.

How to get there

Automatic adjustment mechanisms may offer a technical solution to deal with long-term trends affecting pension systems, but that does not mean that they bypass political processes. AAMs raise questions of how the costs of population ageing are distributed across generations. Setting objectives and deciding on which pension parameters to adjust are therefore fundamentally political decisions, and the introduction of an AAM follows standard law-making procedures. While *not* intervening might appear to be neutral policy, it is what changes redistribution between generations in the face of changing circumstances. As life expectancy increases, a fixed statutory retirement age with unadjusted benefits amounts to redistributing more (and unfinanced) pension income to retirees at the expense of those – most likely future generations – that will have to pay the bill. Hence, the view of AAMs as 'confiscating democracy' or as 'depoliticising' pension policy is mistaken.

AAMs should be politically sustainable in order to fulfil their long-term goals of financial and social sustainability and trust in the pension system: people should be able to rely on the mechanisms remaining in place over a long time. Hence, a government seeking to introduce an AAM should look for a wide parliamentary majority as well as broad public support to ensure that the mechanism survives government or coalition changes and is not subject to attacks from various stakeholders.

That does not mean that politics should no longer matter once AAMs are in place. Policy makers maintain full control over the development of the pension system and can intervene if they deem the triggered adjustments undesirable. This applies in particular when AAMs produce unexpected consequences, for instance during unusually large economic shocks, and it must be possible to change AAMs when preferences in society change. However, AAMs make the trade-off between the short-term and long-term consequences of interventions in the pension system transparent. Furthermore, AAMs can be designed to favour political solutions to sustainability questions as long as they fulfil the predefined objective, as is the case for Canada's automatic backstop mechanism.

Several aspects of AAM design and implementation contribute to political sustainability beyond avoiding real reductions in pensions in payment or long periods between adjustments. Political independence of the body responsible to calculate the indicator and transparency in how it is measured is vital, and all the more so for projection-based indicators. As forecasting is a complex and therefore less transparent exercise, projection-based indicators are more vulnerable to political manipulation through challenging or adjusting forecasting methods or assumptions to change outcomes. Furthermore, the procedure to implement adjustments when the indicator changes or crosses a critical value should be clear.

Finally, clear communication about why AAMs are necessary and what they exactly do is paramount for their political sustainability. The general public should be well informed about the consequences of procrastination when facing these large expected demographic changes. As with all pension reforms, the introduction of AAMs is likely to spark intense political debate as different stakeholders assess whether they stand to gain or lose from them. Hence, the implementation of AAMs is more likely to succeed if they can be perceived by different stakeholders as providing a fair solution across generations.

In the communication on AAMs, it is important to distinguish between the parametric change triggered by AAMs and the automaticity of the trigger. Public resistance against the introduction of AAMs is often not as focused on the automaticity of the change, which is the core component distinguishing AAMs from discretionary adjustments, but on the triggered change in pension parameters itself. For instance, opposition is likely to challenge increasing the statutory retirement age, and not as much the automatic link with life expectancy that triggers this increase. Indeed, any discretionary reforms aiming to improve financial sustainability through adjusting statutory retirement ages or pension benefits will face the same critique. It is therefore important to point out the cost of inaction as well as the difference between AAMs and discretionary reforms following preset timetables. AAMs are conditional and can be designed to maintain the status quo: the statutory retirement age will only increase if life expectancy increases, so as to ensure for example that the ratio of time spent in the labour market over time spent in retirement remains stable over generations. Hence, AAMs by definition offer a clear justification for why pension parameters are adjusted. Reforms following preset timetables cannot promise a solution to the problem of pension financing, nor ensure that adjustments are not sharper than needed to reach financial balance.

Notes

1. Upon parliamentary approval, the triple lock will be suspended for one year in 2022 to avoid that the increase in wages in 2021 compared to 2020, when many workers had a lower income due to COVID-19, causes an 8% hike in pension levels.
2. When pension entitlements are annuitised, longer lives mean more expensive annuities, and therefore lower monthly benefits even if individual longevity risks are still shared among all recipients. As the annuity is set based on life expectancy at retirement, the risk of life expectancy of a cohort growing faster than

predicted after retirement is borne by the pension provider. In the case of lump-sum payments all individual longevity risk is borne by the individual. With longer lives, these lump sums have to finance consumption over a period that is longer on average and uncertain individually.

3. In this generic form, accounts accumulated by people who die before retiring are typically not inherited, thereby increasing the internal rate of return beyond the growth of the contribution base.

4. Moreover, some NDC schemes include survivors' pensions financed by NDC contributions. The generic NDC scheme does not include survivors' benefits, although they can be added. Of all NDC countries, only Italy and Greece have a survivors' pension inside the NDC scheme, while Poland has a survivors' pension outside it (OECD, 2018[44]). In absence of a survivors' pension inside the scheme, NDC schemes generate a 'survivor dividend': the notional accounts of people who pass away before retirement are not accounted for in benefit calculation.

5. Upon the introduction of NDC in 2015, all auxiliary pensions including those in payment were supposed to be transferred to the new NDC scheme, but the Constitutional Court ruled against this. Auxiliary pensions currently make up 12% of total public pension expenditure in Greece.

6. The 'survivor dividend', that is, the notional accumulated capital of people in a cohort who pass away before retirement, would be sufficient to cover the higher pension expenditure due to underestimation of a cohort's longevity gains resulting from the use of period life expectancy (Arnold, Boado-Penas and Godínez-Olivares, 2016[42]).

7. The Czech Republic has a long-term planning policy that somewhat resembles a semi-automatic adjustment of the statutory retirement age to life expectancy. Life expectancy is calculated for every cohort between ages 25 and 54. If for at least one cohort, life expectancy at the statutory retirement age would either be below 24% of total life expectancy or above 26% of total life expectancy, then the report also publishes what the statutory retirement age should be for each cohort for it to fall between these limits. However, even if a clear target is set, there is no formal procedure or mechanism linking this report to effective changes in the statutory retirement age.

8. The increase in statutory retirement age between 2021 and 2050 is faster in Denmark and Estonia than in other countries with a one-to-one link to life expectancy. For Denmark, this is the result of the maximum period people on average can expect to be in retirement having been set at 14.5 years, which is less than what it is expected to be upon introduction of the mechanism, making the retirement age rise faster than life expectancy with the first applications of the link. In Estonia, this is the result of the gradual statutory retirement age increase before the link is applied.

9. For example, Denmark sets a maximum period people can expect to live in retirement, which is at 14.5 years. In Italy, where life expectancy over the last two years is compared to that over the two years prior and the retirement age follows the change in life expectancy between both periods, the statutory retirement age only starts to increase again once life expectancy reaches the level it was at before declining.

10. A longer period between announcement of a change in the statutory retirement age and its implementation is supposed to allow people to better plan their careers as well as their retirement. Moreover, the period has to be longer in Denmark than in other countries with a link as the eligibility ages of various early retirement schemes are linked to the statutory retirement age, the earliest of which being accessible as of six years before the statutory retirement age.

11. Chile, Indonesia and Mexico use gender-specific tables, which lower pensions for women, something that is not allowed in the European Union.

12. By contrast, letting different groups retire at different ages would raise a host of other issues, such as how these groups would be defined and delineated, whether individual health status and behaviours should be taken into account, how retirement ages should be adapted to changing longevity in a group, etc. Many countries in the past allowed for different retirement ages according to occupational risks and these were increasingly closed and replaced by disability pension schemes that grant benefits based on individual health status.

13. The issue is more serious in the US given the very large increase in life-expectancy inequality (Auerbach et al., 2017[46]) but the US is clearly an outlier (Banks et al., 2021[16]).

14. These include Mackenbach et al. (2016[47]), Eurostat (2020[48]) and some country-specific studies: Auerbach et al. (2017[46]), Baker, Currie and Schwandt (2019[49]), Blanpain (2020[50]), Brønnum-Hansen and Baadsgaard (2012[51]), Chetty et al. (2016[52]), Finansministeriet (2017[60]), Khang et al. (2019[53]), Insee (2016[54]), Marshall-Catlin, Bushnik and Tjepkema (2019[55]), van Raalte, Sasson and Martikainen (2018[59]) and studies referenced in GAO (2016[57]).

15. In Finland, inequality in life expectancy increased between the mid-1990s and the late 2000s, but has since remained roughly constant.

16. The longevity measure (such as life expectancy or mortality rates) used to calculate the sustainability factor typically refers to a given age and a given year, and the correction applies to the initial pensions of all people within the same cohort.

17. The annual growth in life expectancy was 0.6% on average over the period (Ministry of Health, Labour and Welfare, 2020[61]). In addition, if the actuarial review conducted every 5 years by the Ministry of Health, Labour and Welfare shows that pension finances can be balanced without the adjustment measures, macroeconomic indexation will be terminated.

18. A "standard pension" is 'the amount of pension benefits received by a household consisting of a husband who works as a salaried worker earning the average wage for 40 years and a wife who is a covered person in the 3rd category for 40 years' (Ministry of Health, Labour and Welfare, 2014, p. 13[45]). The 50% minimum replacement rate refers to the pension this household would receive upon retirement relative to the average net income of men of active age. In 2019, the replacement rate for a "standard pension" was equal to 61.7% according to the Japanese Ministry of Health, Labour and Welfare (2019[58]).

19. Portugal also takes into account GDP growth in the indexation rule but unrelated to ageing prospects. Average annual GDP growth over the last two years is partially taken into account in indexation. If real-GDP growth is above 3%, pensions in payment are indexed by 12.5% of real-GDP growth on top of CPI. Adjustment to GDP does not apply to higher pensions, i.e. pensions above six times the Social Support Index (IAS, currently at EUR 438.81).

20. In every third report (i.e. every nine years), the Canadian Chief Actuary also reports on the CPP Actuarial Factors that adjust benefits to individuals' retirement timing and provides recommendations for adjustments.

21. Moreover, in the calculation of the sustainability factor, the number of both contributors and pensioners is standardised in a way to avoid that the ratio is disproportionately impacted by changes in the amount of people with very low contributions or pensions. The equivalent number of contributors is calculated by dividing total contributions (including those of employees and the unemployed) by contributions that would have been paid by one person earning the average wage (the unemployed are included in calculating the equivalent number of contributors so as to avoid that pensions are affected by economic cycles (Vidal-Meliá, Boado-Penas and Settergren, 2009[1])); the equivalent number of pensioners is calculated by dividing the total pension points of pensioners by the number of points an individual has collected after a 45-year career at average wages (i.e. the 'standard pension').

22. The suspension seems to have been decided officially to avoid that the pension of an average wage worker with a 45-year career would fall below 48%.

23. The commission proposed to maintain both a floor in the replacement rate and a ceiling of the contribution rate, but to revise their levels every seven years. It proposed a 'corridor' within which the replacement rate floor could be set of 44-49% and another 'corridor' for the contribution-rate ceiling of 20-24%.

24. Also the German pension insurance scheme is not allowed to be in debt (Baksa, Munkacsi and Nerlich, 2020[56]).

25. If the contribution rate were to be increased beyond its current level of 24%, then the end-of-year allowance paid to pensioners would be suspended, corresponding to a 1.8% reduction of gross pension after a full career at average wages. This suspension is automatic.

26. Moreover, it decided to prolong the period between announcing an increase in statutory retirement age and the increase taking effect from one to five years (Ministry of Finance of the Slovak Republic, 2020[43]).

27. Even if Norway's indexation rule only involves indexation to average wages and therefore falls outside the scope of this chapter, it is worth noting that it similarly led to a decline of real pension benefit levels between 2015 and 2018 – although for some groups this loss was offset by changes in taxation and minimum and basic pension benefits. In 2021, the subtraction of 0.75% from average wage growth was not applied, and the government is working on a proposal to change the indexation of pensions in payment to the average of wage and price growth as of 2022 (Chapter 1).

28. Moreover, the Agreement also established a temporary early retirement scheme for people in occupations deemed arduous by the social partners, allowing early retirement without penalty three years before the statutory retirement age. As the social partners could not agree on a list of arduous occupations centrally, the social partners at the sectoral level can now propose a list of occupations they consider arduous within the sector. The early retirement scheme is temporary, and will terminate once occupational pension schemes are transformed into FDC schemes.

29. Estonia's one-to-one link of the statutory retirement age to life expectancy will only partially mitigate this effect.

References

[39] Andersen, T. (2021), *Pension adequacy and sustainability – An evaluation of the Finnish pension system*, Finnish Centre for Pensions, Helsinki.

[42] Arnold, S., M. Boado-Penas and H. Godínez-Olivares (2016), "Longevity Risk in Notional Defined Contribution Pension Schemes: A Solution", *The Geneva Papers on Risk and Insurance - Issues and Practice*, Vol. 41/1, pp. 24-52, http://dx.doi.org/*10.1057/gpp.2015.15*.

[46] Auerbach, A. et al. (2017), *How the Growing Gap in Life Expectancy May Affect Retirement Benefits and Reforms*, National Bureau of Economic Research, Cambridge, MA, http://dx.doi.org/*10.3386/w23329*.

[49] Baker, M., J. Currie and H. Schwandt (2019), "Mortality Inequality in Canada and the United States: Divergent or Convergent Trends?", *Journal of Labor Economics*, Vol. 37/S2, pp. S325-S353, http://dx.doi.org/*10.1086/703259*.

[56] Baksa, D., Z. Munkacsi and C. Nerlich (2020), "A Framework for Assessing the Costs of Pension Reform Reversals", *IMF Working Papers*, No. WP/20/132, IMF, Washington, DC.

[31] Baldwin, B. (2020), "Sources of Comfort and Chills: What We Can Learn from CPP Valuation Reports", *Commentary*, No. 587, C.D. Howe Institute, Toronto.

[16] Banks, J. et al. (2021), "The Evolution of Mortality Inequality in 11 OECD Countries: Introduction*", *Fiscal Studies*, Vol. 42/1, pp. 9-23, http://dx.doi.org/*10.1111/1475-5890.12267*.

[24] Barr, N. and P. Diamond (2011), "Improving Sweden's automatic pension adjustment mechanism", *Center for Retirement Research In Brief*, No. 11-2, Center for Retirement Research, Chestnut Hill, MA.

[50] Blanpain, N. (2020), "La mortalité stagne à l'âge adulte pour les générations nées entre 1941 et 1955", *Insee Première*, Vol. 1824, pp. 1-4.

[26] Board of Trustees (2021), *The 2021 Annual Report of the Board of Trustees of the Federal Old-Age and Survivors Insurance and Federal Disability Insurance Trust Funds*, Washington, DC.

[14] Bommier, A. et al. (2005), "Droits à la retraite et mortalité différentielle", *Économie et Prévision*, Vol. 168, pp. 1-16.

[29] Börsch-Supan, A. (2007), "Rational Pension Reform", *The Geneva Papers on Risk and Insurance - Issues and Practice*, Vol. 32/4, pp. 430-446, http://dx.doi.org/*10.1057/palgrave.gpp.2510149*.

[21] Börsch-Supan, A. and J. Rausch (2020), "Corona und Rente", *MEA Discussion Papers*, No. 11-2020, Munich Center for the Economics of Aging, Munich.

[2] Bosworth, B. and R. Weaver (2011), "Social Security on auto-pilot: International experience with automatic stabilizer mechanisms", *Center for Retirement Research Working Papers 2011-18*, Center for Retirement Research, Chestnut Hill, MA.

[28] Boulhol, H. (2019), "Objectives and challenges in the implementation of a universal pension system in France", *OECD Economics Department Working Papers*, No. 1553, OECD Publishing, Paris, *https://dx.doi.org/10.1787/5a476f15-en*.

[40] Boulhol, H. and C. Geppert (2018), *Population ageing: Pension policies alone will not prevent the decline in the relative size of the labour force*.

[11] Boulhol, H., M. Lis and M. Queisser (2022), "Trends in Pension Reforms in OECD Countries", in Bloom, D., A. Sousa-Poza and U. Sunde (eds.), *Handbook on the Economics of Ageing*, Routledge, Abingdon (Forthcoming).

[51] Brønnum-Hansen, H. and M. Baadsgaard (2012), "Widening social inequality in life expectancy in Denmark. A register-based study on social composition and mortality trends for the Danish population", *BMC Public Health*, Vol. 12/1, http://dx.doi.org/*10.1186/1471-2458-12-994*.

[38] Casey, B. (2014), "From pension funds to piggy banks: (Perverse) consequences of the Stability and Growth Pact since the crisis", *International Social Security Review*, Vol. 67/1, pp. 27-48, http://dx.doi.org/*10.1111/issr.12029*.

[52] Chetty, R. et al. (2016), "The Association Between Income and Life Expectancy in the United States, 2001-2014", *JAMA*, Vol. 315/16, p. 1750, http://dx.doi.org/*10.1001/jama.2016.4226*.

[6] Davidoff, T., J. Brown and P. Diamond (2005), "Annuities and Individual Welfare", *American Economic Review*, Vol. 95/5, pp. 1573-1590, http://dx.doi.org/*10.1257/000282805775014281*.

[23] del Carmen Boado-Penas, M., P. Naka and O. Settergren (2020), "Last Lessons Learned from the Swedish Public Pension System", in *Economic Challenges of Pension Systems*, Springer International Publishing, Cham, http://dx.doi.org/*10.1007/978-3-030-37912-4_11*.

[3] Diamond, P. (2004), "Social Security", *American Economic Review*, Vol. 94/1, pp. 1-24, http://dx.doi.org/*10.1257/000282804322970670*.

[13] Diamond, P. and P. Orszag (2004), *Saving Social Security: A Balanced Approach, Washington DC: Brookings Institution Press*, Brookings Institution Press.

[48] Eurostat (2020), *Eurostat database Life expectancy by age, sex and educational attainment level (indicator "demo_mlexpecedu")*.

[4] Fernández, J. (2012), "Explaining the introduction of automatic pension indexation provisions in 17 OECD countries, 1945–2000", *Journal of European Social Policy*, Vol. 22/3, pp. 241-258, http://dx.doi.org/*10.1177/0958928712440202*.

[60] Finansministeriet (2017), *Økonomisk analyse: Stigende levetider for alle befolkningsgrupper*, Finansministeriet, Copenhagen.

[25] Gannon, F., F. Legros and V. Touzé (2020), "Sustainability of pension schemes: Building a smooth automatic balance mechanism with an application to the US Social Security", *Revue de l'OFCE*, Vol. 170/6, pp. 377-401, http://dx.doi.org/*10.3917/reof.170.0377*.

[20] Gannon, F., F. Legros and V. Touzé (2015), "Automatic Adjustment Mechanisms and Budget Balancing of Pension Schemes", *Working paper*.

[57] GAO (2016), *Retirement Security: Shorter Life Expectancy Reduces Projected Lifetime Benefits for Lower Earners*, GAO, Washington, DC.

[9] Geppert, C. et al. (2019), "Labour supply of older people in advanced economies: the impact of changes to statutory retirement ages", *OECD Economics Department Working Papers*, No. 1554, OECD Publishing, Paris, *https://dx.doi.org/10.1787/b9f8d292-en*.

[35] Goss, S. (2010), "The Future Financial Status of the Social Security Program", *Social Security Bulletin*, Vol. 70/3, pp. 111-125.

[34] Guardiancich, I. et al. (2019), "The Politics of NDC Pension Scheme Diffusion: Constraints and Drivers", *Social Protection & Jobs Discussion Papers*, No. 1927, World Bank, Washington, DC.

[5] Hohnerlein, E. (2019), "Pension indexation for retirees revisited – Normative patterns and legal standards", *Global Social Policy*, Vol. 19/3, pp. 246-265, http://dx.doi.org/*10.1177/1468018119842028*.

[54] Insee (2016), *Les inégalités sociales face à la mort*, Insee, Paris.

[27] Inspection générale de la sécurité sociale (2021), "Peer reviews on pension projections: Country fiche for Luxembourg", *Country Fiche on public pensions for the Ageing Report 2021*, European Commission, Brussels.

[53] Khang, Y. et al. (2019), "Trends in inequality in life expectancy at birth between 2004 and 2017 and projections for 2030 in Korea: multiyear cross-sectional differences by income from national health insurance data", *BMJ Open*, Vol. 9/7, p. e030683, http://dx.doi.org/*10.1136/bmjopen-2019-030683*.

[47] Mackenbach, J. et al. (2016), "Changes in mortality inequalities over two decades: register based study of European countries", *BMJ*, p. i1732, http://dx.doi.org/*10.1136/bmj.i1732*.

[55] Marshall-Catlin, E., T. Bushnik and M. Tjepkema (2019), "Trends in mortality inequalities among the adult household population", *Health Reports*, Vol. 30/12, pp. 11-17, http://dx.doi.org/*10.25318/82-003-x201901200002-eng*.

[10] Mastrobuoni, G. (2009), "Labor supply effects of the recent social security benefit cuts: Empirical estimates using cohort discontinuities", *Journal of Public Economics*, Vol. 93/11-12, pp. 1224-1233, http://dx.doi.org/*10.1016/j.jpubeco.2009.07.009*.

[18] Merilä, V. (2019), *The Life Expectancy Coefficient for 2020 according to the Employees Pensions Act*, Finnish Centre for Pensions, Helsinki.

[43] Ministry of Finance of the Slovak Republic (2020), *Country fiche on 2018 pension projections of the Slovak Republic*.

[61] Ministry of Health, Labour and Welfare (2020), "主な年齢の平均余命の年次推移 [Annual change in life expectancy at major ages]", *令和2年簡易生命表の概況 [Overview of the 2020 basic life table]*, No. Reference material 2.

[58] Ministry of Health, Labour and Welfare (2019), "国民年金及び厚生年金に係る財政の現況及び見通し [Current status and outlook of finances related to national pension and welfare pension]", *9th Social Security Council Pension Subcommittee, 27 August 2019*, No. Document 2-1.

[45] Ministry of Health, Labour and Welfare (2014), *Summaries of the 2014 Actuarial Valuation and Reform Options.*

[32] Montserrat Codorniu, J. and G. Rodríguez Cabrero (2018), "Spain: Parliamentary recommendation to revalue the level of pensions in line with the consumer price index", *ESPN Flash Report*, No. 2018/64, European Commission, Brussels.

[7] O'Dea, C. and D. Sturrock (2018), "Subjective expectations of survival and economic behaviour", *IFS Working Papers*, No. W18/14, Institute for Fiscal Studies.

[36] OECD (2020), *OECD Reviews of Pension Systems: Czech Republic*, OECD Reviews of Pension Systems, OECD Publishing, Paris, *https://dx.doi.org/10.1787/e6387738-en.*

[17] OECD (2019), *OECD Reviews of Pension Systems: Portugal*, OECD Reviews of Pension Systems, OECD Publishing, Paris, *https://dx.doi.org/10.1787/9789264313736-en.*

[41] OECD (2019), *Working Better with Age*, Ageing and Employment Policies, OECD Publishing, Paris, *https://dx.doi.org/10.1787/c4d4f66a-en.*

[44] OECD (2018), *OECD Pensions Outlook 2018*, OECD Publishing, Paris, *https://dx.doi.org/10.1787/pens_outlook-2018-en.*

[12] OECD (2017), *Preventing Ageing Unequally*, OECD Publishing, Paris, *https://dx.doi.org/10.1787/9789264279087-en.*

[37] OECD (2012), *OECD Pensions Outlook 2012*, OECD Publishing, Paris, *https://dx.doi.org/10.1787/9789264169401-en.*

[19] Sakamoto, J. (2005), "Japan's Pension Reform", *Social Protection Discussion Paper*, No. 0541, World Bank, Washington, DC.

[15] Sánchez-Romero, M., R. Lee and A. Prskawetz (2019), *Redistributive Effects of Different Pension Systems When Longevity Varies by Socioeconomic Status*, National Bureau of Economic Research, Cambridge, MA, http://dx.doi.org/*10.3386/w25944.*

[22] Sundén, A. (2009), "The Swedish pension system and the economic crisis", *Center for Retirement Research In Brief*, No. 9-25, Center for Retirement Research, Chestnut Hill, MA.

[33] Turner, J. (2009), "Social Security financing: Automatic adjustments to restore solvency", *AARP Research Report*, No. 2009-01, AARP Public Policy Institute, Washington, DC.

[8] Valdes-Prieto, S. (2000), "The Financial Stability of Notional Account Pensions", *Scandinavian Journal of Economics*, Vol. 102/3, pp. 395-417, http://dx.doi.org/*10.1111/1467-9442.03205.*

[59] van Raalte, A., I. Sasson and P. Martikainen (2018), "The case for monitoring life-span inequality", *Science*, Vol. 362/6418, pp. 1002-1004, http://dx.doi.org/*10.1126/science.aau5811.*

[1] Vidal-Meliá, C., M. Boado-Penas and O. Settergren (2009), "Automatic Balance Mechanisms in Pay-As-You-Go Pension Systems", *The Geneva Papers on Risk and Insurance - Issues and Practice*, Vol. 34/2, pp. 287-317, http://dx.doi.org/*10.1057/gpp.2009.2.*

[30] Weaver, K. and A. Willén (2014), "The Swedish pension system after twenty years: Mid-course corrections and lessons", *OECD Journal on Budgeting*, *https://dx.doi.org/10.1787/budget-13-5jxx3sx58x9t.*

Pensions at a Glance 2021
OECD and G20 Indicators

Chapter 3

Design of pension systems

The five indicators in this section look in detail at the design of retirement income systems in OECD countries and other major economies. The first indicator sets out the taxonomy of the different kinds of retirement-income programmes found around the world. It uses this framework to describe the architecture of the pension systems of OECD and G20 countries.

The next four indicators set out the parameters and rules of the pension systems. The second indicator covers first-tier schemes and shows the values and coverage of basic, targeted and minimum pensions. The third indicator looks at the mandatory earnings-related pensions systems and shows how benefits are determined in these schemes and the range of earnings that are covered. The fourth and fifth indicators present, respectively, the current and the future retirement ages by pension scheme for an individual entering the labour market at age 22 and working a full, uninterrupted career.

Key results

Retirement-income regimes are diverse and often involve a number of different programmes. The taxonomy of pensions used here consists of two mandatory "tiers"; the first generates retirement income independent of past earnings level with the second covering earnings-related components. Voluntary provision, be it personal or employer-provided, makes up a third tier.

Figure 3.1 is based on the role of each part of the system. The first tier comprises programmes offering the first layer of social protection in old age, and for which past earnings are irrelevant in the calculation of retirement income. Such schemes often target some absolute, minimum standard of living in retirement. Mandatory earnings-related components (second-tier) contribute to smoothing consumption, and therefore standards of living, between working life and retirement. *Pensions at a Glance* focuses mainly on these mandatory components, although information is also provided on some widespread voluntary, private schemes (third tier).

Table 3.1 shows the architecture of pension systems in OECD countries based on the rules that determine eligibility and benefit level while categorising mandatory earnings-related pensions as public or private in accordance with national accounts. Panel A describes the latest legislation applying to future retirees while Panel B shows where those rules have changed compared to current retirees.

Basic pensions can take two different forms: a residence-based benefit or a benefit that is only available to those who contributed during their career. The level of the benefit may vary with the number of residence or contribution years but is independent of the earnings level during the career. Eight OECD countries have a residence-based basic pension for future retirees while Norway and Sweden are replacing theirs with targeted schemes that involve a means test. Nine OECD countries feature a contribution-based basic pension.

Eligibility for ***targeted*** plans requires meeting some residence criteria. In these plans, the value of the benefit depends on income from other sources and possibly also assets. Hence, poorer pensioners receive higher benefits than better-off retirees. All countries have general safety nets of this type but only those countries are marked in which full-career workers with very low earnings (30% of average) would be entitled. This holds for eight OECD countries, both currently and in the future.

Minimum pensions can refer to either the minimum of a specific contributory scheme, or to all schemes combined and are currently found in 16 OECD countries, with Chile and Italy phasing this scheme out. In most countries, the value of entitlements only takes account of pensions rather than testing for other income. Minimum pensions either define a minimum for total lifetime entitlements, which may increase in level once the length of the contribution period exceeds certain thresholds, or they are based on minimum pension credits that calculate year-by-year entitlements of low earners based on a higher earnings level.

Only Ireland and New Zealand in the OECD do not have mandatory second-tier pensions. In the other countries, there are four kinds of scheme.

For future retirees public pay-as-you-go schemes will follow a general ***defined benefit*** (DB) format in 20 OECD countries, with pension's dependent on the number of years of contributions, accrual rates and individual pensionable earnings. In another eight countries, DB schemes apply to current retirees but they have been closed to new workers (Table 3.1 Panel B). Private occupational DB schemes are mandatory or quasi-mandatory in two OECD countries (the Netherlands and Switzerland).

There are ***points*** schemes in five OECD countries: French occupational plans managed by social partners under pubic supervision and the Estonian, German, Lithuanian and the Slovak public schemes. Workers earn pension points based on their earnings. At retirement, the sum of pension points is multiplied by a pension-point value to convert them into a regular pension payment.

There are ***notional defined contribution*** (NDC) schemes at the core of the pension system in five OECD countries (Italy, Latvia, Norway, Poland and Sweden). In addition, the smaller supplementary component of the pension system in Greece is also NDC. These are pay-as-you-go public schemes with individual accounts that apply a notional rate of return to contributions made, mimicking Funded defined contribution (FDC) plans. The accounts are "notional" in that the balances exist only on the books of the managing institution. At retirement, the accumulated notional capital is converted into a monthly pension using a formula based on life expectancy.

Funded defined contribution (FDC) plans are compulsory for future retirees in 12 OECD countries. In these schemes, contributions flow into an individual account. The accumulation of contributions and investment returns is usually converted into a monthly pension at retirement. In Denmark and Sweden, there are quasi-mandatory, occupational FDC schemes in addition to smaller compulsory public plans.

Figure 3.1. **Taxonomy: Different types of retirement-income provision**

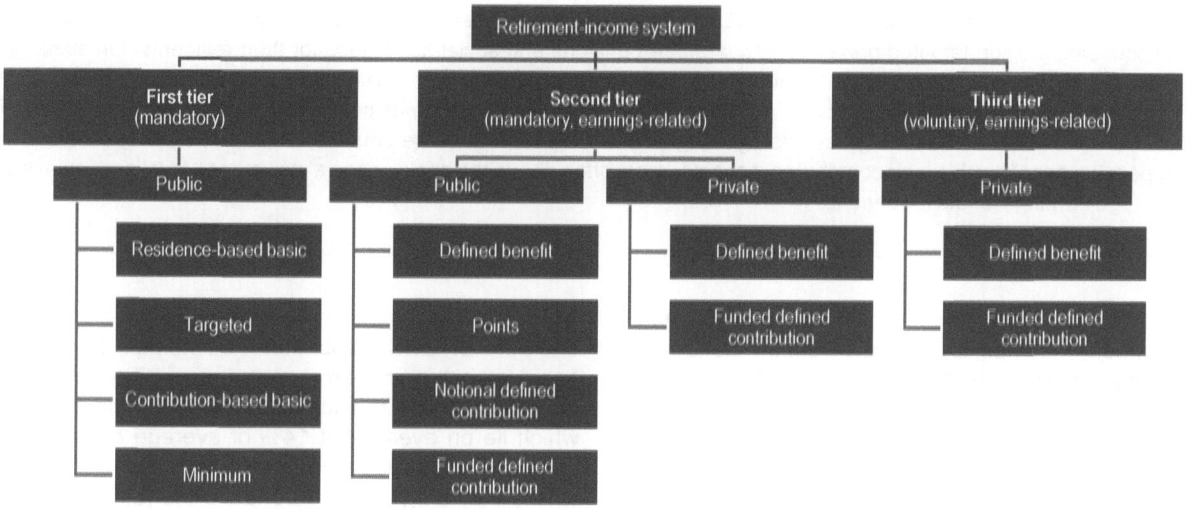

Table 3.1. **Structure of retirement-income provision through mandatory schemes**

	First tier				Second tier			First tier				Second tier	
	Residence-based		Contribution-based					Residence-based		Contribution-based			
	Basic	Targeted	Basic	Minimum	Public	Private		Basic	Targeted	Basic	Minimum	Public	Private
Panel A. Latest legislation (applying to future retirees entering the labour market in 2018 at age 22)													
Australia		✔				FDC	Mexico	✔			✔		FDC
Austria				✔	DB		Netherlands	✔					DB [q]
Belgium				✔	DB		New Zealand	✔					
Canada	✔	✔			DB		Norway		✔			NDC	FDC
Chile		✔				FDC	Poland				✔	NDC	
Colombia				✔	DB	FDC	Portugal				✔	DB	
Costa Rica					DB	FDC	Slovak Republic				✔	Points	
Czech Republic			✔	✔	DB		Slovenia				✔	DB	
Denmark	✔	✔			FDC	FDC [q]	Spain				✔	DB	
Estonia			✔		Points		Sweden		✔			NDC + FDC	FDC [q]
Finland		✔			DB		Switzerland				✔	DB	DB
France				✔	DB + Points		Turkey				✔	DB	
Germany					Points		United Kingdom			✔			FDC [q]
Greece	✔				DB + NDC		United States					DB	
Hungary				✔	DB								
Iceland	✔	✔				FDC [q]							
Ireland			✔				Argentina			✔	✔	DB	
Israel	✔		✔			FDC	Brazil				✔	DB	
Italy					NDC		China				✔	NDC + FDC	
Japan			✔		DB		India				✔	DB + FDC	
Korea			✔		DB		Indonesia				✔	DB + FDC	
Latvia				✔	NDC + FDC		Russian Federation			✔		Points	FDC
Lithuania			✔		Points		Saudi Arabia				✔	DB	
Luxembourg			✔	✔	DB		South Africa		✔				
Panel B. Current legislation where different from Panel A (applying to new retirees in 2020)*													
Chile		✔		✔	DB	FDC	Mexico				✔	DB	
Estonia			✔		DB/Points	FDC	Norway	✔	✔			DB	FDC
Italy				✔	DB + NDC		Poland				✔	DB/NDC	
Latvia				✔	DB/NDC + FDC		United Kingdom			✔		DB	

Note: *Information for non-OECD countries unavailable. A tick for the column "Targeted" is only shown if a full-career worker at 30% of the average wage is eligible. [q] = Quasi-mandatory scheme based on collective agreements with a very high coverage rate, see Chapter 9. DB = Defined benefit, FDC = Funded defined contribution, NDC = Notional defined contribution. The contribution-based basic pension in Israel is a 2% top-up (total maximum 50%) on the residence-based basic pension for each contribution year beyond 10 years. In Switzerland, the government sets contribution rates, minimum rates of return and the annuity rate at which the accumulation is converted into a pension for mandatory occupational plans. This scheme is therefore implicitly defined benefit. In Mexico, the government pays a transfer to the individual private FDC account of a contributing employee every month. In Canada, the basic pension (OAS) is income-tested but only through the tax system ("claw back").
Source: See "Country Profiles" available at *http://oe.cd/pag*.

StatLink *https://stat.link/2xd6uo*

Key results

Residence-based basic pensions exist in ten OECD countries and are, on average, worth 20% of the gross average wage. Almost all OECD countries provide targeted benefits like guarantee pensions and social assistance for their residents. On average in the OECD, people without a contributory record could receive 19% of average earnings from targeted schemes, subject to a means test, and 20% when including residence-based basic pensions. Nine OECD countries provide contribution-based basic pensions, with the full benefit being equal to 14% of the gross average wage on average across these countries. Half of OECD countries provide a minimum pension benefit within their contributory scheme, most often above the basic or social assistance level and, on average, at 27% of average earnings for the full benefit.

There are four main ways in which OECD countries might provide retirement incomes to meet a minimum standard of living in old age (Table 3.2). The left-hand part of the table shows the value of benefits provided under these different types of schemes. Values are presented in *relative* terms – as a percentage of countries' gross average wages – to facilitate comparisons between countries (See the "Average wage" indicator in Chapter 7). The right-hand part of the table shows the number of total recipients as a share of the population aged 65 and over.

Benefit level

Benefit values are shown for a single person. In some cases – in particular for minimum pensions – each partner in a couple can receive an individual entitlement. In other cases – especially for targeted schemes – the household is treated as the unit of assessment and generally receives less than twice the entitlement of a single person.

Only four OECD countries have neither a basic nor a minimum pension: Australia, Finland, Germany and the United States. However, in Germany a new supplemental pension has been introduced to the points scheme, which will provide higher benefits to low earners with long careers. Moreover, almost all OECD countries provide targeted benefits that are subject to further means tests. The existence of multiple programmes in many countries complicates the analysis of effective benefit levels. In some cases, benefits under these schemes are additive. In others, there is a degree of substitution between them.

Figure 3.2 therefore summarises the level of non-contributory, residence-based benefits. Residence-based basic pensions are present in ten countries with an average benefit of 20% of the gross average wage and a maximum of 40% in New Zealand. Norway and Sweden are phasing them out. All OECD countries provide targeted benefits to their residents, but people in Greece, the Netherlands and New Zealand cannot receive such a benefit on top of a full residence-based basic pension. In Canada, Denmark and Iceland, residence-based basic pensions do not reduce the targeted benefit. On average in the OECD, 19% of gross average earnings can be received from targeted schemes subject to further means tests, and a total of 20% when including residence-based basic pensions.

As for the contributory components of first-tier pensions, one-third of OECD countries has neither contribution-based basic nor minimum pensions (Figure 3.3). Nine OECD countries provide contribution-based basic pensions, which lie on average at 14% of average earnings for the full benefit. They range from 6% of average earnings in Israel, where they are paid as a bonus to the residence-based basic pension, to 28% in Ireland. In half of OECD countries, low contributory pensions are topped up to a higher minimum pension level, up to 27% of average earnings on average. These minimum pensions vary between a low of about 7% of the average wage in Hungary and 13% in the Czech Republic and Latvia to a high of about 39% in Luxembourg and 66% in Colombia.

Coverage

The importance of first-tier benefits varies enormously across OECD countries. The percentage of over-65s receiving such benefits is shown in the final four columns of Table 3.2. Different approaches of reporting the number of recipients, for example in case of benefits paid to couples or even households, may blur the data comparability across countries to some extent.

Naturally, residence-based basic pensions have on average the highest coverage. However, contribution-based basic pensions also have very high recipient numbers in most countries that have such a scheme. Sometimes recipient numbers exceed 100% of the population aged 65 and older hinting to recipients younger than 65 or living abroad.

The incidence of receiving a minimum pension is very diverse across countries and positively related to the level of the benefit. Minimum pensions are received by almost 40% of the over-65s in France. In Belgium, Italy and Spain around 30% of the over-65s receive a minimum pension while it is less than 10% in the Slovak Republic and at 2% or under in Hungary, Poland and Slovenia.

The range in targeted schemes is similarly big, with in particular Australia, Chile, Korea and Mexico showing high recipient numbers of more than every second person aged 65 or older.

Table 3.2. **Current level and recipients of first-tier benefits**

	Benefit value in 2020 (% of gross AW earnings)				Recipients in 2018 (% of population aged 65 and over)			
	Residence-based basic	Targeted	Contribution-based basic	Minimum	Residence-based basic	Targeted	Contribution-based basic	Minimum
Australia		27.0				63		
Austria		22.6		28.0		1		10
Belgium		29.0		32.5		5		33
Canada	12.9	19.2			98	32		
Chile		16.5		17.7		60		..
Colombia				65.7				
Costa Rica		13.0		19.0				
Czech Republic		11.5	10.4	12.7			119	
Denmark	17.6	19.6			103			
Estonia		16.0	15.5			1	117	
Finland		21.9				38		
France		28.4		20.2		4		38
Germany		19.3				1		
Greece	21.8				..	..		
Hungary		7.4		6.8		0		1
Iceland	33.3	17.7			67	..		
Ireland		26.4	27.7			14	61	
Israel	11.9	24.7	6.0		88	..	..	
Italy		19.8		22.7		7		32
Japan		18.0	15.1			3	92	
Korea		7.8	11.9			69	43	
Latvia		7.4		12.6		..		..
Lithuania		10.2	13.2			3	109	
Luxembourg		31.1	12.0	39.1			115	
Mexico	11.9			30.1		55		..
Netherlands	29.2				104	1		
New Zealand	39.8				105	2		
Norway	15.4	30.5			103			
Poland				23.6				2
Portugal		27.0		28.6		7		38
Slovak Republic		17.4		30.3		0		6
Slovenia		34.7		33.0				2
Spain		20.4		35.5		3		25
Sweden		22.2			..	35		
Switzerland		22.3		16.3		0		..
Turkey		11.1		33.5				10
United Kingdom		21.6	16.7			16	105	
United States		15.6				2		
Other G20 countries								
Argentina		21.1	12.5	26.4		..	..	41
Brazil		45.3		49.1				..
China				..				..
India				8.0				..
Indonesia				14.6				..
Russian Federation		23.3	14.2			..	..	
Saudi Arabia				23.9				..
South Africa		14.9				..		

Note:. = Data are not available. The benefit level shown is for new pensioners in 2020. The contribution-based basic amounts refer to the benefit level for a full career. People in Greece, the Netherlands and New Zealand cannot receive a targeted benefit on top of a full residence-based basic pension.
Source: Information provided by countries and OECD's Social Recipients database.

StatLink https://stat.link/uxgr8v

Figure 3.2. **Non-contributory first-tier benefits**

Percentage of gross average earnings, 2020

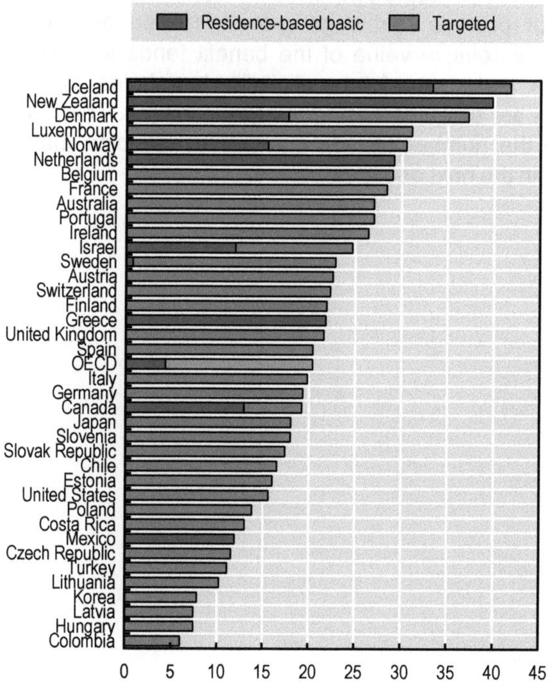

StatLink https://stat.link/kpoilu

Figure 3.3. **Contributory first-tier benefits**

Percentage of gross average earnings, 2020

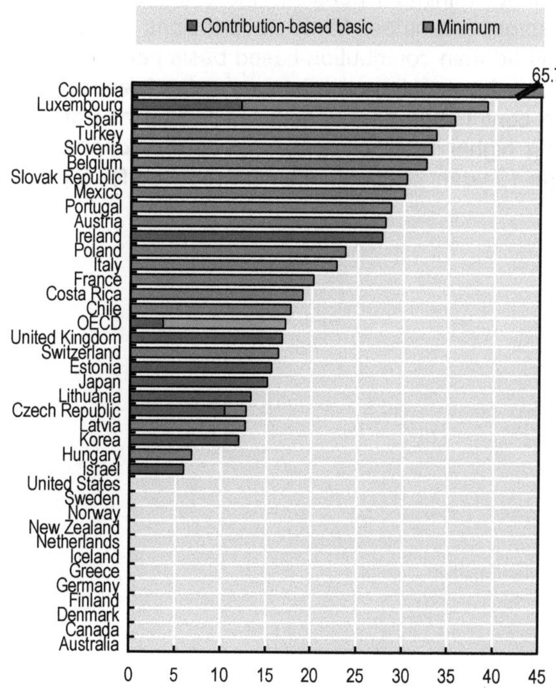

StatLink https://stat.link/k23yri

Key results

On average 34 years of contributions are needed for a full contribution-based basic pension, with 13 years contributions to be entitled to any benefit. The United Kingdom currently requires the shortest contribution period to be eligible for a benefit at one year, while the Czech Republic requires 35 years for eligibility, which is also the same level for the full benefit. Minimum pensions on average require 29 years for a full benefit. Partial benefits are available in France and Switzerland when any payment has been made to the pension system, with at least 15 years required in other OECD countries.

Contribution-based basic pensions

The full rates of first-tier pensions are described in the previous indicator, but these levels are only applicable after full eligibility. In most countries with such systems, partial eligibility is achieved after much shorter careers. For example, whilst full entitlement to the contribution-based basic pension is achieved after 40 years in Canada, Japan and Luxembourg, only 10 years of contribution are required for eligibility for a reduced benefit (Figure 3.4). On average across the OECD countries that have contribution-based basic pensions 34 years are required for a full pension and 13 years for initial eligibility. In both Lithuania and the United Kingdom the eligibility criteria are changing, with Lithuania increasing the period for the full benefit and the United Kingdom increasing the criteria for both eligibility and full benefit. In the Czech Republic 35 years are required for eligibility, with Argentina at 30 years and no other OECD or G20 country requiring more than 15 years. Residence-based basic pensions also have proportionally reduced benefits in many countries but the default assumption for the analysis in this report is full residence irrespective of career breaks.

Minimum pensions

Likewise for minimum pensions there are different eligibility rules across countries. Minimum pensions are much more widespread than contribution-based basic pensions and more commonly have only one monetary value irrespective of the eligible contribution period, with fewer than half of countries applying higher rates for longer careers of contribution. On average 19 years of contribution are required for eligibility to a minimum pension, with 29 years required on average for a full minimum pension. In France and Switzerland, only one period of contribution is required for a minimum pension, whilst over 40 years are required for the full benefit. In the Slovak Republic, the minimum pension is achieved after 30 years, with no explicit maximum duration. Full minimum pensions are eligible with 25 years of contributions or less in Chile, Colombia, Costa Rica, Hungary, Italy, Mexico, Poland, Slovenia, Spain and Turkey.

Indexation

Once eligible for a basic, minimum or targeted pension, how it is indexed in payment is the key factor apart from discretionary adjustments to how these benefits may support future generations of retirees, and be effective to fight against old-age poverty. If benefits are indexed to wages, as is the case for the basic and safety-net benefits in Denmark, for example, then they will hold their value relative to average wages throughout the retirement period, decreasing future poverty risks and maintaining the relative standard of living of the retiree. However, indexing first-tier benefits to wage growth is rare across OECD countries (Table 3.3). Price indexation is a much more common approach, which means that during normal times of positive real-wage growth, fuelled by productivity gains, the relative value of the benefit tends to decline over time. In that case, future eligibility thresholds for targeted benefits are also decreasing relative to wages. This is likely to reduce the number of individuals or households that will be eligible in the next decades.

Figure 3.4. **Number of years required for partial and full contribution-based basic pensions**

Number of years required for initial eligibility and for full contribution-based basic pensions

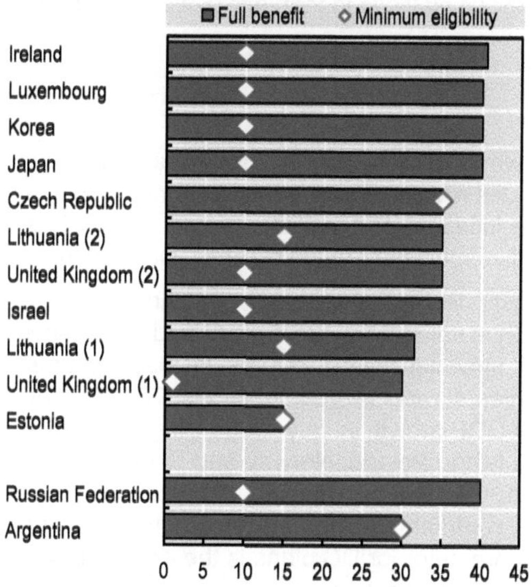

Note: Lithuania (1) and the United Kingdom (1) refer to the rules that apply for those retiring in 2020, whilst Lithuania (2) and the United Kingdom (2) are for those first entering the labour market in 2020.

Source: See "Country Profiles" available at *http://oe.cd/pag.*

StatLink https://stat.link/1geuqx

Figure 3.5. **Number of years required for partial and full minimum pensions**

Number of years required for initial eligibility and for full minimum pensions

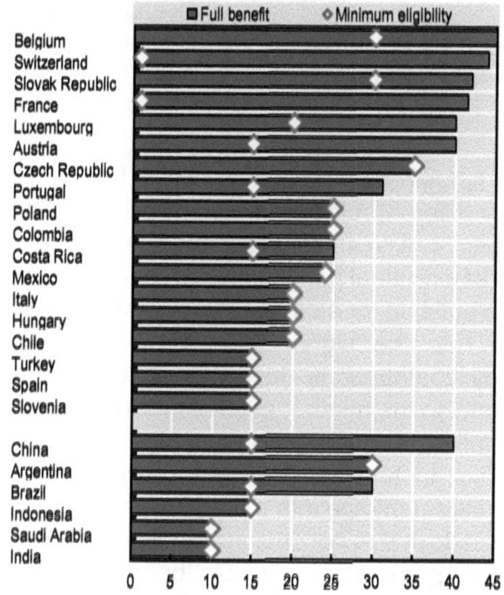

Note: In the Slovak Republic, the full benefit of 42 years recorded in the chart, reflects the full career case from age 22, as there is no explicit maximum duration.

Source: See "Country Profiles" available at *http://oe.cd/pag.*

StatLink https://stat.link/yrfnhu

Table 3.3. **Indexation of pension benefits by component of the system**

	Basic	Minimum	Safety net		Basic	Minimum	Safety net
Australia			Whatever is higher: prices or cost of living	Japan	Wages until age 67, then prices		Cost of living and wages
Austria		Prices	Discretionary	Korea	Prices		Prices
Belgium		Prices	Prices	Latvia		Wages	Wages
Canada	Prices		Prices	Lithuania	GDP		Prices
Chile		Prices	Prices	Luxembourg	Cost of living and annually consider wages	Cost of living and annually consider wages	Cost of living and annually consider wages
Colombia		Wages		Mexico	Prices	Prices	Prices
Costa Rica		Wages	Wages	Netherlands	Legal minimum wage		minimum wage
Czech Republic	Wages	Wages/none	Prices	New Zealand	Prices and periodically net average wage		Prices and periodically net average wage
Denmark	Wages		Wages	Norway	Wages minus 0.75%		Wages minus 0.75%
Estonia	80% wages/20% prices		80% wages/20% prices	Poland		Prices	Prices
Finland			Prices	Portugal		GDP and consumer price index without housing	Prices
France		Prices	Prices	Slovak Republic		Wages	Prices
Germany			Wages	Slovenia		60% wages/40% prices	Wages
Greece	Prices		Prices	Spain		Between 0.25% and (consumer price index + 0.5%)	At least equal to contributory pension increase
Hungary		Prices and net average monthly earnings	Prices and net average monthly earnings	Sweden			Prices
Iceland	Whatever is higher: wages or cost of living		Prices	Switzerland		50% wages/50% prices	50% wages/50% prices
Ireland	Wages		Wages	Turkey		Prices	Prices
Israel	Prices		Prices	United Kingdom	Whatever is highest: prices, wages or 2.5%		Whatever is higher: prices, wages or 2.5%
Italy		Prices	Prices	United States			Prices

Source: See "Country Profiles" available at *http://oe.cd/pag.*

Key results

The second tier of the OECD's taxonomy of retirement-income provision comprises mandatory earnings-related pensions. Key parameters and rules of these schemes determine the value of entitlements, including the long-term effect of pension reforms that have already been legislated.

Generic earnings-related schemes are of four different types governed by different rules of benefit calculation. DB schemes typically specify a nominal accrual rate, expressed as a percentage of individual pensionable earnings, at which benefit entitlements build up for each year of coverage. The higher the contribution rate the higher the accrual rate that can be sustained by contributions. In points schemes, the pension benefit is equal to the number of points accumulated during the career multiplied by the point value. FDC schemes apply an annuity divisor to turn accumulated capital in the individual account at retirement age into a monthly pension benefit. NDC schemes also do that to notional accumulated capital. Table 3.4 presents future parameters and rules for benefit calculation that will apply to people who enter the labour market in 2020, according to the latest legislation.

Nominal accrual rates of at least 2% apply in Colombia, Portugal, Spain and Turkey. Japan and Korea credit the lowest rates of about 0.5%. In half of DB schemes the accrual rate is constant. In the Czech Republic, Portugal, for the public scheme in Switzerland and the United States, entitlements vary with earnings levels, granting higher accrual rates to lower earners. Accrual rates increase with a longer contribution history in Greece and Luxembourg while in Hungary, Slovenia and Spain accruals are higher for the first years of coverage. Moreover, in the Swiss occupational plan accrual rates increase with age as contribution rates do. In some countries, total accrual rates are limited by a ceiling or by a maximum number of years that generate accruals.

Earnings measures used to calculate benefits differ by country. The vast majority of OECD countries uses entire career earnings, with Portugal and the United States coming close by using the best 40 and 35 years, respectively. Only the main scheme in France and public pensions in Colombia, Costa Rica, Slovenia and Spain will be based on a comparatively small fraction of career earnings; the best 25, final 10, final 20, best 24 and final 25 years of earnings, respectively.

All schemes apply a ***valorisation rate*** to past earnings to take account of changes in "living standards" between the time pension rights accrued and the time they are claimed. The most commonly used rate is the growth of average earnings. Belgium, Colombia, Costa Rica, the main scheme in France, occupational DB schemes in the Netherlands and the system in Spain only revalue earnings with price inflation, thereby leading to a negative impact of real-wage growth on replacement rates and making the finances of the system (more) sensitive to real-wage growth (OECD, 2019[1]). Also Finland, Portugal and the United States revalue earlier years' earnings with a mix of price and wage inflation, and in Estonia and Turkey it is a mix of prices and, respectively, wage bill and GDP growth.

The interest rate applied to paid contributions in DC plans is the counterpart to valorisation rates in DB and points schemes. It is based on financial market returns in FDC schemes and on notional interest rates in NDC schemes. The latter are equal to the rate of GDP growth in Italy, wage bill growth in Latvia and a mix of the two in Poland. Norway and Sweden apply earnings growth. On top, Sweden redistributes accrued entitlements of deceased contributors to all other contributors in the system. One key parameter for DC plans is the ***contribution rate*** paid into individual accounts.

Most countries set a limit on the earnings used to calculate pension benefits. Pension schemes in ten countries do not have a ceiling. The highest ceilings apply in the occupational scheme in Colombia, France, Lithuania, Mexico and the Slovak Republic, at over six times average earnings. The lowest ceilings at about 0.75 times average earnings is in Israel and Switzerland, with no other country having a ceiling below the average wage.

Indexation refers to the growth of pensions in payment. Price indexation is most common. However, eight countries uprate benefits with a mix of price inflation and wage growth, and four countries combine inflation and GDP or wage bill growth. Norway indexes to wage growth minus 0.75% while Sweden indexes pensions based on wage growth minus 1.6%.

The ***effective accrual rate*** measures the rate at which benefit entitlements are effectively built for each year of coverage. It is thus closely connected to the replacement rates shown in Chapter 4. For DB schemes, it equals the nominal accrual rate corrected for the effects applying to pensionable earnings (thresholds, valorisation of past earnings, sustainability factors). In FDC and NDC schemes the effective accrual rate depends on contribution rates, rates of returns and annuity factors.

Based on current legislation, the highest future effective annual accrual rates are in Austria (1.72%) and Colombia (1.87%) with Italy, Luxembourg, Portugal, Spain and Turkey also larger than 1.5%. The lowest rates, below 0.2%, are in the points scheme in Lithuania and the FDC schemes of Norway and Sweden, reflecting low contribution rates. The effective accrual rate from mandatory schemes will equal 1.1% on average among OECD countries.

Table 3.4. **Future parameters and rules of mandatory earnings-related pensions, latest legislation**

At the normal retirement age of a full-career worker who entered the labour market at age 22 in 2020

	Type of scheme	DB schemes	DB, points or NDC schemes			FDC or NDC schemes	Ceiling for pensionable earnings (% of average earnings)	Effective accrual rate of a male full-career average earner (% of earnings)
		Nominal accrual rate (% of individual pensionable earnings)	Earnings measure	Valorisation rate	Indexation rate	Total contribution rate (%)		
Australia	FDC					12.0	2.51	0.70
Austria	DB	1.78	L	w	d		1.55	1.72
Belgium	DB	1.33	L	p	p		1.25	0.97
Canada	DB	0.83	L	w	p[c]		1.02	0.73
Chile	FDC					10.0	2.72	0.73
Colombia	DB or FDC	2.56 [w]	F10	p	p	11.5	16.42	1.87
Costa Rica	DB / FDC	1.40 [w]	F20	p	p	4.25	None	1.4 / 0.27
Czech Republic	DB	0.90 [w]	L	w	50%w + 50%p		3.58	0.90
Denmark	FDC (Occ.)					12.0	None	0.97
Estonia	Points		L	w	80%wb + 20%p		None	0.32
Finland	DB	1.50	L	80%w + 20%p	20%w + 80%p		None	1.23
France	DB / points	1.16	B25 / L	p / w	p / p		1.08 / 8.62	1.02 / 0.35
Germany	Points		L	w	w − x		1.59	0.92
Greece	DB / NDC	1.14 [y]	L	p, w / g	p/ 50%p+50%g	6.0	4.30	1.14 / 0.23
Hungary	DB	1.45 [y]	L	w	p		None	1.45
Iceland	FDC (Occ.)					15.5	None	1.15
Ireland	None							
Israel	FDC					12.5	0.76	0.69
Italy	NDC		L	g	p	33.0	3.41	1.52
Japan	DB	0.55	L	w	p or w [a]		2.37	0.50
Korea	DB	0.51	L	w	p		1.31	0.51
Latvia	NDC / FDC		L	wb	p + 50%wb	14.0 / 6.0	4.86 / none	0.54 / 0.47
Lithuania	Points		L	w	wb		6.35	0.18
Luxembourg	DB	1.61 [y]	L	p, w	p, w [c]		2.21	1.61
Mexico	FDC					15.0	6.04	1.07
Netherlands	DB (Occ.)	1.15	L	p[c]	p[c]		None	0.86
New Zealand	None							
Norway	NDC / FDC		L	w	w − 0.75%	18.1 / 2.0	1.14 / 1.93	0.88 / 0.15
Poland	NDC		L	p, wb, g	p, w [c]	19.5	2.57	0.71
Portugal	DB	2.13 [w]	B40	Max(25%w+75%p,p+ 0.5%)	p, d		None	1.63
Slovak Republic	Points		L	w	p		6.56	1.26
Slovenia	DB	1.05 [f/m, y]	B24	w, d	60%w + 40%p		3.25	1.05
Spain	DB	2.70 [y]	F25	p	p		1.81	1.72
Sweden	NDC / FDC / FDC (occ.)		L	w	w − 1.6% [c]	14.9 / 2.3 / 4.5 [w]	1.16 / 1.16 / none	0.8 / 0.16 / 0.28
Switzerland	DB / DB (occ.)	0.66 [w] / 0.67 [a]	L / L	f / r	50%w+50%p / 0%		0.74 / 0.74	0.51 / 0.51
Turkey	DB	2.00	L	p + 30%g	p		3.54	1.70
United Kingdom	FDC					8.0		0.61
United States	DB	1.23 [w]	B35	w or p	p		2.29	0.87

Note: Empty cells indicate that the parameter is not relevant. [a] = varies with age, [c] = valorisation/indexation conditional on financial sustainability, [f/m] = varies by gender, [w] = varies with earnings, [y] = varies with years of service, B = number of best years, F = number of final years, L = lifetime average, d = discretionary valorisation/ indexation, f = fixed-rate, g = growth of gross domestic product; p = price inflation, w = growth of average earnings, wb = wage bill growth. Denmark: typical contribution rate for quasi-mandatory occupational plans. ATP pension only enters the last column. Germany: x depends on changes in both sustainability and contribution factors. Italy: indexation is to price inflation for low pensions and 75% of price inflation for high pensions. Japan: indexation is to earnings growth until age 67 and to price inflation after age 68. Luxembourg: indexation is to price inflation plus a share of real earnings growth, depending on the financial situation of the pension scheme, assumed to be full wage growth until 2027 and 25% thereafter. Poland: indexation is to price inflation + at least 20% of real average-earnings growth in the previous year. Portugal: indexation is higher relative to prices for low pensions and vice versa. Indexation rises with higher GDP growth. Switzerland: in the public scheme, ceiling applies to average earnings measure at retirement rather than annual earnings in the contribution years. United States: valorisation with earnings growth to age 60, no adjustment from 60 to 62, valorisation with price inflation from 62 to 67. Accrual rates applied to average earnings measure at retirement rather than annual earnings in the years of contribution. In some countries accrual stops after a certain number of contribution years or when a certain total accrual rate is reached. This is the case in Belgium (45 years), Canada (40 years), Portugal (40 years), Spain (100%), Turkey (90%) and the United States (35 years). In other countries a maximum pension or a late retirement age may stop accrual too.

Source: See "Country Profiles" available at *http://oe.cd/pag.*

StatLink https://stat.link/4jmihd

Key results

The rules for eligibility to retire and withdraw a pension benefit are complex and often reflect conflicting objectives. This is all mirrored in the different criteria for pension benefit withdrawal in different schemes. The 2020 average normal retirement age across OECD countries for an individual with a full career and who entered the labour market at age 22 was equal to 63.4 years for women and 64.2 years for men. Turkey is an outlier with a normal retirement age of 49 and 52 for women and men, respectively. Except for Turkey, the lowest ages are 57 for women in Colombia and 62 for men in Colombia, Luxembourg and Slovenia. Iceland, Norway and, for men only, Israel have the highest normal age of 67. The largest gender difference was five years in Austria, Colombia, Israel and Poland.

In many OECD countries, different rules apply to different components of the overall retirement-income package. The normal retirement age reflects the age of eligibility to all schemes combined without penalty after a full career from age 22. Therefore, where normal retirement ages differ across pension schemes the maximum across schemes defines the normal retirement age of the country.

Table 3.5 shows the rules for both normal and early retirement for mandatory pension schemes. "Normal" retirement is defined as receiving a full pension without penalties. In some schemes, a pension can be claimed earlier, from the "early" retirement age onwards, implying benefit penalties that adjust for the longer retirement spell. The indicated ages are theoretical, applying to a person entering the labour force at age 22 and working without interruption. Chapter 6 looks at effective ages of labour market exit and employment rates at older ages.

Early age

A very early pension withdrawal is often only possible in occupational pension plans, like in Australia, France and Sweden at age 55. The non-occupational public schemes in both Korea and Lithuania allow receiving benefits before age 60. In the FDC schemes of Chile, Colombia and Mexico and the DB scheme in the Slovak Republic, early retirement requires that the pension entitlements exceed a floor that is a proxy for the subsistence level. In the Slovak Republic, this is only possible within two years to the normal retirement age while no age condition apply in Chile, Colombia and Mexico.

In general, most DB and points schemes specify an early retirement age next to the normal retirement age. Public DB or points schemes typically allow withdrawing a pension between two and five years earlier than the normal retirement age. In Greece and Luxembourg the early and normal retirement ages coincide for the case of an uninterrupted career from age 22.

Only in Austria (for women), Costa Rica, Hungary, Turkey and the United Kingdom do DB schemes currently not include an early retirement option. Basic pensions and targeted schemes often exclude such a possibility as well. Exceptions are found where the public pension consists of both a basic and a DB component, like in the Czech Republic and Japan.

For comparison across countries it is assumed that all pension pots within DC schemes are annuitised, even if this is not the case in practice. Then there is an automatic actuarial adjustment to the remaining life expectancy at the point of initial claim.

Normal retirement age

In many OECD countries, different normal retirement ages apply to different components of the overall retirement-income package. In particular, in those countries where targeted schemes have a higher eligibility age than the earnings-related scheme, the age of pension benefit withdrawal may in practice differ across earnings levels – individuals with high earnings-related pensions might afford to retire before having access to first-tier components. Pension schemes in 10 countries still specify normal retirement ages by gender setting a lower age for women than for men.

The OECD defines the normal retirement age in a given country as the age of eligibility of all schemes combined without penalty, based on a full career after labour market entry at age 22. Women in Chile, for example, are eligible for the defined contribution component at age 60 but they are not eligible to the targeted pension before age 65. The latter is therefore recorded as their normal retirement age in 2020 (Figure 3.6).

In 2020, the OECD average normal retirement age was equal to 64.2 years for men and 63.4 years for women. It ranges from 49 for women and 52 for men in Turkey to 67 in Iceland, Norway and, for men only, Israel. The statutory retirement age in Italy is 64 years 10 months but if the career length and retirement age combined sum to at least 100 then retirement is possible without penalty, at age 62 in 2020, which is therefore the 2020 normal retirement age; this condition is being removed from 2021 onwards. The largest gender difference of five years are in Austria, Colombia, Israel and Poland – the gap is also five years for the DC scheme in Chile but because women are only eligible to the targeted scheme at age 65, this difference is eliminated. In non-OECD G20 countries normal retirement ages tend to be lower, except for men in Argentina and Brazil at 65. Gender differences exist in half of those countries but not in India, Indonesia, Saudi Arabia and South Africa (Figure 3.6).

Table 3.5. **Current early and normal retirement ages by type of pension scheme**

For an individual retiring in 2020 after an uninterrupted career from age 22

		Scheme	Early	Normal
Australia		T	n.a.	66
		FDC	55	..
Austria	men	DB, Min	62	65
	women	DB, Min	n.a.	60
Belgium		DB	63	65
		Min	n.a.	65
Canada		Basic, T	n.a.	65
		DB	60	65
Chile		Min, T	n.a.	65
	men	FDC	any age & SL	65
	women	FDC	any age & SL	60
Colombia	men	DB, Min	n.a.	62
	men	FDC	any age & SL	62
	women	DB, Min	n.a.	57
	women	FDC	any age & SL	57
Costa Rica	men	DB, FDC	n.a.	61.9
	women	DB, FDC	n.a.	59.9
Czech Republic		Basic, DB, Min	60	63.7
Denmark		Basic, T	n.a.	65.5
		FDC (ATP)	65.5	..
		FDC (Occ)	60	..
Estonia		Basic, points	60.8	63.8
		FDC	62	..
Finland		DB	63	65
		T	63.8	65
France		DB, Min	62	63.5
		Points	55	64.5
Germany		Points	63.7	65.7
		T	n.a.	65.7
Greece		Basic, DB, NDC	62	62
Hungary	men	DB, Min	n.a.	64.5
	women	DB, Min	n.a.	62
Iceland		Basic, T	n.a.	67
		FDC (Occ)	65	67
Ireland		Basic	n.a.	66
Israel	men	Basic	n.a.	67
Israel (cont)	men	FDC	67	..
	women	FDC	62	
Italy		NDC / DB	62	62
Japan		Basic, DB	60	65
Korea		Basic, DB	57	62
Latvia		NDC, Min, FDC	61.8	63.8
Lithuania	men	Basic, points	59	64
	women	Basic, points	58	63
Luxembourg		Basic, DB, Min	62	62
Mexico		Min	60	65
		Basic	n.a.	68
		DB, FDC	60 or SL	..
Netherlands		Basic	n.a.	66.3
		DB (Occ)	sector-specific	..
New Zealand		Basic	n.a.	65
Norway		Basic, T	n.a.	67
		DB	62	67
		FDC	62	
Poland	men	DB / NDC, Min	n.a.	65
	women	DB / NDC, Min	n.a.	60
Portugal		DB	62	65.3
		Min	n.a.	65.3
Slovak Republic		Points, Min	60.7 & SL	62.7
Slovenia		DB, Min	60	62
Spain		DB, Min	63	65
Sweden		Basic, T	n.a.	65
		DB / NDC, FDC	62	..
		FDC (Occ)	55	65
Switzerland	men	DB, Min	63	65
	women	DB, Min	62	64
	men	DB (Occ)	58	65
	women	DB (Occ)	58	64
Turkey	men	DB, Min	n.a.	52
	women	DB, Min	n.a.	49
United Kingdom		Basic, DB	n.a.	66
United States		DB	62	66

Note: n.a. = early retirement or deferral of pension is not available; Occ = occupational, Min = minimum pension, SL = subsistence level reached, T = targeted,. = no normal retirement age indicated as benefits automatically adjusted to the age of retirement in an actuarially neutral way. Normal and early retirement ages for a scheme describe the ages at which the receipt of a pension, respectively, with and without penalties is first possible, assuming labour market entry at age 22 and an uninterrupted career. Credits for educational periods are not included.

Source: OECD based on information provided by countries; see "Country Profiles" available at *http://oe.cd/pag*.

StatLink https://stat.link/xl2acr

Figure 3.6. **Current normal retirement age by gender**

For an individual retiring in 2020 after an uninterrupted career from age 22

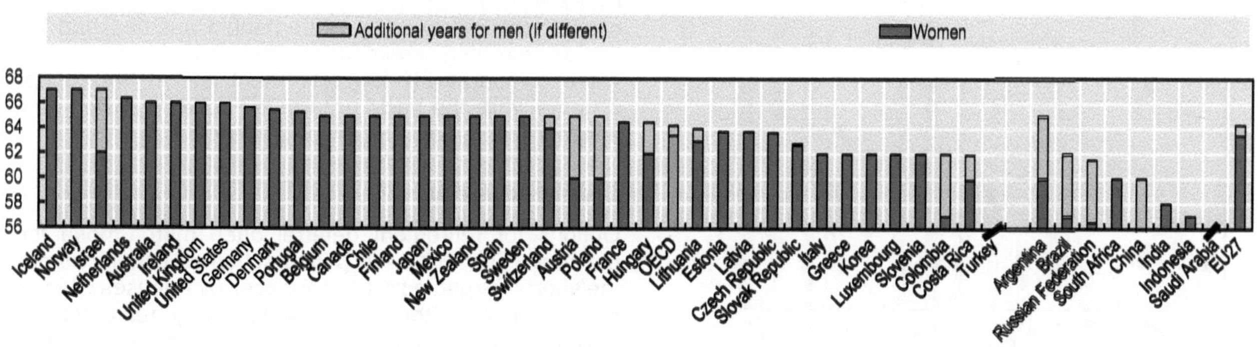

Note: For better visibility, the scale of this chart excludes the lowest observed values, which equal 47 for both men and women in Saudi Arabia, 49 and 52 for women and men, respectively, in Turkey. The retirement age for women in China depends on the type of work and lies between 50 and 60. Credits for educational periods are not included.

Source: OECD based on information provided by countries; see "Country Profiles" available at *http://oe.cd/pag*.

StatLink https://stat.link/3vszen

Key results

Future normal and early retirement ages will continue to rise. Assuming labour market entry at age 22 in 2020 the normal retirement age will increase to 66.1 for men and 65.5 for women on average across all OECD countries against 64.2 and 63.4 years, respectively, for retirement in 2020.

Normal retirement age

Across countries, the average normal retirement age for a man with a full career from age 22 equalled 64.2 years in 2020 (Figure 3.8). For the generation entering the labour market in 2020, this age will increase to 66.1 years (hence around 2064). Meanwhile, the remaining life expectancy of men at age 65 is projected to increase on average from 18.1 to 22.5 years (see Chapter 6). So, the average increase in men's normal retirement ages will account for about half the average increase in old-age life expectancy.

The normal retirement age of men will increase in 20 out of 38 OECD countries. The highest increase is projected for Turkey, from 52 currently to 65 years. Assuming that legislated life expectancy links are applied, also Denmark, from 65.5 to 74 years, and Estonia, from 63.8 to 71 years, will rapidly raise the retirement age. This is also true for Italy where the retirement age will increase from 62 in 2020 (as mentioned earlier, the retirement age in 2020 is temporarily lowered from 64.8 years) to 71 years for the modelled cohort.

The lowest future retirement age for men equals 62 in Colombia, Luxembourg and Slovenia. Normal retirement ages in G20 countries outside the OECD tend to be lower, both today and in the future; in Saudi Arabia even below 50 for both current and future retirees – the statutory retirement age is 58 but individuals can leave without penalty after 25 years so for this model the normal age is 47.

In 2020, gender differences in the normal retirement age existed in nine OECD countries (Figure 3.7). However, for the generation entering the labour market in 2020, gender gaps will have been phased out everywhere in the OECD except in Colombia, Hungary, Israel, Poland, Switzerland and Turkey (the legislated retirement age for women in Hungary is also 65, but they can leave without penalty after 40 years, hence 62 for this case). In Turkey, it will be phased out for those entering in 2028. Marked gender gaps also exist in several non-OECD G20 countries.

Table 3.6 shows the rules for early, normal and late retirement by pension scheme for a person entering the labour force at age 22 in 2020. The lowest normal age will apply in the FDC scheme of Chile for women, equalling 60 years. However, as women in Chile are not eligible to the targeted pension before 65 the latter is recorded as their normal retirement age.

Early retirement

Under the assumption of full annuitisation, FDC schemes benefits are automatically actuarially adjusted to the age at retirement and, therefore, only an early retirement age is specified, like in Norway and Sweden for NDC. The NDC schemes in Italy, Latvia and Poland still specify a standard retirement age indicated as normal age in the table.

All DB and points schemes, except in Colombia, Costa Rica, Hungary and Turkey, will allow to claim a pension early. In Luxembourg the early and normal retirement ages coincide for a full-career worker entering the labour market at age 22. Pension benefits for early retirees are usually reduced to reflect the longer durations in retirement. Only Belgium and Luxembourg do not impose such a penalty.

Residency-based basic and targeted schemes exclude the option for early pension receipt. The contribution-based schemes in the Czech Republic, Estonia, Greece, Japan, Korea and Luxembourg that pay both basic and earning-related components allow early retirement. Countries that combine basic or targeted schemes with occupational pensions typically set a comparatively low retirement age in the occupational scheme while the basic or targeted scheme assures a certain minimum retirement income only above 65.

Late retirement

Options for retirement deferral often mirror those for early pensions. DB, FDC and points schemes usually compensate the shorter expected retirement spell by bonuses which tend to be higher than the penalties for early retirement, with a maximum-rate of about 12% per year in case of a 10-year deferral in the basic/targeted scheme of Denmark and in some exceptional cases for a one-year deferral in the Portuguese DB scheme. Colombia, France in the mandatory occupational scheme, Greece and, again, Belgium and Luxembourg, deviate by not paying a deferral bonus in DB or points schemes. Many basic, minimum and targeted schemes do not pay a bonus either. Late retirement ages, maximum accrual rates and maximum pensions stop accrual of pension rights in some countries (see note of Table 3.4).

Figure 3.7. **Gender gap in current and future normal retirement ages**

Based on a full career from labour market entry at age 22

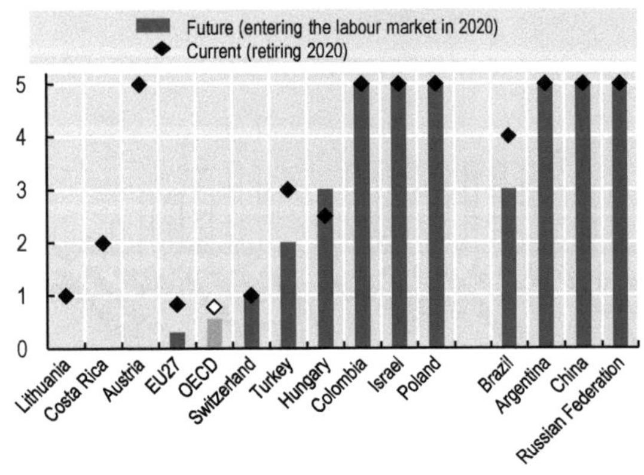

Note: See the StatLink.

Source: OECD based on information provided by countries.

StatLink https://stat.link/2cvxya

Figure 3.8. **Current and future normal retirement ages for a man with a full career from age 22**

Current and future refer to retiring 2020 and entering the labour market in 2020, respectively

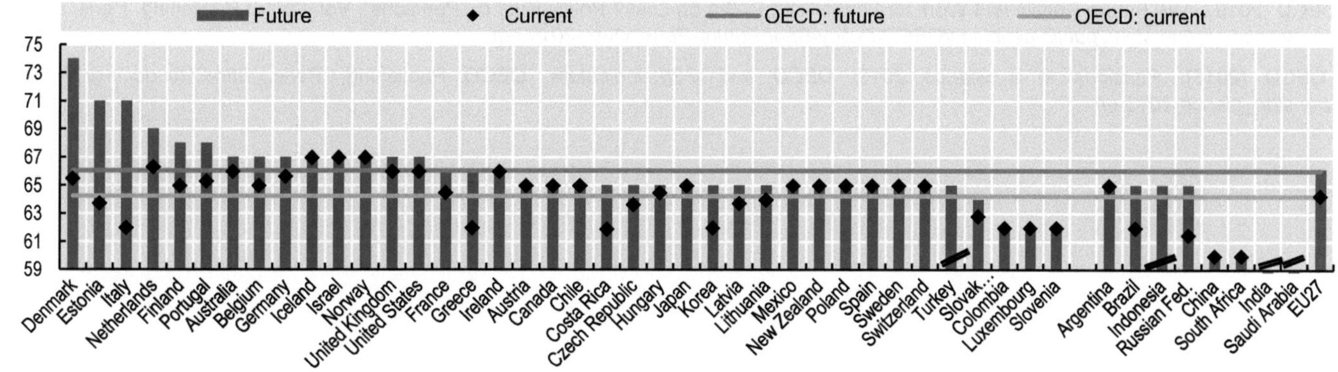

Note: For better visibility, the scale of this chart excludes the lowest observed values of 47 for both current and future in Saudi Arabia, 52 for current in Turkey, 57 for current in Indonesia and 58 for both current and future in India. Credits for educational periods are not included. More notes in the StatLink.

Source: OECD based on information provided by countries; see "Country Profiles" available at *http://oe.cd/pag*.

StatLink https://stat.link/9n57a3

Table 3.6. **Future ages, penalties and bonuses for early, normal and late retirement by type of pension scheme**

For an individual with an uninterrupted career after entering the labour market at age 22 in 2020

		Scheme	Early age	Penalty (p.a.)	Normal age	Bonus (p.a.)
Australia		T	n.a.		**67**	0.0%
		FDC	60	..		..
Austria		DB, Min	62	5.1%	**65**	4.2%
Belgium		DB	n.a.	0.0%	**67**	0.0%
		Min	n.a.		67	0.0%
Canada		Basic	n.a.		**65**	7.2%
		T	n.a.		65	0.0%
		DB	60	7.2%	65	8.4%
Chile		Min, T	n.a.		**65**	0.0%
	(M)	FDC	any age & SL	..	65	..
	(W)	FDC	any age & SL	..	60	..
Colombia	(M)	DB, Min	n.a.		**62**	
	(M)	FDC	any age & SL		62	
	(W)	DB, Min	n.a.		**57**	
	(W)	FDC	any age & SL		57	
Costa Rica		DB, FDC	n.a.		**65**	1.6%
Czech Republic		DB	60	3.6-6% [l]	**65**	6.0%
		Basic, Min	60	0.0%	65	0.0%
Denmark		Basic, T	n.a.		**74**	6.9-11.9% [l]
		FDC (ATP)	74	..		5.0%
		FDC (Occ)	68	..		..
Estonia		Basic, points	66	5.1%	**71**	5.6%
Finland		DB	65	4.8%	**68**	4.8%
		T	n.a.		68	4.8%
France		DB, Min	62	5.0%	65	5.0%
		Points	57	4-5.7.0% [l,y]	**66**	0.0%
Germany		Points	65	3.6%	**67**	6.0%
Greece		Basic, DB, NDC	66	6.0%	**66**	0.0%
Hungary	(M)	DB, Min	n.a.		**65**	6.0%
	(W)	DB, Min	n.a.		**62**	6.0%
Iceland		Basic, T	n.a.		**67**	6.0%
		FDC (Occ)	65	6.6%	67	6.0%
Ireland		Basic	n.a.		**66**	0.0%
Israel	(M)	Basic	n.a.		**67**	5.0%
	(W)	Basic	n.a.		**62**	5.0%
Israel (cont)	(M)	FDC	67			
	(W)	FDC	62			
Italy		NDC	68	..	**71**	..
Japan		Basic, DB	60	6.0%	**65**	8.4%
Korea		Basic, DB	60	6.0%	**65**	7.2%
Latvia		NDC, Min, FDC	63	..	**65**	..
Lithuania		Basic, Points	60	3.8%	**65**	8.0%
Luxembourg		Basic, DB, Min	62	0.0%	**62**	0.0%
Mexico		Basic	n.a.		**65**	
		Min	60		65	0.0%
		FDC	60 or SL	..		..
Netherlands		Basic	n.a.		**69**	0.0%
		DB (Occ)	sector-specific	..		..
New Zealand		Basic	n.a.		**65**	0.0%
Norway		T	n.a.		**67**	0.0%
		NDC	62	..		..
		FDC (Occ)	62	..		..
Poland	(M)	NDC, Min	n.a.		**65**	..
	(W)	NDC, Min	n.a.		**60**	..
Portugal		DB	25	7.8%	**68**	0.0-12.0% [l,w,y]
		Min	n.a.		68	0.0%
Slovak Republic		Points, Min	62 & SL	6.5%	**64**	6.0%
Slovenia		DB, Min	60	3.6%	**62**	3.0%
Spain		DB, Min	63	6.0% [y]	**65**	4.0% [y]
Sweden		T	n.a.		**65**	0.0%
		NDC, FDC	62	..		..
		FDC (Occ)	55	..	65	..
Switzerland	(M)	DB, Min	63	6.8%	**65**	5.2-6.3% [l]
	(W)	DB, Min	62	6.8%	**64**	5.2-6.3% [l]
	(M)	DB (Occ)	58	2.0-3.0% [l]	65	3.9-4.2% [l]
	(W)	DB (Occ)	58	2.0-3.0% [l]	64	3.9-4.2% [l]
Turkey	(M)	DB, Min	n.a.		**65**	0.0%
	(W)	DB, Min	n.a.		**63**	0.0%
United Kingdom		Basic	n.a.		**67**	5.8%
		FDC (Occ)	57		67	
United States		DB	62	6.7-5.0% [l]	**67**	8.0%

Note: See statlink.

Source: OECD based on information provided by countries; see "Country Profiles" available at *http://oe.cd/pag*.

StatLink https://stat.link/qfbnrc

[1] OECD (2019), *OECD Reviews of Pension Systems: Portugal*, OECD Reviews of Pension Systems, OECD Publishing, Paris, *https://dx.doi.org/10.1787/9789264313736-en*.

[2] OECD (2019), "Will Future Pensioners Work for Longer and Retire on Less? Policy Brief on Pensions", Vol. OECD Publishing, Paris, *https://www.oecd.org/pensions/public-pensions/OECD-Policy-Brief-Future-Pensioners-2019.pdf*.

[3] OECD (2015), *Pensions at a Glance 2015: OECD and G20 Indicators*, OECD Publishing, Paris, *https://dx.doi.org/10.1787/pension_glance-2015-en*.

Pensions at a Glance 2021
OECD and G20 Indicators

Chapter 4

Pension entitlements for the base case

Pension entitlements are calculated using the OECD pension models. The theoretical calculations relate to workers entering the labour market in 2020 aged 22 including the full impact of legislated pension reforms. A note on the methodology used and assumptions made precedes the pension indicators.

The indicators begin with the gross pension replacement rate in mandatory pension schemes: the ratio of pensions to individual earnings. The second shows the replacement rates for mandatory and voluntary pension schemes where these schemes have broad coverage. Thereafter follows an analysis of the tax treatment of pensions and pensioners. The fourth and fifth indicators show the net replacement rates, taking account of taxes and contributions. After this follows two indicators of pension wealth: the lifetime discounted value of the flow of retirement benefits. This indicator also takes into account the retirement age, indexation rules, and life expectancy, and is presented in gross and net terms.

Introduction

The indicators of pension entitlements that follow here in Chapter 4 use the OECD cohort-based pension models. The methodology and assumptions are common to the analysis of all countries, allowing the design of pension systems to be compared directly. This enables the comparison of future entitlements under today's parameters and rules.

The pension entitlements that are presented are those that are currently legislated in OECD countries. Reforms that have been legislated before publication are included where sufficient information is available. Changes that have already been legislated and are being phased in gradually are modelled from the year that they are implemented and onwards.

The values of all pension system parameters reflect the situation in 2020 and onwards. The calculations show the pension benefits of a worker who enters the system that year at age 22 – that worker is thus born in 1998 – and retires after a full career. The baseline results are shown for single individuals. All indexation and valorisation rules follow what is legislated in the baseline scenario.

Career length

A full career is defined here as entering the labour market at age of 22 and working until the normal pension age (see indicator on "Future retirement ages"). The implication is that the length of the career varies with the normal retirement age: 40 years for retirement at 62, 45 for retirement at 67, etc.

Coverage

The pension models presented here include all mandatory pension schemes for private-sector workers, regardless of whether they are public (i.e. they involve payments from government or from social security institutions, as defined in the System of National Accounts) or private. For each country, the main national scheme for private-sector employees is modelled. Schemes for civil servants, public-sector workers and special professional groups are excluded.

Schemes with near-universal coverage are also included, provided that they cover at least 85% of employees. Such plans are called "quasi-mandatory" in this report. They are particularly significant in Denmark, the Netherlands, Sweden and the United Kingdom. The United Kingdom has been added to this list for this edition, as 88% of eligible individuals were covered in 2019 (DWP, 2020[1]). More details are given in Box 1.3.

An increasing number of OECD countries have broad coverage of voluntary, occupational pensions and these play an important role in providing retirement incomes. For these countries, a second set of results for replacement rates is shown with entitlements from these voluntary pension plans.

Resource-tested benefits for which retired people may be eligible are also modelled. These can be means-tested, where both assets and income are taken into account, purely income-tested or withdrawn only against pension income. The calculations assume that all entitled pensioners take up these benefits. However, the only applicable asset or income included in the model is from the mandatory, and, if applicable, the voluntary pensions that have been accumulated.

Pension entitlements are compared for workers with a range of different earnings levels from 0.5 times the average worker earnings (AW). This range permits an analysis of future retirement benefits of both the poorest and richer workers.

Economic variables

The comparisons are based on a single set of economic assumptions for all the OECD countries and other major economies analysed. In practice, the level of pensions will be affected by economic growth, rate of return on financial assets, real-wage growth, discount rates and price inflation, and these will vary across countries. A single set of assumptions, however, ensures that the outcomes of the different pension regimes are not affected by different economic conditions. In this way, differences across countries in pension levels reflect differences in pension systems and policies alone. The baseline assumptions are set out below.

Price inflation is assumed to be 2% per year. ***Real earnings*** are assumed to grow by 1.25% per year on average (given the assumption for price inflation, this implies nominal wage growth of 3.275%). ***Individual earnings*** are assumed to grow in line with the economy-wide average. This means that the individual is assumed to remain at the same point in the earnings distribution, earning the same percentage of average earnings in every year of the working life. The net ***real rate of return*** on funded, defined contribution pensions is assumed to be 3% per year. Administrative charges, fee structures and the cost of buying an annuity are assumed to result in a ***defined contribution conversion factor*** of 90% applied to the accumulated defined contribution wealth when calculating the annuity. The ***real discount rate*** (for actuarial calculations) is assumed to be 2% per year. An indicator showing the impact of lower values of economic parameters is shown in Chapter 5; Chapter 4 in the 2015 edition of *Pensions at a Glance* includes a more detailed sensitivity analysis to the various parameters used here.

The baseline modelling uses country-specific projections of ***mortality rates*** from the United Nations population database for every year from 2020 to 2100. The mortality tables used include projected changes in mortality rates after the retirement age (cohort-based mortality projections).

The calculations assume that benefits from defined contribution plans are paid in the form of a price-indexed life annuity at an actuarially fair price assuming perfect foresight. This is calculated from the mortality projections once the conversion factor is taken into account. If people withdraw the money in alternative ways, the capital sum at the time of retirement is the same: it is only the way the benefits are spread that is changed. Similarly, the annuity rate in notional accounts schemes is calculated from mortality data using the indexation rules and discounting assumptions employed by the respective country.

Taxes and social security contributions

Information on personal income tax and social security contributions paid by pensioners, which were used to calculate pension entitlements, are in the "Country Profiles" available at *http://oe.cd/pag*.

The modelling assumes that tax systems and social-security contributions remain unchanged in the future. This constant policy assumption implicitly means that "value" parameters, such as tax allowances or contribution ceilings, are adjusted annually in line with average worker earnings, while "rate" parameters, such as the personal income tax schedule and social security contribution rates, remain unchanged.

General provisions and the tax treatment of workers for 2020 can be found in the OECD's *Taxing Wages* report. The conventions used in that report, such as which payments are considered taxes, are followed here.

Key results

The future gross replacement rate represents the level of pension benefits in retirement from mandatory public and private pension schemes relative to earnings when working. For workers with average earnings and a full career from age 22, the future gross replacement rate at the normal retirement age averages 51.8% for men and 50.9% for women in OECD countries, with substantial cross-country variation. At the bottom of the range, future gross replacement rates from mandatory schemes are below 30% at the average wage in Estonia, Ireland and Lithuania. Colombia, Denmark, Italy and Luxembourg offer replacement rates at 75% or more.

All of the replacement rates are calculated for full-career workers from the age of 22, which means that career lengths differ between countries. Denmark has an estimated long-term retirement age of 74 years for those starting in 2020, whilst in Colombia it will be 57 for women and 62 for men, and in both Luxembourg and Slovenia retirement will still be possible with a full pension at age 62 for both men and women (Table 4.1).

Full career male workers will have a replacement rate of 51.8% on average across OECD countries, with a high of 75% or more in Colombia, Denmark, Italy and Luxembourg and a low of under 30% in Estonia, Ireland and Lithuania. The average for women is slightly lower, at 50.9%.

Most OECD countries aim to protect low-income workers (here defined as workers earning half of average worker earnings) from old-age poverty, which results in higher replacement rates for them than for average earners. Low-income workers would receive gross replacement rates averaging 65%. Some countries, such as Australia and Ireland, pay relatively small benefits to average earners, but are closer to or even above average for low-income workers. Australia, the Czech Republic, Denmark and Ireland record the largest difference between gross replacement rates applying to low-wage and average-wage workers, of about 30 percentage points or more. However, projected replacement rates in eight countries are the same for a full career at average and half-average pay: Austria, Finland, France, Hungary, Italy, Latvia, Spain and Turkey.

At the top of the range, based on current legislation, low earners in Denmark will receive a future gross replacement rate of 125% after a full career; retirement benefits are thus higher than their earnings when working. At the other end of the scale, Lithuania and Poland offer gross replacement rates of 32% to low-income earners, thus implying a gross retirement income around 16% of average earnings after a full career. On average, the gross replacement rate at twice average earnings (here called "high earnings") is 44%. Replacement rates for these high earners equal 70% or more in Colombia, Italy, Portugal and Turkey, while at the other end of the spectrum, Estonia, Ireland, Korea, Lithuania and New Zealand offer a replacement rate lower than 20%.

Gross pension replacement rates differ for women in eight countries, due to a lower future pension eligibility age than for men (Colombia, Hungary, Israel, Poland and Turkey) and the use of sex specific mortality rates to compute annuities (Australia, Chile and Mexico). The replacement rates are expressed as percentage of earnings which are not gender specific. Differences between the sexes are substantial in Australia, Chile, Hungary, and especially Israel and Poland, with replacement rates (i.e. monthly benefits) for women being between 7% and 26% lower than for men.

Gross pension replacement rates fall with age from 52% on average at the time of retirement to 46% at age of 80, a fall of 11% relative to average wages. This difference is due to the indexation of pension benefits in payment, which do not follow wages in many countries. With price indexation from a normal retirement age of 65, the fall is equal to 17% based on the OECD model assumptions. The earlier the normal retirement age the larger the fall with price indexation. The largest fall of about 20% is found in Sweden because the indexation of the NDC schemes is wages minus 1.6%, which is less than price indexation in the OECD model. Countries where the indexation of pension benefits follows wages – Ireland and New Zealand – have the same replacement rate at age 80 than at the normal retirement age. Australia actually shows a large increase in the replacement rate at age 80 compared to normal retirement age, because the means-tested component is not available for average earner retirees at the retirement age as their DC pension has a capital value over the ceiling, but as the capital diminishes eligibility to the Age Pension increases.

Definition and measurement

The old-age pension replacement rate measures how effectively a pension system provides a retirement income to replace earnings, the main source of income before retirement. The gross replacement rate is defined as gross pension entitlement divided by gross pre-retirement earnings. Under the baseline assumptions, workers earn the same percentage of average worker earnings throughout their career. Therefore, final earnings are equal to lifetime average earnings revalued in line with economy-wide earnings growth. Replacement rates expressed as a percentage of final earnings are thus identical to those expressed as a percentage of lifetime earnings.

Table 4.1. **Gross pension replacement rates by earnings, percentage, mandatory schemes**

Individual earnings, multiple of mean for men (women where different)

	Pension age		0.5		1		2	
Australia	67		62.7	(59.8)	31.3	(28.4)	31.3	(28.4)
Austria	65		74.1		74.1		57.3	
Belgium	67		67.5		43.4		29.2	
Canada	65		53.2		38.8		22.3	
Chile	65		41.9	(40.4)	31.2	(28.8)	31.3	(28.8)
Colombia*	62	(57)	100.0		74.8	(73.4)	74.8	(72.4)
Costa Rica	65		73.1		71.9		68.0	
Czech Republic	65		81.2		49.0		32.9	
Denmark	74		125.1		80.0		61.3	
Estonia	71		47.6		27.9		18.1	
Finland	68		56.6		56.6		56.6	
France	66		60.2		60.2		51.9	
Germany	67		46.5		41.5		33.0	
Greece	66		84.7		72.6		66.5	
Hungary	65	(62)	62.5	(58.1)	62.5	(58.1)	62.5	(58.1)
Iceland	67		72.9		51.8		51.8	
Ireland	66		59.4		29.7		14.9	
Israel	67	(62)	61.7	(52.4)	41.5	(34.1)	20.7	(17.0)
Italy	71		74.6		74.6		74.6	
Japan	65		43.2		32.4		26.9	
Korea	65		43.1		31.2		18.6	
Latvia	65		43.4		43.4		43.4	
Lithuania	65		31.5		19.7		13.8	
Luxembourg	62		90.4		76.6		69.7	
Mexico	65		80.9		61.2	(58.2)	53.6	(50.5)

	Pension age		0.5		1.0		2	
Netherlands	69		73.1		69.7		68.0	
New Zealand*	65		65.9		39.8		19.9	
Norway	67		60.6		46.0		28.9	
Poland	65	(60)	31.8	(31.9)	30.6	(23.4)	30.0	(22.8)
Portugal	68		76.3		74.9		72.5	
Slovak Republic*	64		62.6		53.1		46.7	
Slovenia*	62		62.3		42.0		41.4	
Spain	65		73.9		73.9		67.0	
Sweden	65		61.4		53.3		67.2	
Switzerland	65	(64)	53.1	(52.5)	44.1	(43.5)	23.0	(22.7)
Turkey	65	(63)	73.3	(70.3)	73.3	(70.3)	73.3	(70.3)
United Kingdom	67		70.6		49.0		38.2	
United States	67		49.6		39.2		27.9	
OECD	**66.1**	**(65.5)**	**64.5**	**(64.0)**	**51.8**	**(50.9)**	**44.4**	**(43.7)**
Argentina	65	(60)	99.0	(92.7)	76.1	(72.9)	64.6	(63.0)
Brazil	65	(62)	88.4	(93.3)	88.4	(93.3)	84.8	(90.6)
China	60	(55)	90.6	(72.2)	71.6	(55.7)	62.1	(47.5)
India	58		56.4	(55.6)	56.4	(55.6)	37.7	(36.9)
Indonesia	65		55.3	(53.0)	55.3	(53.0)	55.3	(53.0)
Russian Federation	65	(60)	56.9	(53.8)	47.2	(43.4)	42.3	(38.2)
Saudi Arabia	47		59.6		59.6		59.6	
South Africa	60		29.8		14.9		7.4	
EU27	66.0	(65.9)	63.6	(63.4)	53.4	(52.8)	48.1	(47.6)

Note: *Low earners in Colombia, New Zealand, the Slovak Republic and Slovenia are at 66%, 60%, 53% and 55% of average earnings, respectively, to account for the minimum wage level. Due to a change in methodology, the Korean replacement rates are lower than in previous editions (see country profile at *http://oe.cd/pag*).
Source: OECD pension models.

StatLink https://stat.link/b2f0ws

Figure 4.1. **Gross pension replacement rates, percentage: Average earners at retirement age and age 80**

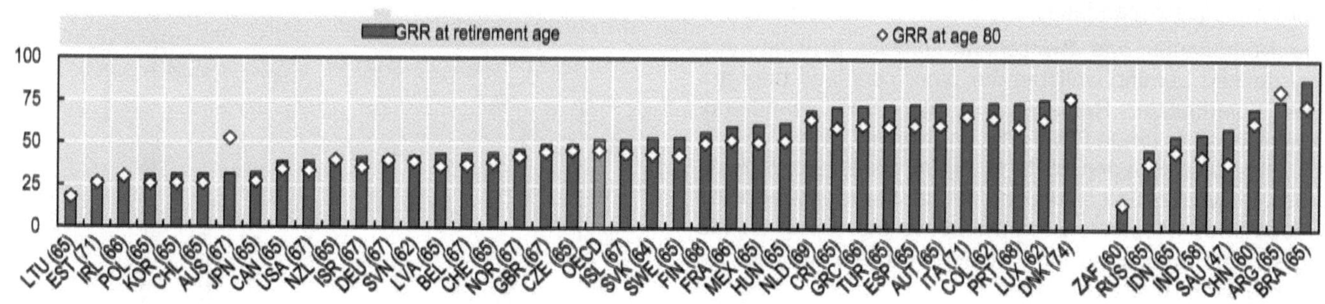

Source: OECD pension models.

StatLink https://stat.link/81n75q

Figure 4.2. **Gross pension replacement rates, percentage: Low and high earners**

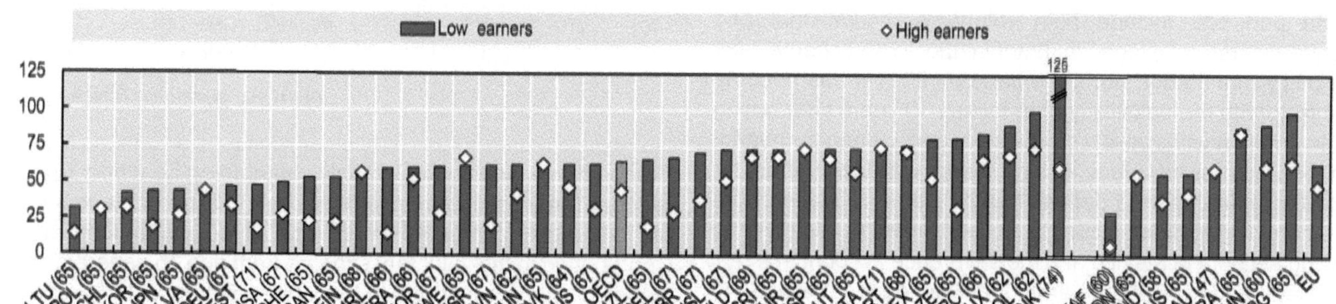

Source: OECD pension models.

StatLink https://stat.link/qv42hy

Key results

Private pensions play a significant role in over one-third of OECD countries. For mandatory schemes, the OECD average for gross replacement rates of an average earner from public schemes alone is 42%, compared with 52% with private pensions included. For the nine OECD countries where voluntary private pensions are widespread the average replacement rate is 56% for an average earner choosing to contribute for the whole career, while it is 58% – which is also the total OECD average – when Israel and Mexico are also included compared with 38% when only mandatory schemes are considered. If the full-career average-wage earner only starts contributing in a voluntary scheme from age 45, the replacement rate is 43% on average among these nine countries.

Table 4.2 shows the interplay between mandatory public, mandatory private and voluntary pension schemes. As shown in the previous indicator, the average replacement rate from mandatory schemes for a full-career average earner is equal to 52%: for the 17 OECD countries where the calculations of entitlements only cover mandatory public pensions, the average replacement rate for an average worker earner is 60%; for the 10 OECD countries with both public and mandatory private provision but no voluntary, the average replacement rate is 53%; and for the last 11 countries with significant voluntary pensions, the replacement rate from the mandatory component alone is 38%.

Mandatory private pensions

Mandatory private pensions exist in 12 countries including Denmark, the Netherlands, Sweden and the United Kingdom where private pensions have near-universal coverage, and are described as "quasi-mandatory".

In the Netherlands and Switzerland, private pensions are mainly defined benefit, whilst in the other countries they are defined contribution. Replacement rates from mandatory private schemes range from 7% in Norway and 12% in Costa Rica and Sweden to 51% in Denmark and 52% in Iceland. In Sweden the contribution rate for the private pension increases from 4.5% below to 30% above the ceiling for the public scheme, hence the total replacement rate is higher for high earners than average earners.

Voluntary private pensions

Voluntary private pensions are shown for nine countries where voluntary private pensions have broad coverage (either assets are above 25% of GDP or coverage is above 75%). Voluntary private pensions include both voluntary occupational and voluntary personal plans. In Estonia the FDC scheme was previously mandatory, but since January 2021 it has become voluntary, with the possibility of re-joining 10 years after opting out. In addition withdrawals of funds have also been permitted, with one-quarter of funds having been withdrawn thus far (Chapter 1). In Japan, a defined benefit plan is modelled, with the others having defined contribution schemes. In addition, the housing account in Mexico and the severance account in Israel have been added as if they are not utilised during the working career, they are then transferred to the pension accounts at retirement.

When voluntary private pensions are taken into account for the whole career in Belgium, Canada, Estonia, Germany, Ireland, Israel, Japan, Lithuania, Mexico, New Zealand and the United States the average replacement, for these 11 countries, is 58% for an average earner compared with 38% when only mandatory schemes are considered. The voluntary component has the largest impact on the replacement rate, more than 30 and 40 percentage points, in Ireland and the United States, respectively.

The length of the contribution period clearly has an impact on the total replacement rate. The chart below compares the full-career full-contribution case with the full-career case but with contributions in the voluntary scheme from age 35 and 45 only, perhaps a more appropriate scenario. The schemes in Israel and Mexico are not considered as contributions are mandatory at all ages to severance and housing accounts respectively.

Gross replacement rate including voluntary contributions from different ages, percentage

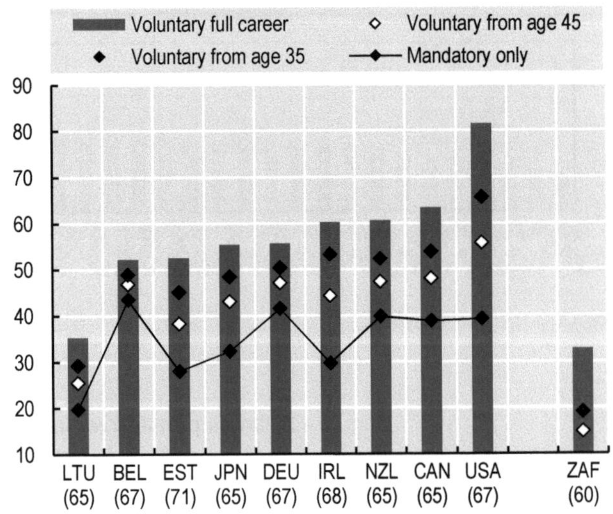

StatLink https://stat.link/oxijbf

Among these nine countries, only contributing from age 35 (45) reduces the gross replacement rate by 7 (13) percentage points on average compared with the full-contribution case. Contributing to the voluntary scheme from age 35 generates the highest replacement rates in the United States, at 66%, above the OECD average for a full career worker.

Table 4.2. **Gross pension replacement rates from mandatory public, mandatory private and voluntary private pension schemes**

Percentage of individual earnings

	Mandatory Public			Mandatory private (DB & DC)			Total mandatory			Voluntary (DB & DC)			Total with voluntary		
	0.5	1	2	0.5	1	2	0.5	1	2	0.5	1	2	0.5	1	2
Australia	31.4	0.0	0.0	31.3	31.3	31.3	62.7	31.3	31.3						
Austria	74.1	74.1	57.3				74.1	74.1	57.3						
Belgium	67.5	43.4	29.2				67.5	43.4	29.2	3.4	8.7	22.7	70.9	52.2	51.9
Canada	53.2	38.8	22.3				53.2	38.8	22.3	24.5	24.5	24.5	70.9	63.3	46.8
Chile	10.8	0.0	0.0	31.1	31.2	31.3	41.9	31.2	31.3						
Colombia*	100.0	74.8	74.8				100.0	74.8	74.8						
Costa Rica	61.3	60.1	56.2	11.8	11.8	11.8	73.1	71.9	68.0						
Czech Republic	81.2	49.0	32.9				81.2	49.0	32.9						
Denmark	74.6	29.5	10.7	50.5	50.5	50.5	125.1	80.0	61.3						
Estonia	47.6	27.9	18.1				47.6	27.9	18.1	27.6	27.6	27.6	70.6	52.4	43.4
Finland	56.6	56.6	56.6				56.6	56.6	56.6						
France	60.2	60.2	51.9				60.2	60.2	51.9						
Germany	46.5	41.5	33.0				46.5	41.5	33.0	14.1	14.1	14.1	60.2	55.7	47.2
Greece	84.7	72.6	66.5				84.7	72.6	66.5						
Hungary	62.5	62.5	62.5				62.5	62.5	62.5						
Iceland	21.1	0.0	0.0	51.8	51.8	51.8	72.9	51.8	51.8						
Ireland	59.4	29.7	14.9				59.4	29.7	14.9	30.5	30.5	30.5	89.9	60.2	45.3
Israel	20.4	10.2	5.1	41.3	31.3	15.6	61.7	41.5	20.7	19.8	15.0	7.5	81.6	56.5	28.2
Italy	74.6	74.6	74.6				74.6	74.6	74.6						
Japan	43.2	32.4	26.9				43.2	32.4	26.9	23.1	23.1	23.1	66.3	55.4	50.0
Korea	43.1	31.2	18.6				43.1	31.2	18.6						
Latvia	43.4	43.4	43.4				43.4	43.4	43.4						
Lithuania	31.5	19.7	13.8				31.5	19.7	13.8	20.6	15.6	13.1	52.0	35.3	26.9
Luxembourg	90.4	76.6	69.7				90.4	76.6	69.7						
Mexico	38.6	15.2	7.6	35.1	46.0	46.0	80.9	61.2	53.6	17.3	17.3	17.3	91.1	78.5	70.9
Netherlands	58.4	29.2	14.6	14.7	40.5	53.4	73.1	69.7	68.0						
New Zealand*	65.9	39.8	19.9				65.9	39.8	19.9	21.8	20.8	20.0	87.7	60.6	39.9
Norway	54.1	39.4	22.5	6.5	6.6	6.4	60.6	46.0	28.9						
Poland	31.8	30.6	30.0				31.8	30.6	30.0						
Portugal	76.3	74.9	72.5				76.3	74.9	72.5						
Slovak Republic*	62.6	53.1	46.7				62.6	53.1	46.7						
Slovenia*	62.3	42.0	41.4				62.3	42.0	41.4						
Spain	73.9	73.9	67.0				73.9	73.9	67.0						
Sweden	49.5	41.3	23.9	12.0	12.0	43.3	61.4	53.3	67.2						
Switzerland	33.3	22.1	12.0	19.8	22.1	11.0	53.1	44.1	23.0						
Turkey	73.3	73.3	73.3				73.3	73.3	73.3						
United Kingdom	43.3	21.6	10.8	27.4	27.4	27.4	70.6	49.0	38.2						
United States	49.6	39.2	27.9				49.6	39.2	27.9	42.1	42.1	42.1	91.8	81.3	70.0
OECD	**55.6**	**42.2**	**34.4**				**64.5**	**51.8**	**44.4**				**70.1**	**57.6**	**50.4**
Argentina	99.0	76.1	64.6				99.0	76.1	64.6						
Brazil	88.4	88.4	84.8				88.4	88.4	84.8						
China	90.6	71.6	62.1				90.6	71.6	62.1						
India	46.7	46.7	28.0	9.6	9.6	9.6	56.4	56.4	37.7						
Indonesia	33.1	33.1	33.1	22.2	22.2	22.2	55.3	55.3	55.3						
Russian Federation	56.9	47.2	42.3				56.9	47.2	42.3						
Saudi Arabia	59.6	59.6	59.6				59.6	59.6	59.6						
South Africa	29.8	14.9	7.4				29.8	14.9	7.4	32.8	32.8	32.8	32.8	32.8	32.8
EU27	58.6	47.4	40.6				63.6	53.4	48.1				65.4	55.3	50.6

Note: DB=defined benefit; DC = defined contribution. *Low earners in Colombia, New Zealand, the Slovak Republic and Slovenia are at 66%, 60%, 53% and 55% of average earnings, respectively, to account for the minimum wage level. Contribution rates for voluntary pensions in Belgium vary by earnings level, see country profile for more details. The OECD average refers to the average of all 38 OECD countries.

Source: OECD pension models.

StatLink https://stat.link/uwc8nt

Key results

The personal tax system plays an important role in old-age support. Pensioners often do not pay social security contributions. Personal income taxes are progressive and pension entitlements are usually lower than earnings before retirement, so the average tax rate on pension income is typically less than the tax rate on labour income. In addition, half of OECD countries give additional tax concessions to pensioners through either increased personal allowances or extra tax credits.

Half of OECD countries provide either higher personal allowances or extra tax credits to older people. In many cases – Canada and the United Kingdom, for example – this additional relief is phased out for older people with higher incomes. This relief is irrespective of the source of income and so will include earned income at older ages.

In addition, 16 OECD countries have specific tax rules for income from pensions, from either public or private schemes. For example, between 15% and 50% of income from public pensions in the United States (social security) is not taxed, depending on the total income of the pensioner. In Australia, benefits derived from pension contributions and investment returns, which have both been taxed, are not taxable in payment for over 60s. This applies to the mandatory defined contribution scheme and voluntary contributions to such plans.

By contrast some countries such as Denmark, Iceland, the Netherlands and Sweden tax earned income from work less than pensions.

Overall, 28 OECD countries have some concession for older people or pension income under their personal income taxes. In only ten countries are the tax rates applied to pensions and pensioners at least equal to those for people of working age.

Virtually all OECD countries levy employee social security contributions on workers: Australia and New Zealand are the only exceptions. In addition to these two countries, a further 19 do not levy social security contributions on pensioners. The rate of contributions in the 17 countries that do levy social security contributions on retirees is always lower than the rate charged on workers. Typically, old-age retirement income is not subject to contributions for pensions or unemployment (for obvious reasons). However, pensioners can be subject to levies to pay for health or long-term care, which can be higher than the level applied to workers, and, in some cases, are liable for "solidarity" contributions to finance a broad range of benefits.

Empirical results

Figure 4.4 shows the percentage of income paid in taxes and contribution by workers and pensioners. Starting with workers, countries have been ranked by the proportion of income paid in total taxes (including social contributions paid by employees) at the average-wage level. This is then compared to the total tax rate paid by a pensioner after a full-career at the average wage, hence receiving the gross replacement rate in the base case (Table 4.1, as set out in the Indicator "Gross pension replacement rates" above).

In 11 OECD countries and six other major economies, such a pensioner would not pay any tax in retirement. In some cases, such as the Slovak Republic and Turkey, this is because pensions are not taxable. In the United States it is because the pension income would be less than the income-tax personal allowance offered to older people. Pensioners with the gross replacement rate of a full-career average earner would pay 10% of their income in taxes and contributions on average across the OECD, and under 1% in the other G20 countries. By comparison, taxes and contributions paid by an average earner – so not including any contributions from the employer – average 26% of the gross wage in OECD countries and 13% in other G20 countries.

The last series in the chart shows how much a pensioner would pay if her income before tax is equal to the gross average wage. The total tax rate is 16% on average in OECD countries, some 10 percentage points lower than what workers pay with the same level of income.

The difference between this 16% rate for pensioners with an income equal to average earnings and the 10% paid in taxes and contributions paid on the income which is equal to the gross replacement rate for an average earner illustrates the impact of progressivity in income-tax systems for pensioners.

Table 4.3. **Treatment of pensions and pensioners under personal income tax and mandatory public and private contributions**

	Extra tax	Full or partial relief for pension income		Mandatory contributions on pension income
	Allowance/credit	Public scheme	Private scheme	
Australia	✓	✓	✓	*None*
Austria				*Low*
Belgium		✓		*Low*
Canada	✓	✓	✓	*None*
Chile	✓			*None*
Czech Republic	✓	✓		*None*
Colombia				*Low*
Costa Rica				*Low*
Denmark				*None*
Estonia	✓			*None*
Finland		✓		*Low*
France				*Low*
Germany		✓	✓	*Low*
Greece				*Low*
Hungary		✓	✓	*None*
Iceland				*None*
Ireland	✓			*Low*
Israel	✓			*Low*
Italy	✓		✓	*None*
Japan	✓	✓	✓	*Low*
Korea	✓	✓		*None*
Latvia	✓			*None*
Lithuania		✓	✓	*None*
Luxembourg	✓			*Low*
Mexico			✓	*None*
Netherlands	✓			*Low*
New Zealand				*None*
Norway	✓	✓		*Low*
Poland				*Low*
Portugal	✓			*None*
Slovak Republic		✓		*None*
Slovenia	✓			*Low*
Spain		✓		*None*
Sweden	✓			*None*
Switzerland				*Low*
Turkey		✓		*None*
United Kingdom	✓			*None*
United States	✓	✓		*None*
Argentina		✓		*Low*
Brazil		✓		*None*
China				*None*
India	✓			*None*
Indonesia				*None*
Russian Federation				*Low*
Saudi Arabia				*Low*
South Africa	✓			*None*

Source: See online "Country Profiles available at *http://oe.cd/pag*.

StatLink https://stat.link/ej4iy2

Figure 4.3. **Personal income taxes and social security contributions paid by pensioners and workers**

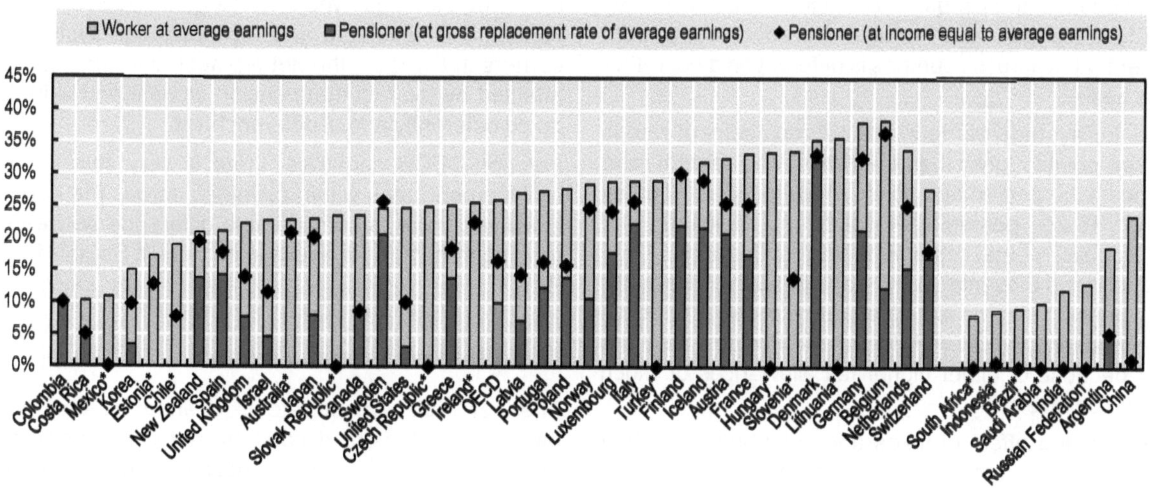

Note: *Pensioners at the gross replacement rate of average earnings have zero income tax and social security. Workers in Colombia at the average earnings pay 8% in taxes and social security contributions, lower than that of pensioners at the gross replacement rate of average earnings.
Source: OECD pension models; OECD tax and benefit models.

StatLink https://stat.link/tzi32g

Key results

Whilst the gross replacement rate gives a clear indication of the design of the pension system, the net replacement matters more to individuals, as it reflects their disposable income in retirement in comparison to when working. For average earners with a full career, the net replacement rate from mandatory pension schemes at the normal retirement age averages 62.4% across the OECD, which is 10.6 percentage points higher than the average gross replacement rate. This reflects the higher effective tax and social contribution rates that people pay on their earnings than on their pensions in retirement, mostly due to the progressivity of tax systems, some tax advantages to pensions and lower social contributions on pension benefits. Net replacement rates vary across a large range, from under 35% in Estonia and Lithuania to 90% or more in Hungary, Portugal and Turkey for average-wage workers. For low earners (with half of average worker earnings), the average net replacement rate across OECD countries is 74.4% while it is 54.9% for high earners (200% of average worker earnings).

The previous indicator of the "Tax treatment of pensions and pensioners" showed the important role that the personal tax and social security contribution systems play in old-age income support. Pensioners often only pay health contributions and receive preferential treatment under the income tax. Tax expenditures and the progressivity of income taxes coupled with gross replacement rates of less than 100% also mean that pensioners have a lower income tax rate than workers. As a result, net replacement rates are generally higher than gross replacement rates.

For average earners, the net replacement rate across the OECD averages 62% for mandatory schemes, from a low of under 35% in Estonia and Lithuania to a high of 103% in Turkey and over 90% in Hungary and Portugal. Moreover, the pattern of replacement rates across countries is different on a net rather than a gross basis.

On average, for average earners, the net replacement rate is 10 percentage points higher than the gross replacement rate. The difference is 30 percentage points in Hungary and Turkey and around 15-25 percentage points in Belgium, the Czech Republic, the Netherlands, Portugal, the Slovak Republic and Slovenia. In Hungary, the Slovak Republic and Turkey, pension income is neither liable for taxes or social security contributions, whilst in Belgium and Portugal they are much lower because of either higher tax allowances or much lower contribution levels.

For low earners, the effect of taxes and contributions on net replacement rates is slightly more muted than for workers higher up the earnings scale. This is because low-income workers typically pay less in taxes and contributions relative to average earners. In many cases, their retirement incomes are below the level of the standard reliefs in the personal income tax (allowances, credits, etc.). Thus, they are often unable to benefit fully from any additional concessions granted to pensions or pensioners under their personal income tax.

The difference between gross and net replacement rates for low earners is 10 percentage points on average. The Czech Republic, Germany, Hungary, Slovenia and Turkey have much higher replacement rates for low earners on a net basis than in gross terms. The net replacement rate for workers earning 200% of the average is highest in Turkey. The lowest replacement rates for high earners are found in Canada, Estonia, Ireland, Israel, Japan, Korea, Lithuania, New Zealand and Switzerland where workers earning 200% of the average will receive net pensions that amount to less than one-third of their net earnings when working. In addition to the higher contribution levels in the occupational system for higher earners in Sweden, the net replacement rates are furthermore affected by the fact that pension income and work income are taxed differently and at different rates.

For non-OECD countries, there is very little variation in net replacement rates within countries across the earnings range. However, there is considerable difference between countries, ranging from 16% for average earners in South Africa to 97% in Brazil.

Definition and measurement

The net replacement rate is defined as the individual net pension entitlement divided by net pre-retirement earnings, taking account of personal income taxes and social security contributions paid by workers and pensioners. Otherwise, the definition and measurement of the net replacement rates are the same as for the gross replacement rate. Details of the rules that national tax systems apply to pensioners can be found in the online Country Profiles available at *http://oe.cd/pag*.

Table 4.4. **Net pension replacement rates by earnings, percentage**

Individual earnings, multiple of mean for men (women where different)

	Pension age		0.5		1		2	
Australia	67		70.3	(67.1)	40.5	(36.8)	39.1	(36.4)
Austria	65		84.4		87.1		67.6	
Belgium	67		83.0		61.9		43.9	
Canada	65		62.0		46.4		28.4	
Chile	65		51.6	(49.8)	38.5	(35.4)	36.6	(33.7)
Colombia*	62	(57)	104.3		73.1	(71.8)	71.5	(69.3)
Costa Rica	65		77.3		76.0		73.2	
Czech Republic	65		100.0		65.2		45.7	
Denmark	74		124.7		84.0		71.4	
Estonia	71		52.0		33.7		23.5	
Finland	68		63.8		63.2		64.3	
France	66		71.3		74.4		64.5	
Germany	67		57.9		52.9		41.9	
Greece	66		94.1		83.6		77.5	
Hungary	65	(62)	94.0	(87.4)	94.0	(87.4)	94.0	(87.4)
Iceland	67		81.3		59.7		59.9	
Ireland	66		67.5		39.9		24.0	
Israel	67	(62)	67.0	(56.3)	51.2	(42.1)	29.6	(24.3)
Italy	71		78.4		81.7		84.6	
Japan	65		49.5		38.7		31.6	
Korea	65		45.8		35.4		22.5	
Latvia	65		55.4		55.3		52.9	
Lithuania	65		44.0		30.7		22.8	
Luxembourg	62		98.9		88.7		80.2	
Mexico	65		82.0		68.6	(65.2)	64.3	(60.6)

	Pension age		0.5		1.0		2	
Netherlands	69		94.3		89.2		87.0	
New Zealand*	65		68.0		43.3		23.7	
Norway	67		76.3		55.7		36.2	
Poland	65	(60)	39.1	(39.3)	36.5	(28.2)	36.8	(28.1)
Portugal	68		88.5		90.3		89.7	
Slovak Republic*	64		76.2		69.4		64.3	
Slovenia*	62		87.3		63.3		59.2	
Spain	65		80.1		80.3		74.7	
Sweden	65		65.1		56.2		75.3	
Switzerland	65	(64)	57.8	(57.0)	50.7	(49.7)	27.9	(27.4)
Turkey	65	(63)	94.8	(90.9)	103.3	(99.1)	110.8	(106.3)
United Kingdom	67		79.2		58.1		47.7	
United States	67		61.0		50.5		39.0	
OECD	**66.1**	**(65.5)**	**74.4**	**(73.7)**	**62.4**	**(61.3)**	**54.9**	**(54.0)**
Argentina	65	(60)	114.1	(106.9)	88.9	(85.3)	86.5	(84.4)
Brazil	65	(62)	95.7	(101.0)	97.3	(102.7)	102.3	(109.3)
China	60	(55)	114.9	(91.8)	92.4	(72.3)	81.0	(63.0)
India	58		64.0	(63.1)	64.0	(63.1)	43.0	(42.1)
Indonesia	65		60.6	(58.1)	60.6	(58.1)	60.6	(58.2)
Russian Federation	65	(60)	65.4	(61.9)	54.2	(49.9)	48.6	(44.0)
Saudi Arabia	47		66.2		66.2		66.2	
South Africa	60		29.8		16.2		8.8	
EU27	66.1	(65.9)	75.7	(75.3)	66.7	(66.0)	60.8	(60.1

Note: * Low earners in Colombia, New Zealand, the Slovak Republic and Slovenia are at 66%, 60%, 53% and 55% of average earnings, respectively, to account for the minimum wage level. Due to a change in methodology, the Korean replacement rates are lower than in previous editions (see country profile at *http://oe.cd/pag*).
Source: OECD pension models.

StatLink https://stat.link/cofr31

Figure 4.4. **Net pension replacement rates: Average earners, percentage**

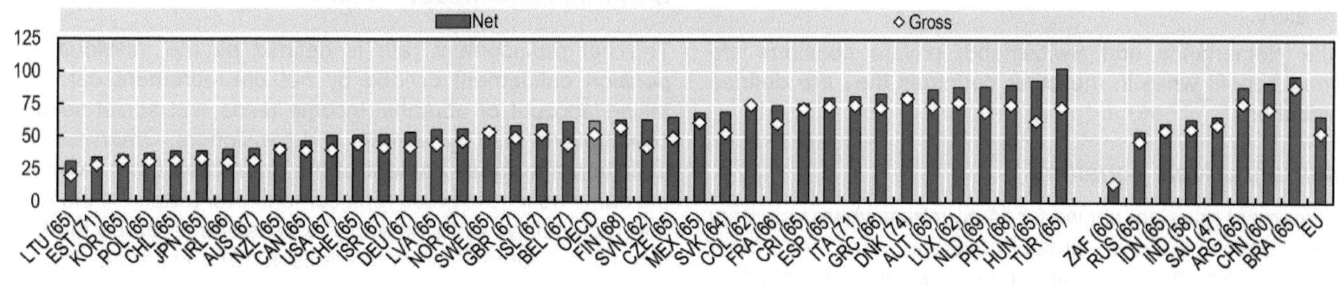

Source: OECD pension models.

StatLink https://stat.link/35c4tz

Figure 4.5. **Net pension replacement rates: Low and high earners, percentage**

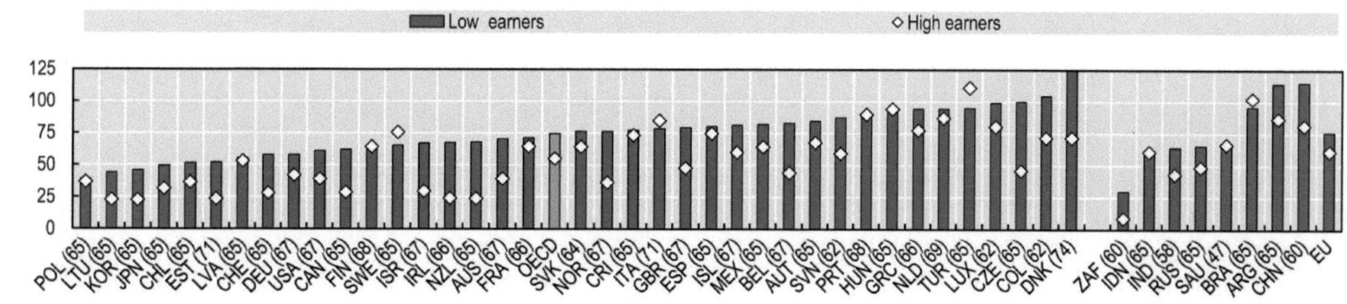

Source: OECD pension models.

StatLink https://stat.link/oher2v

Key results

The OECD average for net replacement rates of an average earner from mandatory (public and private) schemes is 62%. Among the nine OECD countries where voluntary private pensions are widespread, and Israel and Mexico, when voluntary private pensions are taken into account for a full career of contributions, the average net replacement rate is 70% compared with 47% when only mandatory schemes are taken into account.

For the 17 OECD countries where the calculations cover only public pensions, the net replacement rate for a full-career average earner is 73% on average. For the 10 OECD countries with public and mandatory private provision, but no voluntary schemes the average net replacement rate is 61%. In the 11 countries where voluntary pensions are modelled the average net replacement rate is 47% from mandatory schemes and reaches 70% for a worker choosing to contribute for the whole career.

For the other major economies, although there is a wide variation between country and across earnings level, there is a smaller difference between gross and net replacement rates as pensions are not normally liable for any taxation.

Mandatory private pensions

Twelve countries have mandatory private pensions, including a subset of four countries – Denmark, the Netherlands, Sweden and the United Kingdom – having private pensions that ensure near-universal coverage and so are described as "quasi-mandatory.

In the Netherlands and Switzerland, private pensions are defined benefit while in the other countries they are defined contribution.

Voluntary private pensions

Replacement rates are shown for 11 countries where voluntary private pensions have broad coverage. For the other economies South Africa also has a significant voluntary scheme. It is assumed that workers with voluntary private pensions spend a full career in the scheme.

The rules that have been modelled are in the "Country Profiles" available at *http://oe.cd/pag*. In ten of the 11 countries, a defined contribution plan is modelled, with a defined benefit schemes applying in Japan.

In general, both the defined contribution and defined benefit schemes pay a constant gross replacement rate with earnings. (Data on actual contribution rates by earnings are not available for most countries, and so an average or typical rate is assumed across the earnings range). However, progressive tax rules mean that the net replacement rate differs across the earnings range. Whilst the increase in gross replacement rate is generally constant across earnings the net replacement rate tends to increase more with earnings as the previous work earnings are taxed at much higher rates as individuals move up the earnings distribution.

Definition and measurement

The net replacement rate is defined as the individual net pension entitlement divided by net pre-retirement earnings, taking account of personal income taxes and social security contributions paid by workers and pensioners. Otherwise, the definition and measurement of the net replacement rates are the same as for the gross replacement rate. Details of the rules that national tax systems apply to pensioners can be found in the online Country Profiles available at *http://oe.cd/pag*.

Table 4.5. **Gross and net pension replacement rates from mandatory (public and private) and voluntary pension schemes**

Percentage of individual earnings

	Gross mandatory public and private			Net mandatory public and private			Total gross with voluntary			Total net with voluntary		
	0.5	1	2	0.5	1	2	0.5	1	2	0.5	1	2
Australia	62.7	31.3	31.3	70.3	40.5	39.1						
Austria	74.1	74.1	57.3	84.4	87.1	67.6						
Belgium	67.5	43.4	29.2	83.0	61.9	43.9	70.9	52.2	51.9	86.8	74.2	81.3
Canada	53.2	38.8	22.3	62.0	46.4	28.4	70.9	63.3	46.8	76.4	72.0	55.3
Chile	41.9	31.2	31.3	51.6	38.5	36.6						
Colombia*	100.0	74.8	74.8	104.3	73.1	71.5						
Costa Rica	73.1	71.9	68.0	77.3	76.0	73.2						
Czech Republic	81.2	49.0	32.9	100.0	65.2	45.7						
Denmark	125.1	80.0	61.3	124.7	84.0	71.4						
Estonia	47.6	27.9	18.1	52.0	33.7	23.5	70.6	52.4	43.4	77.1	59.3	49.6
Finland	56.6	56.6	56.6	63.8	63.2	64.3						
France	60.2	60.2	51.9	71.3	74.4	64.5						
Germany	46.5	41.5	33.0	57.9	52.9	41.9	60.2	55.7	47.2	75.0	70.2	58.3
Greece	84.7	72.6	66.5	94.1	83.6	77.5						
Hungary	62.5	62.5	62.5	94.0	94.0	94.0						
Iceland	72.9	51.8	51.8	81.3	59.7	59.9						
Ireland	59.4	29.7	14.9	67.5	39.9	24.0	89.9	60.2	45.3	100.3	73.0	61.5
Israel	61.7	41.5	20.7	67.0	51.2	29.6	81.6	56.5	28.2	88.9	68.3	39.5
Italy	74.6	74.6	74.6	78.4	81.7	84.6						
Japan	43.2	32.4	26.9	49.5	38.7	31.6	66.3	55.4	50.0	75.9	60.8	55.3
Korea	43.1	31.2	18.6	45.8	35.4	22.5						
Latvia	43.4	43.4	43.4	55.4	55.3	52.9						
Lithuania	31.5	19.7	13.8	44.0	30.7	22.8	52.0	35.3	26.9	72.8	55.0	44.5
Luxembourg	90.4	76.6	69.7	98.9	88.7	80.2						
Mexico	80.9	61.2	53.6	82.0	68.6	64.3	91.1	78.5	70.9	92.2	88.0	85.0
Netherlands	73.1	69.7	68.0	84.7	85.3	81.0						
New Zealand*	65.9	39.8	19.9	68.0	43.3	23.7	87.7	60.6	39.9	92.9	67.5	47.8
Norway	60.6	46.0	28.9	76.3	55.7	36.2						
Poland	31.8	30.6	30.0	39.1	36.5	36.8						
Portugal	76.3	74.9	72.5	88.5	90.3	89.7						
Slovak Republic*	62.6	53.1	46.7	76.2	69.4	64.3						
Slovenia*	62.3	42.0	41.4	87.3	63.3	59.2						
Spain	73.9	73.9	67.0	80.1	80.3	74.7						
Sweden	61.4	53.3	67.2	65.1	56.2	75.3						
Switzerland	53.1	44.1	23.0	62.2	54.8	29.3						
Turkey	73.3	73.3	73.3	94.8	103.3	110.8						
United Kingdom	70.6	49.0	38.2	79.2	58.1	47.7						
United States	49.6	39.2	27.9	61.0	50.5	39.0	91.8	81.3	70.0	111.7	95.8	83.2
OECD	**64.5**	**51.8**	**44.4**	**74.4**	**62.4**	**54.9**	**70.1**	**57.6**	**50.4**	**80.8**	**69.1**	**62.2**
Argentina	99.0	76.1	64.6	114.1	88.9	86.5						
Brazil	88.4	88.4	84.8	95.7	97.3	102.3						
China	90.6	71.6	62.1	114.9	92.4	81.0						
India	56.4	56.4	37.7	64.0	64.0	43.0						
Indonesia	55.3	55.3	55.3	60.6	60.6	60.6						
Russian Federation	56.9	47.2	42.3	65.4	54.2	48.6						
Saudi Arabia	59.6	59.6	59.6	66.2	66.2	66.2						
South Africa	29.8	14.9	7.4	29.8	16.2	8.8	32.8	32.8	32.8	35.4	38.8	42.6
EU27	63.6	53.4	48.1	75.7	66.7	60.8				78.7	69.9	65.0

Note: *Low earners in Colombia, New Zealand, the Slovak Republic and Slovenia are at 66%, 60%, 53% and 55% of average earnings, respectively, to account for the minimum wage level. The OECD average refers to the average of all 38 OECD countries.

Source: OECD pension models.

StatLink https://stat.link/scxdj3

Key results

Pension wealth relative to individual earnings before retirement measures the total discounted value of the lifetime flow of all retirement incomes in mandatory pension schemes at retirement age. For average earners, pension wealth for men is 9.4 times and for women 10.3 times annual individual earnings on average in OECD countries. Gross pension wealth relative to annual individual earnings is higher for women because of their longer life expectancy. The main determinants of differences across countries are differences in the gross replacement rate, in the length of the retirement period measured by remaining life expectancy at the normal retirement age, and in indexation rules.

Replacement rates give an indication of the pension promise relative to individual earnings, but they are not comprehensive measures of cumulated pension payments; they look only at the benefit level relative to individual earnings at the point of retirement, or more generally at a given, later age. For a full picture, life expectancy, normal retirement age and indexation of pension benefits must also be taken into account. Together, these determine for how long the pension benefit is paid, and how its value evolves over time. Pension wealth – a measure of the stock of future discounted flows of pension benefits – takes account of these factors. It can be thought of as the lump sum needed at the retirement age to buy an annuity giving the same flow of pension payments as that promised by mandatory retirement-income schemes.

In defined benefit systems there is often no or a weak link between the replacement rate and the expected duration of benefit withdrawal. However, in the long run, ensuring financial sustainability imposes a trade-off between the replacement rate and the duration of retirement. When retirement ages and pension benefits are held constant, pension wealth increases with longevity gains. In defined contribution systems there is a more direct link between the size of the benefit and the expected duration of benefit withdrawals. In these systems the pension wealth measure is equal to the accumulated assets and therefore independent of longevity increases as these automatically reduce the monthly benefits.

Gross pension wealth at individual earnings equal to the average wage is highest in Luxembourg at 16.2 times annual individual earnings for men and 17.7 times for women. It is also larger than 14 times for men and 16 times for women in Colombia and Spain. The lowest pension wealth for both men and women is found in Lithuania at 3.2 and 3.7, respectively, due to low replacement rates, while Australia, Chile, Estonia, Korea and Poland also have fewer than 6 times for men, with these countries along with Ireland having fewer than 7 times for women.

This indicator is built based on the gender-specific average mortality rates within countries. It thus assumes away differences in life expectancy across income levels. Given that individuals with low (high) income generally have a lower (higher) life expectancy, this implies that the computed numbers overestimate pension wealth for low earners and underestimate it for high earners. With this caveat in mind, higher individual replacement rates for low earners than for average earners mean that the computed pension wealth relative to individual earnings is also higher for low earners. For men with individual earnings equal to half average-earnings, pension wealth is 11.8 times their annual earnings on average and it is 13.0 times for women. In the countries where pension wealth for low earners is highest (Colombia and Luxembourg), its value is 19 times individual earnings for men and between 21 and 23 times individual earnings for women, with Colombia having a larger increase because of the lower retirement age for women.

Impact of life expectancy

In countries where the duration in retirement is shorter, such as Estonia and Hungary, pension wealth is smaller. The effect is the opposite in Switzerland and some of the Nordic countries, where life expectancy is high. Similarly, since women's life expectancy is longer than men's, pension wealth for women is higher in all countries that use unisex mortality tables to compute annuities or that have defined benefit systems. In addition, some countries still have lower retirement ages for women; this extends the payment period even further.

Impact of indexation

Pension wealth is affected by indexation rules at a given initial replacement rate level. Although most OECD countries now index pensions in payment to prices, there are exceptions: Ireland and New Zealand, for example, link their basic systems to average earnings. Since earnings tend to grow faster than prices pension wealth is higher with wage than price indexation, for a given level of replacement rate. If Ireland, for example, indexed to prices, the pension wealth for an average male earner would decrease from 6.3 to 5.4 with unchanged initial benefit based on the OECD pension model.

Definition and measurement

The calculation of pension wealth uses a uniform real discount rate of 2%. Since the comparisons refer to prospective pension entitlements, the calculations use country-specific mortality rates by age and sex at the year of retirement. Pension wealth is expressed as a multiple of gross annual individual earnings.

Table 4.6. **Gross pension wealth by earnings, multiple of annual earnings**

	Individual earnings, multiple of mean					
	0.5	1.0	2	0.5	1.0	2
	Men			Women		
Australia	11.3	5.7	5.7	11.9	5.7	5.7
Austria	13.7	13.7	10.6	15.0	15.0	11.6
Belgium	11.9	7.6	5.1	13.0	8.4	5.6
Canada	10.0	7.3	4.2	10.3	7.5	4.3
Chile	7.7	5.7	5.8	8.1	5.7	5.8
Colombia*	19.1	14.3	14.3	22.8	16.7	16.5
Costa Rica	13.5	13.3	12.6	14.7	14.5	13.7
Czech Republic	15.3	9.2	6.2	16.7	10.0	6.7
Denmark	17.3	10.9	8.2	19.0	12.0	9.0
Estonia	6.8	4.0	2.6	7.7	4.5	2.9
Finland	9.8	9.8	9.8	11.1	11.1	11.1
France	11.2	11.2	9.9	12.8	12.8	11.3
Germany	9.3	8.3	6.6	10.3	9.2	7.3
Greece	15.6	13.4	12.2	17.1	14.6	13.4
Hungary	10.4	10.4	10.4	11.5	11.5	11.5
Iceland	13.5	9.2	9.2	14.6	9.9	9.9
Ireland	12.5	6.3	3.1	13.5	6.8	3.4
Israel	11.1	7.5	3.7	11.5	7.5	3.7
Italy	11.7	11.7	11.7	13.2	13.2	13.2
Japan	8.3	6.2	5.2	9.7	7.3	6.1
Korea	8.0	5.8	3.5	9.4	6.8	4.1
Latvia	7.0	7.0	7.0	7.9	7.9	7.9
Lithuania	5.1	3.2	2.3	6.0	3.7	2.6
Luxembourg	19.1	16.2	14.8	20.9	17.7	16.1
Mexico	13.5	10.2	8.9	14.4	10.4	9.0

	Individual earnings, multiple of mean					
	0.5	1.0	2	0.5	1.0	2
	Men			Women		
Netherlands	13.7	13.1	12.7	14.9	14.2	13.9
New Zealand*	14.4	8.7	4.3	15.5	9.4	4.7
Norway	12.1	9.2	5.7	13.3	10.1	6.3
Poland	5.7	5.5	5.4	7.3	5.4	5.2
Portugal	12.3	12.0	11.6	13.9	13.6	13.2
Slovak Republic*	10.7	9.1	8.0	11.9	10.1	8.9
Slovenia*	13.4	9.0	8.9	15.0	10.1	10.0
Spain	14.7	14.7	13.3	17.0	17.0	15.4
Sweden	11.4	9.8	12.6	12.2	10.6	13.5
Switzerland	10.7	8.8	4.6	12.1	10.0	5.2
Turkey	13.0	13.0	13.0	14.4	14.4	14.4
United Kingdom	13.2	8.9	6.8	14.7	9.9	7.6
United States	8.7	6.8	4.9	9.2	7.2	5.1
OECD	**11.8**	**9.4**	**8.0**	**13.0**	**10.3**	**8.8**
Argentina	18.6	14.3	12.2	23.1	18.1	15.7
Brazil	15.1	15.1	14.5	19.1	19.1	18.5
China	19.0	15.0	13.0	18.4	14.2	12.1
India	9.7	9.7	6.5	10.5	10.5	6.9
Indonesia	8.2	8.2	8.2	8.8	8.8	8.8
Russian Federation	9.9	8.2	7.4	9.4	7.6	6.7
Saudi Arabia	14.7	14.7	14.7	15.3	15.3	15.3
South Africa	4.5	2.3	1.1	5.6	2.8	1.4
EU27	11.6	9.7	8.8	12.8	10.7	9.6

Note: *Low earners in Colombia, New Zealand, the Slovak Republic and Slovenia are at 66%, 60%, 53% and 55% of average earnings, respectively, to account for the minimum wage level.

Source: OECD pension models.

StatLink https://stat.link/6rkifo

Figure 4.6. **Gross pension wealth for lower earners by gender, multiple of annual earnings**

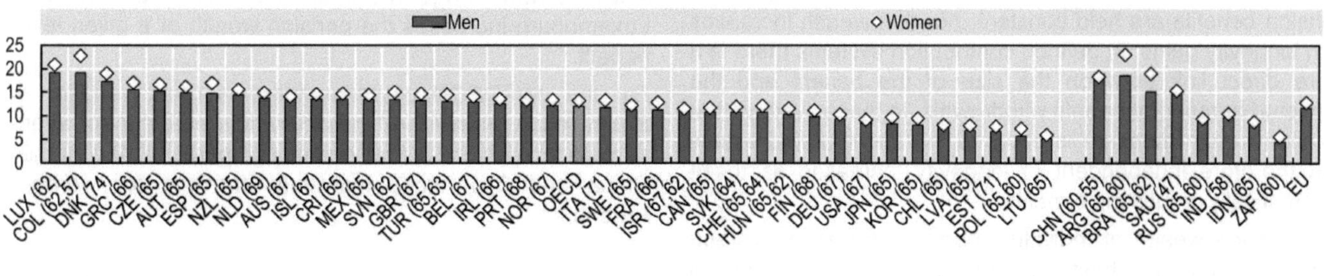

Source: OECD pension models.

StatLink https://stat.link/xpf4bi

Figure 4.7. **Gross pension wealth for average earners by gender, multiple of annual earnings**

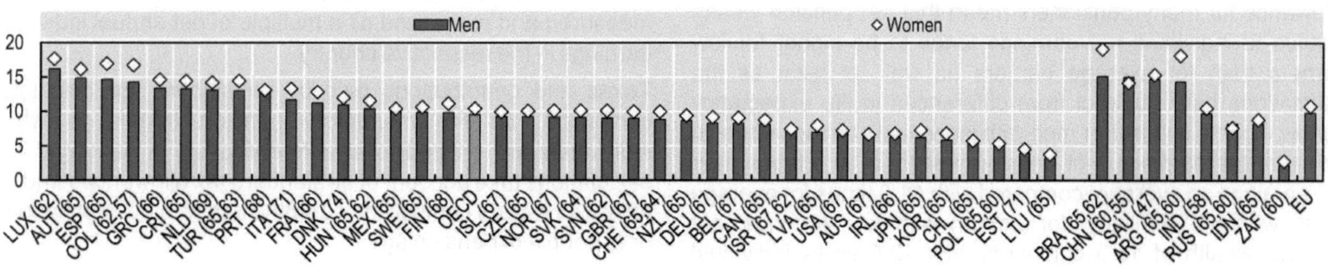

Source: OECD pension models.

StatLink https://stat.link/4ow6bi

Key results

As with gross pension wealth, net pension wealth relative to individual net earnings measures the total discounted value of the lifetime flow of all retirement incomes in mandatory pension schemes at retirement age. For average earners, net pension wealth for men is 11.3 times and for women 12.5 times annual individual net earnings on average in OECD countries. Net pension wealth relative to annual individual earnings is higher for women because of their longer life expectancy. The main determinants of differences across countries are differences in the net replacement rate, in the length of the retirement period measured by remaining life expectancy at the normal retirement age, and in indexation rules.

Replacement rates give an indication of the pension promise relative to individual earnings, but they are not comprehensive measures of cumulated pension payments; they look only at the benefit level relative to individual earnings at the point of retirement, or more generally at a given, later age. For a full picture, life expectancy, normal retirement age and indexation of pension benefits must also be taken into account. Together, these determine for how long the pension benefit is paid, and how its value evolves over time. Net pension wealth – a measure of the stock of future discounted flows of pension benefits after taxes and social contributions – takes account of these factors. It can be thought of as the total net benefits that will be received on average from the mandatory retirement-income schemes.

In defined benefit systems there is often no or a weak link between the replacement rate and the expected duration of benefit withdrawal. Of course, in the long run, ensuring financial sustainability imposes a trade-off between the replacement rate and the duration of retirement. When retirement ages and pension benefits are held constant, pension wealth increases with longevity gains. In defined contribution systems there is a more direct link between the size of the benefit and the expected duration of benefit withdrawals. In these systems the pension wealth measure is equal to the accumulated assets and therefore independent of longevity increases as these automatically reduce the benefits.

Net pension wealth at individual earnings equal to average worker earnings is highest in Luxembourg at 18.8 times annual individual net earnings for men and 20.5 times for women. The lowest pension wealth is found in Lithuania at 5.0 and 5.8 times for men and women respectively, due to low replacement rates.

Higher individual replacement rates and the increased tax allowance for many pensioners mean that net pension wealth relative to individual net earnings tends to be higher for low earners than for average earners as well, at least as the estimations here abstract from differences in life expectancy across income levels. For men with individual earnings equal to half-average earnings, net pension wealth is 13.6 times their net earnings on average, compared with 11.3 times for average wage workers. Similarly, for women with low earnings, net pension wealth of 15.0 compares with 12.5 times individual earnings for average earners.

For higher earners net pension wealth is on average 9.9 for men and 10.9 for women, only slightly lower than that for average earners, with Turkey highest and Lithuania again lowest.

Impact of life expectancy

In countries where the duration in retirement is shorter and where pension benefits are defined benefit, such as Estonia and Hungary, the individual pension wealth is smaller. The effect is the opposite in Switzerland and some of the Nordic countries (in DB systems), where life expectancies are high. Similarly, since women's life expectancy is longer than men's, pension wealth for women is higher in all countries that use unisex mortality tables or that have defined benefit systems. This is simply because in that case the same level of pension benefits can be expected to be paid over a longer retirement period. In addition, some countries still have lower retirement ages for women; this extends the payment period even further. Pension wealth is also affected by pension ages. A low retirement age in a defined benefit system such as in Luxembourg increases the pension wealth at a given level of benefit.

For the non-OECD countries there is great variation with South Africa at only 2.4 times individual earnings for average earners for men and 3.1 for women compared to 19.4 for men in China and 21.2 times individual earnings for women in Argentina.

Definition and measurement

Net pension wealth is the present value of the flow of pension benefits, taking account of the taxes and social security contributions that retirees have to pay on their pensions. It is measured and expressed as a multiple of net annual individual earnings in the respective country.

Taxes and contributions paid by pensioners are calculated conditional on the mandatory pension benefit to which individuals are entitled to at different levels of earnings. The calculations take account of all standard tax allowances and tax reliefs as well as concessions granted either to pension income or to people of pension age.

Details of the rules that national tax systems apply to pensioners can be found in the online "Country Profiles" available at *http://oe.cd/pag*.

Table 4.7. **Net pension wealth by earnings**

	Men 0.5	Men 1.0	Men 2	Women 0.5	Women 1.0	Women 2
	Individual earnings, multiple of mean					
Australia	12.7	7.3	7.1	13.3	7.3	7.2
Austria	15.6	16.1	12.5	17.0	17.6	13.7
Belgium	14.6	10.9	7.7	16.0	11.9	8.5
Canada	11.6	8.7	5.3	12.0	9.0	5.5
Chile	9.5	7.1	6.7	10.0	7.1	6.7
Colombia*	20.0	14.0	13.7	23.8	16.3	15.8
Costa Rica	14.3	14.0	13.5	15.5	15.3	14.7
Czech Republic	18.8	12.3	8.6	20.5	13.4	9.4
Denmark	17.3	11.4	9.6	19.0	12.5	10.5
Estonia	7.4	4.8	3.3	8.5	5.5	3.8
Finland	11.1	11.0	11.2	12.5	12.4	12.6
France	13.3	13.9	12.3	15.2	15.8	14.0
Germany	11.6	10.6	8.4	12.8	11.7	9.2
Greece	17.3	15.4	14.3	18.9	16.8	15.6
Hungary	15.6	15.6	15.6	17.3	17.3	17.3
Iceland	15.1	10.6	10.7	16.2	11.4	11.4
Ireland	14.2	8.4	5.0	15.3	9.1	5.4
Israel	12.1	9.2	5.3	12.4	9.2	5.3
Italy	12.3	12.8	13.3	13.9	14.5	15.0
Japan	9.5	7.4	6.0	11.1	8.7	7.1
Korea	8.6	6.6	4.2	10.0	7.7	4.9
Latvia	8.9	8.9	8.5	10.1	10.1	9.7
Lithuania	7.2	5.0	3.7	8.3	5.8	4.3
Luxembourg	21.0	18.8	17.0	22.8	20.5	18.5
Mexico	13.6	11.4	10.7	14.6	11.6	10.8

	Men 0.5	Men 1.0	Men 2	Women 0.5	Women 1.0	Women 2
	Individual earnings, multiple of mean					
Netherlands	17.7	16.7	16.3	19.2	18.2	17.7
New Zealand*	14.9	9.5	5.2	16.0	10.2	5.6
Norway	15.7	11.4	7.4	17.3	12.6	8.1
Poland	7.0	6.5	6.6	9.0	6.5	6.4
Portugal	14.2	14.5	14.4	16.1	16.4	16.3
Slovak Republic*	13.1	11.9	11.0	14.5	13.2	12.2
Slovenia*	18.7	13.6	12.7	21.0	15.2	14.3
Spain	15.9	16.0	14.8	18.4	18.5	17.2
Sweden	12.3	10.6	14.3	13.3	11.5	15.4
Switzerland	11.7	10.1	5.6	13.1	11.4	6.3
Turkey	16.8	18.3	19.6	18.7	20.4	21.8
United Kingdom	14.8	10.6	8.5	16.5	11.8	9.4
United States	10.7	8.8	6.8	11.3	9.3	7.2
OECD	**13.6**	**11.3**	**9.9**	**15.0**	**12.5**	**10.9**
Argentina	21.5	16.7	16.3	26.6	21.2	21.0
Brazil	16.4	16.7	17.5	20.6	21.0	22.3
China	24.1	19.4	17.0	23.3	18.4	16.0
India	11.0	11.0	7.4	11.9	11.9	7.9
Indonesia	9.0	9.0	9.0	9.6	9.6	9.6
Russian Federation	11.4	9.5	8.6	10.8	8.7	7.7
Saudi Arabia	16.4	16.4	16.4	17.0	17.0	17.0
South Africa	4.5	2.4	1.3	5.6	3.1	1.7
EU27	13.9	12.2	11.2	15.4	13.5	12.3

Note: *Low earners in Colombia, New Zealand, the Slovak Republic and Slovenia are at 66%, 60%, 53% and 55% of average earnings, respectively, to account for the minimum wage level.
Source: OECD pension models.

StatLink https://stat.link/wrlhic

Figure 4.8. **Net pension wealth for lower earners by gender, multiple of annual earnings**

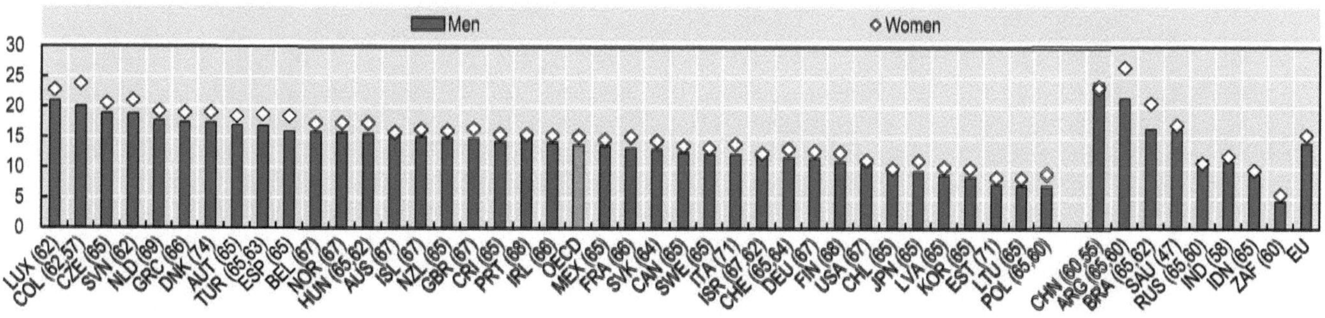

Source: OECD pension models.

StatLink https://stat.link/rd2z83

Figure 4.9. **Net pension wealth for average earners by gender, multiple of annual earnings**

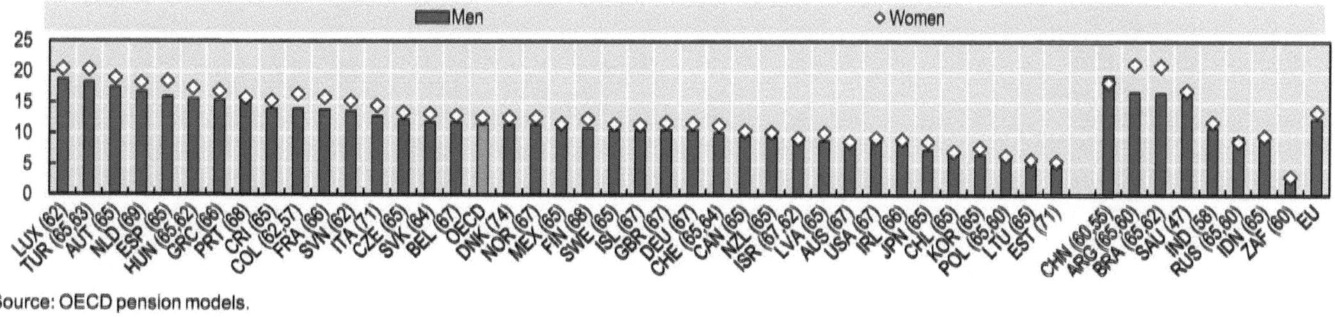

Source: OECD pension models.

StatLink https://stat.link/r49icq

Pensions at a Glance 2021
OECD and G20 Indicators

Chapter 5

Pension entitlements for alternative scenarios

Full-career single individuals being covered in Chapter 4, the analysis turns to those with different career paths or for couples. The indicators start by showing pension entitlements for couples compared to single workers. As people often spend periods out of paid work in unemployment or caring for children the following indicators show the gross pension replacement rates in mandatory pension schemes for first childcare and then unemployment breaks, with breaks of five and ten years, with a later entry also for the longer unemployment period. Next a comparison of gross replacement rates is given for alternative economic assumptions compared with the base case. Finally there is a comparison of the replacement rates for the self-employed with that of dependent employees.

Key results

Most of the indicators of pension entitlements in this report are based on analysis of a single person. In many countries, pension systems are effectively "individualised": the position of a couple is the same as that of two single people with the same level of total earnings. In others, however, being in a couple has an effect on pension entitlements.

There are two ways in which partnership status affects pension entitlements. First, some systems offer "derived" rights: these are benefits for the couple that derive from the working experience and contributions of one spouse. Secondly, some first-tier benefits are calculated based on family status, assessed using the couple as a "pension unit" rather than treating each individual separately. For this analysis the word "couple" refers to the benefit unit that is recognised in each country, be that through marriage, civil partnership or cohabitation.

Table 5.1 shows calculations of pension entitlements for three different family types. In the first two, total gross earnings are held constant at 100% of the economy-wide individual average. A single man with these earnings is compared with a single-earner couple (male earner). The final case shows a couple consisting of two earners, each with 100% of average earnings, compared with two singles, each with average earnings.

There is significant variation between countries in terms of the policy stance adopted for non-workers within a couple. In some countries, benefits are higher for couples than for single people because of basic schemes that pay a higher rate to a couple than to a single person (although less than the entitlement of two single people) as in the Netherlands, for example. In Ireland there are spousal benefits in the basic pension for partners in a couple who do not earn a full basic pension entitlement in their own right.

In Japan and the United States, there are spousal benefits in the public, earnings-related schemes. Again, these higher benefits are paid to couples where one partner has not earned a large entitlement in his or her own right.

On average for couples in which there is a male average earner and a non-working partner, the gross replacement rate is 57.2%, at the normal retirement age, compared to 51.8% for a single male worker at average earnings. Overall just under half of OECD countries provide a higher gross entitlement for one-earner couples at the average wage compared to a single earner. The largest differences are found in Australia, Ireland and Slovenia where single earner couples are at least 24 percentage points higher than for single earners. In Australia, for example, both individuals have entitlement to the first-tier pension (Age Pension), whilst in Ireland the non-working partner is entitled to the non-contributory pension. Lithuania actually has a lower replacement rate as the living alone supplement is withdrawn.

Resource-tested schemes explain why Denmark has higher benefits for one-earner couples than for single people with average earnings. Even at average earnings, both would be eligible for resource-tested benefits. Similarly, in Belgium, Finland and Sweden, a single person on average earnings would not be entitled to a minimum pension. However, a couple with one partner earning the economy-wide average would receive a top-up.

Given an equivalence scale of square root of 2 for a couple (Chapter 7), the single earner couple replacement rate of 57.2% of average earnings provides an equivalent, at the individual level, of 40.4%, so 11 percentage points lower than for single men.

For couples with both earning the average wage, results are only shown for those cases that would give a different pension entitlement than for two single individuals. The only countries with couple specific rules in that case are Denmark, Ireland, Lithuania, the Netherlands and New Zealand. In New Zealand the residence-based basic component is paid at a lower level for each individual in a couple than if they were single. This is also the case in the Netherlands, but there is an additional earnings-related scheme which is calculated individually. In Denmark the rate of withdrawal of the means-tested component is higher for couples than for single individuals. In Ireland and Lithuania, living alone allowances are lost for the couple compared to two single individuals.

Definition and measurement

The old-age pension entitlement measures how effectively a pension system provides a retirement income to replace earnings, the main source of income before retirement. The gross entitlement is defined as gross pension divided by gross pre-retirement earnings.

For the couple analysis, a male and female partner of the same age are assumed to enable easier comparison with the single-earner scenario. For the two-earner couple, both are assumed to retire at the earliest age at which no penalty will apply to their benefits, with the female pensioner then having their benefits indexed until reaching the male retirement age for those countries with lower female retirement age.

Table 5.1. **Gross pension entitlements by earnings: singles versus couples, percentage of average earnings**

	Single, average earner – male (female where different)		Single earner couple – male at average earnings, if different from single male average earner	Couple, each with average earnings, if different from two single average earners
Australia	31.3	(28.4)	56.0	
Austria	74.1			
Belgium	43.4		54.0	
Canada	38.8		46.4	
Chile	31.2	(28.8)		
Colombia	74.8	(73.4)		
Costa Rica	71.9			
Czech Republic	49.0		60.0	
Denmark	80.0		102.0	150.2
Estonia	27.9		39.1	
Finland	56.6		69.0	
France	60.2			
Germany	41.5			
Greece	72.6			
Hungary	62.5	(58.1)		
Iceland	51.8		71.2	
Ireland	29.7		54.1	55.3
Israel	41.5	(34.1)	46.6	
Italy	74.6			
Japan	32.4		43.2	
Korea	31.2			
Latvia	43.4			
Lithuania	19.7		18.3	36.7
Luxembourg	76.6			
Mexico	61.2	(58.2)	76.1	
Netherlands	69.7		88.7	137.3
New Zealand	39.8		60.4	60.4
Norway	46.0		69.1	
Poland	30.6	(23.4)		
Portugal	74.9			
Slovak Republic	53.1			
Slovenia	42.0		75.3	
Spain	73.9			
Sweden	53.3		73.0	
Switzerland	44.1	(43.5)		
Turkey	73.3	(70.3)		
United Kingdom	49.0			
United States	39.2		48.1	
OECD	51.8	(50.9)	**57.2**	**101.3**

Note: Values are only shown for single-earner couples where the pension received differs from that of a single male earner. Values are only shown for couples with average earnings when they differ from the rates that would apply to a single man and single woman combined.
Source: OECD pension models.

StatLink https://stat.link/j1g6p3

Key results

The analysis above has concentrated on showing full-career replacement rates where there has been no period of absence from the labour market. This future gross replacement rate shows the level of pension benefits in retirement from mandatory pension schemes relative to earnings when working. However, many individuals will have interrupted careers because of having children and this indicator shows how this will affect future pension entitlements. Women with average earnings and taking five years out of the labour market to care for two children will have a pension equal to 95% of that for a full-career female worker on average across the 38 OECD countries. Spain offers benefits 5% higher than for the full-career worker, whilst in Australia and Iceland the future benefit is less than 87% of the full-career worker's. For low earners, the impact of such breaks on future pensions is more limited in most countries.

All OECD countries, with the exception of the United States offers credit for periods of maternity, but the analysis presented here covers the period beyond maternity leave, looking specifically at childcare periods. Most OECD countries aim to protect periods of absence from the labour market to care for children. Whilst fathers are becoming increasingly able to access periods of credit the mother is still the primary recipient in many countries and so this analysis has been computed for females only.

Credits for childcare typically cover career breaks until children reach a certain age. They are generally less generous for longer breaks and for older children. Many OECD countries credit time spent caring for very young children (usually up to three or four years old) as insured periods and consider it as paid employment. However, once children are aged six years or older any credit given for this extended period is usually only to determine eligibility for early retirement and the minimum pension. Some countries (the Czech Republic, Greece, Hungary and Luxembourg) factor childcare into assessments of eligibility, but disregard them when computing the earnings base.

The gross pension entitlements of mothers who take time out of employment is illustrated in Figure 5.1 and Figure 5.2 at different earnings levels for breaks from work of five and ten years, respectively. In Spain the benefits are higher with a five-year career break for childcare as a 5% bonus is paid for having two children and would be as high as 15% for four or more children. In the Czech Republic, Ireland, New Zealand and the United States, pensions are not affected by breaks irrespective of earnings. In Ireland the reason is that career breaks to care for children under 12 are considered insured periods up to a maximum of 20 years. Those breaks are therefore excluded from the averaging periods used to compute pension entitlements. In New Zealand, the public pension is simply residence-based, so any period spent out of the labour market does not change the benefits.

In Germany having a child gives one parent a credit of one pension point annually for three years, thereby making it equivalent for pension purposes to earning the average wage throughout the credit period, resulting in a much higher benefit entitlement for low earners. Similarly in Estonia credits are given based on the nationwide average income again resulting in higher benefits for low earners.

On average, a five-year break lowers future benefit entitlements at the average wage by 5%, which increases to 11% for a ten-year break. The average impact is more limited for low earners at 2% for five-year break and 6% for a ten-year break.

In Greece and Slovenia for both five- and ten-year breaks and in France, Hungary, Luxembourg and Portugal for the ten-year break, workers have to retire later to be entitled to a pension without penalty due the rules governing required contribution periods. In Slovenia, for example, a worker who enters paid employment at 22 but takes ten years out of work will have contributed for less than 40 years at age 62, and will therefore have to work until 65 to be able to retire without penalty. Conversely in France for the five-year break and in the Slovak Republic for both five- and ten-year breaks it is possible to retire earlier due to childcare, by one year in the Slovak Republic in both cases and by three years in France for a five-year career break.

Definition and measurement

The OECD baseline full-career simulation model assumes labour market entry at the age of 22. For the childcare career case, women are assumed to embark on their careers as full-time employees at 22, and to stop working during a break of up to ten years from age 30 to care for their two children born when the mother was aged 30 and 32; they are then assumed to resume full-time work until normal retirement age, which may increase because of the career break. Any increase in retirement age is shown in brackets after the country name on the charts, with the corresponding benefits for the full career worker indexed until this age. The simulations are based on parameters and rules set out in the online "Country Profiles" available at *http://oe.cd/pag*.

Figure 5.1. **Gross pension entitlements of low and average earners with a five-year childcare break versus worker with an uninterrupted career**

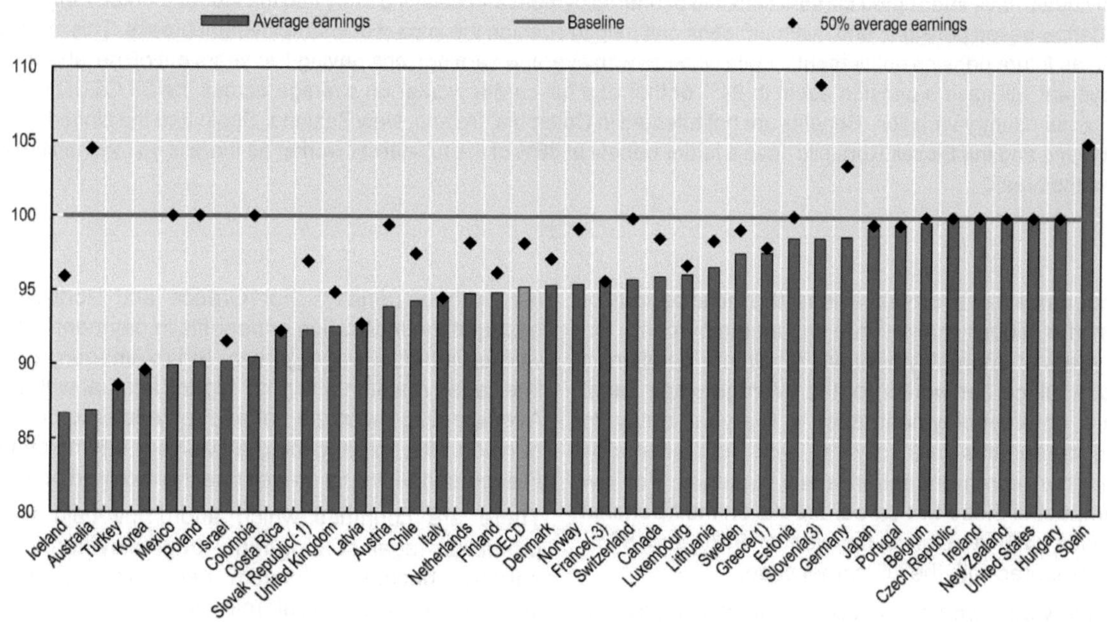

Note: Figure in brackets refers to increase/decrease in retirement age. Individuals enter the labour market at age 22 in 2020. Two children are born in 2028 and 2030 with the career break starting in 2028. Low earners in Colombia, New Zealand, the Slovak Republic and Slovenia are at 66%, 60%, 53% and 55% of average earnings, respectively, to account for the minimum wage level.
Source: OECD pension models.

StatLink https://stat.link/fw3hrg

Figure 5.2. **Gross pension entitlements of low and average earners with a ten-year childcare break versus worker with an uninterrupted career**

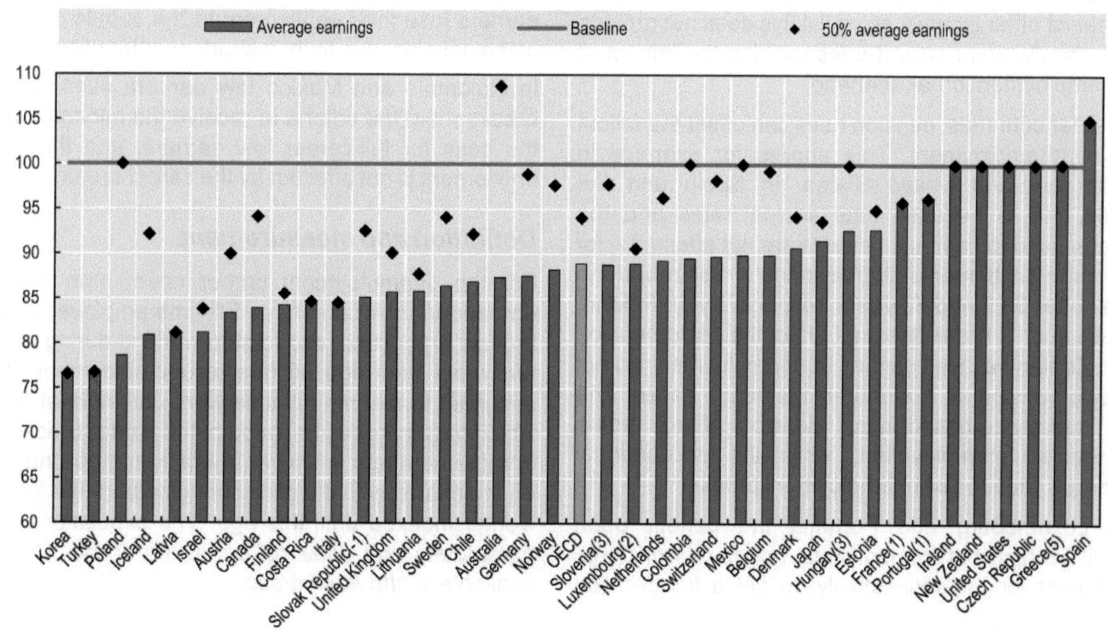

Note: Figure in brackets refers to increase/decrease in retirement age. Individuals enter the labour market at age 22 in 2020. Two children are born in 2028 and 2030 with the career break starting in 2028. Low earners in Colombia, New Zealand, the Slovak Republic and Slovenia are at 66%, 60%, 53% and 55% of average earnings, respectively, to account for the minimum wage level.
Source: OECD pension models.

StatLink https://stat.link/rcfhp2

Key results

Many individuals have interrupted careers because of unemployment and delaying entry into the labour market. Pension credits as well as residence-based pensions and minimum pensions help to cushion the impact of unemployment breaks. This indicator shows how this affects future pension entitlements. Male workers with average earnings and having five years out of the labour market due to unemployment will have a pension equal to 94% of that of a full-career worker on average across the 38 OECD countries with substantial cross-country variation. Benefits are not affected in Colombia, Ireland, New Zealand, Spain and the United States, whilst Australia, Iceland and the Slovak Republic have a future benefit at 88% of the full-career worker as there is no mechanism to cushion the impact of the break.

Most OECD countries aim to protect at least the initial periods of absence from the labour market due to unemployment. On average five years of unemployment will result in a pension of 94% of that of a full-career worker for the average-wage case. With 10 years of unemployment after a five-year delay to beginning the career this falls to 78%, with both scenarios leading to a higher retirement age in a few countries. For low earners, the impact of these two career breaks on their pension benefits is lower, with a relative pension of 96% and 83%, respectively, compared with the full-career case.

For the average-wage worker, pension shortfalls relative to someone with a full, unbroken career varies widely across countries. They are generally larger for longer duration of career absence and for high-earners. In the Slovak Republic the pension loss after a five-year unemployment break is around 12% as there is no instrument to cushion the impact of the unemployment shock on pension. In Latvia there is only minimal protection for the first year. In Australia and Iceland, although there is no protection in the DC pension schemes, both countries have basic pensions that are gradually withdrawn against other income, so whilst this does not provide protection for the five-year case it does cushion the impact of the longer unemployment break scenario.

However, in other countries, pension rules can offset the fallout from spells of unemployment. This applies for example in Ireland, Spain and the United States. In Spain and the United States, this is because total accrual rates and the reference wage used to compute benefits are not affected – for example, pension entitlements stop accruing in Spain and the United States after 38.5 and 35 years, respectively. In Ireland, this is because such a break does not affect the basic pension level. In New Zealand as well periods of unemployment do not affect the basic pension as it is entirely residence based. The Netherlands' residence-based basic pension affords some protection against unemployment, while the occupational pension is sharply reduced by unemployment breaks.

In Greece, Luxembourg and Portugal the benefit upon retirement will be high but the individual needs to work one, three or one year longer, respectively, to get a full pension (i.e. without penalty). For Greece and Portugal this is also because the indexation of benefits in payment to the full-career worker is below wage growth. In Luxembourg contributions at later ages result in a slightly higher accrual with a long career. Average-wage workers have to retire later to benefit from a full pension after experiencing a five-year unemployment break in France and Slovenia as well due the required contribution rules.

There are countries which afford low-paid workers better protection against long-term unemployment than average earners, because minimum pensions and resource-tested schemes play a crucial role in some of them – Australia, Belgium, Canada, Chile, Colombia, Iceland, Mexico, Norway and Poland. Where there is no or limited pension credit provision – in Chile, Estonia, Israel, Korea, Mexico and Turkey, for example – pension losses are more substantial for average-wage earners with effects felt most keenly in countries whose compulsory pension programmes link pensions and earnings closely – e.g. Chile – and at higher earnings levels. By contrast, lower earners in Germany are more affected by the longer unemployment break than average earners, as low earners lose their entitlement to the supplemental component of the pension, due to their shorter contribution period.

In Colombia and Mexico low earners even with long-career breaks meet the criteria to receive the minimum pension, as is the case for full-career low earners, and thus their pension entitlement is not affected by the career break.

Definition and measurement

For the unemployment career case, men are assumed to embark on their careers as full-time employees at 22 or 27 for the late entry case, and to stop working during a break of up to ten years from age 35 due to unemployment; they are then assumed to resume full-time work until normal retirement age, which may increase because of the career break. Any increase in retirement age is shown in brackets after the country name on the charts, with the corresponding benefits for the full career worker indexed until this age. The simulations are based on parameters and rules set out in the online "Country Profiles" available at *http://oe.cd/pag*.

Figure 5.3. **Gross pension entitlements of low and average earners with a five-year unemployment break versus worker with a full career**

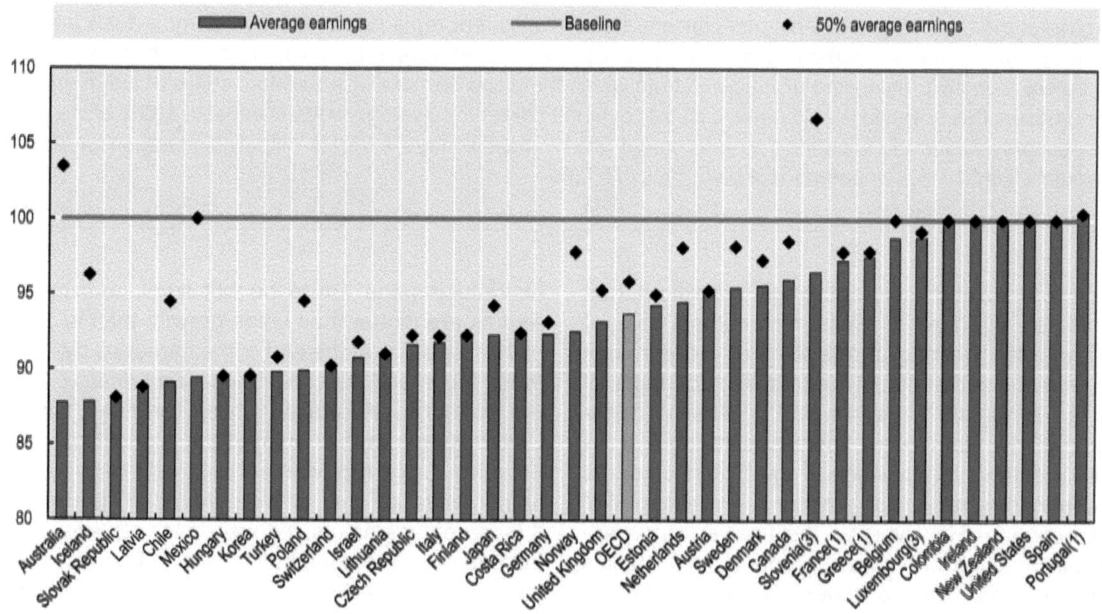

Note: Figure in brackets refers to increase in retirement age due to the career break. Individuals enter the labour market at age 22 in 2020. The unemployment break starts in 2033. Low earners in Colombia, New Zealand, the Slovak Republic and Slovenia are at 66%, 60%, 53% and 55% of average earnings, respectively, to account for the minimum wage level.

Source: OECD pension models.

StatLink https://stat.link/m9wjvq

Figure 5.4. **Gross pension entitlements of low and average earners with a ten-year unemployment break after entering the labour market five years later**

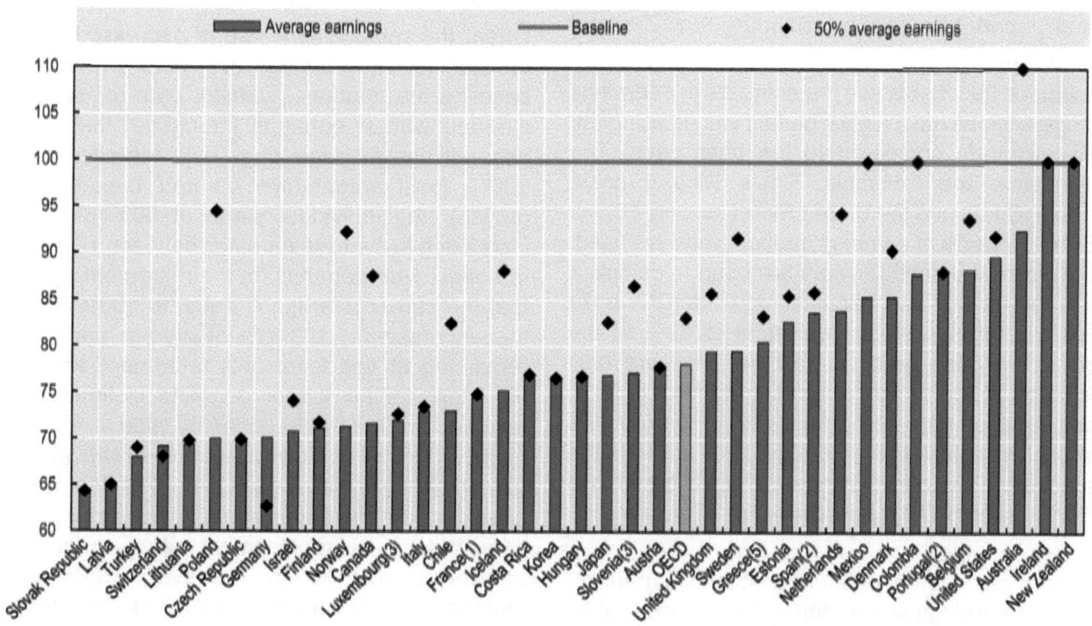

Note: Figure in brackets refers to increase in retirement age due to the career break. Individuals enter the labour market at age 27 in 2025. The unemployment break starts in 2033. Low earners in Colombia, New Zealand, the Slovak Republic and Slovenia are at 66%, 60%, 53% and 55% of average earnings, respectively, to account for the minimum wage level.

Source: OECD pension models.

StatLink https://stat.link/8zopex

Key results

The base case at the beginning of this chapter concentrates on full-career replacement rates when individuals are at a constant level of earnings relative to the average during their whole career. In the alternative earnings profile shown here individuals start at a lower salary before steadily progressing until age 55 from which the wage remains at a constant share of the average wage. For comparison purposes, this scenario is calibrated such that over the career the average wage is equal to 100% of the average wage for the whole economy. Under this scenario the replacement rate for male workers is 53.1%, slightly higher than for the base case at 51.8%. For women, it is 52.1%, compared to the base case of 50.9%.

Full-career male workers at the average wage throughout their career will have, on average, a gross replacement rate of 51.8%, when they start working at age 22. For the earnings profile shown here the replacement rate as a percentage of average earnings is slightly higher at 53.1%. That is, while under this scenario, the relative wage increases throughout the career – from 60% of the average wage at age 22, ensuring the same lifetime earnings – the pension amount is similar to that of the base case scenario. However, as the final earnings are higher under this specific alternative scenario, this implies 43.1% of final earnings. The equivalent figures for female workers are 50.9% for the base case and 52.1% for the earnings profile, equivalent to 42.3% of final earnings.

In some countries, the pension benefit level is identical in the earnings profile and the base cases, as pension systems that have flat-rate benefits, or points systems or constant accrual rates with wage valorisation of past earnings are not affected, as career average earnings are the same and any ceilings to contributions do not come into play. These countries are Austria, Canada, the Czech Republic, Estonia, Germany, Hungary, Ireland, Japan, Lithuania, Luxembourg, New Zealand and the Slovak Republic.

By contrast, countries that do not use the entire career earnings when calculating pensions have higher benefit values using the earnings profile scenario compared to the base case. The countries in question are Colombia, Costa Rica, France, Portugal, Slovenia, Spain and the United States as only 10, 20, 25, 40, 24, 25 and 35 years of earnings, respectively, are used. For example, in Spain the final 25 years are used to calculate the reference wage for pension calculations. Under the base case this gives a reference wage equivalent to 82% of the average wage in the base case as past earnings are only adjusted for inflation, whereas for the earning profile it is 96%, hence the gross replacement rate increases by 17%, from 74% to 86%. The impact is not as large in Portugal because 40 of the 46 years of career are used, nor in France as there is a ceiling to contributions to the general DB scheme at 108% of the average wage.

For countries that have large defined contribution pension schemes, the lower earnings at the start of the career – while having the same average over the career – has a greater effect on reducing the future benefit level, assuming the level of returns are higher than wage growth, than is countered by the higher earnings at the end of the career as there is less time for these increased contributions to accumulate. The largest falls are found in Australia, Chile, Denmark, Iceland and the United Kingdom, but even in the highest case in Iceland the effective future replacement rate only falls by 2.4 percentage points with all the others around 1 percentage points – 1.5 percentage points. In Sweden the replacement rate actually increases as the contribution rate to the occupational pension increases from 4.5% to 30% for earnings above 108% of the average.

Definition and measurement

The old-age pension replacement rate measures how effectively a pension system provides a retirement income to replace earnings, the main source of income before retirement. The gross replacement rate is defined as gross pension entitlement divided by gross pre-retirement earnings.

Often, the replacement rate is expressed as the ratio of the pension to final earnings (just before retirement). Under the baseline assumptions, workers earn the same percentage of average worker earnings throughout their career. However, although the average wage over the career is maintained at 100% (past wages are uprated based on average-wage growth), the individual starts at 60% of average earnings, increasing to average earnings between 12 and 25 years later – the exact year depends on the retirement age so as to ensure that the career average is equal to 100% of average wage -, then increasing to 123.33% of average earnings at age 55 and remaining at this level until retirement age. Therefore, final earnings are no longer equal to lifetime average earnings revalued in line with economy-wide earnings growth. The replacement rates shown are expressed as a percentage of career average earnings. Given that the wage reference is equal for both the base case and the earnings-profile scenario, comparisons of replacement rates amount to comparing pension benefit levels. However, under this scenario, if replacement rates are expressed in terms of the last earnings, numbers in the below table should be divided by 1.2333.

Table 5.2. **Gross and net pension replacement rates by earnings profile**

Percentage of average earnings throughout the career for men (women where different)

	Pension age		GRR				NRR			
			Base case		Earning profile		Base case		Earning profile	
Australia	67		31.3	*(28.4)*	30.3	*(27.5)*	40.5	*(36.8)*	39.3	*(35.7)*
Austria*	65		74.1		74.1		87.1		87.1	
Belgium	67		43.4		42.6		61.9		61.3	
Canada*	65		38.8		38.8		46.4		46.4	
Chile	65		31.2	*(28.8)*	29.8	*(27.9)*	38.5	*(35.4)*	36.8	*(34.4)*
Colombia	62	*(57)*	74.8	*(73.4)*	91.6	*(87.0)*	73.1	*(71.8)*	89.6	*(85.1)*
Costa Rica	65		71.9		81.4		76.0		86.1	
Czech Republic*	65		49.0		49.0		65.2		65.2	
Denmark	74		80.0		78.9		84.0		82.9	
Estonia*	71		27.9		27.9		33.7		33.7	
Finland	68		56.6		57.0		63.2		63.5	
France	66		60.2		64.7		74.4		78.7	
Germany*	67		41.5		41.5		52.9		52.9	
Greece	66		72.6		72.9		83.6		83.8	
Hungary*	65	*(62)*	62.5	*(58.1)*	62.5	*(57.1)*	94.0	*(87.4)*	94.0	*(69.6)*
Iceland	67		51.8		49.4		59.7		57.4	
Ireland*	66		29.7		29.7		39.9		39.9	
Israel	67	*(62)*	41.5	*(34.1)*	40.6	*(33.5)*	51.2	*(42.1)*	50.2	*(41.3)*
Italy	71		74.6		76.0		81.7		83.0	
Japan*	65		32.4		32.4		38.7		38.7	
Korea	65		31.2		30.6		35.4		34.8	
Latvia	65		43.4		43.2		55.3		55.0	
Lithuania*	65		19.7		19.7		30.7		30.7	
Luxembourg*	62		76.6		76.6		88.7		88.7	
Mexico	65		61.2	*(58.2)*	60.7	*(58.2)*	68.6	*(65.2)*	68.1	*(65.2)*
Netherlands	69		69.7		71.4		89.2		90.3	
New Zealand*	65		39.8		39.8		43.3		43.3	
Norway	67		46.0		44.6		55.7		54.7	
Poland	65	*(60)*	30.6	*(23.4)*	31.4	*(23.4)*	36.5	*(28.2)*	37.4	*(28.2)*
Portugal	68		74.9		79.6		90.3		95.1	
Slovak Republic*	64		53.1		53.1		69.4		69.4	
Slovenia	62		42.0		47.6		63.3		70.9	
Spain	65		73.9		86.0		80.3		91.3	
Sweden	65		53.3		55.1		56.2		57.9	
Switzerland	65	*(64)*	44.1	*(43.5)*	43.9	*(43.3)*	50.7	*(49.7)*	50.4	*(49.4)*
Turkey	65	*(63)*	73.3	*(70.3)*	74.4	*(70.5)*	103.3	*(99.1)*	105.0	*(99.5)*
United Kingdom	67		49.0		47.7		58.1		56.8	
United States	67		39.2		41.8		50.5		53.8	
OECD	**66**	***(65.5)***	**51.8**	***(50.9)***	**53.1**	***(52.1)***	**62.4**	***(61.3)***	**63.8**	***(62.1)***
Argentina	65	*(60)*	76.1	*(72.9)*	88.5	*(84.6)*	88.9	*(85.3)*	103.2	*(98.8)*
Brazil	65	*(62)*	88.4	*(93.3)*	91.1	*(95.4)*	97.3	*(102.7)*	100.3	*(105.0)*
China	60	*(55)*	71.6	*(55.7)*	80.3	*(63.3)*	92.4	*(72.3)*	103.3	*(81.9)*
India	58		56.4	*(55.6)*	65.4	*(64.6)*	64.0	*(63.1)*	74.3	*(73.4)*
Indonesia	65		55.3	*(53.0)*	55.3	*(53.2)*	60.6	*(58.1)*	60.7	*(58.3)*
Russian Federation*	65	*(60)*	47.2	*(43.4)*	47.1	*(43.4)*	54.2	*(49.9)*	54.2	*(49.9)*
Saudi Arabia	47		59.6		N/A		66.2		N/A	
South Africa*	60		14.9		14.9		16.2		16.2	

Note: * Individuals have the same gross benefit under both the base case and earnings profile scenarios.

Source: OECD pension models.

StatLink https://stat.link/yixmlu

Key results

The base case at the beginning of this chapter concentrates on showing full-career replacement rates under the standard economic parameters that apply within the report, and reflect those used in the last few editions. This indicator focuses on an alternative set of economic assumptions that may better reflect the possibility of an extended period of low growth and low interest rates, which might be in part driven by population ageing. For workers with average earnings and a full career from age 22, the future gross replacement rate at the normal retirement age averages 51.6% for men and 50.6% for women in the 38 OECD countries under this alternative scenario, which is very similar to the base case figures. However, this similar average masks significant differences across countries.

Full career male workers at the average wage throughout their career will have, on average, a gross replacement rate of 51.8%, when they start working at age 22. These estimates are based on the standard economic parameters described in Chapter 4. As an alternative these standard parameters have been lowered to account for the possibility of a low economic growth and low interest rates scenario over the long term, which might be partly related to population ageing (Table 5.3). Within the alternative assumptions all the parameter values have been lowered.

Table 5.3. **Annual economic assumptions**

Economic assumptions that apply every year from 2020

	Base case assumptions	Alternative scenario
Discount rate	2.0%	1.0%
Price inflation	2.0%	1.0%
Real wage growth	1.25%	1.0%
Real rate of return	3.0%	2.0%
GDP growth	Country specific	Adjusted downward by 0.25%

As a consequence the gross replacement rate for male workers at average earnings decreases slightly to 51.6%, with the corresponding value for women also decreasing from 50.9% under the base assumptions to 50.6% under the alternative scenario. These reasonably stable values, however, hide the country specific impact, which can be quite significant.

Firstly, there are seven OECD countries, the Czech Republic, Germany, Ireland, Japan, Italy, New Zealand and Slovenia, as well as South Africa amongst G20 countries that have the same replacement rate under both scenarios. In all these countries there is either just a basic pension linked to earnings growth, or all parameters of the pension system are linked to wage (or GDP) growth, resulting in a steady state replacement rate if the earnings are at a constant proportion of the average.

The largest increases in replacement rates are found in Belgium, France, Greece, the Netherlands, Spain and Turkey, with increases of between 2.3 percentage points and 3.8 percentage points. In these countries past earnings are valorised to prices (Belgium, France, Greece for the first five years, the Netherlands and Spain) or the basic pension is indexed to prices, holding a higher relative value as a result of lower earnings growth (Greece) or past earnings are increased partially by GDP (Turkey). In both instances under the alternative economic parameters, wage growth is lower thereby increasing the value of the pension at retirement relative to average earnings.

Conversely, in countries that have large DC pension schemes the replacement rate decreases as the rate of return under the alternative scenario is only 1.0 percentage points higher than real wage growth, compared to 1.75 percentage points under the baseline assumptions. Australia, Chile, Denmark, Iceland, Israel, Latvia and Sweden all have a fall in their replacement rate of between 2.7 percentage points and 4.7 percentage points.

Definition and measurement

The old-age pension replacement rate measures how effectively a pension system provides a retirement income to replace earnings, the main source of income before retirement. The gross replacement rate is defined as gross pension entitlement divided by gross pre-retirement earnings.

Often, the replacement rate is expressed as the ratio of the pension to final earnings (just before retirement). Under the baseline assumptions, workers earn the same percentage of average worker earnings throughout their career. Therefore, final earnings are equal to lifetime average earnings revalued in line with economy-wide earnings growth. Replacement rates expressed as a percentage of final earnings are thus identical to those expressed as a percentage of lifetime earnings.

Table 5.4. **Gross pension replacement rates by different economic assumptions**

Percentage of average earnings

Full career male workers at average earnings (women where different)

	Pension age		Base case		Sensitivity		Difference	
Australia	67		31.3	*(28.4)*	27.0	*(24.6)*	*-4.2*	*(-3.8)*
Austria	65		74.1		75.0		*0.9*	
Belgium	67		43.4		45.9		*2.4*	
Canada	65		38.8		40.4		*1.6*	
Chile	65		31.2	*(28.8)*	28.5	*(27.3)*	*-2.7*	*(-1.5)*
Colombia	62	*(57)*	74.8	*(73.4)*	75.8	*(74.3)*	*1.0*	*(0.9)*
Costa Rica	65		71.9		71.5		*-0.4*	
Czech Republic*	65		49.0		49.0		*0.0*	
Denmark	74		80.0		75.9		*-4.1*	
Estonia	71		28.0		29.0		*0.9*	
Finland	68		56.6		57.3		*0.6*	
France	66		60.2		62.7		*2.5*	
Germany*	67		41.5		41.5		*0.0*	
Greece	66		72.6		75.5		*2.9*	
Hungary	65	*(62)*	62.5	*(58.1)*	63.3	*(47.7)*	*0.8*	*(-10.4)*
Iceland	67		51.8		47.1		*-4.7*	
Ireland*	66		29.7		29.7		*0.0*	
Israel	67	*(62)*	41.5	*(34.1)*	37.4	*(31.7)*	*-4.1*	*(-2.4)*
Italy*	71		74.6		74.6		*0.0*	
Japan*	65		32.4		32.4		*0.0*	
Korea	65		31.2		31.2		*0.1*	
Latvia	65		43.4		40.1		*-3.3*	
Lithuania	65		19.7		19.8		*0.1*	
Luxembourg	62		76.6		77.3		*0.7*	

	Pension age		Base case		Sensitivity		Difference	
Netherlands	69		69.7		72.0		*2.3*	
New Zealand*	65		39.8		39.8		*0.0*	
Norway	67		46.0		44.9		*-1.1*	
Poland	65	*(60)*	30.6	*(23.4)*	30.7	*(23.5)*	*0.1*	*(0.1)*
Portugal	68		74.9		71.5		*-3.3*	
Slovak Republic	64		53.1		52.6		*-0.5*	
Slovenia*	62		42.0		42.0		*0.0*	
Spain	65		73.9		77.7		*3.8*	
Sweden	65		53.3		50.4		*-2.9*	
Switzerland	65	*(64)*	44.1	*(43.5)*	44.6	*(44)*	*0.4*	*(0.5)*
Turkey	65	*(63)*	73.3	*(70.3)*	76.9	*(73.6)*	*3.6*	*(3.3)*
United Kingdom	67		49.0		49.8		*0.8*	
United States	67		39.2		40.2		*1.0*	
OECD	**66.1**	**(65.5)**	**51.8**	**(50.9)**	**51.6**	**(50.6)**	*-0.2*	*(-0.3)*
Argentina	65	*(60)*	76.1	*(72.9)*	73.8	*(71.3)*	*-2.3*	*(-1.6)*
Brazil	65	*(62)*	88.4	*(93.3)*	93.0	*(97.8)*	*4.5*	*(4.5)*
China	60	*(55)*	71.6	*(55.7)*	66.8	*(52.9)*	*-4.8*	*(-2.8)*
India	58		56.4	*(55.6)*	56.8	*(56.1)*	*0.4*	*(0.5)*
Indonesia	65		55.3	*(53)*	53.4	*(51.5)*	*-1.9*	*(-1.5)*
Russian Federation	65	*(60)*	47.2	*(43.4)*	54.0	*(49.2)*	*6.9*	*(5.8)*
Saudi Arabia	47		59.6		60.7		*1.1*	
South Africa*	60		14.9		14.9		*0.0*	

Note: * Individuals have the same gross benefit under both the base case and alternative economic assumption scenarios.

Source: OECD pension models.

StatLink https://stat.link/6m4tau

Key results

Self-employed workers with a taxable income (i.e. net of social security contributions) equal to the net average wage before tax (gross wage net of employee's contributions) can, on average in the OECD, expect to receive an old-age pension equal to 75% of the pension of the average-wage dependent worker in the private sector.

While the self-employed are required to participate in earnings-related pension schemes in most countries, they only contribute in a similar way to employees in Canada, Costa Rica, the Czech Republic, Estonia, Korea, Lithuania, Luxembourg, Portugal, Slovenia and the United States. Even in these countries, insufficient compliance with rules may undermine pension coverage.

In 19 countries, while self-employed workers are mandatorily covered by earnings-related schemes, pension coverage is limited because they are allowed to contribute less than employees, through reduced contribution rates (Austria, Belgium, Chile, France, Iceland, Israel, Italy, Latvia, Norway, Sweden and Switzerland), a flat-rate contributions (Colombia, Greece, Hungary, Poland, Spain and Turkey) or minimum income thresholds below which they are exempt from contribution obligations (Austria, Chile, Finland, Latvia, the Slovak Republic and Turkey). In Australia, Denmark, Germany, Japan, Mexico and the Netherlands, the self-employed are, in contrast to employees, not required to join earnings-related schemes. Finally, in Ireland, the self-employed participate in contribution-based basic schemes on similar terms as employees while the earnings-related schemes are voluntary for all.

In countries where the self-employed are not required to contribute to earnings-related pension schemes the relative pension level is among the lowest as the old-age pension of the self-employed is limited to first-tier benefits. In the full-career case, the relative pension of the self-employed is about half that of employees or even much lower in Mexico (32%), Japan (34%) and also Denmark, Germany, the Netherlands and the United Kingdom. Among countries with no mandatory contributions to earnings-related pensions by the self-employed, Australia stands out, as the means-tested basic pension gives the self-employed 86% of what average-wage employees get from the mandatory earnings-related scheme.

Low relative pensions for the self-employed - between 40% and 65% of employees' pensions - are also projected in Greece, Poland, Spain and Turkey where only flat-rate contributions to earnings-related schemes are mandatory for the self-employed, and in Latvia, where mandatory contributions above the minimum wage are reduced substantially. In Hungary, almost 60% of the self-employed pay taxes under the so-called KATA flat-rate regime that allows them to pay low flat-rate mandatory contributions, which leads to the lowest future relative pensions of 18%.

Lower contribution rates and a reduced contribution base result in lower pensions from mandatory earnings-related schemes for the self-employed relative to employees with the same taxable earnings in many countries. For example, in France (points scheme) and Italy, reduced contribution rates directly affect entitlements within the public system while in Norway, Sweden and Switzerland pensions are lower because the self-employed pay no or reduced contributions to mandatory funded schemes. As a result, pensions of the self-employed relative to employees reach 49% in Switzerland; around 65% in Israel and Italy; between 75% and 90% in Belgium, Chile, the Czech Republic, France, Norway, Portugal, the Slovak Republic, Slovenia and Sweden; and above 90% in Canada, Costa Rica, Estonia, Iceland, Korea and Lithuania.

Lower contributions of the self-employed do not always result in proportionally lower pensions. For example in the Czech Republic, progressive replacement rates result in the relative theoretical pensions of the self-employed reaching 85% even though the contribution base is set at only 50% of taxable income. In Belgium and Norway, the reduced contribution rates to public schemes do not reduce the benefits implicitly while in Austria and Costa Rica the reduced contributions of the self-employed are explicitly topped up with taxes.

Some countries calculate pensions of the self-employed based on gross income, i.e. income before deducting contributions. This leads to higher pensionable earnings "all else equal" in the case studied here (taxable income of the self-employed equal to the net wage before tax) when the contribution rate paid by the self-employed is higher than the employee part for dependent workers. Hence, the theoretical pension of the self-employed is slightly higher than that of employees in Austria and Luxembourg. The United States allow the self-employed to deduct half of social security contributions before calculating the contribution base. Given that employees and employers pay equal shares of contributions, this deduction equalises theoretical pensions between the self-employed and employees.

Definition and measurement

Theoretical pensions of a self-employed worker relative to an employee assumes that both have a taxable income (net income or net wage before taxes) equal to the average net wage before taxes, their career starts at age 22 in 2020, they do not face any interruptions and they retire at the normal retirement age. They contribute the amount that is (quasi) mandatory to pensions.

Table 5.5. **Contributions requirements to mandatory and quasi-mandatory pensions for the self-employed**

Mandatory or quasi-mandatory contributions to earnings-related schemes				Mandatory contributions to basic pensions only	No mandatory pension contributions
Employee-like	Reduced contribution rate	Only flat-rate contributions mandatory	Regular contributions mandatory only above income threshold		
Canada	Austria	Colombia	Austria	Ireland	Australia
Costa Rica	Belgium	Greece	Chile	Japan	Denmark
Czech Republic	Chile	Hungary	Finland	Netherlands	Germany
Estonia	France	Poland	Latvia	United Kingdom	Mexico
Korea	Iceland	Spain	Slovak Republic		
Lithuania	Israel	Turkey	Turkey		
Luxembourg	Italy				
Portugal	Latvia				
Slovenia	Norway				
United States	Sweden				
	Switzerland				

Note: Employee-like means that self-employed are covered by the same or equivalent schemes as employees, have the same contribution rates and thresholds, and that their contributions are income based. In Ireland neither self-employed nor dependent workers are covered by mandatory or quasi-mandatory earnings-related schemes but basic pensions are financed with contributions.
Source: Country Profiles available at *http://oe.cd/pag*.

StatLink https://stat.link/z3f0ut

Figure 5.5. **Theoretical relative pensions of the self-employed as % of those of employees**

Theoretical pensions of a self-employed worker relative to an employee having both a taxable income (net income or net wage before taxes) equal to the average net wage before taxes, for individuals with a full career from age 22 in 2018 and contributing only the amount that is (quasi) mandatory to pensions

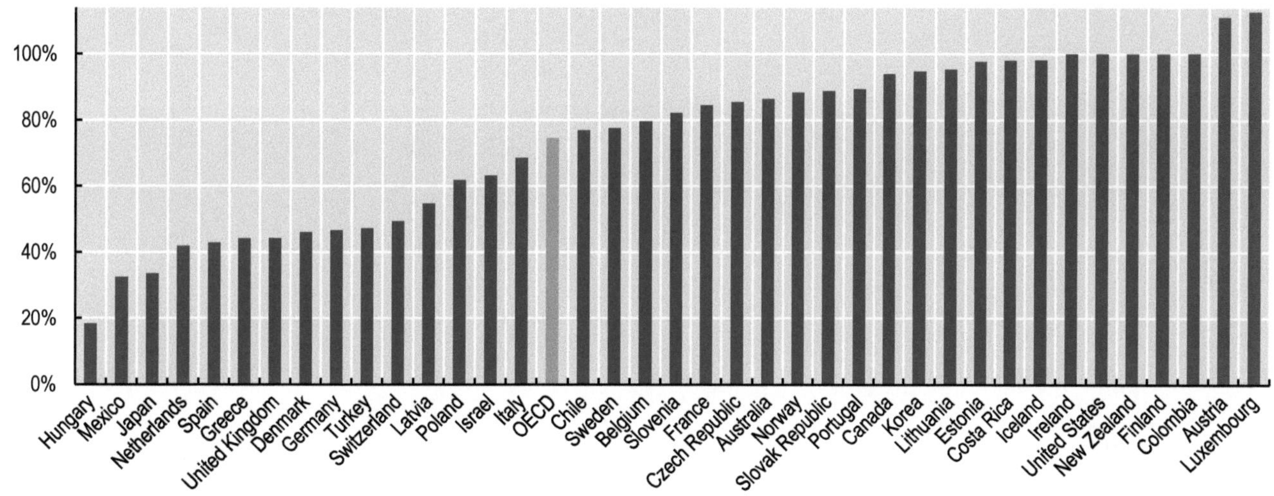

Source: OECD pension models.

StatLink https://stat.link/bnf5s1

Pensions at a Glance 2021
OECD and G20 Indicators

Chapter 6

Demographic and economic context

Population ageing has been one of the main driving forces behind changes in pension policies. Ageing is the result of demographic trends in fertility and life expectancy. The first indicator looks into the number of births per woman and its development over the last 50 years. Changes in life expectancy – at birth and at age 65 – are shown as the second indicator. The third looks into the degree of ageing measured as the level of and change in the number of people aged 65 and above relative to the number of people of working age (20-64). The fourth indicator looks at the employment rates of older workers. The fifth indicator presents calculations for the age at which people leave the labour market – the "Effective age of labour market exit", with the last indicator measuring the expected life years from this age by combining life expectancy with the previous indicator.

Key results

The total fertility rate is below the estimated replacement level – the number of children per woman needed to keep the total population constant – of about 2.1 in developed countries, in 36 out of 38 OECD countries. Exceptions are Israel with a total fertility rate of 3.04 and Mexico at 2.14 in 2020. Fertility rates fell sharply in the second half of the 20th century, and have stabilised in the OECD on average over the last two decades. In more than half of OECD countries, fertility rates have slightly increased since the early 2000s. Fertility rates have a profound implication for pension systems because they, along with life expectancy, are the drivers of substantial shifts in demographic structures. Since 1960, there has been a steady convergence of fertility rates across countries, which is expected to be prolonged in the next decades.

Fertility rates currently average 1.67 across OECD countries, well below the level that ensures population replacement. The trend to fewer children has been going on since the late 1950s, but stopped around the turn of century on average. The fall in fertility rates reflected changes in individuals' lifestyle preferences, in family formation, and in the constraints of everyday living, such as those driven by labour market insecurity, difficulties in finding suitable housing and unaffordable childcare.

Another effect might come from changes in women's aspiration regarding partnership and childbearing norms, especially in countries such as Japan and Korea where there is a strong link between marriage and maternity. However, the childbearing patterns of unmarried men and women have also changed. For example, half or more of births now occur outside of marriage in France, Iceland, Norway and Sweden. The average proportion of births outside marriage in OECD countries is now one-third of the total.

Over the last 50 years, there has been a steady convergence in fertility rates across OECD countries. In 1960, Korea, Mexico and Turkey had rates around twice the OECD average, with Hungary and Latvia not much over half, and an overall standard deviation of 1.2. This latter figure has decreased considerably over time, falling to 0.3 by 2020 and forecast to be only 0.1 by 2060.

Since 2000, the fertility rates in 21 out of 38 countries have slightly increased while the average has decreased slightly. The increases from a very low level have been the strongest in a few countries, including the Czech Republic (+0.47), Latvia (+0.54) and Slovenia (+0.35). The largest declines have been observed in Colombia (-0.88), Costa Rica (-0.85) and Mexico (-0.71).

This recent increase in fertility rates is forecasted to continue in more than two-thirds of OECD countries, albeit very slowly, and the average rate will be 1.71 across OECD countries by 2060 according to the median forecast of the United Nations Population Prospects. However, forecast uncertainty is considerable, with the 20th percentile of probabilistic projections for the OECD average at only 1.39 and the 80th percentile close to reproduction at 1.96 (Figure 6.1).

Low fertility rates have wider social and economic consequences. The old-age to working-age ratio will increase sharply placing additional burdens on the working-age population to finance pay-as-you-go pensions and health care for older people. Moreover, the workforce will also age over time and so might be less adaptable to technological change.

Among the other major economies, Argentina, India, Indonesia, Saudi Arabia and South Africa all currently have fertility rates well above the replacement level of 2.1. However, the downward trend is expected to continue in these countries as well as in Brazil, with fertility rates going below the natural replacement rate by 2030. By contrast, the trough was reached at low levels in China and the Russian Federation about 20 years ago.

Definition and measurement

The total fertility rate is the number of children that would be born to each woman if she were to live to the end of her child-bearing years and if the likelihood of her giving birth to children at each age was the currently prevailing age-specific fertility rate. It is generally computed by summing up the age-specific fertility rates defined over a five-year interval. A total fertility rate of 2.1 children per women – the replacement level – broadly ensures a stable population size, on the assumptions of no migration flows and unchanged mortality rates.

Table 6.1. **Total fertility rates, 1960-2060**

	1960	1980	2000	2020	2040	2060		1960	1980	2000	2020	2040	2060
Australia	3.41	1.99	1.79	1.83	1.73	1.72	Netherlands	3.10	1.60	1.60	1.66	1.72	1.74
Austria	2.57	1.65	1.39	1.53	1.65	1.71	New Zealand	4.07	2.18	1.95	1.90	1.77	1.73
Belgium	2.50	1.70	1.60	1.71	1.75	1.77	Norway	2.84	1.81	1.86	1.68	1.73	1.75
Canada	3.88	1.73	1.56	1.53	1.52	1.61	Poland	3.47	2.23	1.51	1.42	1.57	1.66
Chile	4.75	2.94	2.20	1.65	1.57	1.61	Portugal	3.12	2.55	1.46	1.29	1.49	1.61
Colombia	6.68	4.16	2.70	1.82	1.61	1.63	Slovak Republic	3.24	2.46	1.40	1.50	1.65	1.71
Costa Rica	6.65	3.70	2.61	1.76	1.61	1.65	Slovenia	2.38	2.16	1.25	1.60	1.71	1.75
Czech Republic	2.38	2.36	1.17	1.64	1.75	1.78	Spain	2.70	2.55	1.19	1.33	1.51	1.61
Denmark	2.55	1.68	1.76	1.76	1.79	1.80	Sweden	2.25	1.66	1.56	1.85	1.84	1.83
Estonia	1.99	2.06	1.33	1.59	1.71	1.75	Switzerland	2.39	1.54	1.48	1.54	1.61	1.65
Finland	2.77	1.66	1.74	1.53	1.53	1.63	Turkey	6.50	4.69	2.65	2.08	1.82	1.73
France	2.70	1.86	1.76	1.85	1.84	1.83	United Kingdom	2.49	1.73	1.74	1.75	1.77	1.77
Germany	2.27	1.51	1.35	1.59	1.67	1.71	United States	3.58	1.77	2.00	1.78	1.80	1.81
Greece	2.42	2.42	1.31	1.30	1.37	1.54	**OECD**	**3.37**	**2.35**	**1.72**	**1.67**	**1.68**	**1.71**
Hungary	2.32	2.25	1.38	1.49	1.63	1.70							
Iceland	4.17	2.45	2.06	1.77	1.67	1.68							
Ireland	3.58	3.25	1.90	1.84	1.70	1.69	Argentina	3.13	3.40	2.63	2.27	2.02	1.87
Israel	3.89	3.47	2.93	3.04	2.63	2.32	Brazil	6.06	4.24	2.47	1.74	1.56	1.59
Italy	2.29	1.89	1.22	1.33	1.42	1.53	China	5.48	3.01	1.62	1.69	1.73	1.76
Japan	2.17	1.83	1.37	1.37	1.49	1.59	India	5.90	4.97	3.48	2.24	1.92	1.76
Korea	6.33	2.92	1.50	1.11	1.25	1.48	Indonesia	5.67	4.73	2.55	2.32	2.00	1.85
Latvia	1.95	1.89	1.17	1.72	1.78	1.80	Russian Federation	2.82	1.94	1.25	1.82	1.83	1.83
Lithuania	2.66	2.10	1.47	1.67	1.75	1.78	Saudi Arabia	7.18	7.28	4.40	2.34	1.83	1.65
Luxembourg	2.23	1.49	1.72	1.45	1.52	1.61	South Africa	6.05	5.05	2.88	2.41	2.07	1.88
Mexico	6.78	5.33	2.85	2.14	1.80	1.71	EU27	2.67	2.08	1.49	1.56	1.64	1.70

Note: The data refers to 5-year periods whose end-point is indicated in the first row of the table.

Source: United Nations, Department of Economic and Social Affairs, (2019). World Population Prospects 2019, Online Edition (for future periods: medium-variant forecast).

StatLink https://stat.link/dgsfk8

Figure 6.1. **Uncertainty about total fertility-rate projections**

Low, medium and high variant projections for 2050-55

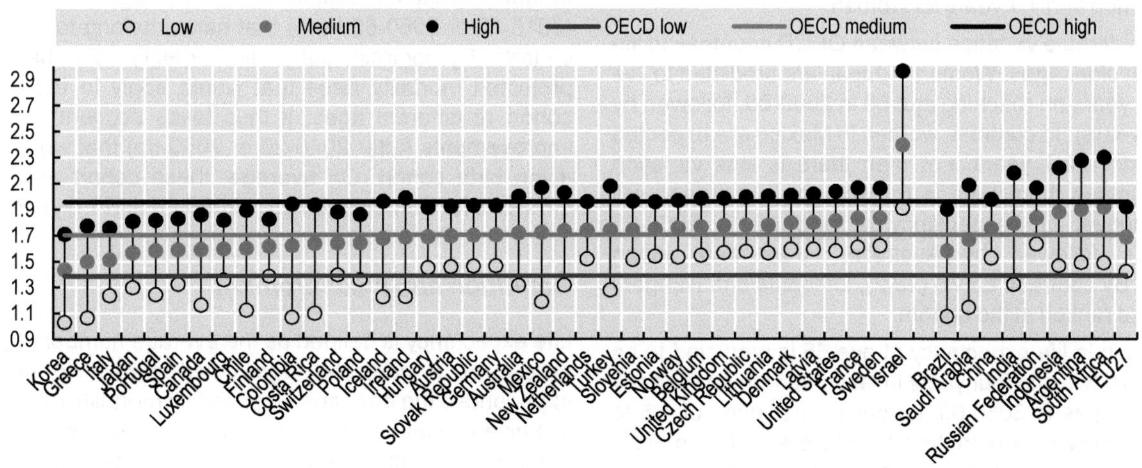

Note: Low, medium and high variant projections correspond to the 20%, 50% and 80% percentiles of probabilistic projections, respectively.

Source: United Nations, Department of Economic and Social Affairs (2019). Probabilistic Population Projections based on the World Population Prospects 2019: *http://population.un.org/wpp/*.

StatLink https://stat.link/x1r2bs

Key results

The remarkable increase in life expectancy is one of the greatest achievements of the last century. Lives continue to get longer, and this trend is predicted to continue although the pace of improvement in old age has slowed slightly. In 2015-20, life expectancy at birth averaged 77.9 years for men and 83.1 years for women. Among women, the figure was highest in Japan (87.5 years) and lowest in Mexico (77.8 years). For men, life expectancy at birth was highest in Switzerland (81.6 years) and lowest in Latvia and Lithuania (69.9 and 70.0 years, respectively). On average across OECD countries, remaining life expectancy at age 65 is projected to increase by 3.9 years among women and 4.5 years among men by 2065.

Remaining life expectancy at 65 significantly contributes to well-being at older ages. It also influences the finances of retirement-income systems. In 2015-20, on average in OECD countries, women aged 65 could expect to live an additional 21.3 years, which is forecast to increase to 25.2 years by 2060-65. Men of the same age could expect to live 18.1 more years in 2015-20, with a projected increase of 4.5 years by 2060-65 to reach about 22.5 years. Gender gaps are therefore expected to decrease slightly over the next 45 years (from 3.3 to 2.7 years on average in OECD countries). However, the improvement in remaining life expectancy at age 65 has recently slowed from a period of fast longevity gains (Box 1.1, Chapter 1). This slowdown began around 2010, for both men and women, and represents a structural break in the series. Between the mid-1990s and 2010 the increase in life expectancy at age 65 was fast at around 1.6 years for men per decade and 1.4 years for women. Since 2010, this has fallen to 1.3 years for men and 1.1 years for women.

There is considerable variation between OECD countries in life expectancy at older ages. Women in Japan are predicted to live another 28.8 years on reaching age 65 in 2060-65, followed by Korea (27.4 years). In contrast, women in Mexico are expected to live an extra 22.1 years. For men there is less variation between countries than there is for women. Switzerland will have the longest life expectancy at age 65 in 2060-65 (23.9 years), followed by Australia, Israel and Japan (23.8 years). By contrast, Latvia (19.2), Lithuania and Hungary (both 19.9) are ranked at the bottom.

The gender gap in life expectancy at age 65 is predicted to be between almost two and four years in favour of women in nearly all OECD countries in 2060-65. Larger gender gaps of 4.5 to 5 years are observed in both Japan and Korea. The smallest gender gap are forecasted for the United States and the United Kingdom at 1.5 and 1.7 years respectively.

Given this trend, many OECD countries have increased or legislated to increase their pension benefit eligibility ages: see Chapter 1 on "Recent Pension Reforms". Others have introduced elements into their retirement-income provision that will automatically adjust the level of pensions as people live longer. Overall longevity gains are due to rising living standards, but also greater access to quality health services.

Turning to the non-OECD major economies, life expectancy is generally lower than the OECD average. Life expectancy at birth is by far the lowest in South Africa at 60.2 years for men and 67.1 years for women. The highest life expectancy at birth is found in Argentina for women at 79.8 years and in China at 74.5 years for men. Life expectancy at 65 is the lowest for South African women (14.7 years) and men (11.5 years). By 2060-65 those aged 65 will live longest in Brazil at 23.7 years for women and 21.1 years for men.

The above numbers refer to period life expectancy, which measures life expectancy (current or projected) based on mortality rates for people of different ages at a given time (2015-20 or 2060-65 here) that hence belong to different birth cohorts. By contrast, cohort life expectancy is based on the projected mortality rates that would apply to the same birth cohort at different ages. It thus takes account of continuing improvements (after 2015-20 or 2060-65) that would benefit a given birth cohort. On average, these cohort estimates add 1.5 years for women aged 65 in 2060-65 and 1.0 years for men.

Definition and measurement

Life expectancy is defined as the average number of years that people of a particular age could expect to live if they experienced the age- and sex-specific mortality rates prevalent in a given country in a particular year: in this case, 2015-20 and 2060-65. Since the determinants of longevity change slowly, life expectancy is best analysed over a long time horizon. Cohort life expectancy takes account of the projected changes in mortality estimates for a given cohort.

Figure 6.2. **Current life expectancy at birth for men and women, in years**

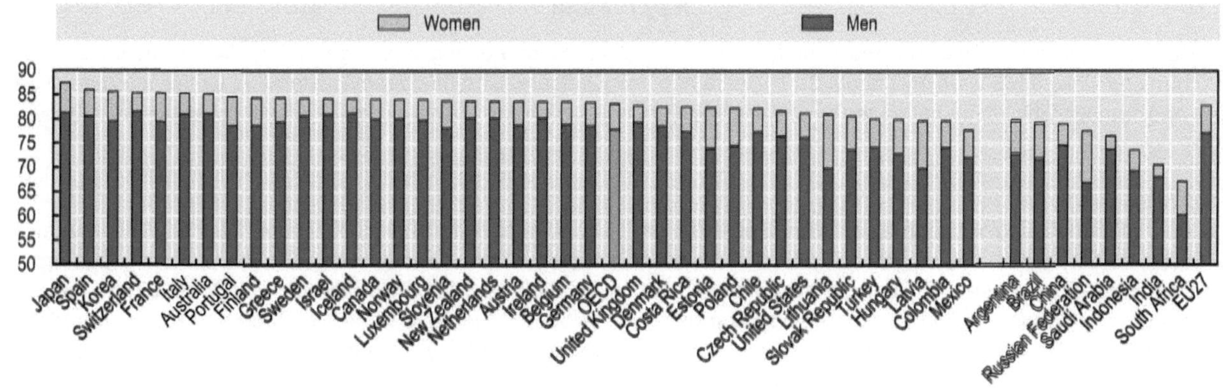

Note: Shown is period life expectancy that is computed from mortality rates that apply in a specific period, here 2015-20, rather than to a specific birth cohort.
Source: United Nations, Department of Economic and Social Affairs, (2019). World Population Prospects 2019, Online Edition.

StatLink https://stat.link/w21i4r

Figure 6.3. **Remaining life expectancy at age 65 for women, current and projections, in years**

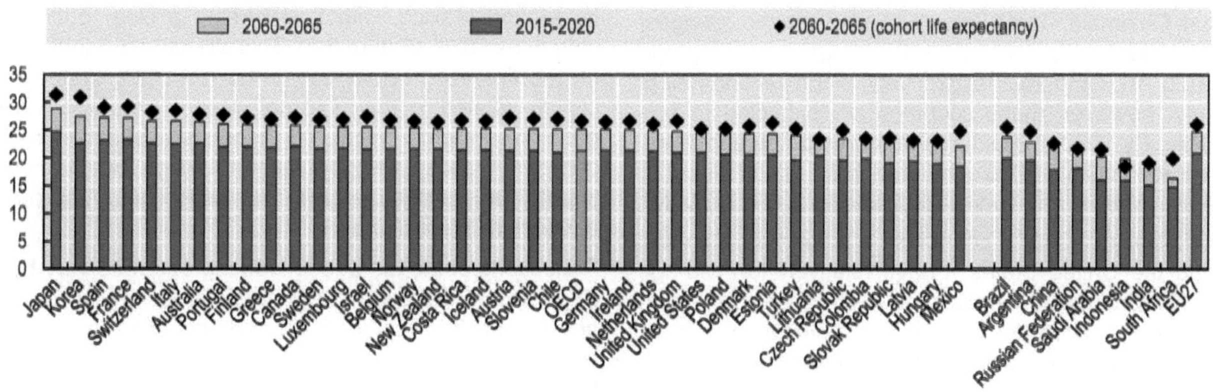

Source: United Nations, Department of Economic and Social Affairs, (2019). World Population Prospects 2019, Online Edition.

StatLink https://stat.link/ndzcm3

Figure 6.4. **Remaining life expectancy at age 65 for men, current and projections, in years**

Based on mortality rates of the indicated period or cohort

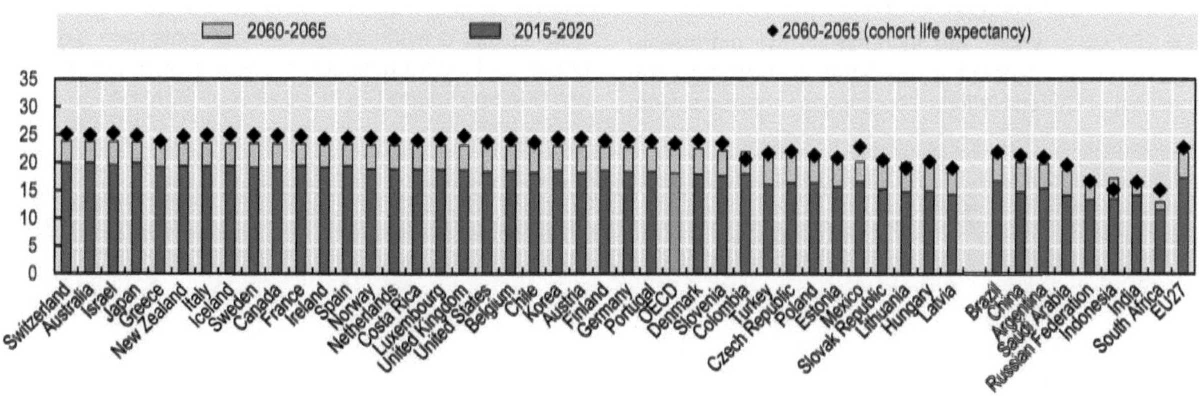

Source: United Nations, Department of Economic and Social Affairs, (2019). World Population Prospects 2019, Online Edition.

StatLink https://stat.link/6vpu5m

Key results

There are 30 individuals aged 65 and over for every 100 persons of working age (ages 20 to 64) on average across all OECD countries while there were only about 20 30 years ago. Population ageing has been accelerating as this average old-age to working-age demographic ratio – computed by keeping age thresholds constant – is projected to reach 53 over the next 30 years.

The evolution of old-age to working-age ratios depends on mortality rates, fertility rates and migration. OECD countries have seen prolonged increases in life expectancy that most analysts project to continue, implying an increasing number of older people and most likely of pensioners too.

Currently, the demographically oldest OECD country is Japan, with an old-age to working-age ratio equal to 52.0 (meaning 52 individuals aged 65 and over for 100 persons of working age defined as 20 to 64). Finland and Italy also have high old-age ratios, of about 40. By 2050, the old-age to working-age ratio is expected to reach more than 70 in Greece (75.0), Italy (74.4), Japan (80.7), Korea (78.8), Portugal (71.4) and Spain (78.4).

By contrast, Colombia, Costa Rica and Turkey are the youngest countries based on this indicator, with old-age to working-age ratios of 15.0, 16.6 and 15.2 respectively, In the second half of this century, however, these countries are expected to age considerably. By 2080, the old-age ratio would rise above the OECD average in Chile (67.5 compared to 61.1) and closer to the average in Mexico and Turkey (50.9 and 58.2, respectively).

Four Anglo-Saxon OECD countries – Australia, Canada, Ireland and the United States – have relatively low old-age ratios, between 25 and 30. This is partly due to inward migration of workers and – except for Canada – to comparatively high fertility rates just below replacement level in recent decades.

There have also been substantial declines in fertility, which, of course, will eventually diminish the number of workers entering the labour market. For example, fertility rates fell below the replacement level on average in OECD countries around the mid-1980s, implying shrinking populations in the long term. In the future, however, there is a great deal of uncertainty over how fertility rates will evolve (Figure 6.1).

For the OECD as a whole, the increase in the old-age to working-age ratio is projected to continue according to the medium forecast of United Nations Populations Prospects, from 30.4 in 2020 to 52.7 in 2050 and 61.1 in 2080. By far, Korea is facing the most rapid population ageing among OECD countries. The old-age ratio would increase from 7.6 in 1960, 23.6 in 2020 to 94.6 in 2080 and Korea would move from being the fifth youngest country in the OECD in 2020 to the oldest in 2080.

The projected working-age population (20-64) will decrease by 10% in the OECD on average by 2060, i.e. by 0.26% per year. It will fall by 35% or more in Greece, Japan, Korea, Latvia, Lithuania and Poland, and also by more than 25% in Estonia, Hungary, Italy, Portugal, Slovenia, the Slovak Republic and Spain. It is projected to increase by more than 20% in Australia, Israel and Mexico, with Israel being a clear outlier with an increase of 67% (Figure 6.5). This will have a significant impact on the financing of pay-as-you-go (PAYGO) systems as it is closely related to their internal rates of return. Even funded pension systems might be negatively affected by rapidly declining working-age populations through its effect on labour supply, in turn potentially lowering output growth and equilibrium interest rates.

Projections of the old-age to working-age ratio vary by source (Figure 6.6). Although the projections for the EU22 countries are virtually identical for 2020 and only differ by 2 percentage points in 2050 this is not the case for all the individual countries. In 15 of the countries the UN data is higher for 2050, with seven countries having a higher figure for the Eurostat data. In Latvia the Eurostat data is 9 percentage points higher in 2050, whereas in Spain the UN data is 14 percentage points higher.

Definition and measurement

The old-age to working-age demographic ratio is defined as the number of individuals aged 65 and over per 100 people of working age defined as those at ages 20 to 64.

Table 6.2. **Demographic old-age to working-age ratio: Historical and projected values, 1950-2080**

	1950	1960	1990	2020	2050	2080		1950	1960	1990	2020	2050	2080
Australia	14.0	16.0	18.8	27.7	41.6	49.4	Netherlands	13.9	16.8	20.6	34.3	53.3	62.2
Austria	17.3	21.0	24.3	31.3	56.0	60.2	New Zealand	16.3	17.0	19.5	28.3	43.8	57.5
Belgium	18.1	20.3	24.8	33.1	51.3	56.8	Norway	16.0	19.8	28.5	29.6	43.4	53.4
Canada	14.0	15.1	18.4	29.8	44.9	54.0	Poland	9.4	10.5	17.3	30.5	60.3	68.6
Chile	7.2	7.9	10.9	19.7	44.6	67.5	Portugal	13.0	14.8	23.9	38.6	71.4	72.3
Colombia	7.5	7.2	8.4	15.0	36.0	64.3	Slovak Republic	11.9	12.6	18.2	26.5	54.6	58.1
Costa Rica	6.8	7.1	9.0	16.6	41.6	69.4	Slovenia	12.5	13.7	17.3	34.7	65.0	60.7
Czech Republic	13.9	16.3	22.0	33.8	55.9	52.8	Spain	12.8	14.6	23.1	32.8	78.4	74.4
Denmark	15.6	19.0	25.9	34.9	44.6	52.4	Sweden	16.8	20.2	30.9	35.9	45.5	53.4
Estonia	19.3	17.7	19.7	34.9	54.9	63.2	Switzerland	15.8	17.6	23.6	31.3	54.4	56.7
Finland	11.9	13.5	22.0	40.1	51.4	65.0	Turkey	6.5	7.0	9.4	15.2	37.0	58.2
France	19.5	20.8	24.0	37.3	54.5	62.2	United Kingdom	17.9	20.2	26.9	32.0	47.1	55.1
Germany	16.2	19.1	23.5	36.5	58.1	59.5	United States	14.2	17.3	21.6	28.4	40.4	51.1
Greece	12.4	12.2	22.9	37.8	75.0	79.7	**OECD**	**13.6**	**15.0**	**20.0**	**30.4**	**52.7**	**61.1**
Hungary	13.2	15.5	22.9	33.4	52.6	55.4							
Iceland	14.1	16.4	19.0	26.6	46.2	64.5							
Ireland	20.9	22.8	21.6	25.0	50.6	60.0	Argentina	7.5	10.1	17.3	20.2	30.3	45.5
Israel	7.1	9.1	17.8	23.9	31.3	39.9	Brazil	6.5	7.1	8.4	15.5	39.5	63.7
Italy	14.3	16.4	24.3	39.5	74.4	79.6	China	8.5	7.6	10.2	18.5	47.5	60.6
Japan	9.9	10.4	19.3	52.0	80.7	82.9	India	6.4	6.4	7.9	11.3	22.5	40.8
Korea	6.3	7.6	8.9	23.6	78.8	94.6	Indonesia	8.6	7.6	7.7	10.6	27.3	41.0
Latvia	18.1	17.7	19.9	35.5	53.0	49.9	Russian Federation	8.7	10.5	17.2	25.3	41.7	41.9
Lithuania	17.5	14.0	18.4	34.7	55.7	55.7	Saudi Arabia	7.5	8.4	6.1	5.3	28.2	44.8
Luxembourg	15.8	17.6	21.1	22.3	43.8	50.1	South Africa	8.5	8.4	8.7	9.6	17.4	26.8
Mexico	8.0	8.3	9.6	13.2	28.9	50.9	EU27	14.6	16.0	21.6	33.6	56.7	62.0

Note: The demographic old-age to working-age ratio is defined as the number of individuals aged 65 and over per 100 people aged between 20 and 64.
Source: United Nations, Department of Economic and Social Affairs (2019), World Population Prospects 2019, Online Edition (for future periods: medium-variant forecast).

StatLink https://stat.link/7bkwjc

Figure 6.5. **The working-age population will decline in a large number of OECD countries**

Change in the working age population (20-64), 2020-60

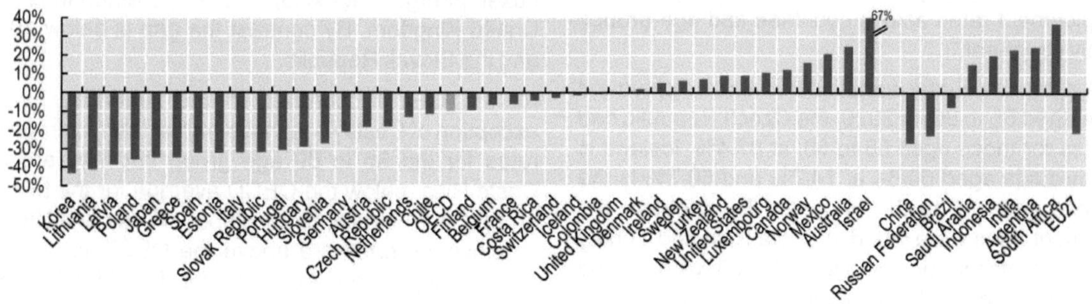

Source: United Nations World Population Prospects: The 2019 Revision.

StatLink https://stat.link/4id2ql

Figure 6.6. **Demographic old-age to working-age ratio projections differ based on data sources**

Difference in population projections for 2050 (EU – UN data source), in percentage points

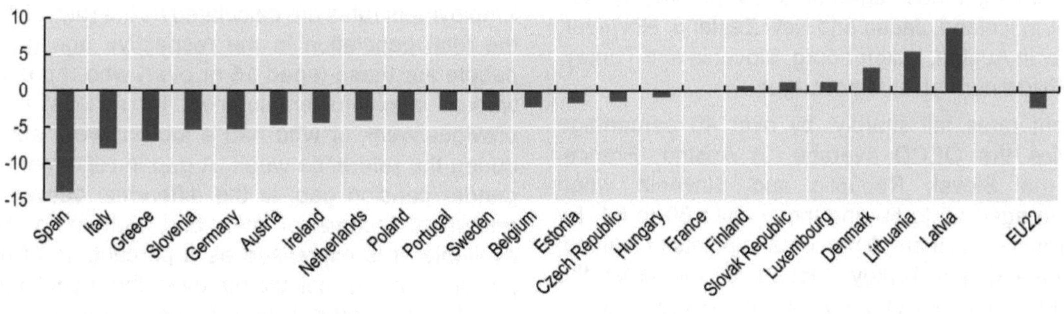

Note: The demographic old-age to working-age ratio is defined as the number of individuals aged 65 and over per 100 people aged between 20 and 64.
Source: United Nations, Department of Economic and Social Affairs (2019), World Population Prospects 2019, Online Edition (for future periods: medium-variant forecast). Eurostat population projections, EUROPOP 2019.

StatLink https://stat.link/nc2y58

Key results

The COVID-19 crisis has had a big impact on employment from 2020 in many countries. Yet, the broad pattern of employment rates across countries and age groups remains structural. The employment rate falls with age in all OECD countries, often sharply. For individuals aged 55 to 59, the average employment rate across all OECD countries was 71.9% in 2020, 50.7% for the 60-64 age group and 22.9% for those aged 65-69. Employment rates for men are higher than for women among older workers in all but two OECD countries, Estonia and Finland, averaging 14 percentage points across all countries. Resulting gender gaps in pensions range from 3% in Estonia to 47% in Japan, with an OECD average of 26%, with men receiving higher levels in all countries.

Recent employment rates have been affected by COVID-19 (Chapter 1), with the impact felt across all age groups. For those aged 55-64 the employment rate decreased by an average of 1.6 percentage points between 2019 and 2020 (Figure 6.10). The greatest decreases were in Chile (-9.9 percentage points), Colombia (-7.0 percentage points) and Costa Rica (-8.0 percentage points). Canada, Mexico, Turkey and the United States were also deeply affected. Conversely in most Central and Eastern European countries, the impact on employment has been lower with employment rates actually increasing. The largest increases were in Hungary (+2.9 percentage points), Poland (+2.3 percentage points) and Slovenia (+1.9 percentage points), with another seven European countries also showing growth of over 1 percentage point Those countries with a smaller decline in employment rates tend to be those that provided greater protection for workers during the COVID-19 crisis. Yet, the pattern of employment rates across countries and age groups remains broadly structural.

There are large cross-country variations in the employment rates of people aged 55 to 69. In 2020, the Czech Republic had the highest rates for those aged 55 to 59, at 87.4%, Iceland is highest for individuals aged 60-64 at 74.7% and 50.7% is the highest for those aged 65 to 69, in Japan. By contrast, the lowest employment rates were found in Costa Rica and Turkey where employment rates for people aged 55 to 59 were around 55%. At ages 60-64 and 65-69 Luxembourg recorded the lowest employment rates in 2020, with 20.2% and 5.7% respectively.

On average across the OECD the employment rate falls with age, from a high of 71.9% for those aged 55 to 59, falling to 50.7% for those aged 60 to 64 and then to 22.9% for those aged 65 to 69. Amongst those aged 60 to 64 the employment rate is over 70% in Iceland, Japan and New Zealand. However, it is 30% or lower in Austria, Luxembourg, Slovenia and Turkey, all countries with low normal retirement ages.

The employment rates fall sharply, by over 40 percentage points, i.e. twice the OECD average, in Austria, France, Luxembourg, the Slovak Republic and Slovenia when comparing those aged 55 to 59 and those aged 60 to 64. By contrast the fall is by less than 10 percentage points in Iceland, Israel, New Zealand and Turkey, though for the latter the employment rates are 35% or under across all the age groups.

Employment rates for women are lower than that for men in all countries for the 25 to 54 age group with only Estonia and Finland reversing this pattern for the older 55 to 64 age group, at 10 percentage points and 2 percentage points higher for women, respectively. For older workers the OECD average gender gap is 14 percentage points, slightly higher than for the prime age group at 12 percentage points The greatest differences in gender gaps for older workers are found in Chile, Colombia, Costa Rica and Mexico, all of which are above 30 percentage points. Only France, Latvia and Lithuania have gender gaps in employment rates for older workers below 5 percentage points

These high employment differences between men and women lead to large differences in pension entitlements, especially as employment gender gaps have historically been even wider. Across the 34 OECD countries where data are available pension payments for men are 26% higher than those for women. The level is 40% or larger in Austria, Japan, Luxembourg, Mexico, the Netherlands and the United Kingdom. By contrast the gap is below 10% in Estonia and the Slovak Republic.

All the OECD countries in the Americas, with the slight exception of Costa Rica, have higher than average employment rates for the 65 to 69 age group but they are all, including Costa Rica, below the OECD average for the two younger age groups. In Australia, Israel, Japan, Korea and New Zealand the employment rates are above the OECD for each age group, except slightly for Australia for the 55-59 age group. By contrast, the employment rates are below the OECD average for all age groups considered in Belgium, Greece, Italy, Luxembourg, Poland, Spain and Turkey.

Definition and measurement

Employment rates are calculated as the ratio of the employed to the total population in the respective age group. Employed people are those (aged 15 or over) who report that they have worked in gainful employment for at least one hour in the previous week or who had a job but were absent from work during the reference week. A gap in retirement income, i.e. a gender pension gap, is the difference between the average retirement income of men and women in the latest year available. It is expressed as a percentage of men's average pension and is calculated over the population of pension beneficiaries aged 65+ for comparability purposes across countries.

Figure 6.7. **Employment rates of workers aged 55-59, 60-64 and 65-69 in 2020**

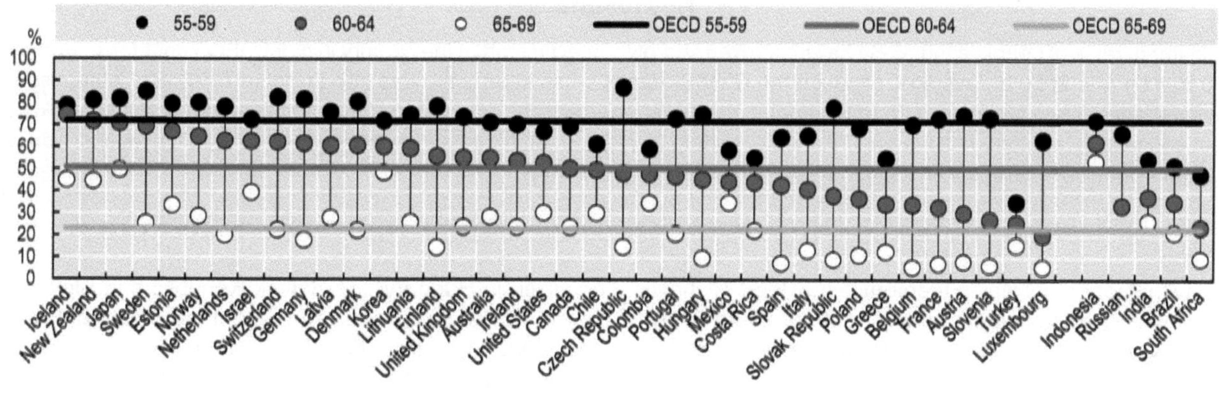

Note: Data for India and Indonesia refer to year 2019. Age group 65-69 data for Russian Federation are unavailable.
Source: OECD database Labour Market Statistics by sex and age: employment-population ratio.

StatLink https://stat.link/rm6z5a

Figure 6.8. **Gender gap in employment rates by age group, 2020**

Percentage-point difference (male – female)

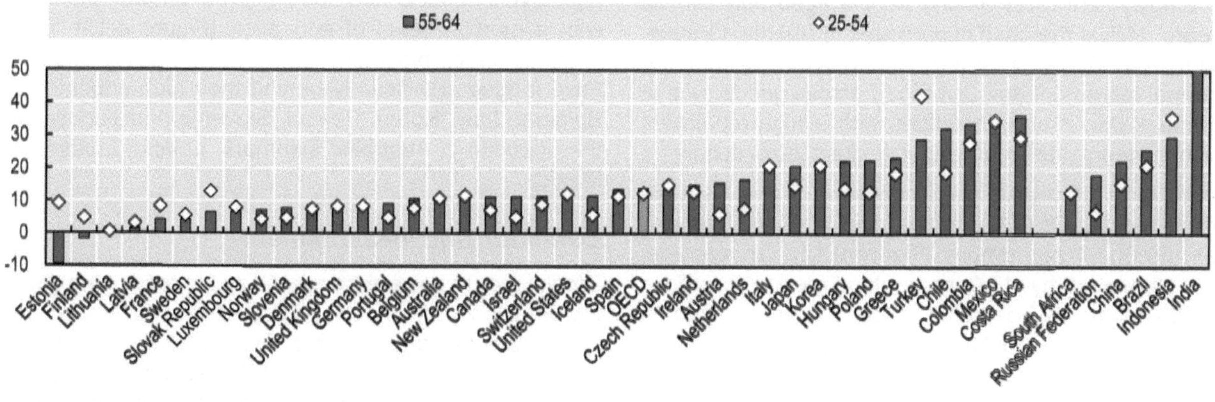

Note: Data for Germany, India and Indonesia refer to 2019. China is for 2010.
Source: OECD database Labour Market Statistics by sex and age: employment-population ratio.

StatLink https://stat.link/lpu1fy

Figure 6.9. **Gender gap in pensions in selected OECD countries, latest year available**

Relative difference between men and women aged 65+ (among pension beneficiaries)

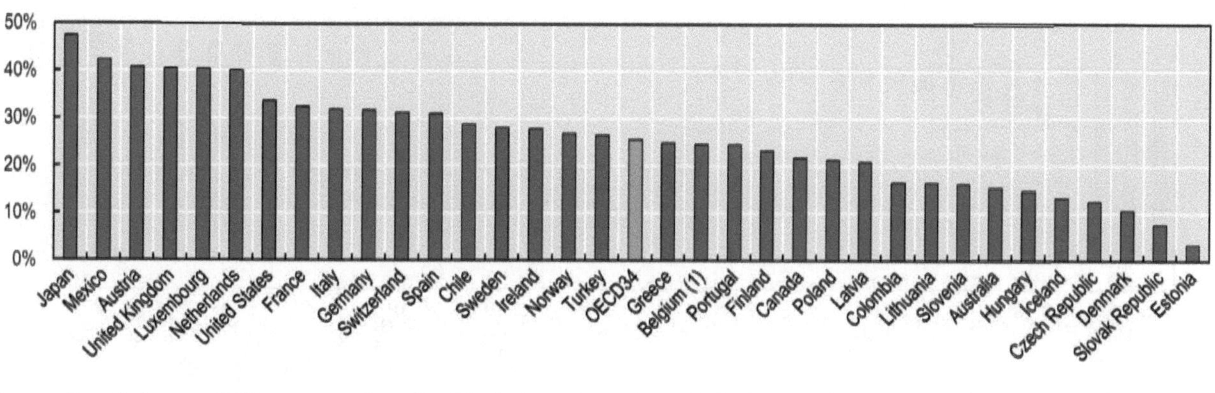

Note: Data come from the latest available survey, conducted in: 2013 for Japan, Luxembourg, the Netherlands, Norway and the Slovak Republic; 2014 for Australia; 2015 for Hungary and Slovenia; and after 2015 for all the other countries. Data refer to 2017 for Iceland and 2018 for Turkey.
(1) In Belgium when partner A's pension rights are less than 25% of those of partner B, the pension of A is not paid out and B receives a family pension (calculated at 75% of wages instead of 60%).
Source: OECD (2021[1]), *Towards Improved Retirement Savings Outcomes for Women*, https://dx.doi.org/10.1787/f7b48808-en.

StatLink https://stat.link/lgw3k6

Key results

Employment rates of people aged 55-64 have improved sharply since the start of the century in most OECD countries, from 43.8% in 2000 to 61.4% in 2020 on average, although the COVID-19 crisis has interrupted this trend (Figure 6.10). By comparison, the employment rate among those aged 25 to 54 only increased by 3 percentage points since 2000. On average, 55-64 year-olds at all levels of educational attainment have experienced a marked increase in employment, with those with a medium level of education doing slightly better on average than those with low or high levels of education.

Countries with higher normal retirement ages tend to have higher employer rates for older workers, but there are a few exceptions (Figure 6.11). Iceland and Norway have retirement ages of 67 years for both men and women and also have among the highest employment rates for those age 60 to 64, at 75% and 65%, respectively, well above the OECD average of 51%.

Except for Colombia, Costa Rica and Korea where informality in the labour market is high or the pension system has not yet matured, countries with low normal retirement ages tend to have low employment rates among people aged between 60 and 64 years. This is the case in particular in Austria, Greece, Luxembourg, the Slovak Republic and Slovenia where the current normal retirement age (averaged across genders) is at 62.5 years or lower. Among countries with a high retirement age, the employment rate among older workers is low in Italy.

Employment rates of people aged between 55 and 64 have improved in almost all OECD countries since 2000, both among the 55-59 and 60-64 age groups (Figure 6.12). On average, they have increased by 17.0 percentage points for those aged 55 to 59 and by 18.8 percentage points for those aged 60 to 64, reaching 71.9% and 50.7% in 2020, respectively. By comparison, the employment rate in the 25-to-54 age group only increased, on average, from 76.5% in 2000 to 79.5% in 2020. The greatest increases for the 55-to-59 age group occurred in Hungary, the Slovak Republic and Slovenia, all of which increased by over 40 percentage points between 2000 and 2020. For the 60-to-64 age group Germany and the Netherlands also increased by over 40 percentage points Conversely, In Iceland and Turkey, for those aged 55-59 and 60-64 the employments rate declined over the 20-year period, as was also the case for those aged 60-64 in Mexico.

On average, 55-64 year-olds at all levels of educational attainment have experienced a marked increase in employment between 2000-19, averaging 13 percentage points for low and high levels of education and by 17 percentage points for those with a medium level of education (Figure 6.13). In terms of changes in employment rates, low-educated older workers have lagged significantly behind their high-educated peers in Belgium, Italy, Korea, Poland, Slovenia and Turkey, while it is the opposite in Australia, Denmark, Ireland, Luxembourg and Mexico.

Definition and measurement

Employment rates are calculated as the ratio of the employed to the total population in the respective age group. Employed people are those (aged 15 or over) who report that they have worked in gainful employment for at least one hour in the previous week or who had a job but were absent from work during the reference week.

Figure 6.10. **COVID-19 has impacted the employment rates of those aged 55 to 64**

Percentage point change in employment rate between 2019 and 2020 for those aged 55 to 64

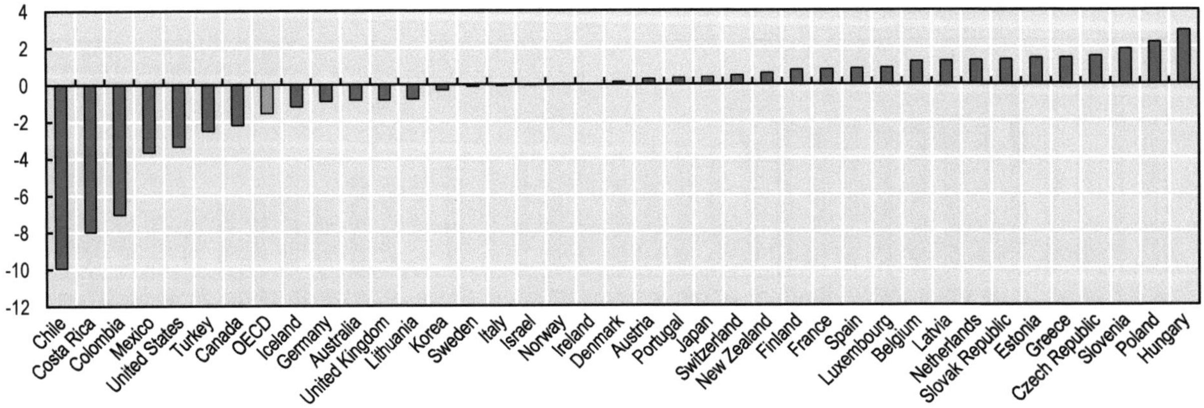

Source: OECD database Labour Market Statistics by sex and age: employment-population ratio.

StatLink https://stat.link/lc34qt

Figure 6.11. **Employment rate at ages 60-64 vs. normal retirement age in 2020**

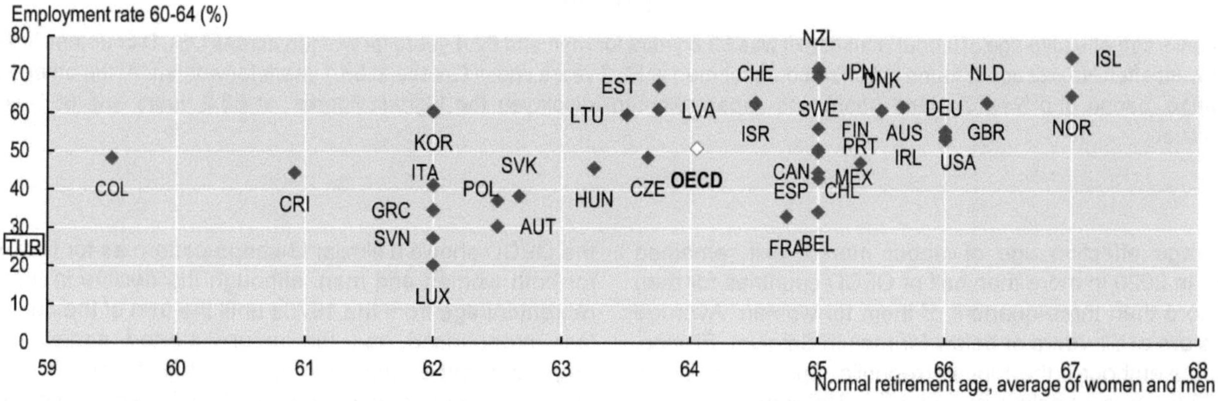

Note: For better visibility, the scale of this chart excludes the lowest observed value for the normal retirement age in Turkey, which is 50.5 (average of 49 and 52 for women and men respectively), with the employment rate equalling 25.7%.

Source: OECD database Labour Market Statistics by sex and age: employment-population ratio. Normal retirement age data: See Chapter 3.

StatLink https://stat.link/bysdok

Figure 6.12. **Change in employment rates of older workers and prime-age workers, 2000-20**

Percentage-point difference

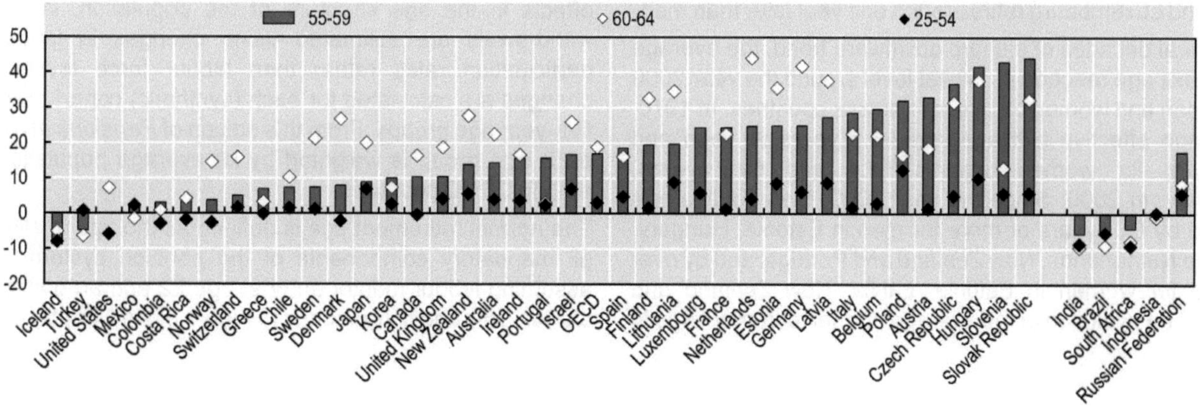

Note: Data for Brazil, Indonesia and South Africa refer to period 2001-20, 2000-19 and 2001-20 respectively.

Source: OECD database Labour Market Statistics by sex and age: employment-population ratio.

StatLink https://stat.link/e50qwg

Figure 6.13. **Growth of employment rates of older workers by education level**

Change in employment rates, 2000-19, percentage points

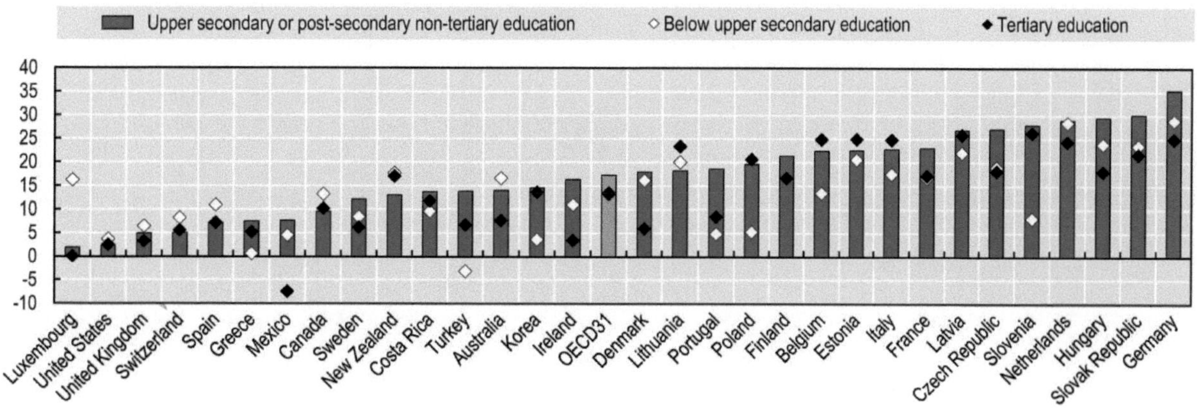

Source: OECD.Stats database, Labour Force Survey.

StatLink https://stat.link/dy9ub4

Key results

The average effective age of labour market exit was 63.8 years for men and 62.4 years for women across OECD countries in 2020. The lowest effective exit age is found in Luxembourg for men at 59.2 years and in Greece at 58.1 years for women. At the other end of the range, Japan and New Zealand (men) and Japan (women) displayed the highest figures, at 68.2 years and 66.7 years, respectively.

The average effective age of labour market exit remained below 64 in 2020 in more than half of OECD countries for men and in more than three-quarters of them for women. Average exit ages are at 61 years or below for men in Belgium, France, Greece, Luxembourg, the Slovak Republic, Spain and Turkey and at 60.5 years or below for women in Belgium, Colombia, Greece, Hungary, Luxembourg, Poland, the Slovak Republic, Slovenia, Spain and Turkey. By contrast, men in Japan and New Zealand withdrew from the labour market after age 68 on average, with women withdrawing after age 65 in Estonia, Japan and New Zealand. In all but six OECD countries, men exit the labour market after women, with the largest difference observed in Colombia (6.4 years). By contrast women in both Estonia and Luxembourg retire around one year later than men.

After several decades of a sharp downward trend, the average effective exit age reached its lowest level around the year 2000 for both men and women on average across countries. In 1970, the average effective exit age was 66.3 years for men and 64.9 years for women, against 61.4 and 59.7 years, respectively, in 2000. Since the year 2000, the effective age increased by four years or more for men in Estonia, Hungary, Latvia, the Netherlands, New Zealand and Portugal and by over six years for women in Estonia, Latvia, New Zealand and Slovenia. The evolution of the average normal retirement age in the OECD shows a similar U-shape pattern as for the exit age, for both women and men, although the decline in the normal retirement age from the 1970s until the turn of the century was less pronounced and the upturn started earlier – at the beginning rather than the end of the 1990s. The current average labour market exit ages are very close to levels reached in the early 1980s.

Definition and measurement

The average effective age of labour market exit is defined as the average age of exit from the labour force for workers aged 40 and over. In order to abstract from compositional effects in the age structure of the population, labour force withdrawals are estimated using changes in labour force participation rates rather than labour force levels. These changes are calculated for each (synthetic) cohort divided into five-year age groups. From this edition of *Pensions at a Glance*, each age group is weighted by its average population share among OECD countries.

The normal retirement age is defined as the age of eligibility to all mandatory components of the pension system in 2020, assuming labour market entry at age 22 and an uninterrupted career. This age corresponds to Figure 3.4 in Chapter 3.

Figure 6.14. **Average effective age of labour market exit and normal retirement age in 2020**

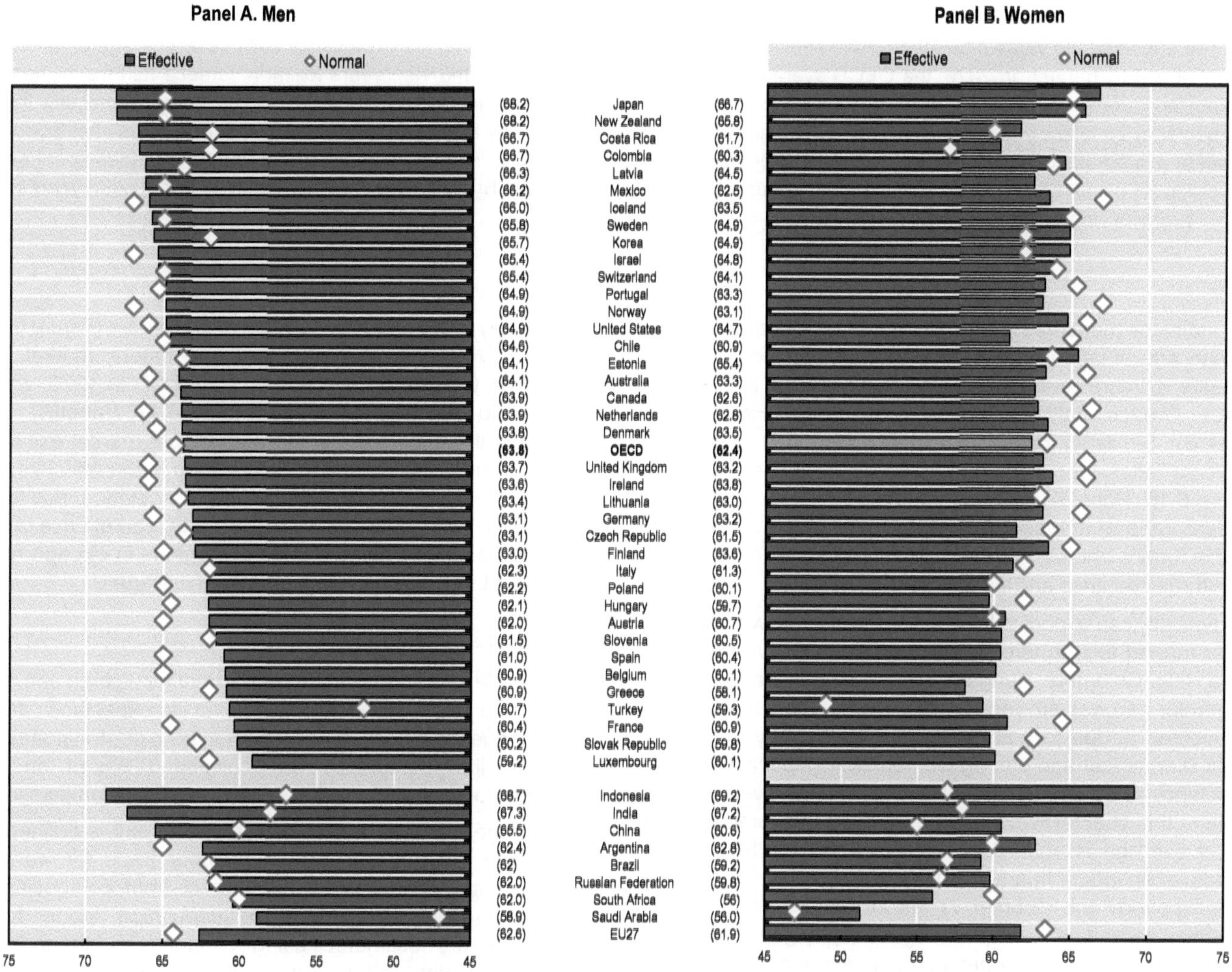

Note: Effective labour market exit age is shown for the five-year period 2015-20. Normal retirement age is shown for individuals retiring in 2020 after a full career from labour market entry at age 22.

Source: OECD estimates based on the results of national labour force surveys and the European Union Labour Force Survey. Normal retirement age: See Chapter 3.

StatLink https://stat.link/kftyqv

Figure 6.15. **Average effective age of labour market exit in OECD countries, 1970-2020**

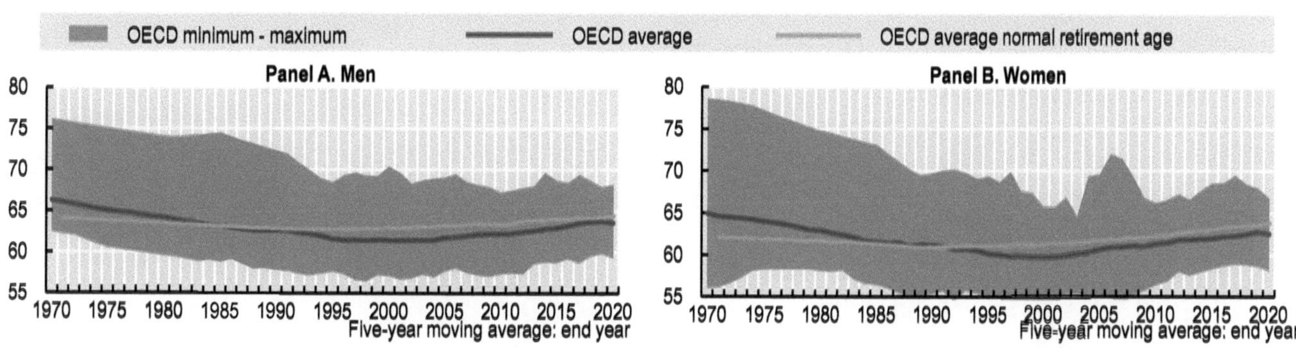

Source: OECD estimates based on the results of national labour force surveys, the European Union Labour Force Survey and, for earlier years in some countries, national censuses. Normal retirement age: Estimate based on data provided by countries.

StatLink https://stat.link/zqsnht

Key results

The expected life years after labour market exit indicator measures the remaining life expectancy at the average age of labour market exit by gender. In 2020, the OECD average was 23.8 years for women and 19.5 years for men. Greece had the highest expected duration for women equal to 28.4 years, with Luxembourg highest for men at 24.0 years. The lowest remaining life expectancy equalled 14.0 years for men and 20.1 years for women in Latvia. The average number of expected life years after labour market exit across OECD countries has sharply increased over time. In 1970, women and men in the OECD countries spent on average 16.0 and 12.0 years of their life after labour market exit, respectively. By 2020, this had increased by about eight years to 23.8 years for women and 19.5 years for men.

This indicator measures the remaining life expectancy at the average age of labour market exit. Women can expect to live 26 years or more after exiting the labour market in Belgium, France, Greece, Italy, Luxembourg and Spain (Figure 6.16, Panel B). Similarly, men can expect to survive more than 22 years after labour market exit in the same countries (Figure 6.16, Panel A). Women's remaining life expectancy at the average age of labour market exit was below 21 years in Estonia, Latvia and Mexico, and men's was below 17 years, in these three countries and in Lithuania.

Men typically can expect to live 4.3 years less than women after labour market exit on average in the OECD (Figure 6.16). In Costa Rica, Colombia, Hungary, Latvia, Lithuania and Poland, the gender gap was six years or more. This gap between men and women is due to both higher life expectancy and lower labour market exit age among women. The gender gap in life expectancy at 65 years is equal to 3.2 years on average (see above in this chapter) while the gender gap in average labour market exit age is equal to 1.4 years (Figure 6.14). Longer periods after labour market exit expose women to old-age income poverty (cf. Chapter 7), as in some countries price indexation magnifies the impact of gender pay gaps, observed in all OECD countries, on pension benefits and of longer life expectancies.

The average length of life after labour market exit has increased over time. In 1970 men in the OECD countries spent on average 12.0 years after their exit from the labour market while by 2020 they could expect a duration of 19.5 years (Figure 6.17, Panel B). Women's life expectancy at labour market exit equalled 16.0 years on average in the OECD in 1970, which increased to 23.8 years in 2020 (Figure 6.17, Panel A). The increase in the expected lifetime after labour market exit from 1970 to around 2000 is due to both a drop in the effective exit age from the labour force and increased longevity. Since then, expected life years after exit from the labour market have rather stabilised as continuing life expectancy gains in old age have been offset by increases in labour market exit ages.

Definition and measurement

Expected life years after labour market exit for women and men is measured as the respective remaining life expectancy at the average age of effective labour market exit. Estimates of remaining life expectancy are calculated based on the UN World Population Prospects – The 2019 Revision dataset.

The average effective age of labour market exit is defined as the average age of exit from the labour force for workers aged 40 and over. In order to abstract from compositional effects in the age structure of the population, labour force withdrawals are estimated using changes in labour force participation rates rather than labour force levels. These changes are calculated for each (synthetic) cohort divided into five-year age groups. From this edition of *Pensions at a Glance*, each age group is weighted by its average population share among OECD countries.

Figure 6.16. **Remaining life expectancy at average labour market exit age, by gender in 2020**

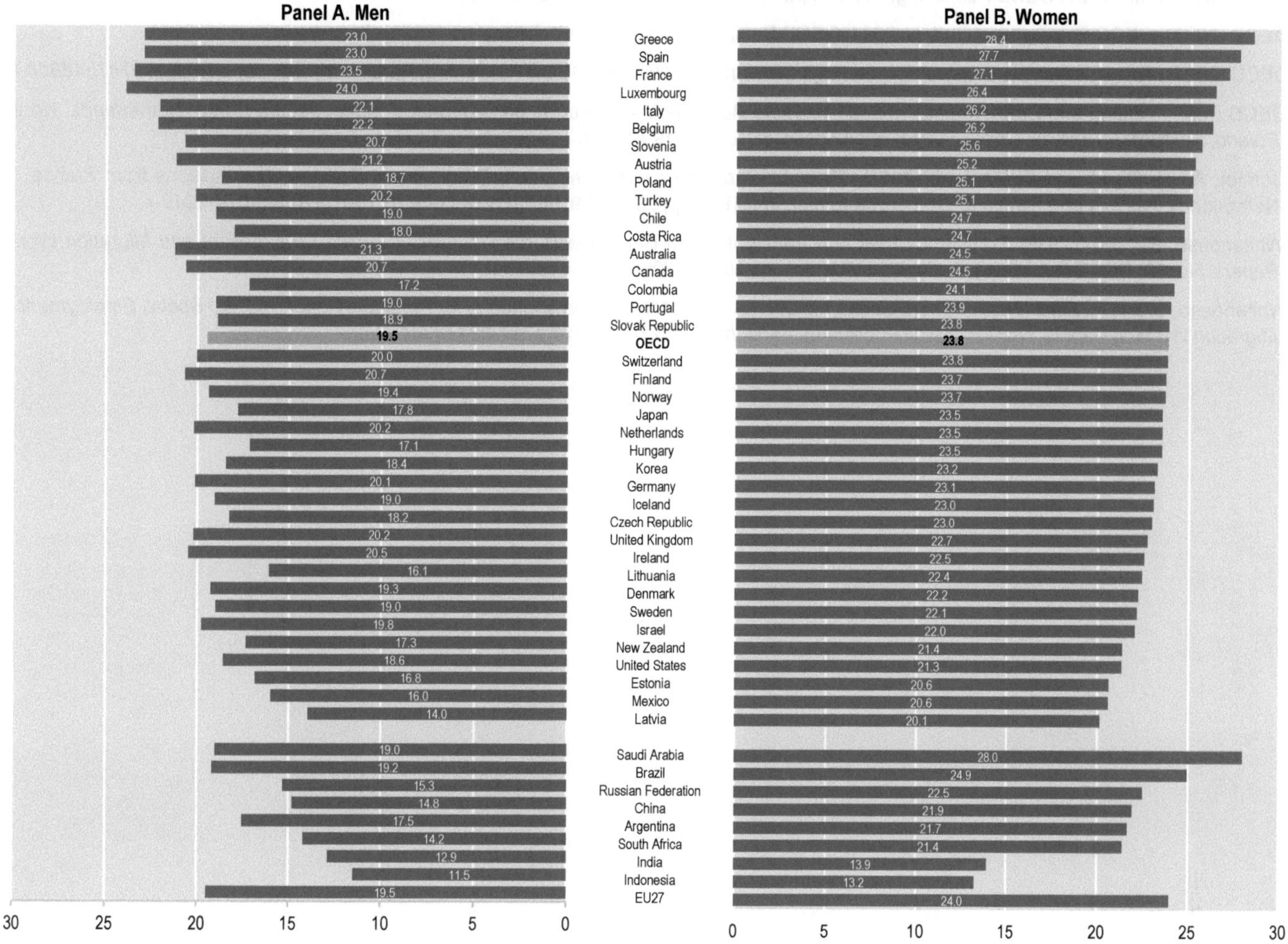

Note: Numbers in parenthesis indicate the average effective age of labour market exit in 2020 by gender. Life expectancy at labour market exit is based on period-specific mortality rates.

Source: OECD calculations based on United Nations Population Prospects: 2019 Revision, exit ages: see previous section.

StatLink https://stat.link/ej5ixw

Figure 6.17. **Expected life years after labour market exit, OECD average 1970-2020**

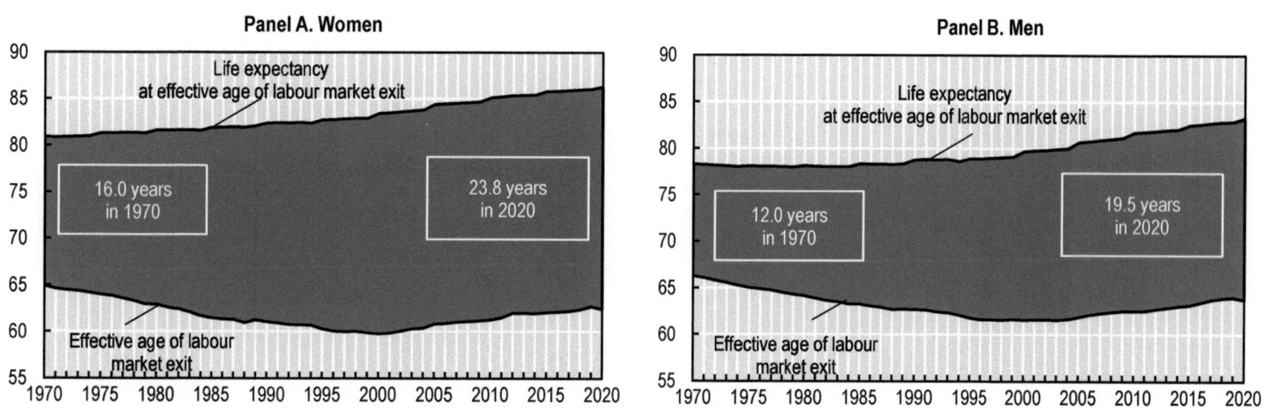

Note: Life expectancy at labour market exit is based on period-specific mortality rates.

Source: OECD calculations based on United Nations Population Prospects: 2019 Revision, exit ages: see previous section.

StatLink https://stat.link/j79e2q

[2] D'Addio, A. and M. d'Ercole (2005), "Trends and Determinants of Fertility Rates: The Role of Policies", *OECD Social, Employment and Migration Working Papers*, No. 27, OECD Publishing, Paris, *https://dx.doi.org/10.1787/880242325663*.

[7] OECD (2021), *OECD Employment Outlook 2021*, OECD Publishing, Paris, *https://doi.org/10.1787/5a700c4b-en*.

[1] OECD (2021), *Towards Improved Retirement Savings Outcomes for Women*, OECD Publishing, Paris, *https://dx.doi.org/10.1787/f7b48808-en*.

[5] OECD (n.d.), "Ageing and Employment Policies", *Working Better with Age reports on Denmark, France, Japan, Korea, Netherlands, Norway, Poland, Switzerland and the United States*, *https://doi.org/10.1787/19901011*.

[6] Sonnet, A., H. Olsen and T. Manfredi (2014), "Towards More Inclusive Ageing and Employment Policies: The Lessons from France, The Netherlands, Norway and Switzerland", *De Economist*, Vol. 162/4, pp. 315-339, http://dx.doi.org/*10.1007/s10645-014-9240-x*.

[4] Whitehouse, E. (2007), "Life-Expectancy Risk and Pensions: Who Bears the Burden?", *OECD Social, Employment and Migration Working Papers*, No. 60, OECD Publishing, Paris, *https://dx.doi.org/10.1787/060025254440*.

[3] Whitehouse, E. and A. Zaidi (2008), "Socio-Economic Differences in Mortality: Implications for Pensions Policy", *OECD Social, Employment and Migration Working Papers*, No. 71, OECD Publishing, Paris, *https://dx.doi.org/10.1787/231747416062*.

Pensions at a Glance 2021
OECD and G20 Indicators

Chapter 7

Incomes and poverty of older people

These four indicators look at the economic situation of older people. The first examines the income of older people, comparing them with the population as a whole. It also shows whether the income comes from publicly provided benefits, private occupational transfers, work, or private personal pensions and other savings.

The second looks at relative income poverty of older people. It shows the proportion of older people living on incomes of less than half the national median disposable income and their average income gap to the poverty line.

The third looks at income inequality among older people, showing Gini and percentile ratios for people aged 66+, also comparing them to the total population and across time.

The final indicator presents the "Average worker earnings" that underpin pension modelling. They are used throughout the report and many parameters and all modelling results are reported as percentages of national average worker earnings.

Key results

Disposable incomes of older people are on average lower than those of the total population. The over-65s had incomes of 88% of the total population's in 2018 on average, broken down into 94% for the 66-75 and 80% for the over-75s. Among the over-65s, the range goes from about 75% or less in Australia, the Czech Republic, Estonia, Korea, Latvia and Lithuania to about 100% or more in Costa Rica, France, Israel, Italy, Luxembourg and Portugal. In 23 out of 37 OECD countries, public transfers provide more than half of gross income after age 65.

People over 65 had incomes amounting at 88% of population incomes on average in 2018 or latest (Table 7.1). Older people fared best in Costa Rica, France, Israel, Italy, Luxembourg and Portugal in relative terms where incomes for the over-65s were about or slightly higher than for the total population. Older people also had high relative incomes on average in Greece, Iceland, Spain and Turkey in international comparison. In Estonia, Korea and Latvia, by contrast, the income of older people was about one-third lower.

Average incomes tend to fall with age after retirement. Lower incomes for older retirees are partly explained by cohort effects given growth trends in real earnings across cohorts due to productivity gains. Over time this translates into higher earnings for each successive cohort and therefore higher pensions in retirement if past wages are not uprated in line with average wage growth and if pensions in payment are not indexed to wage growth. As for the latter, while price indexation protects purchasing power, it tends to lower relative income over time. This particularly affects older women who live longer, which adds to their lower own entitlements due to lower past employment and wages compared to men. Moreover, older people live alone more often, which lowers their equivalised disposable income given household economies of scale.

The income of people aged over 65 has increased relative to that of the total population in more than two-thirds of OECD countries over the past decades, and on average by 6.0 percentage points across all countries. Driven by a maturing pension system, the over-65s in Israel have seen the strongest rise in their relative income, about 22 percentage points, from 81% in 2000 to 103% in 2018. Norway records a similarly strong increase as well as Portugal since 2005. The sharpest decline (-10 percentage points) is reported for the over-65s in Poland since 2005, from 95.7 to 85.7, with Chile is next at -8 percentage points since 2006.

Sources of income

Of the four main sources of income on which older people draw, public transfers (earnings-related pensions, resource-tested benefits, etc.) and private occupational transfers (pensions, severance payments, death grants, etc.) account for around two-thirds of the total income (Figure 7.1). Public transfers account for 57% and private occupational transfers represent 7% of older people's incomes on average. The countries where over-65s are most reliant on public transfers are Austria, Belgium, Finland and Luxembourg: more than 80% of their incomes come from that source. Public transfers represent only 5% and 18% of all income in Mexico and Chile, respectively. Private occupational transfers are of particular importance in 13 OECD countries, with the Netherlands being highest at 39%.

Work accounts for 26% and capital for about 10% of older people's incomes on average. Work is especially important in Korea and Mexico, where it accounts for more than half of old-age income; it also represents a large share of income in Chile, Costa Rica, Estonia, Iceland, Israel, Japan, Latvia, Lithuania, New Zealand, Poland, the Slovak Republic and the United States. Also, as incomes are measured at the household level, work is likely to be a more important income source for older people where many of them live in multi-generational households.

Capital, mostly private pensions, represents 40% of all income sources of older people in Canada. In Denmark, Korea and New Zealand, capital represents over 20% of all income.

Definition and measurement

Incomes of older people groups all incomes from employment, self-employment, capital and public transfers. The data shown are for disposable incomes (i.e. net of personal income tax and social security contributions). Incomes are measured on a household basis and equivalised with the square-root equivalence scale to adjust for differences in household size. See OECD Income Distribution Database for more details on definitions and data sources. The special chapter on "Incomes and poverty of older people" in OECD (2013[1]) provides a more detailed analysis.

Table 7.1. **Incomes of older people, latest available year**

Average income by age group in percentage of average income of total population

	All aged over 65	Age 66-75	Aged over 75	All aged over 65: 2000 or earliest thereafter		All aged over 65	Age 66-75	Aged over 75	All aged over 65: 2000 or earliest thereafter
Australia	75.2	82.7	63.5	5.9	Latvia	67.1	75.1	58.8	-5.4
Austria	94.0	95.4	92.1	6.9	Lithuania	70.5	75.1	65.7	-2.7
Belgium	80.0	85.0	73.2		Luxembourg	107.8	111.4	101.9	
Canada	90.8	95.1	83.8	2.3	Mexico	92.2	97.9	83.1	6.0
Chile	93.5	95.8	90.0	-8.0	Netherlands	85.6	91.2	76.9	1.0
Colombia					New Zealand	86.2	95.4	71.1	5.5
Costa Rica	107.8	112.6	100.5		Norway	91.4	100.6	77.4	20.2
Czech Republic	73.3	76.2	68.2	-5.1	Poland	85.7	85.6	85.8	-10.0
Denmark	81.3	86.6	73.1	9.9	Portugal	99.1	106.9	90.2	18.7
Estonia	67.4	74.5	59.5		Slovak Republic	87.0	89.2	82.5	7.2
Finland	82.6	89.9	72.2	4.3	Slovenia	85.3	88.7	80.2	1.0
France	99.8	103.9	94.5	1.9	Spain	95.8	102.4	88.1	14.8
Germany	88.8	92.5	85.5	0.8	Sweden	86.3	97.5	70.8	8.2
Greece	95.0	101.2	87.8	13.4	Switzerland	82.8	87.9	76.5	1.1
Hungary	93.2	94.3	91.3	6.2	Turkey	97.6	101.5	91.3	7.4
Iceland	95.0	103.8	77.5	14.6	United Kingdom	81.3	86.4	74.3	8.3
Ireland	83.9	91.1	74.4	13.9	United States	93.8	102.1	80.9	10.7
Israel	103.4	110.9	91.6	21.9	**OECD**	**87.9**	**93.5**	**80.0**	**6.0**
Italy	100.0	109.3	90.6	14.5					
Japan	85.2	91.8	78.0	-4.5	Russian Federation	84.3	86.4	81.3	
Korea	65.8	73.1	56.0		South Africa	95.8	94.3	99.2	

Notes: Data for 2000 except for Greece and Turkey (2004), Chile and Switzerland (2006), the Czech Republic, Iceland, Ireland, Latvia, Lithuania, Poland, Portugal, the Slovak Republic and Slovenia (2005), Austria and Spain (2007). Most recent data are for 2018 except for the following countries: Costa Rica (2020), Canada, France, Sweden and the United Kingdom (2019), Chile, Denmark, Hungary, Iceland, Russian Federation, Switzerland and the United States (2017), the Netherlands (2016), South Africa (2015) and New Zealand (2014). Due to a break in series, 2006-data for Chile are scaled with a factor measuring the age-specific effect of the series break on income levels using data from 2011 or closest available. = Historical data for Belgium, Estonia, Korea and Luxembourg are not comparable due to breaks in series and those for Costa Rica, the Russian Federation and South Africa are unavailable and are not shown here. Data for Colombia is unavailable.

Source: *OECD Income Distribution Database, http://www.oecd.org/social/income-distribution-database.htm*.

StatLink *https://stat.link/32iwc9*

Figure 7.1. **Income sources of older people, latest available year**

Percentage of total equivalised gross household income and transfers

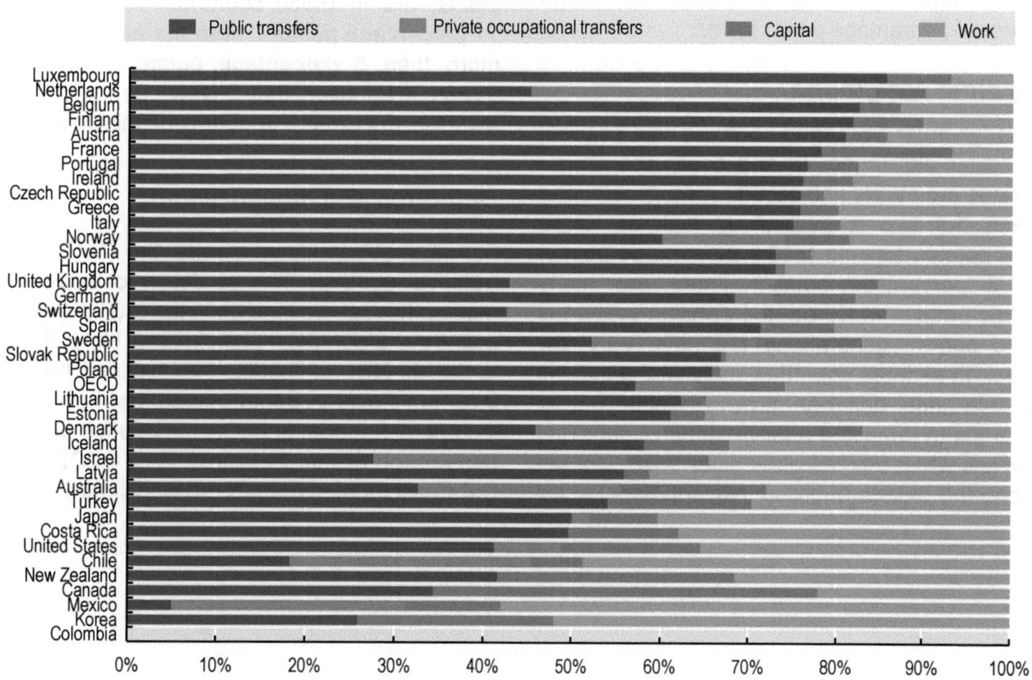

Note: Income from work includes both earnings (employment income) and income from self-employment. Private occupational transfers include pensions, severance payments, death grants and other. Capital income includes private personal pensions and income from the returns on non-pension savings. Data are for 2018 except for some countries; see note of Table 7.1.

Source: OECD Income Distribution Database, *http://www.oecd.org/social/income-distribution-database.htm* (July 2021 version).

StatLink *https://stat.link/lqhcun*

Key results

On average in the OECD, 14.1% of individuals aged over 65 live in relative income poverty, defined as having an income below half the national median equivalised household disposable income. Their income gap to the relative poverty line is 23.8% on average. Poverty rates are higher for older people than for the population as a whole, which averages 11.6%. However, this result is driven by a handful of countries. In 16 out of 37 OECD countries, the old-age income poverty rate is lower than for the population as a whole. It tends to rise with age during retirement and is higher for women. In recent decades, relative poverty has tended to shift from people aged over 65 to people aged 18 to 25.

According to the latest available figures, relative poverty rates of people aged over 65 exceeded 40% in Korea, were above 30% in Estonia and Latvia, and more than 20% in Australia, Lithuania, Mexico and the United States. By contrast, the Czech Republic, Denmark, France, Iceland, the Netherlands, Norway and the Slovak Republic have the lowest relative poverty rates, below 5%. The first-tier pension level is an important factor influencing old-age poverty rates (see the indicator on "Basic, targeted and minimum pensions" in Chapter 4). There are considerable country differences in wealth (housing or otherwise) held by older people, which is not reflected in income poverty rates.

In 20 OECD countries, older people are more likely to be income poor than the total population (Figure 7.2). The largest difference between old-age and total-population poverty rates is found in Korea where older people have 27 percentage-point higher poverty rates than the total population, followed by Latvia and Estonia. Older people are less likely to be poor than the total population in several countries, especially France, Greece, Luxembourg, the Netherlands and Spain where the old-age poverty rate is at least 4 percentage points lower.

Poverty among older age groups

Poverty among the "younger old" (aged 66-75) is less frequent than among the "older old" (aged 75 and over); the OECD average poverty rates are 12.2% and 16.6%, respectively. The difference between the two is particularly high in Korea (+20.5 percentage points), Estonia (+18.7 percentage points) and Latvia (+11.3 percentage points). There are many explanations for this pattern. In Korea, the pension system is still maturing, and current generations still have very low pensions. Moreover, in all three countries, individual pensions are indexed to less than earnings growth (Table 3.3 in Chapter 3). This tends to lower the relative value of pensions compared to earnings when retirees grow older. Also, women predominate among the older age group. Nevertheless, in six OECD countries – Austria, Chile, Germany, Hungary, Iceland and Poland – the over 75s fare slightly better than their younger counterparts do. Pension reforms that have reduced the generosity of pension systems typically lower the relative income of new generations of retirees.

Poverty and gender

Older women are at greater risk of poverty than older men in all countries except Chile where risks are nearly equal, while in Spain the gender difference is minimal. The average old-age poverty rates for women and men in the OECD equal 16.2% and 11.6%, respectively. Lower earnings-related pension income and longer life expectancy are among the main drivers of higher poverty incidence among women than among men.

The smallest gender differences in the poverty rate apart from Chile and Spain are observed in Brazil, Costa Rica, Denmark, France and the Netherlands with less than 2 percentage points. The largest gender differences, more than 15 percentage points, are in Baltic countries, followed by Korea at about 11 percentage points. There are also significant differences of more than 5 percentage points in Australia, Canada, the Czech Republic, Italy, New Zealand, Poland, Slovenia, Sweden, the United Kingdom and the United States.

Definition and measurement

For international comparisons, the OECD treats poverty as a "relative" concept. The yardstick for poverty depends on the median household income in the total population in a particular country at a particular point in time. Here, the poverty threshold is set at 50% of median, equivalised household disposable income. Poverty depth measures how much the average income of the poor is below the relative poverty threshold, as a percentage of this threshold. See OECD Income Distribution Database for more details on definitions and data sources.

Table 7.2. Income poverty rates by age and gender, latest available year

Percentage with income lower than 50% of median equivalised household disposable income

	Older people (aged over 65)							Older people (aged over 65)					
	All	By age		By gender		Total population		All	By age		By gender		Total population
		Age 66-75	Aged over 75	Men	Women				Age 66-75	Aged over 75	Men	Women	
Australia	23.7	21.6	27.1	21.0	26.2	12.4	Latvia	39.0	33.4	44.7	29.1	43.7	17.5
Austria	10.0	10.6	9.2	7.4	12.1	9.4	Lithuania	25.2	23.3	27.1	11.3	32.1	15.5
Belgium	8.5	7.1	10.3	7.2	9.5	8.2	Luxembourg	7.1	6.7	7.9	5.2	9.2	11.4
Canada	12.3	10.2	15.7	9.3	15.0	11.6	Mexico	26.6	23.9	31.0	25.5	27.6	15.9
Chile	17.6	17.7	17.4	17.6	17.5	16.5	Netherlands	3.1	2.0	4.9	2.8	3.5	8.3
Colombia							New Zealand	10.6	7.7	15.2	6.6	14.0	10.9
Costa Rica	17.0	16.4	17.8	17.8	16.3	20.5	Norway	4.3	2.5	7.2	2.2	6.2	8.4
Czech Republic	10.4	9.4	12.2	4.7	14.8	6.1	Poland	12.8	13.4	11.9	8.1	15.8	9.8
Denmark	3.0	2.0	4.5	2.2	3.7	6.1	Portugal	9.0	8.0	10.2	7.0	10.5	10.4
Estonia	37.6	28.8	47.5	24.6	44.2	16.3	Slovak Republic	5.0	4.5	6.0	2.6	6.5	7.7
Finland	7.2	4.3	11.3	6.0	8.2	6.5	Slovenia	12.1	9.6	15.9	7.2	15.7	7.5
France	4.4	4.0	4.9	3.3	5.2	8.4	Spain	10.2	9.2	11.3	10.1	10.2	14.2
Germany	9.1	9.6	8.8	7.6	10.4	9.8	Sweden	11.4	8.5	15.4	7.5	14.8	9.3
Greece	7.5	7.2	7.7	6.0	8.7	12.1	Switzerland	16.5	14.0	19.6	14.7	18.0	9.2
Hungary	4.9	5.3	4.2	3.0	6.1	8.0	Turkey	11.1	9.0	14.6	9.2	12.5	14.4
Iceland	3.1	4.0	1.1	4.5	1.7	4.9	United Kingdom	15.5	12.8	19.2	12.6	18.0	12.4
Ireland	7.4	6.4	7.5	5.2	8.3	7.4	United States	23.1	19.7	28.3	19.6	25.9	17.8
Israel	20.6	16.8	26.4	18.0	22.6	16.9	**OECD**	**13.1**	**11.4**	**16.3**	**10.1**	**15.1**	**11.3**
Italy	11.3	10.4	12.2	8.1	13.7	14.2							
Japan	20.0	16.4	23.9	16.4	22.8	15.7	Russian Federation	12.0	13.2	10.3	7.0	14.5	11.5
Korea	43.4	34.6	55.1	37.1	48.3	16.7	South Africa	20.7	20.5	21.1	13.3	24.7	26.6

Notes: Data are for 2018 except for some countries; see note of Table 7.1 for details. Data for Colombia is unavailable.
Source: *OECD Income Distribution Database*, *http://www.oecd.org/social/income-distribution-database.htm* (July 2021 version).

StatLink *https://stat.link/4sgc2z*

Figure 7.2. Income poverty rates by age: older vs. total population, latest available year

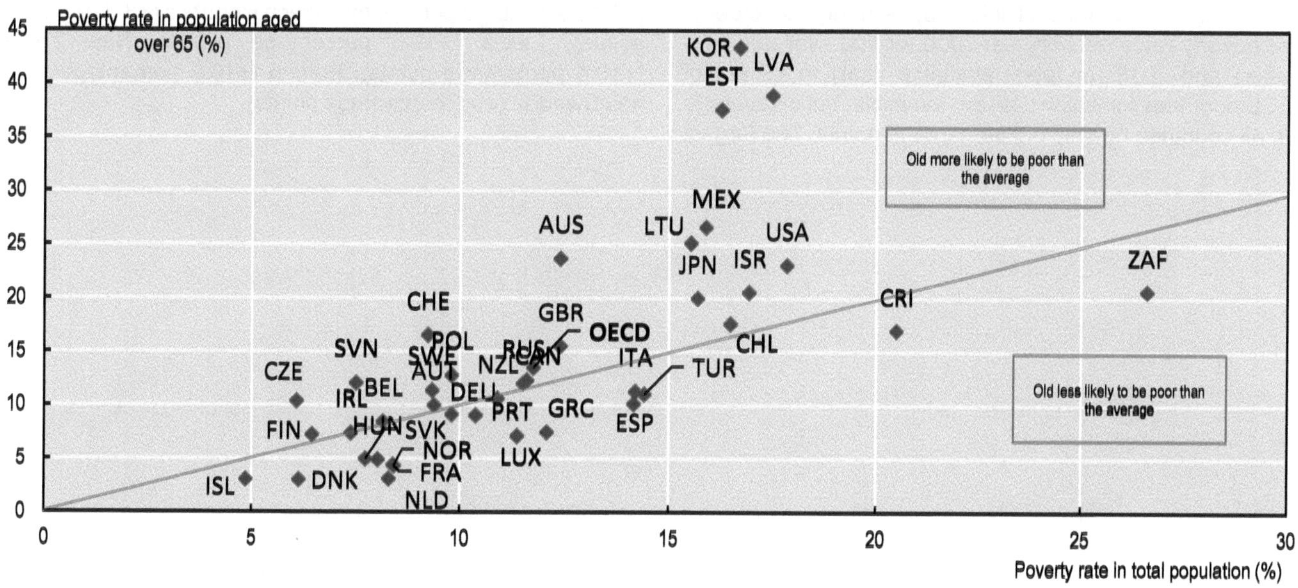

Note: Data are for 2018 except for some countries; see note of Table 7.1 for details.
Source: *OECD Income Distribution Database*, *http://www.oecd.org/social/income-distribution-database.htm* (July 2021 version).

StatLink *https://stat.link/ocju6r*

Poverty depth

Substantial country differences exist in the so-called poverty depth measured by the gap between the average income of the poor and the relative poverty line, here defined as 50% of median income (Figure 7.3). Among the elderly, the largest poverty depth – more than 35% of the income at the poverty threshold – is in Iceland, Korea, Mexico, Turkey and the United States. This means that in these countries the average income of those aged 66+ who are relatively poor is less than 65% of the relative poverty line income. In Austria, Israel, Japan, Luxembourg and the Netherlands, the poverty depth of the 66+ also exceeds 30%. The lowest average gaps, of less than 15%, are reported in Canada, the Czech Republic, Denmark, Finland, New Zealand, Norway, the Slovak Republic and Sweden.

Poverty depth is smaller for the elderly (23.8%) than for all poor (29.8%). This is the opposite in only Iceland, Korea, Mexico and Turkey as well as, but to a smaller extent, in Austria, Belgium and Luxembourg.

A higher poverty incidence tends to coincide with larger poverty depth in OECD countries. This effect is even stronger for the total population (coefficient of correlation of 0.40) than for the over-65s (0.32).

Change in poverty in recent decades

The incidence of poverty has substantially changed over time, at least in some countries (Table 7.3). Among the elderly, relative poverty rates fell between 2000 (or first available year thereafter) and 2018 (or latest available year) in 18 out of 32 OECD countries for which data are available, but on average among all countries by only 0.7 percentage points. The largest declines were observed in Greece (-12.3 percentage points), Ireland (-11.6 percentage points) and Spain (-9.7 percentage points) while poverty rates increased substantially in Latvia (+15.2 percentage points) and New Zealand (+8.9 percentage points).

Poverty rates increased over recent decades for other age groups – and in particular for young adults. The poverty rate of the 18 to 25-year-olds increased in 21 out of 32 countries between 2000 and 2018 and by 1.0 percentage points on average. It declined most in Iceland (-5.1 percentage point), Ireland (-2.3 percentage points), Latvia (-2.3 percentage points), Poland (-2.5 percentage points) and Sweden (-3.5 percentage points) and increased strongly in Denmark (+5.5 percentage points), Finland (+5.7 percentage points), Greece (+5.7 percentage points), the Netherlands (+7.4 percentage points) and Norway (+6.1 percentage points).

As a result, poverty shifted from the old, who used to have the highest poverty incidence, to young adults. The poverty shift, measured by the difference in poverty-rate changes for the over-65s and the 18-25s, averaged -1.7 percentage points for the OECD-32 between 2000 and the latest available data. The most extreme shift in poverty from the old to the young happened in Denmark (-12.8 percentage points), Greece (-18.1 percentage points), Norway (-14.2 percentage points), Portugal (-10.9 percentage points) and Spain (-13.8 percentage points) since 2000. The strongest poverty shifts in the opposite direction, hence from young to old, were in Canada (+7.1 percentage points), the Czech Republic (+8.7 percentage points), Latvia (+17.6 percentage points), New Zealand (+10.4 percentage points), Poland (+10.9 percentage points) and Sweden (+8.6 percentage points).

Figure 7.3. **Income poverty depth by age: older vs. total population, latest available year**

Poverty depth is measured as mean income gap of poor population to income at poverty line, percentage

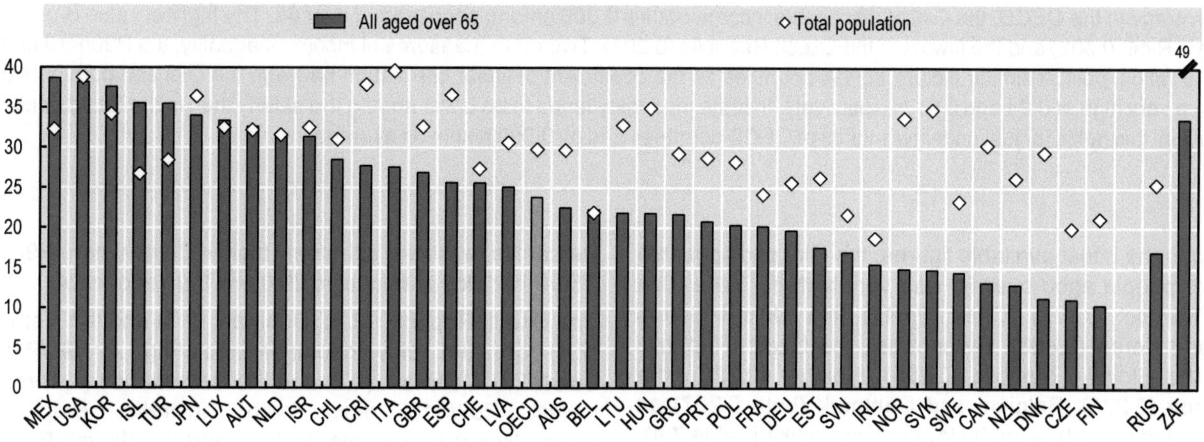

Note: Data are for 2018 except for some countries; see note of Table 7.1 for details. In Spain, for example, the average income of the poor aged over 65 is 25.7% below the income threshold that determines whether a person counts as poor, which equals 50% of the median income in the total population here. That is, their average income is equal to 37.2% of median income. The average income of all poor in Spain is 36.6% below that poverty line. Due to scale, the total population figure of 48.5% for South Africa is not shown on the graph.

Source: *OECD Income Distribution Database, http://www.oecd.org/social/income-distribution-database.htm* (July 2021 version).

StatLink https://stat.link/3ipsaw

Table 7.3. **Change in relative income poverty rates between 2000 and latest available year by age**

Percentage-point change in share with income lower than 50% of median equivalised household disposable income

Country (change since 2000 or latest thereafter)	Aged over 65	Age 0-17	Age 18-25	Age 26-65	Total	Poverty shift: aged over 65 vs. 18-25	Country change since 2000 or latest thereafter)	Aged over 65	Age 0-17	Age 18-25	Age 26-65	Total	Poverty shift: aged over 65 vs. 18-25
Australia	2.1	-1.2	1.2	-0.6	0.0	0.9	Korea						
Austria*	-3.3	-0.1	0.0	0.5	-0.3	-3.3	Latvia*	15.2	-8.5	-2.3	-3.0	-0.1	17.6
Belgium							Lithuania*	9.7	-2.3	1.0	-0.8	1.0	8.7
Canada	7.1	-3.5	0.0	-0.8	-0.4	7.1	Luxembourg						
Chile*	0.5	-4.7	0.3	-3.7	-3.6	0.2	Mexico	-0.2	-4.2	-1.8	-2.6	-3.2	1.5
Colombia							Netherlands	0.3	1.3	7.4	2.0	1.9	-7.1
Costa Rica							New Zealand	8.9	-0.5	-1.5	1.0	1.4	10.4
Czech Republic*	8.0	-3.3	-0.7	0.0	0.6	8.7	Norway	-8.2	5.0	6.1	2.8	2.2	-14.2
Denmark	-7.3	2.5	5.5	2.2	1.2	-12.8	Poland*	8.4	-10.5	-2.5	-2.4	-2.6	10.9
Estonia							Portugal*	-9.0	-2.3	1.9	-0.8	-2.2	-10.9
Finland	-1.1	0.5	5.7	1.1	1.2	-6.8	Slovak Republic*	-2.4	2.8	2.3	0.3	0.5	-4.7
France	1.1	2.5	1.1	0.9	1.2	0.1	Slovenia*	-2.6	-0.2	2.0	0.9	0.4	-4.6
Germany	-0.1	2.4	3.9	2.8	2.3	-4.0	Spain*	-9.7	-0.5	4.1	1.8	-0.2	-13.8
Greece	-12.3	1.4	5.7	2.4	-0.3	-18.1	Sweden	5.1	5.8	-3.5	4.7	4.5	8.6
Hungary	3.1	0.1	0.5	1.6	1.5	2.6	Switzerland*	-1.3	1.0	-0.8	-1.1	-0.5	-0.6
Iceland*	-1.4	-2.3	-5.1	0.0	-1.4	3.7	Turkey	-3.9	-1.0	-1.9	-2.1	-2.6	-2.0
Ireland*	-11.6	-5.9	-2.3	-2.8	-4.2	-9.3	United Kingdom	-7.2	-2.1	0.3	0.9	-0.6	-7.5
Israel	-5.0	7.7	2.7	2.5	3.8	-7.7	United States	2.0	-0.3	0.1	-0.3	-0.5	1.9
Italy	-5.6	5.2	2.9	3.5	1.9	-8.5	**OECD19**	**-1.2**	**1.1**	**1.8**	**1.1**	**0.8**	**-3.0**
Japan							**OECD32***	**-0.7**	**-0.5**	**1.0**	**0.3**	**0.1**	**-1.7**

Notes: Data are for 2018 except for some countries; see note of Table 7.1 for details. Historical data for Belgium, Estonia, Korea and Luxembourg are not comparable due to breaks in series and are not shown here. Data for Colombia and Costa Rica are unavailable.

Source: OECD calculations based on *OECD Income Distribution Database, http://www.oecd.org/social/income-distribution-database.htm* (July 2021 version).

StatLink https://stat.link/inafdm

Key results

On average in the OECD, the Gini of disposable income equals 0.309 among people aged over 65. The highest value is observed for Costa Rica (0.502) and the lowest in the Czech Republic (0.201). Two other measures of income inequality, the P90/P10 and the P50/P10 ratios, paint a similar picture across countries as the coefficient of linear correlation between the Gini and both percentile ratios are very high at 0.94 and 0.81, respectively. Income inequality tends to be lower among the elderly than in the total population. For the Gini this holds for just under two-thirds of OECD countries and by 0.009 points on average.

According to the latest available figures, the Gini of disposable income for people aged over 65 was very high in Costa Rica (0.502), Mexico (0.473), Chile (0.441), the United States (0.411) and Korea (0.406). By contrast, the Czech Republic (0.201), the Slovak Republic (0.205), Norway (0.226), the Netherlands (0.235), Belgium and Denmark (both 0.237) as well as Finland (0.240) have the lowest Gini values (Table 7.4). Such a range means that there are huge differences in the level of old-age income inequality across OECD countries.

In 23 OECD countries, income inequality for the total population (measured by the Gini index) is higher than among older people. The largest difference equalling 0.050 between the two Ginis is found in the Netherlands, followed by the Czech Republic, Luxembourg and Greece. Important factors that explain a lower level of inequality in old-age are first-tier pension benefits, other redistributive features of earnings-related pension schemes and ceilings on pensionable earnings (Chapter 3). Yet, older people are more unequal than the total population in 14 countries, most notably Korea and Mexico.

Except for the Russian Federation, income Ginis for people over 65 in G20-countries lie far above the OECD average. The age pattern is similar to the OECD average except for China and India where Ginis for the over-65s markedly exceed those for the total population.

P90/P10 and P50/P10 ratios

The coefficient of correlation between the Gini and both the 90/10 and the 50/10 percentile ratios are very high (0.94 and 0.81, respectively), indicating a very similar country ranking of income inequality as for the Gini. Also the age pattern follows mostly the one observed for the Gini.

On average in the OECD, a person at the 90th percentile of the disposable income distribution among the over-65-year-olds has an income equal to 4.0 times the one at the tenth percentile. At the fiftieth percentile, the income is 1.9 times the P10 level. Among OECD countries, highest P90/P10 ratios for older people are again in Costa Rica (9.9), Mexico (9.8), the United States (6.9) and Chile (6.6). For the P50/P10 ratio, the United States and Chile rank highest, followed by Israel. Percentile ratios are extremely high in China where P90/10 and P50/P10 ratios are equal to 29.0 and 8.9, respectively.

The Czech Republic (2.4), Denmark (2.3) and the Netherlands (2.4) are the only countries reporting a P90/P10 ratio below 2.5. Denmark (1.3) and the Netherlands (1.4) report the lowest P50/P10 ratios with Australia, Belgium, the Czech Republic, Estonia, Iceland and the Slovak Republic at 1.5.

Change of inequality over time

Income inequality among people older than 65 has barely changed on average over recent decades. The average Gini index has been broadly stable between 2000 and the latest available data, with an average Gini increase of 0.004. The same is true for income inequality for the total population since 2000, with an average Gini decrease of -0.005 (Figure 7.4).

While the average movements in inequality at older ages were moderate in the OECD, there are substantial country differences. Inequality among older people decreased markedly since 2000 in Greece, Israel, Mexico and the Slovak Republic (by more than 0.05 in the Gini index). At the other end of the country range, New Zealand and (albeit from a very low level) Sweden report large increases in inequality since 2000 (by more than 0.07).

Definition and measurement

Gini and percentile ratios are core measures of inequality, here based on the distribution of equivalised household disposable income. The Gini index is defined between 0 (complete equality between all) and 1 (complete inequality, i.e. one person receives all income). Percentile ratios indicate the ratio of incomes of two persons who are at different positions in the disposable income distribution. The P90/P10 ratio compares the income at the 90th percentile to the one at the tenth percentile while the P50/P10 uses accordingly the 50th percentile in the numerator. See OECD Income Distribution Database for more details on definitions and data sources.

Table 7.4. **Income inequality by age: older vs. total population, latest available year**

Gini coefficient, P90/P10 and P50/P10 ratios of the distribution of equivalised disposable household income

	Gini		P90/P10 ratio		P50/P10 ratio			Gini		P90/P10 ratio		P50/P10 ratio	
	Aged over 65	Total population	Aged over 65	Total population	Aged over 65	Total population		Aged over 65	Total population	Aged over 65	Total population	Aged over 65	Total population
Australia	0.346	0.325	3.5	4.3	1.5	2.2	Luxembourg	0.272	0.318	3.4	4.1	1.9	2.1
Austria	0.271	0.280	3.4	3.5	1.9	2.0	Mexico	0.473	0.418	9.8	6.4	3.2	2.5
Belgium	0.237	0.258	2.6	3.2	1.5	1.9	Netherlands	0.235	0.285	2.4	3.4	1.4	1.9
Canada	0.292	0.301	3.4	4.0	1.8	2.1	New Zealand	0.354	0.349	3.8	4.3	1.6	2.1
Chile	0.441	0.460	6.6	7.2	2.5	2.5	Norway	0.226	0.262	2.6	3.1	1.6	1.9
Colombia							Poland	0.263	0.281	3.2	3.6	1.9	2.0
Costa Rica	0.502	0.497	9.9	11.0	2.4	3.0	Portugal	0.336	0.317	4.2	4.1	1.8	2.0
Czech Republic	0.201	0.249	2.4	3.0	1.5	1.8	Slovak Republic	0.205	0.236	2.5	3.0	1.5	1.8
Denmark	0.237	0.264	2.3	3.0	1.3	1.8	Slovenia	0.251	0.249	3.1	3.1	1.7	1.8
Estonia	0.297	0.305	3.4	4.7	1.5	2.4	Spain	0.300	0.330	3.7	4.8	1.9	2.4
Finland	0.240	0.269	2.7	3.1	1.6	1.8	Sweden	0.295	0.280	3.1	3.4	1.6	2.0
France	0.275	0.292	3.0	3.5	1.7	1.9	Switzerland	0.306	0.299	3.9	3.7	2.0	1.9
Germany	0.269	0.289	3.1	3.6	1.7	2.0	Turkey	0.369	0.397	4.6	5.4	2.1	2.3
Greece	0.265	0.306	3.2	4.1	1.8	2.2	United Kingdom	0.331	0.366	3.8	4.5	1.9	2.2
Hungary	0.255	0.289	2.8	3.4	1.6	1.9	United States	0.411	0.390	6.9	6.2	2.7	2.7
Iceland	0.275	0.250	2.6	2.8	1.5	1.7	**OECD**	**0.309**	**0.318**	**4.0**	**4.4**	**1.9**	**2.2**
Ireland	0.281	0.292	3.1	3.5	1.6	1.9							
Israel	0.382	0.348	6.0	5.3	2.6	2.6							
Italy	0.315	0.330	4.0	4.6	2.0	2.4	Brazil	0.440	0.470	5.5	8.7	1.9	3.0
Japan	0.339	0.334	4.8	5.2	2.4	2.6	China	0.545	0.514	29.0	23.0	8.9	7.8
Korea	0.406	0.345	6.5	5.5	2.5	2.7	India	0.536	0.495	13.2	9.4	3.7	2.9
Latvia	0.362	0.351	4.5	5.3	1.7	2.6	Russian Federation	0.292	0.317	3.5	4.3	1.7	2.1
Lithuania	0.322	0.361	3.7	5.4	1.8	2.4	South Africa	0.600	0.620	12.5	25.6	2.4	4.8

Notes: Data are for 2018 except for some countries; see note of Table 7.1 for details.

Source: *OECD Income Distribution Database*, *http://www.oecd.org/social/income-distribution-database.htm* (July 2021 version).

StatLink https://stat.link/zg2eo8

Figure 7.4. **Change in income inequality over time: older vs total population**

Change in Gini of disposable income between 2000 and latest available year

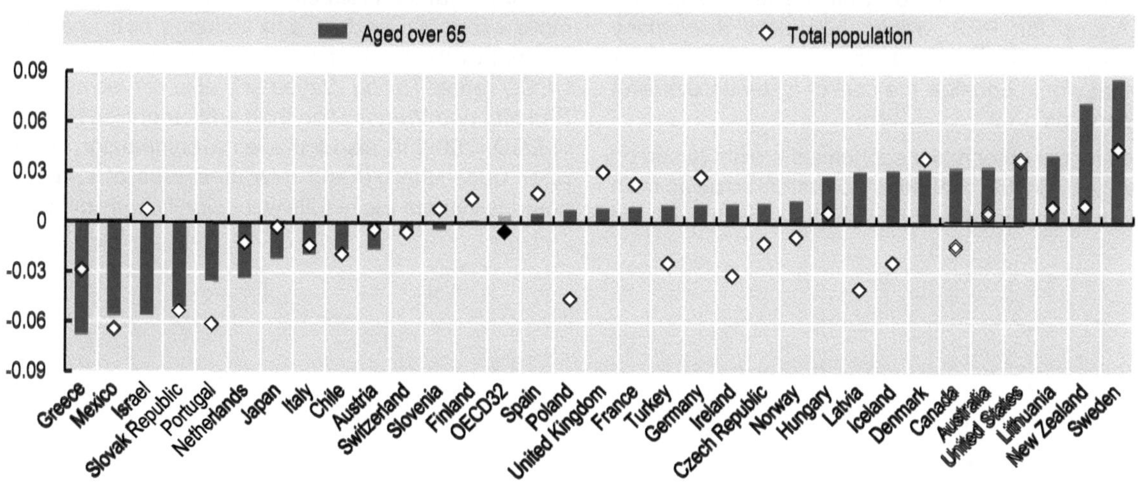

Note: Disposable income here refers to equivalised disposable household income. Data are for 2018 except for some countries; see note of Table 7.1 for details. Historical data for Belgium, Estonia, Korea and Luxembourg are not comparable due to breaks in series and are not shown here. Data for Colombia and Costa Rica are unavailable.

Source: *OECD Income Distribution Database*, *http://www.oecd.org/social/income-distribution-database.htm* (July 2021 version).

StatLink https://stat.link/gyijv0

Key results

"Average wage (AW)" is an important metric as all pension modelling results are presented as multiples of this measure. The average for all OECD countries was USD 39 178 in 2020 and USD 46 520 in PPP terms.

Table 7.5 reports the OECD's full-time average wage (AW) levels for the year 2020. The wage earnings are defined as gross wages before deductions of any kind (including personal income taxes and social security contributions), but including overtime pay and other cash supplements paid to employees.

Average wages are displayed in national currencies and in US dollars (both at market exchange rates and at purchasing power parities, PPP). The PPP exchange rate adjusts for the fact that the purchasing power of a dollar varies between countries: it allows for differences in the price of a basket of goods and services between countries.

Wage earnings across the OECD countries averaged USD 39 178 in 2020 at market exchange rates. Switzerland has the highest level at USD 93 049. This is over 20 times the level recorded in Colombia, at USD 4 339, and 15 times that of Mexico at USD 6 105.

At PPP wages averaged USD 46 520. Switzerland is again highest amongst OECD countries, at USD 76 377, with, Germany, Norway and Luxembourg next at USD 69 968, USD 67 438 and USD 67 162 respectively. Colombia is again the lowest, at USD 11 861, followed by Mexico at USD 13 799. The higher figure for PPP wages suggests that many OECD countries' exchange rates with the US Dollar were lower than the rate that would equalise the cost of a standard basket of goods and services.

Average wages for the other major economies are not based on the average wage definition or another consistent basis as such series are unfortunately not available. Data have been collected from national sources and thus vary between average individual income, average covered wage and average wage for a particular group of workers as available. The figures used range from a low of USD 2 024 in India to a high of USD 26 614 in Saudi Arabia, at market exchange rates.

Between 2019 and 2020, the impact of COVID-19 on wawage figures varied considerably. In Colombia, for example, the average wage, in national currency, decreased by 13%, but it increased by more than 5% in Hungary, Lithuania and the United States, and 21% in Turkey (Figure 7.5). Across the OECD as a whole wages increased slightly by an average of 0.6%, while it had increased by 4.0% on average per year since 2000.

Definition and measurement

The "average worker" earnings series (AW), defined as the average full-time adult gross wage earnings, was adopted from the second edition of *Pensions at a Glance* (OECD, 2007[2]). This concept is broader than the previous benchmark of the "average manual production worker" (APW) because it covers more economic sectors and includes both manual and non-manual workers. The new AW measure was introduced in the OECD report *Taxing Wages* and also serves as benchmark for *Benefits and Wages*. The third edition of *Pensions at a Glance* (OECD, 2009[3]) also included a comparison of replacement rates under the old and new measures of earnings for eight countries where the results were significantly different.

Table 7.5. **Average wage (AW), 2020**

	OECD measures of average wages			Exchange rate, national currency per USD	
	National currency	USD, market exchange rate	USD, PPP	Market rate	PPP
Australia	90861	62530	62166	1.45	1.46
Austria	48658	55577	64027	0.88	0.76
Belgium	47720	54506	63287	0.88	0.75
Canada	57292	42718	47819	1.34	1.20
Chile	10279535	12967	24423	792.73	420.90
Colombia	16033240	4339	11861	3694.85	1351.78
Costa Rica	9360000	16003	27413	584.90	341.44
Czech Republic	402261	17331	31320	23.21	12.84
Denmark	437094	66812	65626	6.54	6.66
Estonia	16637	19002	31219	0.88	0.53
Finland	45719	52220	53498	0.88	0.85
France	38188	43618	51569	0.88	0.74
Germany	52104	59513	69968	0.88	0.74
Greece	21139	24145	38749	0.88	0.55
Hungary	5011590	16272	34406	308.00	145.66
Iceland	9247101	68284	64167	135.42	144.11
Ireland	46685	53324	57211	0.88	0.82
Israel	157093	45635	42619	3.44	3.69
Italy	30233	34532	45190	0.88	0.67
Japan	5185181	48562	50141	106.77	103.41
Korea	46020316	38991	52954	1180.28	869.06
Latvia	12913	14749	26249	0.88	0.49
Lithuania	16426	18761	36481	0.88	0.45
Luxembourg	58040	66293	67162	0.88	0.86
Mexico	131163	6105	13799	21.49	9.51
Netherlands	54843	62641	68994	0.88	0.79
New Zealand	64150	41600	43965	1.54	1.46
Norway	627370	66603	67438	9.42	9.30
Poland	60915	15620	33633	3.90	1.81
Portugal	19478	22247	33921	0.88	0.57
Slovak Republic	13200	15077	24755	0.88	0.53
Slovenia	20424	23329	35931	0.88	0.57
Spain	26934	30764	43130	0.88	0.62
Sweden	465767	50570	52317	9.21	8.90
Switzerland	87363	93049	76377	0.94	1.14
Turkey	74751	10666	35375	7.01	2.11
United Kingdom	41807	53599	58369	0.78	0.72
United States	60220	60220	60220	1.00	1.00
OECD		39178	46520		
Argentina	586615	8316	28320	70.54	20.71
Brazil	27696	5372	11985	5.16	2.31
China	100000	14491	23805	6.90	4.20
India	150000	2024	7026	74.10	21.35
Indonesia	28774200	1973	6159	14582.20	4671.89
Russian Federation	480000	6657	19795	72.10	24.25
Saudi Arabia	99802	26614	56403	3.75	1.77
South Africa	150000	9106	21903	16.47	6.85

Note: USD = the United States of America Dollar, PPP = purchasing power parity.

Source: OECD (2021[4]), *Taxing Wages 2021*, *https://dx.doi.org/10.1787/83a87978-en* and *OECD's National Accounts Database*.

StatLink https://stat.link/f2v8ds

Figure 7.5. **Change in average wage, national currency**

Percentage change in average wage between 2019 and 2020

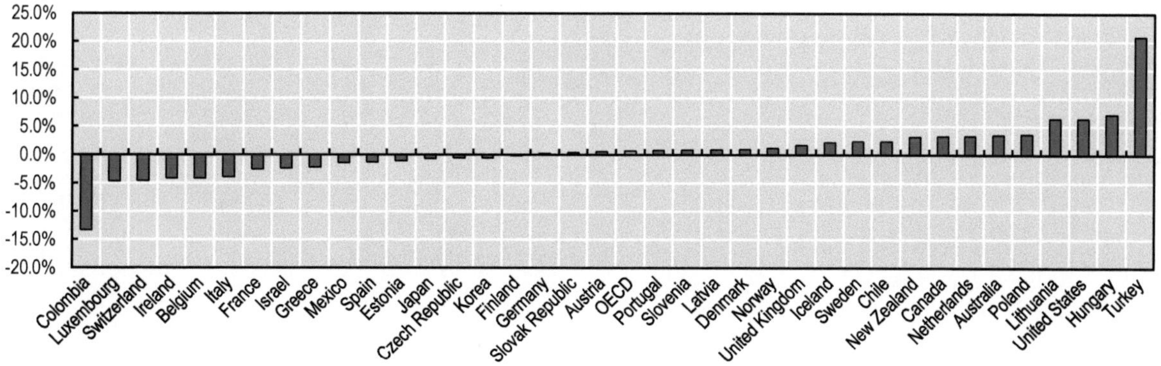

Source: OECD (2020[5]), *Taxing Wages 2020, https://dx.doi.org/10.1787/047072cd-en*; OECD (2021[4]), *Taxing Wages 2021*, *https://dx.doi.org/10.1787/83a87978-en*.

StatLink https://stat.link/tnfpj2

[7] OECD (2021), *Income Distribution Database*, *http://www.oecd.org/social/income-distribution-database.htm* (accessed on 15 July 2021).

[4] OECD (2021), *Taxing Wages 2021*, OECD Publishing, Paris, *https://dx.doi.org/10.1787/83a87978-en*.

[5] OECD (2020), *Taxing Wages 2020*, OECD Publishing, Paris, *https://dx.doi.org/10.1787/047072cd-en*.

[8] OECD (2019), *Will Future Pensioners Work for Longer and Retire on Less? Policy Brief on Pensions*, *https://www.oecd.org/pensions/public-pensions/OECD-Policy-Brief-Future-Pensioners-2019.pdf*.

[6] OECD (2017), *Preventing Ageing Unequally*, OECD Publishing, Paris, *https://dx.doi.org/10.1787/9789264279087-en*.

[1] OECD (2013), *Pensions at a Glance 2013: OECD and G20 Indicators*, OECD Publishing, Paris, *https://dx.doi.org/10.1787/pension_glance-2013-en*.

[3] OECD (2009), *Pensions at a Glance 2009: Retirement-Income Systems in OECD Countries*, OECD Publishing, Paris, *https://dx.doi.org/10.1787/pension_glance-2009-en*.

[2] OECD (2007), *Pensions at a Glance 2007: Public Policies across OECD Countries*, OECD Publishing, Paris, *https://dx.doi.org/10.1787/pension_glance-2007-en*.

Pensions at a Glance 2021
OECD and G20 Indicators

Chapter 8

Finances of retirement-income systems

The indicators in this chapter look at the finances of pension systems. The first indicator presents an overview of the "Mandatory pension contributions" that workers have to pay towards their future pension entitlements.

The second indicator looks at the "Public expenditure on pensions". It shows how much of gross domestic product is allocated towards national public pensions and the overall share of public pensions in the government budget. The third indicator focuses on private pension spending and looks at the total benefit spending on mandatory, quasi-mandatory and voluntary private schemes.

The final indicator presents long-term projections of pension spending and in particular the evolution of public expenditure on pensions in the period 2018-19 to 2050.

Key results

Total mandatory effective pension contribution rates for an average earner averaged 18.2% in 2020 for the 35 OECD countries that have specific pension contributions. In Ireland, Spain and the United Kingdom, mandatory contributions are not earmarked for pensions and cover social insurance.

Most of the measures presented in *Pensions at a Glance* look at the benefits side of the pension system. The indicators here look at the contribution side, mapping out how much workers contributed towards their pension in 2020. Tax-financed pension benefits are not covered here. Since different pension components in a country can be financed through different income sources, mapping out the pension's contribution terrain is very important but it can also be difficult.

Table 8.1 presents the 34 OECD countries where pension contributions are mandatory, either public or private, and New Zealand where there is no mandatory contributions. Countries that belong to this group have pension systems where the contribution rate paid is more directly linked to the pension system. However, there are still 11 countries within this group, Austria, the Czech Republic, Denmark, Finland, Germany, Iceland, Italy, Lithuania, Luxembourg, Slovenia and Turkey, where contributions also finance disability or invalidity benefits. The average effective contribution rate in this group equalled 18.2% at the average-wage level in 2020. The highest total mandatory contribution rates are found in Italy at 33.0%. The Czech Republic, France and Greece also have high effective contribution rates, around 26-28%. By contrast the mandatory contribution in Mexico amounts to only 6.275%, but will increase to 15% over the next few years (Chapter 1). In Korea and Lithuania, the contribution rates are also 9% or lower, with Lithuania having recently moved all contributions to employees with no obligation for the employer. In both Australia and Canada, tax-financed components play a large role and so contribution rates to earnings-related schemes are close to 10%. The same is true for New Zealand, but as there is no mandatory earnings-related scheme the contribution level is zero.

The average effective contribution rate to the public schemes is 15.4% compared to 2.8% for private schemes, which makes a total of 18.2%. Within the public scheme employee contributions are around two-thirds of those of employers, representing effective contribution rates of 6.2% and 9.2%, respectively. In Slovenia, the split is almost reverse, as employees pay 15.5% compared to 8.85% for employers. In Australia and Estonia, all mandatory contributions are paid by employers, while in Lithuania employees pay total contributions.

Table 8.2 looks at social insurance contribution rates that apply for a private-sector worker in Ireland, Spain and the United Kingdom. For these three countries it is difficult to separate the pension contributions from the other parts of social insurance such as survivor's benefits, disability benefits, unemployment, etc. In addition, individuals have to contribute fully to all parts. Within this group, for an average earner in 2020, the contribution rate is 15.1% in Ireland, 20.4% in the United Kingdom and 28.3% in Spain.

Countries with higher pension contribution rates often have above average pension benefits (as in the case of France, Italy and the Netherlands). The choice of the contribution level should be the result of trading off lower net wages against higher future pensions. However, in addition higher mandatory contribution rates might hurt the competitiveness of the economy, and lower total employment while potentially increasing informality.

Table 8.1. **Mandatory pension contribution rates for an average worker in 2020**

	Nominal rate					Ceiling (multiple of gross average earnings), public / private	Effective rate on average earnings
	Employee, public	Employer, public	Employee, private	Employer, private	Total		
Australia			0.0	9.5	9.5	2.51	9.5
Austria*	10.25	12.55			22.8	1.55	22.8
Belgium	7.5	8.9			16.4	1.25	16.4
Canada	5.25	5.25			10.5	1.02	10.5
Chile			11.3	1.6	12.8	2.72	12.8
Colombia	3.5	10.6			14.1	16.42	14.1
Costa Rica	4.0	5.3	1.0	3.3	13.5	None	13.5
Czech Republic*	6.5	21.5			28.0	3.58	28.0
Denmark*			4.0	8.0	12.0	None	12.8
Estonia	0.0	20.0			20.0	None	20.0
Finland*	7.15 [a]	15.2			22.4 [a]	None	22.4 [a]
France	11.3 [w]	16.5 [w]			27.8 [w]	1.08 / 8.62	27.8
Germany*	9.3	9.3			18.6	1.59	18.6
Greece	6.7	19.8			26.5	4.30	26.5
Hungary	10.0	11.8			21.8	None	21.8
Iceland*	0.0	6.35	4.0	11.5	21.9	None	21.9
Israel	7.0 [w]	7.6 [w]	6.0	6.5	27.1 [w]	0.76 / 3.36	19.2
Italy*	9.19	23.81			33.0	3.41	33.0
Japan	9.15	9.15			18.3	2.37	18.3
Korea	4.5	4.5			9.0	1.31	9.0
Latvia	10.0	10.0			20.0	4.86	20.0
Lithuania*	8.72	0.0			8.7	6.35	8.7
Luxembourg*	8.0	8.0			16.0	2.21	16.0
Mexico			1.1	5.2	6.3	6.04	6.3
Netherlands	18.0	0.0	7.7 [w]	14.8 [w]	x [w]	0.63 / none	25.1
New Zealand					0.0		0.0
Norway	8.2	13.0	0.0	2.0	23.2	None / 1.93	23.2
Poland*	9.8	9.8			19.5	2.57	19.5
Portugal	7.2	15.5			22.7	None	22.7
Slovak Republic	4.0	18.8			22.8	6.56	22.8
Slovenia*	15.5	8.85			24.4	None	24.4
Sweden	7.0	10.8	0.0	4.5 [w]	22.3 [w]	1.08 / none	22.3
Switzerland	4.2	4.2	6.25 [a,w]	6.25 [a,w]	20.9 [a,w]	None / 0.98	17 [a]
Turkey	9.0	11.0			20.0	3.54	20.0
United States*	5.3	5.3			10.6	2.29	10.6
OECD35							**18.2**

Note: *Contribution rate also finances disability or invalidity benefits. [a] and [w]: rate varies by age and earnings level respectively. In the private occupational schemes of the Netherlands and Switzerland contributions are only paid on the part of individual earnings exceeding 39% and 27% of average earnings respectively. Therefore, the total nominal contribution rate in the Netherlands equals 18% below 39% of average earnings, 40.5% between 39% and 66% of average earnings and 22.5% above. For occupational schemes in Denmark and the Netherlands, contribution rates are fund-specific, so typical rates are shown. In France, Latvia and Sweden, the indicated public contribution rates include contributions to mandatory occupational or personal pension schemes. Flat-rate contributions to the ATP scheme in Denmark are only included in the effective contribution rate. Public pensions in Finland are partly funded and privately managed while national accounts define them as public. For France, the total nominal rate drops from 27.8% to 26.4% at 108% of average earnings and – once the ceiling of the occupational scheme is reached (862% of average earnings for AGIRC-ARRCO) – it drops further to 1.9% without ceiling. For Israel, the public nominal rate for earnings below 48% of average earnings equals 3.95% compared to 14.6% above. For the Slovak Republic the employer contribution is split 14.0% for pensions and 4.75% for a reserve fund which is used to cover the deficit in the basic social insurance funds and so is not pension specific. For Sweden, the nominal rate in the private occupational scheme rises from 4.5% to 30% at 108% of average earnings. The indicated nominal rate in the private occupational scheme in Switzerland is an average of the age-specific rates (7% at ages 25-34, 10% at 35-44, 15% at 45-54 and 18% at 55-64). Likewise for employee contributions to the public scheme in Finland (7.85% between 53 and 62, otherwise 6.35%). For Latvia, contributions are assumed to be equally split between employee and employer as legislation does not make such a split explicit. For Chile, the indicated values include a 1.57%-rate for disability and survivor pensions and a 1.25%-rate for administrative costs. In Hungary employer contributions are levied for pensions and health care together of which 71.6% go to the pension budget. For Mexico, contribution rates shown exclude contributions paid by the government to the private individual account in form of both a 0.225%-contribution and the social quota, which is an amount that varies with the wage level. Also contributions for public survivor and disability benefits of 0.625% (employee) + 1.75% (employer) + 0.125% (government) are not included. Also in Luxembourg (8%) and Israel (0.25%) the government pays contributions to mandatory pension schemes, which are excluded here.

Source: Country profiles and OECD Taxing Wages 2021.

StatLink https://stat.link/h4uwj7

Table 8.2. **Social insurance contribution rates for an average worker in 2020**

	Nominal rate					Ceiling (multiple of gross average earnings), public / private	Effective rate on average earnings
	Employee, public	Employer, public	Employee, private	Employer, private	Total		
Ireland	4.0	11.05			15.1	None	15.1
Spain	4.7	23.6			28.3	1.81	28.3
United Kingdom	12 [w]	13.8 [w]			25.8 [w]	None	20.4

Note: The indicated rates cover different social security schemes across countries. Ireland: All schemes excluding for sickness and maternity benefits in kind. Spain: All schemes except for unemployment. United Kingdom: Old age, survivor, disability, sickness and maternity, work injury and unemployment. In the United Kingdom, contributions are only paid on the part of individual earnings exceeding 21% of average earnings. Moreover, the employee contribution drops from 12% to 2% at 120% of average earnings.

Source: Country profiles and OECD Taxing Wages 2021.

StatLink https://stat.link/9oqgj4

Key results

Public spending on cash old-age pensions and survivors' benefits in the OECD increased from an average of 6.6% of gross domestic product (GDP) to 7.7% between 2000 and 2017. Public pensions are often the largest single item of social expenditure, accounting for 18.4% of total government spending on average in 2017.

Greece and Italy spent the largest proportion of national income on public pensions among OECD countries in 2017, at around 15.5% of GDP. Other countries with high gross public pension spending are in continental Europe, with Austria, France and Portugal around 13%-14% of GDP. Public pensions generally account for between one-quarter and one-third of total public expenditure in these countries.

At the other end of the spectrum, Chile, Iceland, Korea and Mexico spent less than 3% of GDP on public pensions. Chile and Mexico have relatively young populations. Moreover, in Mexico, low spending also reflects the relatively narrow coverage of pensions (only around 35% of employees). In Iceland, much of retirement income is provided by compulsory occupational schemes (see the next indicator of "Pension-benefit expenditures: Public and private"), leaving a lesser role for public pensions; in addition the retirement age is high at age 67. Korea's pension system is not mature yet: the public, earnings-related scheme was only established in 1988 and the new targeted basic pension was only introduced in 2014.

Spending also tends to be low in countries with favourable demographics, such as Australia, Canada, Ireland and New Zealand. However, this is not always the case: Turkey spends 7.4% of GDP on public pensions despite being the second youngest OECD country in demographic terms. This is more than the Netherlands, Switzerland and the United Kingdom, but these three countries have extensive private pension schemes. For Turkey, the expenditure can be explained by the historically low retirement ages, resulting in longer periods in retirement than in many other countries.

Trends

Public pension spending increased from an OECD average of 6.6% of gross domestic product (GDP) to 7.7% between 2000 and 2017. It is estimated that population ageing captured by the shift in demographic structures alone would have triggered an increase in pension expenditure of 2.5% of GDP on average, with higher employment lowering total pension expenditure by 1.1% of GDP on average (Chapter 1). Public pension spending was relatively stable as a proportion of GDP over the period 2000-17 in 16 countries: Australia, Canada, the Czech Republic, Estonia, Germany, Iceland, Ireland, Israel, Lithuania, the Netherlands, New Zealand, Poland, Slovenia, Sweden, Switzerland and the United Kingdom. It increased by more than 4 percentage points of GDP between 2000 and 2017 in Finland, Greece and Portugal, and by 2 or 4 percentage points in France, Italy, Japan, Norway, Spain and Turkey.

Gross and net spending

The penultimate column of the table shows public spending in *net* terms: after taxes and contributions paid on benefits. Net spending is significantly below gross spending in Austria, Denmark, Finland, Italy, Luxembourg and Sweden, due to taxes on pension benefits. Gross and net spending are similar where pensions are not taxable such as in the Slovak Republic and Turkey or where public benefits are generally below basic tax reliefs (Australia, the Czech Republic, Iceland, Ireland and Slovenia).

Non-cash benefits

The final column of the table shows total gross public spending on older people, including non-cash benefits. In Denmark, Finland, Japan, Norway and Sweden, non-cash benefits exceed 1.5% of GDP. The most important are housing benefits. These are defined as "non-cash benefits" because they are contingent on particular expenditure by individuals. Australia and Belgium also record high figures for non-cash benefits.

Table 8.3. **Public expenditure on old-age and survivors benefits**

	Level (% of total government spending)		Level (% of GDP)						Change of level	Level in net terms (% of GDP)	Total including non-cash (% of GDP)
	2000	2017	1990	2000	2005	2010	2015	2017	2000-17	2017	2017
Australia	12.8	10.9	3.1	4.7	3.7	3.8	4.3	4.0	-0.7	4.0	5.0
Austria	23.3	26.4	11.3	11.9	11.9	13.0	13.3	13.0	1.1	10.8	13.6
Belgium	17.8	20.2	9.0	8.8	8.9	9.9	10.5	10.5	1.7	9.3	11.5
Canada	10.1	11.6	4.2	4.2	4.0	4.3	4.7	4.8	0.6	4.5	4.8
Chile			8.0	5.0	3.7	3.4	2.9	2.8	-2.2	2.8	2.8
Colombia		13.1				5.5	5.9	5.9		5.9	5.9
Costa Rica		14.4						4.9		4.9	4.9
Czech Republic	16.8	19.8	5.5	6.8	6.6	8.0	8.0	7.7	0.9	7.7	7.9
Denmark	12.0	15.7	6.1	6.3	6.5	7.1	8.1	8.0	1.7	5.9	9.6
Estonia	16.5	16.5		6.0	5.3	7.5	6.9	6.5	0.5	6.4	6.6
Finland	15.4	22.0	7.2	7.4	8.0	9.8	11.5	11.8	4.5	9.8	13.4
France	22.2	24.2	10.4	11.5	12.0	13.2	13.8	13.6	2.2	12.3	14.1
Germany	22.8	23.0	9.5	10.9	11.2	10.7	10.1	10.2	-0.7	9.8	10.2
Greece	21.9	32.6	9.5	10.2	11.4	14.2	16.8	15.5	5.3	14.4	15.5
Hungary	15.7	18.2		7.4	8.3	9.6	9.1	8.5	1.1	8.5	9.0
Iceland	5.1	6.2	2.2	2.1	1.9	1.5	2.0	2.6	0.6	2.6	3.0
Ireland	9.3	14.2	4.8	2.9	3.1	4.8	3.6	3.7	0.8	3.6	3.8
Israel	9.9	11.9		4.5	4.7	4.8	4.7	4.7	0.2	4.7	5.3
Italy	28.9	32.1	11.3	13.5	13.7	15.4	16.2	15.6	2.2	12.8	15.7
Japan		24.2	4.7	7.0	8.1	9.6	9.4	9.4	2.4	8.9	11.3
Korea		9.4	0.7	1.3	1.4	2.0	2.8	2.8	1.5	2.8	3.0
Latvia	23.3	17.5		8.7	5.5	9.3	7.0	6.8	-1.9	6.5	7.2
Lithuania	17.9	18.7		7.1	5.7	7.7	6.7	6.2	-0.9	6.2	6.4
Luxembourg	18.8	20.2	7.8	7.1	7.8	8.0	8.4	8.5	1.4	7.0	8.5
Mexico		10.2	0.4	0.8	1.0	1.6	2.2	2.7	1.9	2.6	2.7
Netherlands	11.0	12.2	6.2	4.6	4.6	4.9	5.3	5.2	0.6	4.7	6.0
New Zealand	13.1	12.8	7.2	4.9	4.2	4.6	5.0	4.9	0.0	4.2	4.9
Norway	11.1	13.6	5.5	4.7	4.8	5.2	6.6	6.9	2.2	5.8	9.2
Poland	24.9	25.6	5.0	10.5	11.3	11.1	11.1	10.6	0.1	9.8	10.6
Portugal	18.3	28.1	4.8	7.8	10.0	12.0	13.3	12.7	4.9	12.7	12.8
Slovak Republic	11.8	17.6		6.2	6.0	6.7	7.2	7.3	1.1	7.3	7.6
Slovenia	21.8	23.6		10.4	9.8	10.9	11.1	10.4	0.1	10.4	10.5
Spain	21.5	26.5	7.7	8.4	8.0	9.2	11.0	10.9	2.5	10.4	11.4
Sweden	12.8	14.6	7.2	6.8	7.2	7.2	7.1	7.2	0.4	5.7	9.4
Switzerland	18.0	19.5	5.2	6.1	6.2	6.2	6.6	6.7	0.6	5.3	6.9
Turkey		21.5	0.7	3.9	6.0	7.4	7.1	7.4	3.5	7.4	7.4
United Kingdom	13.4	13.7	4.5	4.8	5.0	6.2	6.1	5.6	0.9	5.4	6.0
United States	16.4	18.6	5.8	5.7	5.7	6.6	7.0	7.1	1.4	6.6	7.1
OECD	**16.6**	**18.4**	**6.3**	**6.7**	**6.8**	**7.6**	**7.9**	**7.7**	**1.0**	**7.1**	**8.2**

Note: See Adema, W. and M. Ladaique (2009), "How Expensive is the Welfare State? Gross and Net Indicators in the OECD Social Expenditure Database (SOCX)", *OECD Social, Employment and Migration Working Paper*, No. 92, OECD, Paris, *http://dx.doi.org/10.1787/220615515052* for more details on the data, sources and methodology.

Source: OECD Social Expenditures Database (SOCX); OECD Main Economic Indicators Database.

StatLink *https://stat.link/92exj3*

Key results

Payments from private pension schemes were worth 1.5% of gross domestic product (GDP) on average in 2017, representing about one-sixth of total – public and private – spending, and having increased from 0.7% of GDP in 1990 and 1.2% in 2005.

Private pensions are mandatory or achieve near-universal coverage through industrial relations agreements ("quasi-mandatory") in less than half of the 38 OECD countries. In others, voluntary private pensions – either individual ("personal") or employer-provided ("occupational") – have broad coverage.

The biggest flow of private-pension payments is in the Netherlands: 5.6% of GDP in 2017. Added to public spending, total benefits are 10.8% of GDP. Canada is next at 5.5% followed by Switzerland and the United States at 5.3% of GDP. While Swiss occupational plans are compulsory, the data on private-pension payments include benefits from voluntary schemes above the statutory minimum level. Next is the United Kingdom at 5.2% when summing both the mandatory and voluntary components.

The next three countries – Australia, Iceland and Sweden – record private-pension payments of between 3.1% and 5.0% of GDP. Japan (where private pensions are voluntary) also has high levels of expenditure on private pensions, at 2.6% of GDP. Iceland has the highest share of private in total pension expenditure at 61%.

Many countries introduced compulsory private pensions in the 1990s: Australia, Estonia, Mexico, Poland, the Slovak Republic and Sweden. In some cases – particularly in Central and Eastern Europe – these new schemes were mainly taken up by younger workers. Many of them have yet to begin paying benefits and some have since reversed the decision with mandatory private schemes removed in Poland and becoming voluntary in Estonia and the Slovak Republic. Much of the private benefit pay-outs recorded in Australia and Sweden relate to voluntary and quasi-mandatory (respectively) schemes that were already in place before private pensions were made compulsory. In all these cases, it will be some decades before all retirees have spent a full career in compulsory private pension plans.

Trends

The countries that have recorded an increase larger than 1 percentage point of GDP between 2000 and 2017 are Australia, Canada, Iceland, the Netherlands, Sweden, Switzerland and the United States. In some cases such as Australia and Switzerland, the occupational pensions became compulsory in 1993 and 1985, respectively, which extended coverage significantly. This is now being reflected in the rapid growth in private pension entitlements as each successive generation of retirees has spent longer, on average, covered by private pensions. Overall in the OECD, private pensions accounted for 10% of total pension expenditure in 1990, increasing to 15% by 2000 with that share being broadly stable since.

Tax breaks

Many OECD countries offer favourable tax treatment to retirement savings made through private pension plans. Often, individual contributions are fully or partially deductible from income and investment returns are fully or partially relieved from tax. Some countries offer tax relief on pension payments (see "Tax treatment of pensions and pensioners" in Chapter 4).

The cost of these fiscal incentives is measured in many OECD countries using the concept of "tax expenditures", developed in the 1960s. This attempts to quantify the value of the preferential tax treatment relative to a benchmark tax treatment. The idea is that this is the amount of revenue forgone as a result of the tax incentives.

Data on tax expenditures for retirement savings are available for 23 OECD countries. Just under half of these figures are 0.2% of GDP or less. And in only six countries – Australia, Canada, Germany, Israel, Switzerland and the United States – are reported tax expenditures worth 1% of GDP or more.

Tax expenditure figures come with important caveats: they are not comparable between countries because of differences in the benchmark tax system chosen. Despite their name, they are not equivalent to direct expenditures and so should not be added to numbers for public pension spending.

Table 8.4. **Private pension-benefit expenditures**

	Scheme type	Level (% of GDP)						Change of level	Public and private benefit spending (% of GDP)	Tax breaks (% of GDP)
		1990	2000	2005	2010	2015	2017	2000-17	2017	2017
Australia	m	0.0	2.9	1.9	3.4	4.6	5.0	2.1	9.0	2.1
Austria	v	0.4	0.6	0.5	0.6	0.7	0.7	0.1	13.7	0.0
Belgium	v	1.0	1.3	1.5	1.1	1.1	1.1	-0.2	11.6	0.2
Canada	v	2.5	3.9	4.1	3.7	4.6	5.5	1.6	10.3	2.2
Chile	m	0.3	1.1	1.2	1.3	1.4	1.5	0.4	4.3	0.2
Colombia	m				0.4	0.4	0.4		6.3	
Costa Rica	m					0.2	0.2		5.1	
Czech Republic	m	0.0	0.2	0.2	0.4	0.3	0.4	0.2	8.1	
Denmark	q/m	0.0	0.0	0.0	1.7	2.2	1.8		10.4	
	v	1.6	2.4	2.5	1.2	0.8	0.6	-1.9		
Estonia									6.5	0.7
Finland	v	0.1	0.3	0.2	0.2	0.2	0.2	-0.1	12.0	0.0
France	v	0.3	0.3	0.3	0.3	0.3	0.3	0.0	13.9	0.1
Germany	v	0.7	0.7	0.8	0.8	0.8	0.8	0.1	11.0	1.1
Greece	v	0.3	0.0	0.1	0.1	0.1	0.1	0.0	15.6	
Hungary									8.5	0.1
Iceland	m	1.4	2.3	2.7	3.3	3.9	4.1	1.8	6.7	0.0
Ireland	v	0.9	2.8	1.5	1.8	1.1	1.0	-1.8	4.7	0.3
Israel	v	0.0	0.7	1.5	1.3	1.3	1.3	0.5	6.0	1.2
Italy	v	1.1	1.1	1.1	1.3	1.2	1.1	0.0	16.8	0.1
Japan	m	0.2	0.4	0.4	0.6	0.5	0.3	-0.1	11.9	
	v	0.0	2.8	2.1	2.6	2.3	2.2	-0.6		
Korea	m	0.2	0.5	0.3	0.4	0.7	0.7	0.1	3.5	
Latvia									6.8	0.1
Lithuania									6.2	
Luxembourg									8.5	
Mexico									2.7	0.2
Netherlands	q	3.6	4.5	4.8	5.5	5.8	5.6	1.0	10.8	
New Zealand									4.9	
Norway	v/m	0.6	0.6	0.6	0.6	1.0	1.0	0.5	7.9	0.3
Poland									10.6	
Portugal	v	0.3	0.2	0.3	0.2	0.7	0.6	0.4	13.4	0.0
Slovak Republic	v	0.0	0.2	0.4	0.3	0.4	0.3	0.1	7.6	
Slovenia									10.4	0.6
Spain	v	0.0	0.0	0.0	0.5	0.5	0.4		11.3	0.0
Sweden	q/m	1.1	1.7	1.9	2.5	3.1	3.1	1.5	10.3	
Switzerland	m	2.3	4.0	4.5	4.7	5.1	5.3	1.3	12.0	1.3
Turkey									7.4	
United Kingdom	m	0.1	0.4	0.5	0.6	0.7	0.7	0.3	10.9	0.9
	v	4.0	5.4	4.3	4.2	4.2	4.6	-0.9		
United States	v	2.6	3.7	3.6	4.4	5.2	5.3	1.6	12.4	1.0
OECD		**0.7**	**1.2**	**1.2**	**1.3**	**1.5**	**1.5**	**0.3**	9.2	**0.5**

Note: m = mandatory private scheme, q = quasi mandatory; and v = voluntary. Blank cells indicate missing values.

Source: *OECD Social Expenditures Database* (SOCX); *OECD Main Economic Indicators Database*. See Adema and Ladaique (2009) for more details on the data, sources and methodology.

StatLink https://stat.link/kp4d5j

Key results

Public spending on pensions has been on the rise in most OECD countries for the past decades, as shown in Table 8.3. Long-term projections show that public pension spending is projected to go on growing in 18 OECD countries, for which information is available, and fall in 11. On average public pension expenditure would increase from 9.0% of GDP in 2018-20 to 10.4% of GDP in 2050 onwards among 29 OECD countries.

The main driver of growing pension expenditures is demographic change. The projections shown in Table 8.5 are derived either from the European Commission's *2021 Ageing Report* – which covers the EU27 members plus Norway – or from countries' own estimates. In the main table, data are presented forwards to 2060 for those countries where the figures are available. However, data are only available for 2040 for Japan and 2030 for Switzerland and not available at all in seven OECD countries.

Long-term projections are a crucial tool in planning pension policy: there is often a long time lag between when a pension reform occurs and when it begins to affect expenditure. There are some differences in the range of different programmes covered in the forecasts, reflecting the complexity and diversity of national retirement-income provision. For example, data for a number of countries do not include special schemes for public-sector workers while in others they are included. Similarly, projections can either include or exclude spending on resource-tested benefits for retirees. The coverage of the data also differs from the *OECD Social Expenditures Database* (SOCX), from which the data on past spending trends in the previous two indicators were drawn. The numbers for 2018-20 may differ between the SOCX database and the sources used here because of the different range of benefits covered and the definitions used.

Pension spending is projected to grow from 9.0% of GDP to 10.4% of GDP by 2040 on average across all OECD-29 countries. The OECD-29 average only refers to the countries for which data is available across the entire timeframe, so both Japan and Switzerland are not included. In the EU27 it is projected to increase from 9.9% of GDP in 2020 to 11.3% of GDP in 2050, after which it is effectively flat. This would be a significant achievement given the demographic change throughout the time period. The indicator of the "Demographic Old-Age to Working-Age Ratio" in Chapter 7 shows a 95% increase in the number of people above age 65 per 100 people aged between 20 and 64 from today until 2050. Cuts in benefits for future retirees at least relative to wages, through lowered indexation and valorisation of benefit formulae, together with increases in the age at which individuals can first claim pension benefits, will reduce growth in public pension expenditure.

Public pension expenditure is expected to increase in 18 OECD countries by 2050. In Korea, the rapid increase reflects both the ageing process and the still maturing pension system. In Slovenia, public spending is projected to keep rising from above the OECD average at 10.0% of GDP in 2018-20, to 15.7% of GDP by 2050, with the Slovak Republic also showing an increase of over 5 percentage points. According to these projections, five other countries would record an increase of about 3 percentage points or more of GDP: Belgium, the Czech Republic, Hungary, Ireland and Luxembourg. Conversely, Denmark, Estonia and Portugal would have a fall of around 2 percentage points of GDP, and Greece of more than 3 percentage points.

Table 8.5. **Projections of public expenditure on pensions, 2018-60, percentage of GDP**

	2018-20	2025	2030	2035	2040	2045	2050	2055	2060
Australia	2.6	2.6	2.5	2.5	2.4	2.3	2.3	2.2	2.1
Austria	13.3	14.6	15.1	15.4	15.1	14.9	14.7	14.7	14.6
Belgium	12.2	13.2	14.0	14.6	14.9	15.1	15.2	15.2	15.2
Canada	5.3	6.0	6.4	6.5	6.4	6.3	6.2	6.3	6.3
Chile									
Colombia									
Costa Rica									
Czech Republic	8.0	8.8	8.8	9.1	9.8	10.7	11.4	11.8	11.8
Denmark	9.3	8.9	8.5	8.3	8.1	7.8	7.6	7.4	7.2
Estonia	7.8	7.1	6.9	6.6	6.5	6.3	6.1	6.0	5.8
Finland	13.0	13.6	13.7	13.4	12.8	12.6	12.7	13.0	13.5
France	14.8	15.4	15.6	15.5	15.2	14.6	14.3	13.8	13.4
Germany	10.3	10.9	11.5	12.0	12.0	12.1	12.2	12.4	12.5
Greece	15.7	14.2	13.8	13.7	14.0	13.7	13.6	12.7	12.0
Hungary	8.3	8.6	8.3	8.8	9.7	10.8	11.2	11.5	11.9
Iceland									
Ireland	4.6	5.3	5.9	6.4	6.9	7.2	7.5	7.5	7.5
Israel									
Italy	15.4	16.2	17.3	17.9	17.8	17.3	16.2	15.0	14.1
Japan	10.1	9.3			9.3				
Korea	1.3	2.0	2.5	3.2	4.2	5.1	5.9	6.5	7.5
Latvia	7.1	7.1	6.9	6.8	6.6	6.3	6.3	6.4	6.2
Lithuania	7.1	7.5	7.9	8.2	8.4	8.3	8.2	8.2	8.1
Luxembourg	9.2	10.3	11.4	12.3	13.0	13.9	14.8	15.8	16.7
Mexico									
Netherlands	6.8	7.3	8.1	8.8	9.1	9.0	8.9	8.8	8.9
New Zealand	4.7	5.1	5.6	6.0	6.3	6.4	6.6	6.9	7.5
Norway	11.0	11.7	12.3	12.6	12.6	12.6	12.7	13.0	13.2
Poland	10.6	11.4	11.0	10.6	10.5	10.6	10.7	10.8	10.8
Portugal	12.7	13.3	14.2	14.6	14.4	13.7	12.6	11.4	10.5
Slovak Republic	8.3	9.7	10.2	10.7	11.6	12.5	13.4	14.2	14.5
Slovenia	10.0	10.1	10.8	12.1	13.6	14.8	15.7	16.1	16.1
Spain	12.3	12.7	12.3	12.5	12.8	13.2	13.0	12.5	11.7
Sweden	7.6	7.7	7.4	7.2	7.0	7.0	7.0	7.3	7.4
Switzerland	6.5	6.4	6.8						
Turkey									
United Kingdom	7.7	8.0	8.0	8.4	8.6	8.3	8.3	8.6	8.9
United States	5.0	5.3	5.7	5.9	5.9	5.8	5.8	5.8	5.8
OECD-29	**9.0**	**9.5**	**9.7**	**10.0**	**10.2**	**10.3**	**10.4**	**10.4**	**10.4**
Brazil	8.5	8.5	8.8	9.4	10.2	11.3	12.3	13.2	13.9
EU27	9.9	10.5	10.7	10.9	11.1	11.2	11.3	11.3	11.3

Note: EU27 figure is a simple average of member states (not the weighted average published by the European Commission). Pension schemes for civil servants and other public-sector workers are generally included in the calculations for EU member states: see European Commission (2021), *2021 Ageing Report*.

Source: European Commission (2021), 2021 Ageing Report for all EU countries and Norway; Australia: Chapter 4, Retirement Income Review – Final Report, November 2020; Canada: 16 Actuarial Report on the Old Age Security Program, 30 Actuarial Report of Canada Pension Plan, Actuarial Valuation of the Québec Pension Plan as at 31 December 2018 (QPP data for 2018, 2023 etc. has been used for 2020, 2025 etc.); Japan: About future social security reform – Looking ahead to 2040; Korea: 2018 National Pension Actuarial Valuation Long-Term Actuarial Projection for the National Pension Scheme; New Zealand: Review of retirement income policies 2019 – Facing the future; Switzerland: BSV – Financial perspectives of the AHV; the United Kingdom: European Commission (2018), 2018 Ageing Report; the United States: The 2020 OASDI Trustees Report.

StatLink https://stat.link/luypts

[1] Adema, W. and M. Ladaique (2009), "How Expensive is the Welfare State?: Gross and Net Indicators in the OECD Social Expenditure Database (SOCX)", *OECD Social, Employment and Migration Working Papers*, No. 92, OECD Publishing, Paris, *https://dx.doi.org/10.1787/220615515052*.

[5] European Commission (2021), *2021 Ageing Report; Economic and budgetary projections for the 27 EU Member States (2019-2070)*, *https://ec.europa.eu/info/publications/2021-ageing-report-economic-and-budgetary-projections-eu-member-states-2019-2070_en*.

[3] OECD (2021), *Taxing Wages 2021*, OECD Publishing, Paris, *https://dx.doi.org/10.1787/83a87978-en*.

[4] OECD (2018), *Financial Incentives and Retirement Savings*, OECD Publishing, Paris, *https://dx.doi.org/10.1787/9789264306929-en*.

[2] OECD (2010), *Tax Expenditures in OECD Countries*, OECD Publishing, Paris, *https://dx.doi.org/10.1787/9789264076907-en*.

Pensions at a Glance 2021
OECD and G20 Indicators

Chapter 9

Retirement savings and public pension reserve funds

This chapter provides eight indicators on retirement savings arrangements (i.e. funded and private pensions) and public pension reserve funds.

The first indicator looks at the proportion of the working-age population covered by a retirement savings plan. The second indicator shows the legislated contribution rates and the average effective contributions paid by member (or by account) relative to average wages.

The third indicator reports assets in retirement savings plans and public pension reserve funds. The fourth indicator focuses on the way these assets are invested, while the fifth indicator analyses their investment performance in the latest year available and over longer periods.

The sixth indicator shows the different types of pension plan across countries. The seventh indicator looks at the fees charged to members in selected defined contribution plans. The final indicator focuses on defined benefit funding ratios, presented over the period 2010-20.

Key results

In the OECD area, 19 countries had mandatory or quasi-mandatory plans in 2020, covering over 75% of the working-age population in 12 of them. In ten OECD countries, voluntary private pensions (occupational and personal) covered more than 40% of the working-age population. Automatic-enrolment programmes are increasingly popular.

In 2020, 19 of the 38 OECD countries had some form of mandatory or quasi-mandatory retirement savings arrangements in place. These arrangements cover over 75% of the working-age population in 12 of these countries, such as in Finland and Switzerland where employers must operate an occupational pension scheme and contribution rates are set by the government. In some countries, the obligation is not set out at the national level but the decision is rather left at the industry or branch level. Through industry-wide or collective bargaining agreements, employers establish schemes that employees must join. As not all sectors may be covered by such agreements, these arrangements are classified as quasi-mandatory (e.g. Denmark, the Netherlands and Sweden). In these countries, the coverage is close to the one in countries with mandatory occupational arrangements. By contrast, in Turkey, participation in a plan is mandatory only for certain employees (e.g. OYAK for military personnel), accounting for the relatively low proportion of the working-age population in a mandatory plan.

Mandatory personal accounts are prevalent in Latin America (e.g. Chile, Colombia, Costa Rica and Mexico) and some other OECD countries [e.g. Denmark (ATP), Estonia (until end-2020) and Sweden (premium pension system)]. While coverage is over 70% in Mexico and over 80% in Chile, Costa Rica, Denmark, Estonia and Sweden, it is not the case in Colombia where people can choose to participate either in the public pay-as-you-go or private funded pension system. A high incidence of informal employment may also account for the relatively lower coverage level in Colombia (52%) than in other similar systems.

Coverage of voluntary occupational pension plans varies across countries. These plans are voluntary because employers, in some countries jointly with employees, are free to set up an occupational plan. Personal pension plans are voluntary when individuals can freely decide whether to join them or not. The coverage of voluntary pension plans (occupational or personal) is above 40% in Belgium, the Czech Republic, Germany, Iceland, Ireland, Japan, Poland, the Slovak Republic, Slovenia and the United States. By contrast, the coverage of voluntary pension plans is very low (below 5%) in countries such as Greece.

Six countries have introduced automatic-enrolment programmes in a retirement savings plan, with an opt-out option, at the national level: Italy (2007), Lithuania (2019), New Zealand (2007), Poland (2019), Turkey (2017) and the United Kingdom (2012). New Zealand has achieved a coverage rate close to 80% in the "KiwiSaver" scheme. In the United Kingdom that initiated its auto-enrolment programme more recently than New Zealand, 49% of the working-age population was covered by an employer-sponsored plan in 2020. In Italy, since 2007 the severance pay provision (so-called Trattamento di Fine Rapporto – TFR) of private-sector employees is automatically paid into an occupational pension plan unless the employee makes an explicit choice to remain in the TFR regime. However, a vast majority of workers has chosen to do so, and only 11% of the working-age population is now covered by an occupational pension plan. Poland and Turkey are still in the early stages of automatic enrolment, probably accounting for the relatively low coverage in 2020. By contrast, Lithuania has already a relatively high coverage in the second pension pillar (over 75%) despite the recent introduction of its automatic enrolment programme in 2019. Before 2019, employees in Lithuania could choose to opt in the second pension pillar voluntarily but could not leave if they did so. Automatic enrolment is also encouraged by regulation in Canada and the United States but at the firm level. Germany also recently introduced an automatic enrolment programme in 2018 for occupational defined contribution pension plans for private-sector employees in the case of deferred compensation. Automatic enrolment needs to be specified in collective agreements.

Definition and measurement

The term "retirement savings plans" refers to private pension arrangements (funded and book reserves) and funded public pension arrangements (e.g. ATP in Denmark).

Several measures of coverage coexist. To be a member of a pension plan from the perspective proposed here, an individual must have assets or have accrued rights in a plan. The proportion of individuals having a plan may be higher than the proportion of individuals actively saving for retirement and paying contributions to the plan.

Counting individuals more than once may arise when using administrative data as individuals can be members of both occupational and personal voluntary pension plans. Therefore, the overall coverage of voluntary pension plans cannot be obtained by summing the coverage rates of occupational and personal plans.

Table 9.1. Coverage of retirement savings plans in selected OECD and other jurisdictions, latest year available

As a percentage of the working-age population (15-64 years)

	Mandatory / Quasi-mandatory	Auto-enrolment	Voluntary		
			Occupational	Personal	Total
Australia	75.2	x	x	..	..
Austria	x	x	15.0	17.9	..
Belgium	x	x	54.0	..	..
Canada	x	..	26.8	24.2	..
Chile	83.0	x	..	..	..
Colombia	52.4	x	x	..	..
Costa Rica	82.9	x	..	4.8	..
Czech Republic	x	x	x	63.6	63.6
Denmark	ATP: 91.9 / QMO: 65.3	x	..	17.0	17.0
Estonia	90.6	x	x	19.8	19.8
Finland	93.0	x	7.0	18.0	25.0
France	x	x	22.1	10.5	..
Germany	x	..	54.0	30.0	66.0
Greece	..	x	<5	..	..
Hungary	x	x	..	18.4	..
Iceland	83.2	x	x	45.4	45.4
Ireland	x	x	56.7	19.6	64.7
Israel	85.4	x	..	..	..
Italy	x	..	10.7	13.8	23.2
Japan	..	x	52.5	16.8	56.5
Korea	17.0	x	x	..	..
Latvia	~100	x	1.1	22.1	..
Lithuania	x	75.7	x	4.2	4.2
Luxembourg	x	x	5.2	..	..
Mexico	70.3	x	2.0	..	..
Netherlands	88.0	x	x	28.3	28.3
New Zealand	x	78.5	..	..	..
Norway	61.2	x	..	24.7	..
Poland	x	6.3	2.7	66.3	..
Portugal	x	x	4.5	<=13.2	13.2
Slovak Republic	x	x	x	44.1	44.1
Slovenia	x	x	..	..	41.5
Spain	x	x	..	..	26.8
Sweden	PPS: ~100 QMO: ~90	x	x	24.2	24.2
Switzerland	77.2	x	x	..	..
Turkey	1.5	12.1	..	12.6	..
United Kingdom	x	49.0	..	5.0	..
United States	x	..	48.1	19.8	..
Argentina	..	..	..	..	..
Brazil	x	x	2.0	12.0	..
China (People's Republic of)	..	..	..	..	..
India	..	..	..	..	..
Indonesia	..	x	0.4	1.6	..
Russian Federation	79.3	x	..	..	..
Saudi Arabia	..	..	..	..	..
South Africa	..	..	..	..	..

Note: QMO = Quasi-mandatory occupational; PPS = Premium Pension System; ".." = Not available; "x" = Not applicable; "~" = Approximately.

Coverage rates are provided with respect to the total working-age population (i.e. individuals aged 15 to 64 years old), unless specified otherwise in the detailed notes of this table. In Korea, the retirement benefit system is mandatory and can take two forms: a severance payment system and an occupational pension plan. The obligation of the employer is to provide a severance payment system, but, by labour agreement, the company can set up an occupational pension plan instead.

Source: OECD Global Pension Statistics; ABS Household Income and Wealth 2017-18 (Australia); FSMA Annual Report 2020 (Belgium); Statistics Canada; ATP Annual Report 2020 and Danish Insurance Association (Denmark); DREES (France); Survey on Pension Provision 2019 of the Federal Ministry of Labour and Social Affairs (Germany); Central Statistical Office (Ireland); Ministry of Health, Labour and Welfare (Japan); OECD Pensions Outlook 2012 (Netherlands); Finance Norway; Polish Financial Supervision Authority (Poland); 2017 edition of the survey "Inquérito à Situação Financeira das Famílias (ISFF)" (Portugal); Spanish Survey of Household Finances (EFF) 2017 of the Bank of Spain; Statistics Sweden for voluntary personal plans; DWP's Family Resources Survey 2019/20 (United Kingdom); 2019 National Compensation Survey (United States).

StatLink https://stat.link/gkvjah

Key results

Regulation usually defines a contribution rate for mandatory and auto-enrolment plans, varying across countries. Some countries have provided flexibility around contribution rates in the context of COVID-19. The actual effective amount of contributions per member was sometimes higher than mandatory rates in 2020 though, through additional voluntary contributions.

Regulation usually defines a (minimum) contribution rate for mandatory and auto-enrolment plans. The responsibility to pay the contributions may fall on the employees (e.g. in Chile), on the employers (e.g. in Australia, Korea, Norway, the Slovak Republic) or on both (e.g. in Estonia, Iceland, Switzerland). This obligation may only apply to certain employees or under certain conditions (e.g. earning threshold in Australia, planned to be removed from 1 July 2022). Contributions may be topped by state matching contributions (e.g. New Zealand, Turkey) or subsidies (e.g. Mexico).

Mandatory contribution rates vary across countries. Iceland sets the highest mandatory contribution rate at 15.5% of salary, split between employers (11.5%) and employees (4%). Mandatory contribution rates also represented over 10% of the salary in Colombia, Denmark (defined in collective agreements), and Israel. By contrast, Norway has the lowest mandatory contribution rate (2% paid by the employer). Employers and employees can however agree on whether employees have to contribute on top of employer contributions. These mandatory contribution rates sometimes vary by income (e.g. ITP1 and SAF-LO plans in Sweden) or by sector in which employees work (e.g. public or private in Mexico).

Some countries have been flexible regarding mandatory contribution rates in response to COVID-19, allowing temporary reductions, postponements or suspensions of mandatory contributions to retirement savings plans. In Finland, employer contributions were lowered by 2.6 percentage points from 1 May 2020 and until the end of 2020. Employers and self-employed in Finland could also agree with their pension provider to postpone the payment of pension contributions into earnings-related pension plans by three months. In Colombia, mandatory contributions to the personal pension system were reduced from 16% to 3% for April and May 2020, but missing contributions are due within 36 months from 1 June 2021. Estonia suspended employer contributions of 4% of salary to the second pension pillar between 1 July 2020 and 31 August 2021. Members were also given the possibility to stop their own contributions between 1 December 2020 and 31 August 2021.

On top of the minimum mandatory contributions, individuals or their employers may have the option of making additional voluntary contributions. In New Zealand, the minimum contribution rate for KiwiSaver plans for employees is 3%. Members can however select a higher personal contribution rate of 4%, 6%, 8% or 10% of salary. In Poland, the minimum contribution rate for employee capital plans (PPK) is 2% for employees and 1.5% for employers. Employers and employees have the option of making additional contributions of up to 2.5% (for employers) and 2% (for employees). In Australia, employees have no obligation to contribute to a plan but can make voluntary contributions on top of their employer's contributions.

In voluntary plans, there may be no required nor minimum amount of contributions expected at the national level. Personal plans may however include a ceiling to benefit from tax advantages. Occupational plans may define specific contribution rates for employees and employers in the plan rules. The contribution rates may vary according to the funding of the plan in the case of defined benefit (DB) plans.

The average effective annual contributions per member (relative to average annual wages) vary a lot across countries. The largest amount of contributions per member in 2020 were paid in Australia, Canada and Switzerland (over 12% of the average wage per member), given the relatively high coverage rate in these countries, high contribution rates, and programmes to support the wages of people during the pandemic. Additional voluntary contributions from employees into superannuation schemes may also account for the high rate in Australia, above the mandatory 9.5% contribution rate. Contributions per member (relative to the average wage) are lower in other countries, and sometimes lower than the minimum mandatory contribution rates such as in Chile and Mexico, which may be due to some people not making contributions in a plan (even if they have one).

Definition and measurement

Average effective annual contributions may be expressed per account instead of member, as the exact number of members holding one (or several) pension plans is sometimes unknown. This is the case for instance in France where individuals can have an occupational (e.g. PER Collectif) and a personal plan (e.g. PER Individuel).

The population holding a pension plan may not be representative of the population on which the average annual wages were calculated and used for the assessment of the average effective annual contributions per member (or account).

Figure 9.1. **Minimum or mandatory contribution rates (for an average earner) in mandatory and auto-enrolment plans (unless specified otherwise), 2020 (or latest year available)**

As a percentage of earnings

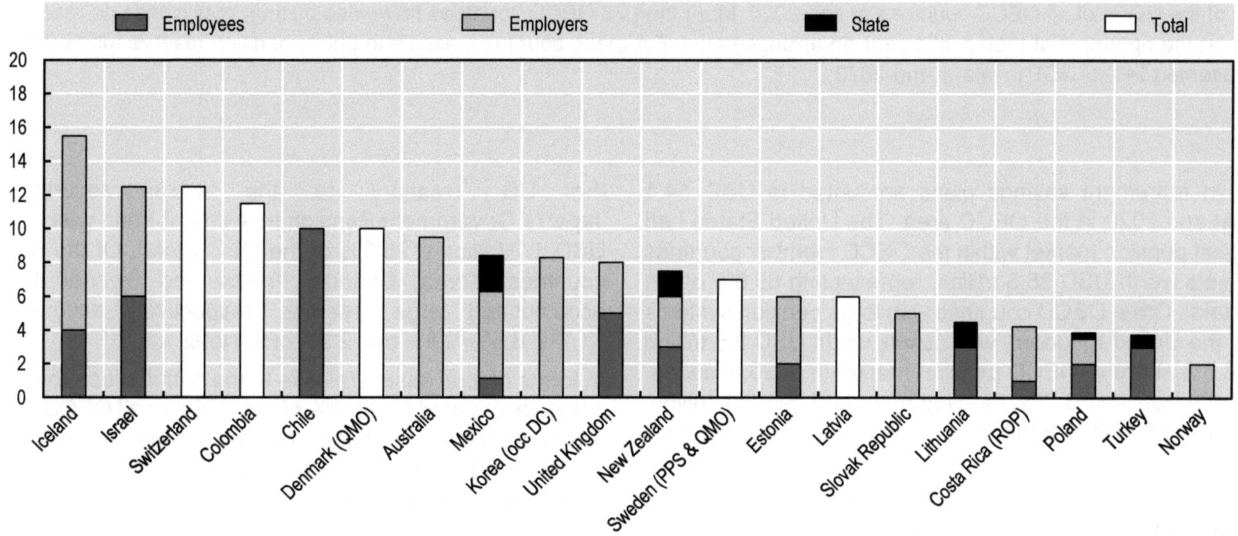

Note: The category "Total" shows the cases where the contribution rates cannot be split precisely between employer, employee (and state). "occ DC" means occupational defined contribution plans. "PPS" means premium pension system. "QMO" means quasi-mandatory occupational plans. "ROP" refers to a mandatory supplementary pension scheme.

Source: ISSA Social Security Country Profiles and other sources.

StatLink https://stat.link/8gtspo

Figure 9.2. **Average annual contribution per active account or member in selected OECD and other jurisdictions, latest year available**

As a percentage of average annual wages

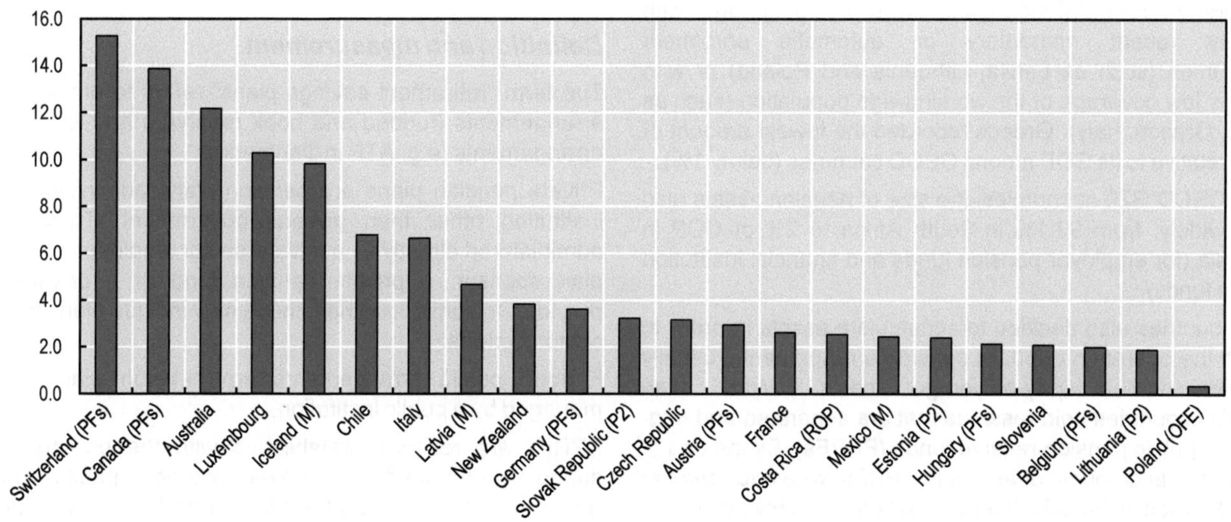

Note: "M" means mandatory. "OFE" means open pension funds. "P2" means second pension pillar. "PFs" means pension funds. "ROP" refers to a mandatory supplementary pension scheme in Costa Rica.

Source: OECD Global Pension Statistics and other sources.

StatLink https://stat.link/symobc

Key results

Substantial pension assets have been provisioned around the world. Assets in retirement savings plans amount to as much as the sum of the GDPs of all OECD countries at end-2020. More than 20 OECD countries have also built up public pension reserves to support the operation of their public pension arrangements. For these countries, assets in public pension reserve funds (PPRFs) represented 14% of GDP in total at end-2020.

Assets in retirement savings plans amounted to USD 54.1 trillion at end-2020 in the OECD area. The United States had the largest pension market within the OECD member countries with assets worth USD 35.5 trillion, representing 65.6% of the OECD total. Other OECD countries with large pension systems include the United Kingdom, with assets worth USD 3.6 trillion and a 6.6% share of OECD pension market in 2020; Canada, USD 3.1 trillion and 5.7%; the Netherlands, USD 2.1 trillion, 3.9%; Australia, USD 1.8 trillion and 3.3%; and Japan, USD 1.6 trillion and 2.9%.

Pension assets in the OECD amount to as much as the sum of the GDPs of all OECD countries at end-2020, but their prominence domestically varies across countries. In three countries, assets exceeded more than twice the size of the GDP: Denmark (229.4%), the Netherlands (212.7%) and Iceland (206.9%). Six additional OECD countries achieved asset-to-GDP ratios higher than 100% – Canada (179.7%), the United States (169.9%), Switzerland (167%), Australia (131.7%), the United Kingdom (126.8%) and Sweden (108.9%). These countries have private pensions from long ago, and most of them have mandatory or quasi-mandatory private pension systems. By contrast, the asset-to-GDP ratios were below 20% in 16 OECD countries, including some with relatively recent mandatory or automatic enrolment programmes (such as Latvia, Lithuania and Poland) or with relatively low coverage of the working-age population (such as France, Greece, Italy). Greece recorded the lowest amount of assets relative to its GDP among OECD countries (below 1%).

In non-OECD G20 economies, the size of pension assets also varied widely, from 92.1% in South Africa to 2% of GDP in Indonesia (for employer pension funds and financial institution pension funds).

Many countries also decided to accumulate assets in order to support the operation of public pension arrangements, usually financed on a pay-as-you-go basis. More than 20 OECD countries hold reserves that are separated and ring-fenced in public pension reserve funds (PPRFs). By the end of 2020, the total amounts of assets in PPRFs were equivalent to USD 6.8 trillion in the OECD area. The largest reserve was held by the US social security trust fund at USD 2.8 trillion, accounting for 41.5% of total OECD assets in PPRFs, although the assets consist of non-tradable debt instruments issued by the US Treasury to the social security trust. Japan's Government Pension Investment Fund was second at USD 1.7 trillion – 25.3% of the OECD total. Of the remaining countries, Korea, Canada, France and Sweden had also accumulated large reserves, respectively accounting for 11.7%, 6.5%, 2.8% and 2.5% of the total.

In terms of total assets relative to the national economy, PPRF assets accounted for 13.9% of the GDPs of all OECD countries with reserves at end-2020. The highest ratio was observed for the Korean National Pension Fund with 45.1% of GDP. Other countries where the ratio was of a significant size include Finland with 33.6%, Luxembourg with 33.6%, Japan with 33% and Sweden with 31.8%. The expansion of these pools of assets are forecast to continue over the coming years in some countries (such as Canada, Japan and New Zealand) but assets in some other PPRFs have started or will fall in the near future (such as in France (FRR) and Spain). Belgium that used to have a PPRF (Zilverfonds) closed it in 2017, while Ireland converted its own (the Irish National Pension Reserve Fund) into a sovereign wealth fund (Ireland Strategic Investment Fund) in 2014, with a broader mandate than financing pay-as-you-go pension plans.

Definition and measurement

The term "retirement savings plans" refers to private pension arrangements (funded and book reserves) and funded public arrangements (e.g. ATP in Denmark).

Private pension plans are pension plans administered by an institution other than general government. They may be administered directly by a private-sector employer acting as the plan sponsor, a private pension fund or a private sector provider. In some countries, these may include plans for public-sector workers.

Funded public arrangements are pension plans that are managed by a public institution.

PPRFs are reserves established with the primary goal to support unfunded / pay-as-you-go public pension arrangements. They could act as a short-term liquidity buffer, a temporary buffer against shocks (such as a demographic change) or as a permanent smoothing vehicle between the inflows and outflows of public pension arrangements.

Table 9.2. **Assets in retirement savings plans and public pension reserve funds in OECD countries and other major economies, in 2020 or latest year available**

As a percentage of GDP and in USD million

	Retirement savings plans		Public pension reserve funds	
	as a percentage of GDP	USD million	as a percentage of GDP	USD million
Australia	131.7	1 794, 300	8.2	110571
Austria	6.6	30634	x	x
Belgium	40.4	223702	x	x
Canada	179.7	3081679	25.6	438314
Chile	75.8	208482	4.4	10787
Colombia	32.0	93053	..	..
Costa Rica	36.9	21657	..	..
Czech Republic	9.5	25347	x	x
Denmark	229.4	882109	x	x
Estonia	21.8	7170	x	x
Finland	64.1	186741	33.6	97939
France	12.2	344114	6.7	186400
Germany	8.2	338469	1.2	45492
Greece	1.0	2016	x	x
Hungary	5.6	8922	x	x
Iceland	206.9	47842	x	x
Ireland	35.5	162459	x	x
Israel	68.9	300489	17.0	73253
Italy	12.7	256417	5.4	107828
Japan	30.1	1564587	33.0	1714783
Korea	31.7	560037	45.1	795652
Latvia	19.5	7004	x	x
Lithuania	9.5	5723	1.6	959
Luxembourg	2.9	2246	33.6	23943
Mexico	22.8	264022	0.2	1965
Netherlands	212.7	2088702	x	x
New Zealand	34.1	80111	13.5	28272
Norway	12.3	49398	7.5	26366
Poland	7.9	48934	2.5	15209
Portugal	22.0	54606	8.5	19898
Slovak Republic	14.4	16192	x	x
Slovenia	8.0	4605	x	x
Spain	14.5	199627	0.2	2419
Sweden	108.9	663486	31.8	171626
Switzerland	167.0	1331372	6.2	46702
Turkey	3.4	23069	x	x
United Kingdom	126.8	3593710	1.8	47282
United States	169.9	35491205	13.4	2811716
Total OECD	**99.9**	**54064238**	**13.9**	**6777376**
Argentina	..	..	12.8	41649
Brazil	28.2	404028	x	x
China	2.2	344259	2.9	447239
India	9.3	249050	..	..
Indonesia	2.0	21701	..	..
Russian Federation	6.1	87489	x	x
Saudi Arabia	..	..	..	..
South Africa	92.1	312355	x	x

Note: ".." means not available. "x" means not applicable. The line "OECD" shows the total assets in millions of USD and the total assets over the total of the GDPs of all reporting OECD countries.

Source: OECD Global Pension Statistics, websites and annual reports of reserve funds or other national authorities.

StatLink https://stat.link/qi2ev9

Key results

Assets in retirement savings plans and in public pension reserve funds are invested mostly in traditional asset classes (primarily bonds and equities). Proportions of equities and bonds vary considerably across countries but there is, generally, a greater preference for bonds.

In most countries, bonds and equities were the two main asset classes in which pension assets were invested at the end of 2020, accounting for more than half of investments in 35 out of 38 OECD countries, and in four reporting non-OECD G20 jurisdictions. The combined proportion of bonds and equities was the highest (relatively to the size of the portfolio) in Chile (97.8%), Estonia (96.9%) and Mexico (96.5%). Pension assets may have been invested in these instruments either directly or indirectly through collective investment schemes (CIS). For some countries, the look-though of the investments of collective investment schemes was not available, such as for the Slovak Republic (where 31.5% of assets were invested in CIS), Sweden (67.7% of investments) and the United States (32% of investments). Only the direct investments in bonds and equities were known for these countries (e.g. 62.5% for the Slovak Republic, 27.1% for Sweden, 54.6% for the United States). The overall exposure of pension assets to fixed income securities and equities was probably higher in these countries.

The proportion of equities and bonds varied considerably across countries at end-2020. Although there was in general a greater preference for bonds, the reverse was true in 11 OECD countries and in South Africa where equities outweighed bonds (e.g. by 41.8% to 14.7% in Australia, by 74.4% to 20.6% in Lithuania).

Public sector bonds, within bond investments as opposed to corporate bonds, represented a larger share of the combined direct bond holdings (i.e. excluding investment via collective investment schemes) in a number of countries at end-2020. For example, public sector bonds accounted for 89% of total direct bond holdings in Israel and the Czech Republic but only 22% in Norway and 14% in New Zealand.

Cash and deposits also accounted for a significant share of pension assets in some OECD countries and in Indonesia at end-2020. For example, the proportion of cash and deposits was 28.7% of pension assets in Indonesia, 19.4% in Korea and 15% in Australia. Pension funds in Australia held more assets in cash and deposits in 2020 than in 2019 (12.7%) to face potential outflows from COVID-19 related early withdrawals.

In most reporting countries, loans, real estate (land and buildings), unallocated insurance contracts and private investment funds (shown as "other" in the chart) only accounted for relatively small shares of the investments of pension assets at end-2020 despite some exceptions. Real estate was a significant component of the portfolios of pension providers (directly or indirectly through collective investment schemes) in some countries such as Canada (11.9% of total assets) and Switzerland (20.1%).

Fixed income and equities were also the predominant asset classes within PPRF portfolios. The 22 reporting PPRFs invested 46.2% of their assets in fixed income and 30.2% in listed equities on average. There was a stronger appetite for listed equities in some reserve funds, which probably reflects their greater investment autonomy and long-term investment outlook. For example, at end-2018, Norway's Government Pension Fund invested 55.3% of its assets in equities and 41.5% in fixed income. New Zealand Superannuation Fund also invests more than half of its portfolio in listed equities, compared to 14.7% in fixed income. Japan's Government Pension Investment Fund has sought to diversify its asset allocation and achieve better risk-adjusted returns, reducing the proportion of assets invested in bonds to 47% while increasing the share of listed equities to 47% of its portfolio by the end of the financial year 2019. By contrast, reserve funds in Chile, Poland and Portugal for instance invested much more in bonds than listed equities.

The extreme case is the one of the US PPRF, which is by law fully invested in government bonds.

Some PPRFs also invested in real estate and non-traditional asset classes like private equity and hedge funds. For example, over 20% of the reserves of the Canada Pension Plan are invested in private equity. In Finland, the State Pension Fund (VER) held 6% of its assets in REITs, unlisted real estate and infrastructure investments at end-2018.

Definition and measurement

The term "retirement savings plans" refers to private pension arrangements (funded and book reserves) and funded public arrangements (e.g. ATP in Denmark).

Data on asset allocation include both direct investment in equities, bills and bonds and cash and deposits, and indirect investment through Collective Investment Schemes (CIS) when possible. The OECD Global Pension Statistics exercise collects data on the investments in CIS, as well as the look-through of these investments in equities, bills and bonds, cash and deposits, and other. When the look-through was not provided by reporting countries, only the direct investments in equities, bills and bonds and cash and deposits are known and shown; investments in CIS are shown separately in that case.

Figure 9.3. **Allocation of assets in retirement savings plans in selected asset classes and investment vehicles, 2020**

As a percentage of total investment

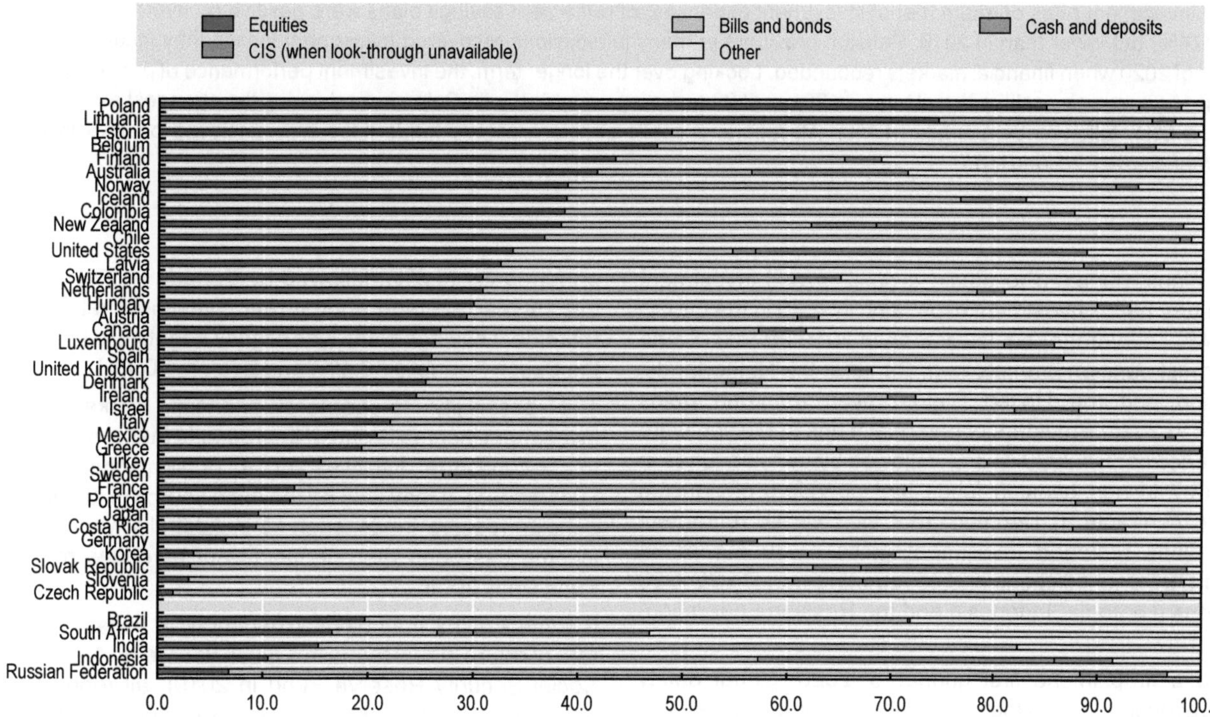

Source: OECD Global Pension Statistics.

StatLink https://stat.link/c7r0h2

Figure 9.4. **Asset allocation of selected reserve funds (latest year available)**

As a percentage of total investment

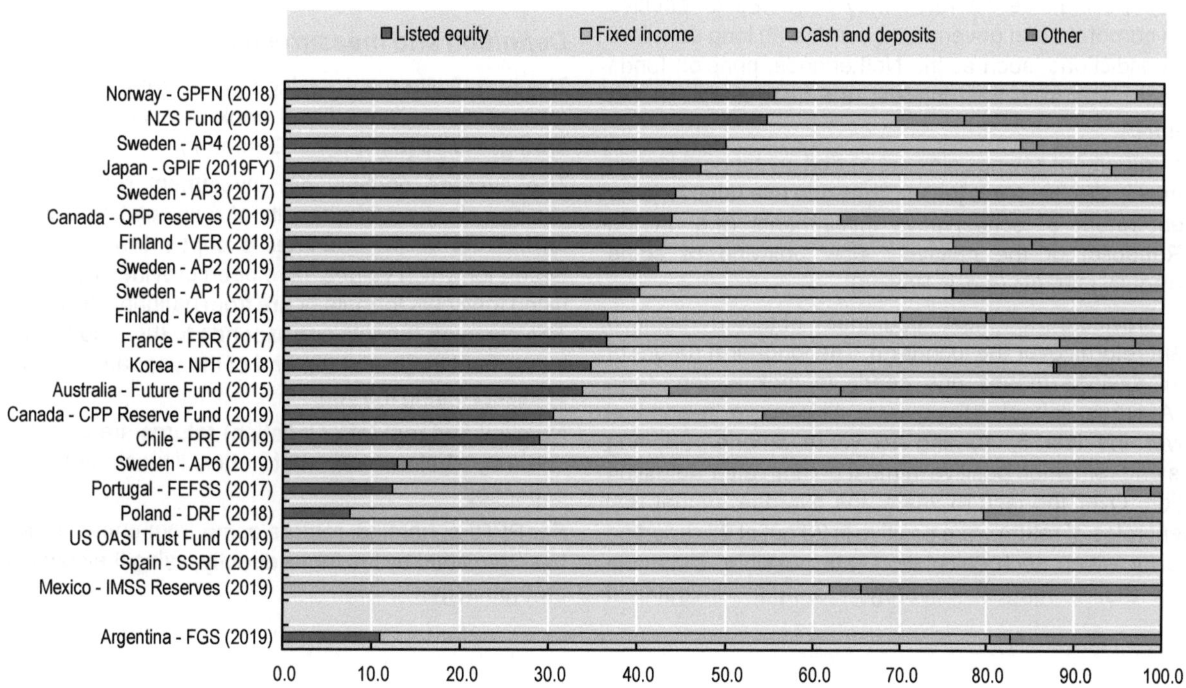

Source: OECD Annual Survey of Public Pension Reserve Funds; Annual report of the Korean NPF; and official websites.

StatLink https://stat.link/b1kzu2

Key results

Real investment rates of return (net of investment expenses) of retirement savings plans were positive on average in 2020 in the OECD (4%) but lower than in 2019. Pension providers in many jurisdictions recovered investment losses they incurred in the first quarter of 2020 when financial markets rebounded. Looking over the longer term, the investment performance of pension plans over the last 15 years was positive in real terms in 20 out of 23 reporting countries, with Colombia achieving the strongest average annual return (5.3%), followed by Canada (4.7%). All reporting public pension reserve funds have also achieved positive investment performance over the long term.

Pension plans managed to obtain a positive real investment rate of return, net of investment expenses, in 2020 in the OECD area (at 4% on average) but lower than in 2019 (at 8%). Some of the largest pension markets (e.g. Canada, the Netherlands, Switzerland and the United States) even recorded gains above 5% in 2020. Providers of personal plans in Mexico were the top performers in 2020 (9.3%), followed by pension funds in Iceland (8.7%) and pension funds and providers of pension insurance contracts in Denmark (8.7%). Overall, retirement savings plans recorded investment gains in 30 out of 34 reporting OECD jurisdictions and all reporting non-OECD G20 jurisdictions (i.e. India, Indonesia and the Russian Federation) in 2020.

Following a drop in the first quarter of 2020, global equity markets recovered during the rest of the year, enabling pension providers in many jurisdictions to recover investment losses from the first quarter. This rebound was driven by sectors that thrived during the pandemic (e.g. tech companies), stimulus from Central Banks to keep borrowing costs low (e.g. decline in interest rates), and positive prospects during the year (development of vaccines and their approval by health authorities). Falling interest rates may have led to positive returns on corporate and government bonds with long duration. In some jurisdictions, such as the Netherlands, pension funds also earned gains from their interest rate hedges as interest rates dropped.

However, retirement savings plans recorded investment losses in real terms in 2020 in a few jurisdictions due to a relatively low investment return of conservative investments (e.g. in the Czech Republic) or the relatively slow upswing of some domestic equity markets (e.g. in Poland).

Pension providers in most countries obtained positive investment returns over the long-term. The long-term nature of retirement savings means one needs to look at long-term returns. Average annual returns were all positive in nominal terms over the last 5, 10 and 15 years among reporting countries and remained positive in most of them after adjusting for inflation. Over the last 15 years, the average annual real investment rates of return were positive in 20 out of 23 reporting countries for which such calculation was possible. Colombia recorded the strongest average annual investment performance (5.3%), followed by Canada (4.7%). By contrast, the 15-year average annual real investment rate of return of retirement savings plans was slightly negative in Latvia (-0.3%), the Czech Republic (-0.4%) and Estonia (-0.7%).

The possibility to harness financial markets and earn investment income is one of the reasons that can lead countries to prefund the liabilities of a public scheme, such as Luxembourg. It may also be the main source of funding of public pension reserve funds, such as in Australia where investment income has been the only source of revenues of the Future Fund since 2008.

If some PPRFs may have experienced a negative investment rate of return in real terms in a given year (e.g. -1.1% for Spain's Social Security Reserve Fund in 2019), all reporting PPRFs have achieved to earn positive investment income over the longer time period (e.g. 10-year period from December 2009 to December 2019, and 15-year period from December 2014 to December 2019). New Zealand Superannuation Fund recorded the strongest real return on average over the 10-year period (11.3%) and over the 15-year period (8.6%) among all reporting PPRFs.

Definition and measurement

The term "retirement savings plans" refers to private pension arrangements (funded and book reserves) and funded public arrangements (e.g. ATP in Denmark).

The average nominal net investment returns of retirement savings plans are the results of a calculation using a common formula for all the countries except a few ones (e.g. Ireland, Israel) for which values have been provided by the jurisdictions using their own formula or are from national official publications. The common formula corresponds to the ratio between the net investment income at the end of the year and the average level of assets during the year.

Nominal and real (after inflation) returns are calculated in local currency before tax but after investment management expenses.

For PPRFs, nominal returns come from annual reports or have been provided by the funds directly, using their own formula and methodology.

Table 9.3. **Geometric average annual investment rates of return of retirement savings plans in 2020 and over longer time periods (%)**

	Nominal				Real			
	2020	5-year average	10-year average	15-year average	2020	5-year average	10-year average	15-year average
Australia	-0.5	6.0	7.5	6.2	-0.1	4.7	5.6	3.9
Austria	2.5	3.5	3.7	2.9	1.4	1.8	1.8	1.0
Belgium	4.1	5.1	5.7	5.1	3.7	3.5	4.1	3.3
Canada	6.3	6.4	6.9	6.4	5.6	4.7	5.3	4.7
Chile	5.7	6.8	6.4	6.8	2.7	4.0	3.2	3.4
Colombia	9.0	9.3	7.4	9.5	7.2	5.4	3.6	5.3
Costa Rica	9.1	8.3	9.2	9.4	8.1	6.7	6.5	4.6
Czech Republic	1.1	0.9	1.4	1.7	-1.2	-1.4	-0.4	-0.4
Denmark	9.2	6.1	6.3	5.4	8.7	5.4	5.3	4.0
Estonia	4.0	3.3	3.0	2.1	4.8	1.3	1.3	-0.7
Finland	4.7	5.3	..	..	4.5	4.5	..	..
Germany	2.9	3.4	3.7	3.8	3.2	2.3	2.5	2.5
Greece	2.1	4.6	..	..	4.5	4.7	..	..
Hungary	3.9	5.0	..	..	1.1	2.2	..	..
Iceland	12.6	8.1	8.6	7.3	8.7	5.3	5.5	2.6
Ireland	5.0	6.6	..	..	6.0	6.3	..	..
Israel	5.0	5.5	5.4	5.6	5.8	5.3	4.8	4.3
Italy	2.8	2.5	3.1	2.9	3.0	1.9	2.2	1.7
Japan	-1.3	..	..	..	-0.1	..	..	..
Korea	3.0	..	..	..	2.5	..	..	..
Latvia	2.3	2.5	2.8	2.7	2.8	0.8	1.3	-0.3
Lithuania	5.4	3.8	4.1	..	5.2	1.7	2.4	..
Luxembourg	2.8	2.7	3.5	2.9	2.3	1.4	2.1	1.2
Mexico	12.7	7.3	6.7	6.7	9.3	3.0	2.8	2.6
Netherlands	7.5	7.3	7.6	6.1	6.5	5.7	5.9	4.4
Norway	7.5	6.0	5.9	5.7	6.0	3.7	3.9	3.5
Poland	-2.3	2.6	..	..	-4.4	0.6	..	..
Portugal	3.9	3.3	3.4	3.3	4.1	2.7	2.5	2.1
Slovak Republic	2.7	2.8	2.3	..	1.1	1.1	0.7	..
Slovenia	2.4	3.5	4.5	..	3.5	2.6	3.5	..
Spain	1.3	2.4	3.5	..	1.8	1.6	2.6	..
Switzerland	4.3	4.5	4.3	3.3	5.1	4.3	4.5	3.1
Turkey	19.6	14.5	10.1	11.9	4.3	1.0	-0.6	1.8
United States	8.1	5.9	4.9	3.1	6.7	3.9	3.1	1.2
India	13.4	..	..	..	8.4	..	..	..
Indonesia	8.7	8.6	8.2	..	7.0	5.6	3.9	..
Russian Federation	5.1	6.4	..	..	0.2	2.3	..	..

Note: ".." means not available. The 2020 and the last 5, 10 and 15-year annual averages are calculated over the periods Dec 2019-Dec 2020, Dec 2015-Dec 2020, Dec 2010-Dec 2020 and Dec 2005-Dec 2020 respectively, except for Australia (from June to June) and Japan (March 2019-March 2020).
Source: OECD Global Pension Statistics.

StatLink https://stat.link/okni78

Table 9.4. **Geometric average annual investment rates of return of PPRFs in 2019 and over longer time periods (%)**

Country	Public pension reserve fund	Nominal				Real			
		2019	Dec 2014-Dec 2019	Dec 2009-Dec 2019	Dec 2004-Dec 2019	2019	Dec 2014-Dec 2019	Dec 2009-Dec 2019	Dec 2004-Dec 2019
Australia	Future Fund	14.3	8.8	9.7	..	12.2	6.9	7.5	..
Canada	CPP Reserve Fund	12.6	10.5	10.5	8.4	10.1	8.5	8.6	6.5
Canada	QPP reserves	10.6	8.7	9.7	..	8.2	6.7	7.9	..
Chile	Pension Reserve Fund	19.9	8.1	7.2	..	16.4	4.9	3.9	..
Finland	Keva	12.8	5.8	6.8	..	11.8	5.1	5.4	..
Finland	VER	13.8	5.5	6.2	5.5	12.8	4.8	4.8	4.0
France	FRR	9.7	3.8	4.8	4.0	8.1	2.8	3.6	2.7
Japan	Government Pension Investment Fund	-5.2	0.9	3.7	3.0	-5.6	0.5	3.2	2.7
Korea	National Pension Fund	11.3	5.3	5.6	5.6	10.5	4.1	3.8	3.4
Korea	Government Employees Pension Fund	9.3	4.5	..	..	8.5	3.3	..	..
Luxembourg	FDC	14.2	4.8	5.5	..	12.3	3.3	3.8	..
Mexico	IMSS Reserve	8.3	6.6	5.8	6.4	5.4	2.5	1.8	2.2
New Zealand	New Zealand Superannuation Fund	21.1	11.3	13.0	10.8	18.9	9.9	11.3	8.6
Norway	Government Pension Fund – Norway	12.4	7.7	8.7	7.7	10.9	5.1	6.5	5.5
Spain	Social Security Reserve Fund	-0.3	0.2	3.0	3.3	-1.1	-0.7	1.8	1.6
Sweden	AP1	15.1	7.3	8.1	7.0	13.1	5.8	6.9	5.7
Sweden	AP2	15.9	7.4	8.4	7.3	13.9	5.9	7.2	6.0
Sweden	AP3	17.6	8.5	8.7	7.3	15.6	6.9	7.4	6.0
Sweden	AP4	21.7	9.3	9.9	8.2	19.6	7.7	8.6	6.9
Sweden	AP6	8.2	9.7	7.5	6.8	6.3	8.2	6.2	5.5
Switzerland	AHV Central Compensation Fund	10.8	3.8	4.0	..	10.6	3.7	4.1	..
United States	Social Security Trust Fund	2.8	3.0	3.6	4.1	0.5	1.2	1.8	2.0

Note: ".." means not available. Returns are calculated over March 2019-March 2020, March 2015-March 2020, March 2010-March 2020 and March 2005-March 2020) for Japan.
Source: OECD Annual Survey of Public Pension Reserve Funds, Annual Reports and Financial Statements of reserve funds.

StatLink https://stat.link/l7zxcn

Key results

The pension landscape includes various types of retirement savings plans worldwide. Occupational and personal plans coexist in most OECD countries and in other jurisdictions. The size of occupational plans in terms of assets varied greatly across countries at end-2020. In most cases, pension funds would administer these plans although there are some notable exceptions (e.g. Denmark and France). Personal plans and occupational defined contribution plans are gaining importance at the expense of occupational defined benefit plans.

The pension landscape includes various types of retirement savings plans worldwide. For example, pension plans may be accessed through employment or by individuals directly without any involvement of their employers. When plans are accessed through employment and were established by employers on behalf of their employees or by social partners, these plans are considered as occupational. The OECD taxonomy classifies plans as personal when access to these plans does not have to be linked to an employment relationship and these plans are established directly by a pension fund or a financial institution acting as pension provider without any intervention of employers.

Occupational and personal plans coexist in most reporting countries: 33 out of the 38 OECD countries, as well as Brazil, India, Indonesia, the Russian Federation and South Africa, have both occupational and personal plans. Individuals may be members of several occupational pension plans through different jobs during their career, and several personal pension plans that they have opened directly with a pension provider. The prominence of occupational plans in terms of assets varied greatly across countries at end-2020. Assets in occupational plans represented 90% of all pension assets in Finland and Switzerland, but only 1% in Latvia where the funded system is mostly based on personal plans.

Depending on how pension benefits are calculated and who bears the risks, occupational pension plans can be either defined benefit (DB) or defined contribution (DC). In DC plans, participants bear the brunt of risk, while in traditional DB plans sponsoring employers assume all the risks. Employers in some countries have introduced hybrid and mixed DB plans, which come in different forms, but effectively involve some degree of risk sharing between employers and employees. For example, in the Netherlands, benefit levels may be conditional on the funding status of the pension fund. Cash balance plans (another type of hybrid DB plan) provide benefits based on a fixed contribution rate and a guaranteed rate of return (the guarantee is provided by the sponsoring employer, hence these plans are classified as DB). Such plans are part of the pension landscape in Belgium (where by law, employers must provide a minimum return guarantee), Japan and the United States. Mixed plans are those where the plan has two separate DB and DC components that are treated as part of the same plan. There are also DC plans such as those in Denmark that offer guaranteed benefits or returns. They are classified as DC as there is no recourse to the sponsoring employer in case of underfunding.

The proportion of assets in DC plans and in personal plans is higher than in DB plans in most of the reporting countries. More than 50% of assets are held in DC plans or personal plans in 20 out of 24 reporting OECD economies, and in Brazil.

DC plans and personal plans have been gaining prominence at the expense of DB plans even in countries with a historically high proportion of assets in DB plans such as the United States. One of the fastest shift away from DB plans over the last decade happened in Israel (from 77% in 2010 to 51% in 2020) where DB plans have been closed to new members since 1995. Some other countries also closed the access to certain DB plans to new members, such as Italy since 1993. New members had the possibility (in Italy) or the obligation (in Israel) to join DC plans instead. More recently, Iceland reformed a pension plan for state and municipal employees at the end of 2016, converting it from DB to DC.

Definition and measurement

The term "retirement savings plans" refers to private pension arrangements (funded and book reserves) and funded public arrangements (e.g. ATP in Denmark).

The OECD has established a set of guidelines for classifying pension plans (see OECD (2005[1])) on which this analysis is based.

In most OECD countries, pension funds are the main vehicle to fund occupational pensions. In some countries, pension insurance contracts (e.g. Belgium, Denmark, France, Korea, Norway and Sweden) or book reserves that are provisions on sponsoring employers' balance sheets (e.g. Austria and Germany) are also used to finance occupational pension plans. Personal pension plans are often funded through pension insurance contracts or financial products provided by banks and asset managers (see OECD (2021[2])).

Table 9.5. **Types of pension arrangements available in the OECD area and selected non-OECD G20 countries according to the OECD taxonomy, 2020**

		Occupational plans			
		DB only	Both DB and DC	DC only	None
Personal plans	Yes	Finland, Israel, Switzerland	Australia, Austria, Belgium, Canada, Costa rica, Denmark, France, Germany, Iceland, Ireland, Italy, Japan, Korea, Luxembourg, Mexico, the Netherlands, New Zealand, Norway, Portugal, Spain, Sweden, turkey, United Kingdom, United States, Brazil, India, Indonesia, Russian Federation, South Africa	Chile, Greece, Hungary, Latvia, Poland, Slovenia	Colombia, the Czech Republic, Estonia, Lithuanaia, the Slovak Republic
	No				

StatLink https://stat.link/l71vwb

Figure 9.5. **Split of pension assets by type of plan, 2020 or latest year available**

As a percentage of total assets

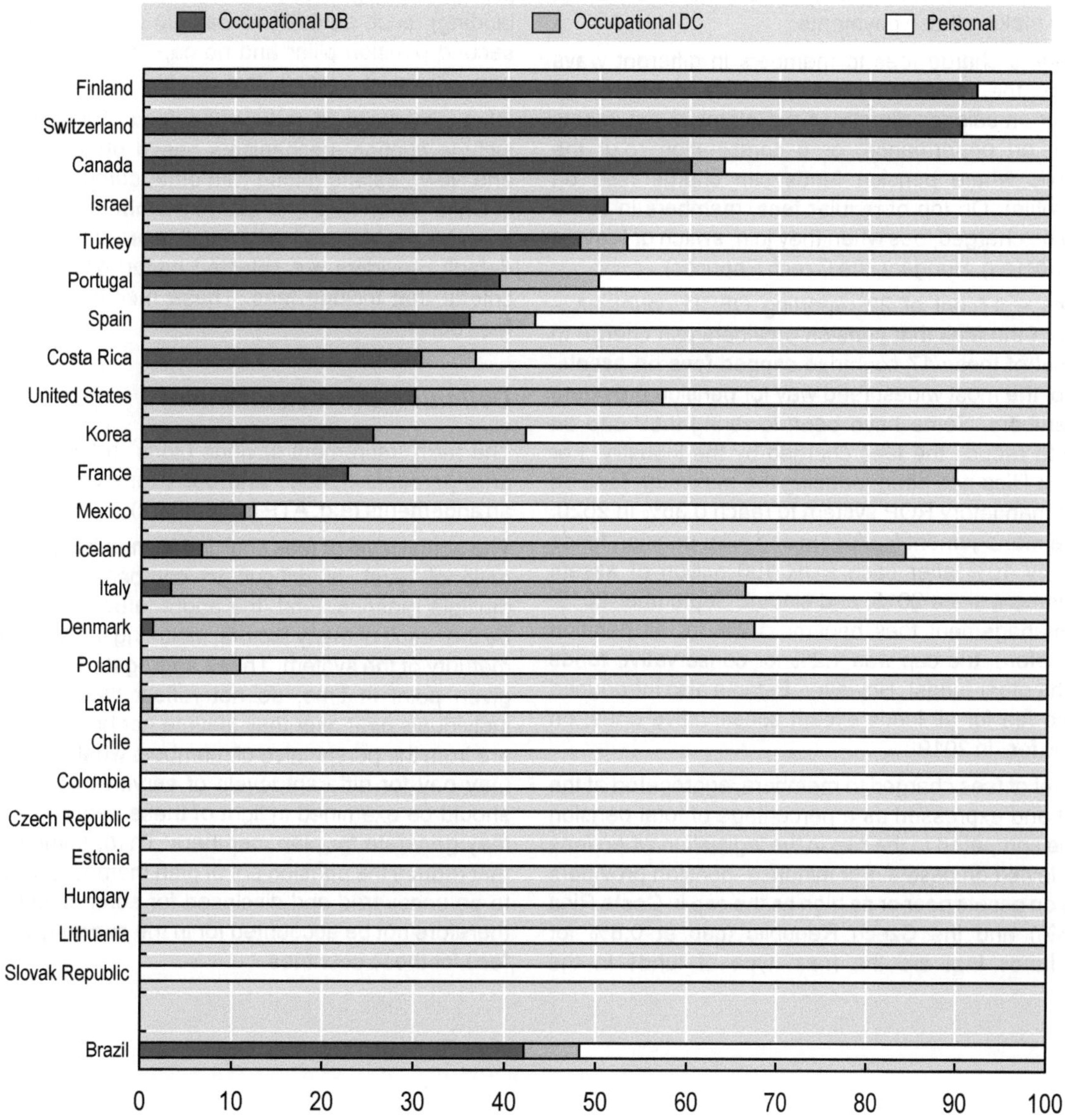

Source: OECD Global Pension Statistics.

StatLink https://stat.link/qa9gpc

Key results

Pension providers charge fees to members to cover their operating expenses for running pension plans. Most countries cap fees, generally fees on assets, which can be charged to members. In some countries, the actual amount of fees levied on assets is close to this cap (such as in Costa Rica and the Czech Republic) while in some others, the cap does not seem too binding as pension providers charge less (such as in Estonia and Hungary). Other initiatives to reduce the fees charged by the industry include auction mechanisms based on fees such as in Chile and in New Zealand (along with other criteria).

Pension providers charge fees to their members to cover their operating expenses. Operating expenses include marketing the plan to potential participants, collecting contributions, sending contributions to investment fund managers, keeping records of accounts, sending reports to participants and supervisors, investing the assets, converting account balances to benefit payments, and making these payments.

Pension providers charge fees to members in different ways depending on the country. Fees can be charged on contributions or on salaries directly (e.g. Colombia), on assets (e.g. Estonia), on performance, or a combination (e.g. the Czech Republic where pension funds can charge fees on assets and profits). On top of regular fees, members in some countries can be charged fees when they join, switch or leave a pension provider (e.g. Hungary, the Czech Republic).

Most countries – 17 out of 22 reporting OECD countries – capped some of the fees that pension providers can charge to members. Most of these 17 countries capped fees on assets, which is one of the most widespread way for pension providers to charge members. Some have been lowering their cap on fees recently to reduce the fees charged by the industry. For instance, Costa Rica has been reducing the maximum fees on assets for the mandatory ROP system to reach 0.35% in 2020. In Estonia, the management fee for second pillar pension funds must decline by 10% after each EUR 100 million of assets under management since 2015, and since 2 September 2019, the cap for management fees became 1.2% for all pension funds (while before, the cap was 1.2% for conservative funds only, 2% for the other funds). However, Estonia also introduced a performance fee for all funds except conservative ones, on top of the basic fee, in 2019.

The actual level of fees charged to members, aggregated at the national level and expressed as a percentage of total pension assets, can be compared to the cap in the legislation when fees are precisely levied on assets. For instance, pension providers charged fees on assets near or as high as the cap in Costa Rica (cap at 0.35%) and the Czech Republic (cap at 0.8% for transformed funds that are the main type of funds in the country). The choice of the level of the cap is therefore important but challenging. If the cap is too high, charges may rise to the level of this cap. If the cap is too low, pension providers may try to lower costs and could lower the quality of the services they provide. In some other countries, pension providers charge less on assets than the cap (which may not be binding), such as 0.6% in Estonia (with a cap at 1.2% for the second pension pillar and no cap for the third pension pillar), and 0.3% in Hungary (with a cap at 0.8%).

Other initiatives to reduce the fees charged by the industry include auction mechanisms based on fees such as in Chile and New Zealand (along with other criteria). Pension providers in Chile bid on fees charged to members. The winning pension provider receives all new eligible entrants. In New Zealand, default providers are selected based on a range of selection criteria that include fees. These mechanisms intend to drive fees down.

Definition and measurement

The term "retirement savings plans" refers to private pension arrangements (funded and book reserves) and funded public arrangements (e.g. ATP in Denmark).

The actual level of fees charged to members, aggregated at the national level, is difficult to compare across countries for multiple reasons. First, the aggregated amounts of fees could be the result of many factors, including the fee structure and the maturity of the system. These aggregated amounts, shown at a given point in time, do not reflect the amount of fees that individuals bear over their lifetime nor how expensive DC plans are from the perspective of members whatsoever. Second, fees may pay for different levels of services across countries and should be examined in light of these services and of the value they generate for plan members. Third, some indirect charges that reduce the pension pot of plan members may also still need to be uncovered and disclosed for some countries, and would therefore not be accounted for in the currently available data on fees for these countries.

Table 9.6. **Fee structure in selected OECD and other major economies**

	Fees on salaries	Fees on contributions	Fees on assets	Fees on returns / performance	Other fees (e.g. exit fees, entry fees, switching fees)
Australia (except MySuper)	No cap	No cap	No cap except for low balances	No cap	No cap
Chile	No cap	x	Capped	x	x
Colombia	Capped	x	x	x	Capped
Costa Rica – ROP	x	x	Capped	x	x
Czech Republic – transformed funds	x	x	Capped	Capped	Capped
Czech Republic – participation funds	x	x	Capped	Capped	Capped
Denmark	No cap	No cap	No cap	No cap	No cap
Estonia – 2nd pension pillar	x	x	Capped	Capped	Redemption fee could be charged
Estonia – 3rd pension pillar	x	x	No cap	x	No cap
Hungary – voluntary personal pension funds	x	Capped	Capped	x	Capped
Ireland	No cap	No cap	No cap	No cap	No cap
Israel	x	Capped	Capped	x	x
Italy	x	No cap	No cap	Possible but rare	Capped
Korea – occupational DC	x	x	No cap	x	x
Latvia – state funded scheme	x	Capped	Capped	Capped	x
Latvia – private pension funds	x	No cap	No cap	No cap	x
Lithuania – 2nd pillar	x	x	Capped	x	Capped
Lithuania – 3rd pillar	x	No cap	No cap	No cap	Capped
Mexico – personal plans	x	x	No cap	x	x
Poland – open pension funds	x	Capped	Capped	Capped	x
Poland – PPK	x	x	Capped	Capped	No cap
Portugal	No cap	No cap	No cap	No cap	Capped
Slovak Republic – 2nd pillar	x	Capped	Capped	Capped	x
Slovak Republic – 3rd pillar	x	x	Capped	Capped	Capped
Slovenia	x	Capped	Capped	x	Capped
Spain	x	x	Capped	No cap	x
United Kingdom – default funds	x	x	Capped	x	x
United States	No cap	No cap	No cap	No cap	No cap
Brazil – open pension entities	x	Capped	No cap	No cap	Capped

Note: "x" means that the type of fee does not exist or is not allowed in the country.
Source: OECD Pension Markets in Focus 2021.

StatLink https://stat.link/lhz89w

Table 9.7. **Annual fees charged to members, by type of fee, 2020**

As a percentage of total assets

	Fees on salaries	Fees on contributions	Fees on assets	Fees on returns / performance	Other fees (e.g. exit fees, entry fees, switching fees)
Australia			0.4		
Chile	0.5	x	0.3	x	x
Colombia	0.4	x	x	x	0.2
Costa Rica	x	x	0.3	x	x
Czech Republic	x	x	0.8	0.1	0.0
Estonia	x	x	0.6	0.1	0.0
Hungary	x	0.3	0.3	x	..
Korea	x	x	0.5	x	x
Lithuania	x	..	0.6	..	0.0
Mexico	x	x	0.8	x	x
Poland	x	0.0	0.4	0.0	x
Slovak Republic	x	0.1	0.4	0.2	0.0
Slovenia	x	..	0.8	x	..
Spain	x	x	1.0	..	x

Note: "x" means that the type of fee does not exist or is not allowed in the country. "." means missing data. All the fees are expressed in this Table as a percentage of total assets, even when fees are levied on salaries, contributions or investment income.
Source: OECD Global Pension Statistics.

StatLink https://stat.link/w2o5gz

Key results

Funding ratios, which measure the amount of liabilities that available assets cover in defined benefit (DB) pension plans, have evolved differently over the years across countries. Funding ratios withstood well the instability in financial markets in 2020, with most countries recording an improvement of the solvency of DB plans at end-2020 compared to end-2019. Funding levels of DB plans were above 100% at the end of 2020 (or latest available date) in all reporting countries but five: Iceland, Mexico, the United Kingdom and the United States among OECD countries, and Indonesia. Funding levels are calculated using national (regulatory) valuation methodologies of liabilities and hence cannot be compared across countries.

Funding ratios of DB plans, which measure the amount of liabilities that available assets cover, have evolved differently over the years across countries. Over the last decade or so, the funding position of DB plans improved by 25 percentage points in Germany (from 108% in 2010 to 133% in 2020), 11 percentage points in Finland (from 118% in 2011 to 129% in 2020), 11 percentage points in Ireland (from 105% in 2016 to 116% in 2020) and 9 percentage points in Switzerland (from 103% in 2010 to 112% in 2020). The funding ratio of DB plans also improved in Luxembourg, Norway and the United States between 2010 and 2020. However, the opposite trend was observed in Iceland, Indonesia, Mexico, the Netherlands and the United Kingdom where the funding ratio deteriorated between 6 percentage points (in Indonesia) and 22 percentage points (in Mexico) over the last decade.

The funding ratio of DB plans improved in 2020 in most reporting jurisdictions, with the strongest improvement recorded in Finland (from 125% at end-2019 to 129% at end-2020). Yet, national authorities and private-sector companies that monitored the funding ratio of DB plans closely in 2020 had usually found a deterioration of this ratio in the first quarter of 2020 such as in Finland, the Netherlands, Switzerland and the United Kingdom. This decline was partly due to the fall in the asset values of DB plans during the first quarter while liabilities may have also even been increasing in some cases. However, the recovery of financial markets after Q1 2020 has supported the improvement of the funding ratios during the rest of 2020, with assets increasing faster than liabilities at the end in most reporting jurisdictions in 2020. Exceptions include Ireland, the Netherlands and the United Kingdom.

Funding levels of DB plans were above 100% at the end of 2020 (or latest available date) in all reporting countries but five: Iceland (33%), Mexico (62%), the United Kingdom (95%) and the United States (64%) among OECD countries, and Indonesia (97%). Assets in DB plans in these five countries would not enable to cover the pension liabilities (the way they are calculated).

Funding levels are calculated using national (regulatory) valuation methodologies of liabilities and hence cannot be compared across countries. Some countries like Finland, Iceland and Luxembourg use fixed discount rates (at 3%, 3.5% and 5% respectively), while others like the Netherlands, the United Kingdom and the United States use market rates as a discount rate. In the Netherlands, pension funds can use an Ultimate Forward Rate (UFR) for the valuation of liabilities. The UFR is an extrapolation of the observable term structure to take into account the very long duration of pension liabilities. The Pension Protection Fund in the United Kingdom uses conventional and index-linked gilt yields to calculate the liabilities of the DB plans in the scope of its index (PPF 7 800). Discount rates of single-employer pension plans in the United States are determined by reference to high-quality corporate bonds. The choice of the discount rate that is used to express in today's terms the stream of future benefit payments can have a major impact on funding levels.

Definition and measurement

The funding position of DB plans is assessed in this publication as the ratio between the investments and the technical provisions (net of reinsurance) of DB plans. Investments of DB plans may be a low estimate of assets of DB plans as they would not include receivables and claims against the plan sponsor to cover the funding shortfall. Technical provisions represent the amount that needs to be held to pay the actuarial valuation of benefits that members are entitled to. This is the minimum obligation (liability) for all DB pension plans.

Liabilities are estimated using country-specific methodologies. Methodologies differ across countries with respect to the formula used, the discount rate (e.g. a market discount rate, or a fixed discount rate), or with the way future salaries are accounted for (e.g. liabilities can be based on current salaries or on salaries projected to the future date that participants are expected to retire) for example.

Figure 9.6. **Assets and liabilities of DB plans (in billions of national currency) and their ratio (percentage) in selected jurisdictions, 2010-20**

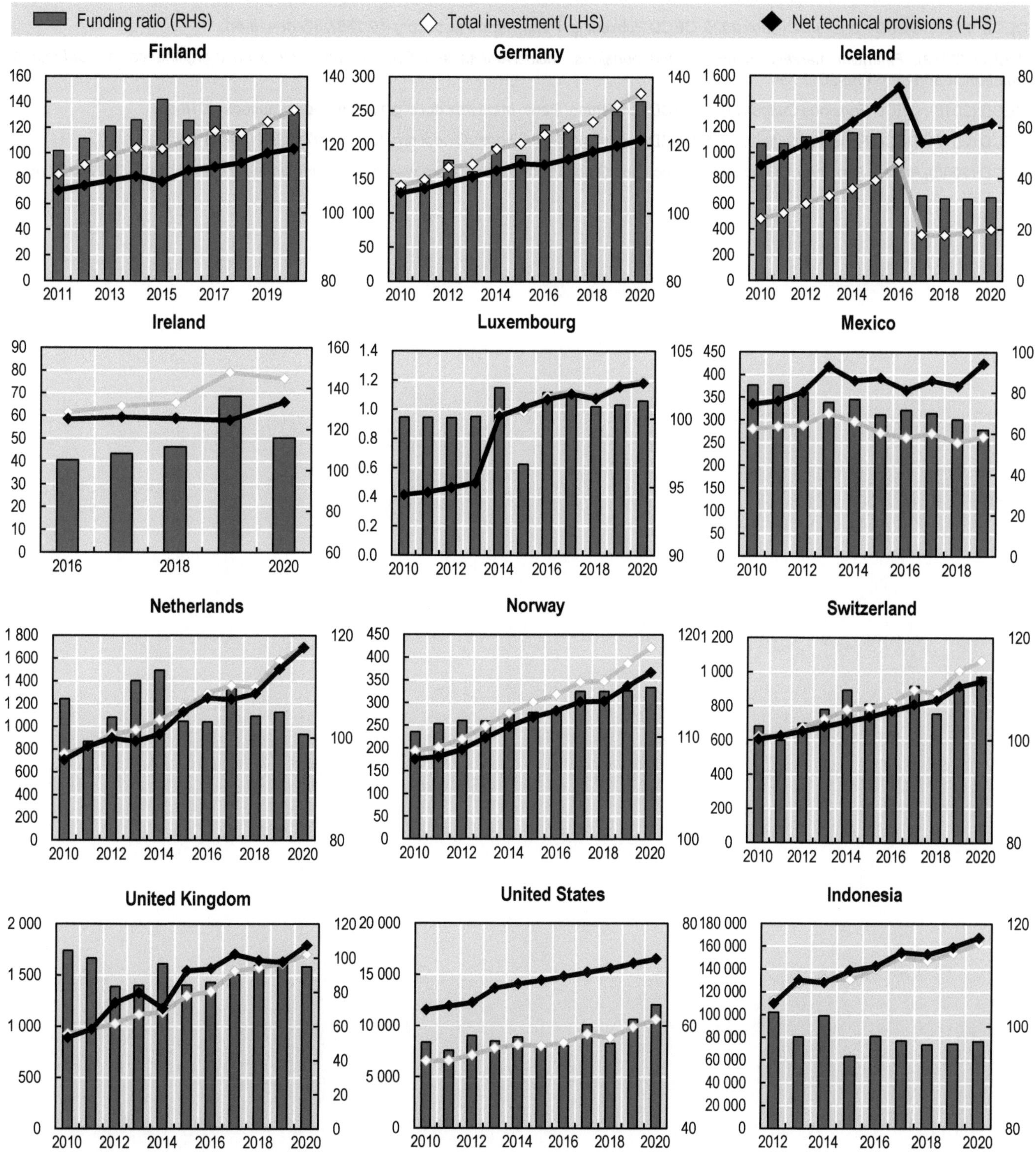

Note: LHS: left-hand side axis. RHS: right-hand side axis.
Source: OECD Global Pension Statistics.

StatLink https://stat.link/vlmga1

[6] International Organisation of Pension Supervisors (2018), *2018 Update on IOPS work on fees and charges, IOPS Working Papers on Effective Pensions Supervision, No. 32, http://www.iopsweb.org/WP-32-2018-Update-on-IOPS-work-on-fees-and-charges.pdf.*

[2] OECD (2021), *Pension Markets in Focus 2021, https://www.oecd.org/finance/private-pensions/pensionmarketsinfocus.htm.*

[3] OECD (2020), *OECD Pensions Outlook 2020*, OECD Publishing, Paris, *https://dx.doi.org/10.1787/67ede41b-en.*

[4] OECD (2019), *Financial markets, insurance and pensions: Inclusiveness and Finance, https://www.oecd.org/finance/financial-markets-insurance-and-pensions-2019.htm.*

[7] OECD (2018), *OECD Pensions Outlook 2018*, OECD Publishing, Paris, *https://dx.doi.org/10.1787/pens_outlook-2018-en.*

[5] OECD (2012), *OECD Pensions Outlook 2012*, OECD Publishing, Paris, *https://dx.doi.org/10.1787/9789264169401-en.*

[1] OECD (2005), *Private Pensions: OECD Classification and Glossary*, http://dx.doi.org/*www.oecd.org/finance/private-pensions/38356329.pdf.*

Printed by Libri Plureos GmbH in Hamburg,
Germany